SCIENCE VS SPOOK

BPSC 101: 50 Lessons in Black American
Political Science and Culture

CONTENTS

1

Introduction

My journey into Black American politics started when I was seventeen and took a bus from South Central Los Angeles, California to the Million Man March on October 16, 1995. It wasn't until more than two decades later that I realized I knew very little about how the system worked. I wasn't intimate with the money; the lobbying; the conflicts of interests; how diversity, equity, and inclusion (DEI) politics could be weaponized against Black Americans and turned into a net negative; and spook.

Spook, in this book's context, is defined as imaginary beliefs in people, leaders, and concepts that are far from what is real or scientific. The opposite of spook is science—a commitment to measuring results, analyzing costs versus benefits, and making decisions based on evidence rather than emotion or symbolism.

Historically, in Black America, the concept of spook was taught by Elijah Muhammad (1897–1975) and a splinter group founded by Clarence 13X (Father Allah, 1928–1969), the Five-Percenters. Malcolm X was firmly grounded in the concept of spook as part of his harsh critique on "pie-in-the-sky" Christian religion. The critique brilliantly diagnosed part of the Black American problem: waiting for a white Jesus in the sky was unacceptable while white America enjoyed so much heaven in the present and gave us hell in the living reality we could see and hear. There were material distortions in our approach to religion that were holding us back from money, good homes, and friendships in all walks of life. Material things. Nation-like things, such as our own schools, farms, banks, national newspapers, international trade, grocery stores, apartment complexes, and hospitals. We could have these things on a collective-good basis only if we put the spook down, better understood how things work, and leaned further into reality.

I understood the spook concept well as a teenager and later, as an adult, as religious critique. However, the gift of lived experience showed me this critique didn't go far enough. Spook can be political, cultural, financial, or economic. Spook has different manifestations, and I realized spook could be easily seen within American politics.

When I examine the period from 1995-2025, I see a pattern where Black America has often traded substantive policy gains for symbolic victories. We've celebrated 'firsts' while our economic position has stagnated or declined. We've focused on representation while the rules of the political and economic game were being rewritten against our interests.

For example, I was only spooky and overly optimistic about the promise of Barack Obama's presidency because I didn't understand how America worked. To understand what is spook and what is science, I would need to better understand the material factors underneath the system—in particular, the money and underbelly of American politics that remains a mystery to most. I was so spooky about the hope of Barack Obama that when valid criticism was presented during his presidency, I would make up things in my head, such as, "Barack Obama will come after the Black American agenda more forcefully once he gets out of office."

Looking back, coming under the messianic-like spook spell of Barack Obama had everything to do with Black religious vulnerabilities and my religious upbringing—areas that stand opposite to science and more scientific thinking.

As part of my research for this book, I interviewed the chairman of the political science department at Howard University and asked him if his department teaches any courses on corruption and lobbying in politics. He told me no. If you were never taught about some of the key concepts in this book, don't worry—political science graduates across the United States, including myself (who completed graduate-level courses at the University of Virginia in political science), haven't either.

The more I researched about the rise of the political influence of Meta (Facebook), Google (Alphabet), Amazon, influential government contractors such as Raytheon and Lockheed Martin, and lobby groups like the American Israel Public Affairs Committee (AIPAC), the pieces on the Monopoly board started coming together. Specifically, how corporations and an enormous amount of money, corruption, promiscuous conflicts of interest, and lobbying fatally weaken and undermine Black American politics. The factors of this political weakness during the period of 1995–2025 haven't been carefully isolated and audited. For example, we know a lot about the perceived benefits of Barack Obama but not much about the costs to Black America. The intention of *BPSC 101: 50 Lessons in Black Political Science and Culture* is to give you a clearer picture and accounting of the political balance sheet.

Science versus Spook is organized into six thematic sections. "Prescriptive Politics" offers forward-looking solutions for building powerful new institutions. "Obama and the New Blacks" examines the costs and benefits of the Obama era. "The Nation of Islam and Modern Black Nationalism" evaluates the achievements and limitations of nationalist movements. "Understanding Political Mechanics" demystifies how power truly operates in American politics. "Pure Reparations" establishes the mathematical case for lineage-based Reparations. "Monetary Science and The Federal Reserve" connects macroeconomic policy to Black American political analysis and outcomes. "Culture and Social Control" examines how cultural forces can shape Black American political orientation, from Amy Wax's flawed paralysis parable to hip-hop's evolution into a system that promotes low impulse control and undermines scientific thinking.

This Black American political renaissance must be programmed with more scientific thinking and less symbolism. More cost-benefit analysis and less spook. More strategy and less hope. More accountability, action, strategy, and planning and fewer articulate speeches and sermons. More political efficiency and fewer promises. More science and less symbolism.

The path forward requires us to be clear-eyed about how power truly operates in America. It demands that we evaluate our leaders and strategies not by how they make us feel, their identity, but by what they actually deliver against a Black American political agenda. And it requires us to build new organizations with the economic foundations needed to advance a Black American agenda that produces measurable results.

Although this book is written with specialization and focus on Black American politics, the concepts could be applied by readers of all walks of life who seek to get more scientific and less emotional about American politics.

The Scientific Orientation Framework

Throughout this work, I use "science" and "scientific orientation" in ways that may differ from strict academic convention. This is intentional. My approach draws from scientific thinking principles—evidence-based analysis, pattern recognition, and systematic observation—while adapting these methods for political analysis within the Black American experience.

To understand is to go underneath. A scientific orientation means digging beneath surface-level explanations to examine the underlying factors, financial relationships, and power structures that drive political and economic outcomes. When I describe something as having a scientific orientation, it follows core principles:

- **Evidence over emotion**: Measurable data and observable patterns rather than wishful thinking

- **Multifactor analysis**: Breaking down problems and issues into factors rather than one-dimensional, black and white, good or bad thinking

- **Risk/reward analysis**: Calculating potential costs and benefits of political strategies

- **Cost/benefit relationships**: Understanding what resources produce what outcomes

- **Quantifying in percentages**: Formulating estimates like "80% probability" or "30% support needed"

- **Following the money**: Tracking financial relationships and conflicts of interest

- **Pattern recognition**: Identifying recurring themes in political behavior
- **Proportion analysis**: Understanding relative scale and mathematical relationships
- **Material outcomes over symbolism**: Focusing on measurable results rather than symbolic gestures
- **Skeptical verification**: Not taking politicians' words at face value but examining who funds them and writes their speeches

A scientific orientation doesn't accept what politicians say or preach at face value. Instead, it examines who is funding them, their biggest donors, and why we must discount what they say on particular policy issues when conflicts exist. For example, a scientific orientation means quickly searching who wrote Joe Biden's Presidential victory speech (Presidential Historian Jon Meacham) after he promised to "always have Black America's back" and credited his victory to Black Americans. Understanding authorship reveals whether promises reflect genuine commitment or skilled speechwriting.

A scientific orientation doesn't leave critical questions to mystery. Why don't Black Americans press Wells Fargo on historical anti-Black American discrimination that cost Black America billions in stealth racial taxes—predatory fees, discriminatory lending rates, and wealth extraction mechanisms that disproportionately target our communities? Through research, going underneath the surface, we discover Wells Fargo sent millions in checks to the NAACP, Marc Morial's Urban League, T.D. Jakes, and other influential organizations, compromising the natural checks and balances that should regulate corporate behavior affecting Black America.

PRESCRIPTIVE POLITICS - BUILDING A NEW FRAMEWORK

Artificial Intelligence Is Political

> *"The advance of artificial intelligence is going to be the biggest technological revolution in the history of mankind."* —Bill Gates

> *"I grew up around anti-Blackness in Missouri. I thought I'd gotten rid of it in college; I had definitely not. I still haven't fully—I'm still noticing new ways I've overlooked Black realities—but I sure want to. Pretending otherwise gets in the way of getting better."* —OpenAI (Owner of Chat GPT) Co-Founder and CEO Sam Altman, Jun 2, 2020

In 1995, the Cerritos Public Library's screens in Los Angeles County became portals to a vast new digital world. There, my insatiable curiosity for Malcolm X, Black nationalism, Black Islam, and African history—including ancient Nubia and Egypt—found unlimited resources at my fingertips. They say when you take the goldfish out of the bowl and put it in a bathtub, it will swim like it's still restricted, like it never left the bowl. But the Yahoo! search engine freed my intellectual curiosity to instantly swim across oceans of knowledge. I felt I was relatively early in heavily using the internet.

My bus trips to use the internet at the library were just as good for me as going to a teen hip-hop party and helped set the foundation for eventually becoming a successful digital media entrepreneur and developing one of the fastest-growing media companies in the United States. [1] The education I received from my own searches on the Yahoo! search engine was better and more motivating than the more restricted curriculum goldfish bowl of the classroom. My more recent experiences with artificial intelligence reminded me of my days at the library.

While attending an advertising conference in Cannes, France, in 2023, two British engineers warned me about AI's impact—junior engineering jobs could be completely wiped out, they told me. (They taught us to get an engineering degree and you will have a job!) They shared that the best engineers within their network couldn't believe the power and flexibility of this new technology. I was skeptical of all the hype as I knew some scamming companies were tricking customers in 2019-2021 about artificial intelligence claims but they didn't really have the goods.[2] Was this another crypto-bubble wave, adding very little value in the material world? When I returned stateside and began using ChatGPT (My favorite AI tool now is Claude by Anthropic), the possibilities astounded me. This isn't just another tech wave; it's a profound opportunity for Black Americans to substantially correct our historic exclusion from the digital revolution.

After experimenting, I thought of artificial intelligence tools as potential equalizers that could help Black America leapfrog institutional and financial barriers, and help us plan, strategize, organize, and execute faster and more efficiently. These tools could be the great equalizer to help us reset our political orientation and organizations, as well as achieve better political outcomes, freedom, justice, and equality. While most large companies and entire industries will eliminate a massive number of jobs due to efficiencies gained with AI, the opposite is true for us as individuals and as a collective. If companies will need fewer employees due to AI, maximizing these tools gives you the ability to effectively have a team of employees or even executives helping you. With AI, individuals will need less or a small amount of capital to accomplish big things.

Consider the numbers: Goldman Sachs projects disruptions to nearly 300 million jobs: 46 percent of office and administrative support roles at risk, 44 percent of legal industry positions facing transformation, and 37 percent of engineering roles potentially affected. Bill Gates sees AI as an indispensable "white-collar worker."[3] JPMorganChase's Jamie Dimon predicts a 3.5-day work week under AI's influence.[4] But we've heard promises before. During Silicon Valley's rise, Obama cultivated ties with tech titans—Eric Schmidt, Mark Zuckerberg, Jeff Bezos—while the broader tech wave marginalized Black Americans. The multitrillion-dollar Silicon Valley boom from 2008–2016 was largely an exclusive white and Asian party, with club security routinely turning away Black Americans who had lined up to get in. The only reason I mention these titans of business is that I like to watch how the biggest players who have the most skin in the game, the most to lose, place their bets with their own pockets. They generally have the best insider information. For example, Schmidt, the former Google chairman/CEO, had predicted China and DeepSeek's AI chatbot would shock everyone months before a historical 2025 reset in the AI industry.[5]

Why is AI adoption crucial for Black Americans? Consider the gun-slave hypothesis: European gunpowder technology, which originated in China, played a pivotal role in the African holocaust.[6] Technological disadvantage led to dire repercussions. Today, AI is both an economic and political weapon. Future wealth distribution will likely follow AI adoption. I see future political strength, with economic power and hyper-organization as foundations, being AI-adjacent. To avoid being left behind as we were during previous technological revolutions, we must institutionalize AI within Black American culture and make AI proficiency hipper than the latest fashion, hip-hop, or sports trends. This technology is so important, there is no political path into a political renaissance in Black America without AI.

While others focus solely on AI's potential for algorithmic discrimination, such as biased banking algorithms, we must also seize its transformational opportunities. Think bigger: AI-powered cooperative economics, automated wealth generation, and data-driven political strategy. Countries from China to Israel are aggressively planting their flags in the AI arms race. Similarly, we must view AI through the lens of future resource distribution and political influence.

Elijah Muhammad would teach, "Study the white man and see why he is successful." Well, that goes for people doing significant things in all walks of life. The elite groups with AI advantages will likely favor their own affinity groups and design updates to the Monopoly board in their favor. We need a sophisticated collective response that isn't dependent on government protection. This starts with education and experience with AI technology. In terms of the potential for using AI as part of a broader Black American political renaissance, here are some areas of interests:

- Strategic analysis

- Resource optimization

- Political planning

- Surgical district voting optimization

- Community organization

- Economic modeling

- Wealth-building strategies

- AI-powered auditing of organization finances and general accountability

- AI-enhanced measurement—what's working; what isn't working

Later in this book, you will see how we have been playing mostly defense with our politics. The AI technological revolution will allow us to access the truth and build organizations and economic enterprises faster without as much anti-Black American biases and obstruction. It's not that the obstruction and barriers disappear, it's just that we have weapons to build, be creative, organize, mobilize, execute, and better fight back. Once we better understand reality and have the weapons to capitalize on reality, we have advantages and can start playing more offense and negotiate our political affairs on better terms. As we'll explore in Lesson #37, AI tools are already helping uncover historical truths about broken promises like '40 Acres and a Mule' by analyzing millions of documents that reveal exactly how land titles were systematically revoked from formerly enslaved people—transforming abstract historical claims into precise mathematical calculations of what is owed.

AI can revolutionize how we target our limited political resources for maximum impact. Instead of spreading our efforts thinly, AI can analyze voting patterns, demographics, and economic data to pinpoint exactly where our political dollars and energy will yield the highest returns.

Think of it like smart money in politics: AI might show that $50,000 invested in organizing a specific Philadelphia suburb delivers the same impact as $2 million spent in a major city center. It identifies "multiplier districts" where victories create ripple effects through key committee members or influential swing votes.

Most importantly, AI helps us transcend traditional party loyalties by identifying politicians across the spectrum who might support specific elements of a Black American agenda under the right conditions. This shifts us from intuition-based to data-driven strategy – applying Wall Street-level analytical precision to our political investments. Just as we'd demand a return on financial capital, AI helps us maximize the return on our political capital.

To give you an example of the many real-life cases of AI, my small business was impacted by fraud perpetrated by a marketing vendor. I was buying clicks to get more traffic to my website, and the software picked up over ninety-two thousand fake clicks, or bots, within a thirty-day period. To help determine what had happened and then navigate the legal process to fight a public company with over $1 billion of revenue, I used AI tools to unpack systematic fraud and a broader conspiracy in my industry. When facing such gross economic and institutional disparity, there was no way this David could have taken on that Goliath without heavy use of AI.

My lawsuit was closely watched in my industry, and by the looks of things, there have been broader investigations into the $143 billion ad fraud industry since my pursuit of justice began. AI helped me fight my legal case like no other weapon I could think of, and the various tools cost me less than $60 a month. There was no legal counsel in America that could help me examine my unique situation and the various nuanced technical factors better and on my restricted legal budget. It's not that AI should replace lawyers; it should be used as a complementary weapon. If a lawyer is charging $600 per hour in Manhattan, maybe I run my questions through multiple AI tools and be more efficient with my questions and possibly save $300. When you're using AI in key areas of your professional or business life, the efficiencies can exponentially add up.

I remember seeing tech influencers laugh about AI getting some questions and problems wrong (what they call "hallucinating"), but they were missing the point. AI is not about perfection. It's about efficiency gains, helping human beings and organizations complete tasks and projects faster and more cost-effectively. These types of tools have the potential to add advantages for those who lack resources and institutional proximity to power. If you want to use AI to help bust up some tricknology, it can do that. If you want to use the tools to contemplate a personal, financial, or organization matter, it can help you organize your thoughts and provide recommendations and suggestions you may have not considered. Some of it is free (the free version of ChatGPT, DeepSeek),[7] and some come with privacy features where your AI chats are not saved.

The Inversion Paradox: Job Killer as Superpower

The technology eliminating jobs is the same technology granting individuals unprecedented capabilities. When fighting a billion-dollar corporation over fraud, professional legal counsel at $600 per hour remained financially out of reach. Yet $60-per-month AI tools delivered the equivalent of an entire legal research team—one person confronting a Goliath through AI-amplified capability. This is the inversion at work:

the same artificial intelligence eliminating legal research positions simultaneously democratized legal research capabilities. AI will displace millions of jobs across industries—this displacement is real, measurable, and already underway. But that identical job-eliminating power grants individuals the capabilities of entire departments for a fraction of traditional costs. *The technology making employees unnecessary is the technology that makes you not need employees.* You now face a choice shaped by this paradox: AI doesn't just threaten your job—it offers you the tools to transcend traditional institutional barriers and employment structures entirely. The implications for developing new, more efficient and impactful organizations that move faster, with less capital requirements, are revolutionary. We should think about AI not just defensively (what are they going to do to us) but we should be playing offense: How do we weaponize it for good, to set up the next generation of Black Americans, with better organizations, better community organizing, more independent and economically sustainable institutions, and better politics.

Here are some suggestions on how to use AI chatbot tools.

Don't Be Stingy

If you see promise in a free version, try a paid version for better analysis and experiences. Think of it this way: If you paid $150,000 for a college degree, a $30 monthly AI subscription may be the best educational investment you'll ever make. If you could pay $10,000 or $150,000 for your college degree, look at premium AI tools at $30 a month as the steal and deal of your lifetime. The investment in the more advantaged models with better thinking abilities will give you room for longer chats and projects.

Train Your Own AI

Help the AI chatbot get smart really fast about your specific project or problem. Upload the key facts and factors of your specific project and questions before asking questions or for estimates and recommendations.

For example, Claude AI has a knowledge base where you can upload text or documents for it to reference while chatting with you. You can copy and paste research or news articles to enhance your thinking experiences. The better the data you give the AI bot about your problem or situation, the better the thinking.

For example, I wanted to better understand where stock in NVIDIA was likely to head and the macroeconomic picture with so much volatility and policy changes, so I uploaded relevant Bloomberg, Financial Times, Yahoo! News, and Reuters articles on the relevant questions. I like to feed my own AI chats rich, nuanced information and then have it give me analysis and estimates. Now, you can't be a pig where you take the AI output as the Bible truth and gobble up everything it spits out, but it helps augment your thinking. It's like having the equivalent of hundreds of intellectual sparring partners helping you prepare for the big event so you can perform better. AI enhanced my stock and macroeconomic analysis and helped get me ahead of everyone else on a big move in NVIDIA and the broader stock market.(So, AI can be your armchair analyst and economist too?) Yes, but in most cases, those who come to the table with deep experience, curiosity, and knowledge will get the most out of AI tools. Sam Altman, the co-founder of OpenAI, has suggested general knowledge will become less important while those who can ask insightful questions will become more valuable. Paradoxically, these effective question prompts still emerge from deep, nuanced knowledge combined with imaginative curiosity.

Don't Be Too Biased

You may approach your project or problem with a desired outcome, so you feed your AI chatbot overly biased facts and factors. These chatbots have the ability to technologically jerk you off after you trick it for more biased outputs, although it started from a neutral point of reference. The more balanced your facts and factors are, the better the thinking output, analysis, recommendations, estimates, and solutions. Be sure to de-risk biases as much as you can to get the cleanest thinking possible about your problem or project. Two-sided arguments (or more) will yield better results.

Use Screenshots

There are many screenshot tools, but I like to use Awesome Screenshot, the Chrome browser plug-in.[8] I can quickly screenshot whatever is on my screen, upload the image to the chatbot, and help train it on the graphical material.

Use Multiple Tools

When elections are held, the averages of multiple polls are often considered more statistically reliable than a single poll. If one poll goes over the cliff with defects, that doesn't mean you go with it. Several polls are averaged to capture whatever dominant trend that can be identified.

For bigger projects, I compare analysis and feedback with the same information and was blown away how one tool looked at the problem very differently than the other. Not only did it give me a differentiated perspective from the other AI tool, it started going off, explaining why it was so confident in its analysis. The predictive analysis was later confirmed with facts and multiple material events. This technology is so powerful, you must make sure you are using it in a way that is commensurate with the problem or project you're dealing with.

For complex problems, consider it best practice to consult multiple AI models, just as you would seek second and third opinions for critical medical decisions. There are some projects where you will want to run two or even three different AI models side by side and then average the analysis and look for insights from one that are missing from the other or others. It may not be about one AI tool being better in general, but which AI model is better for a specific problem or project at any given time.

Never Feed AI Sensitive Information

Avoid sharing personal identifiers (such as Social Security numbers or detailed personal addresses), financial credentials, private health data, or confidential business information. Even with AI that promises privacy, practice caution with your most sensitive data. You should also estimate by default, the U.S. government and intelligence agencies have added an "AI chat tap" vs phone tap to its list of surveillance arsenals. Whatever you chat about, assume zero privacy from government surveillance and that agencies likely have direct API connection to your favorite AI tool.

Evangelize

If it works well for you, evangelize to others AI literacy and the latest tools or the techniques. Start with your family and move on to friends. And while you're at it, tell them about *Science versus Spook*!

The Science

- AI is this generation's gunpowder: Those who master it gain massive advantages; those who don't get left behind
- Future wealth distribution will follow AI adoption: Just as Silicon Valley created trillions while locking out Black Americans, AI will determine who gets rich next
- AI can level the playing field: Unlike previous tech waves that required massive capital, AI tools can give individuals the power of entire teams
- Start now, start cheap: Basic AI subscriptions ($30/month) may be the best educational investment you'll ever make
- Don't wait for permission: While others debate AI ethics, start using it to solve your problems and build your advantages

[1] Inc. Magazine, "Moguldom Media Group," Inc. 5000, ranked No. 882 (2014), No. 1195 (2015), No. 4414 (2016), listed as one of the fastest-growing private companies in America. https://www.inc.com/profile/moguldom-media-group

[2] Ann Brown, "A Warning To Black America About Scammy 'Artificial Intelligence' Hype: 5 Things To Know," The Moguldom Nation, November 18, 2021, https://moguldom.com/382263/a-warning-to-black-america-about-scammy-artificial-intelligence-hype-5-things-to-know/

[3] Goldman Sachs, "Generative AI Could Raise Global GDP by 7 Percent," Goldman Sachs Research, April 5, 2023.

[4] Jennifer Liu, "JPMorgan CEO Jamie Dimon Says AI Could Bring a 3½-Day Workweek," CNBC, October 3, 2023.

[5] Eric Schmidt, Interview by George Stephanopoulos, "This Week," ABC News, December 15, 2024.

[6] Warren C. Whatley, "The Gun-Slave Hypothesis and the 18th Century British Slave Trade," Explorations in Economic History 67 (2018): 80-104.

[7] Columbia School of Law, "A Survey of Free AI Tools: Chat GPT and Deep Seek," Columbia Law Technology Review, May 15, 2024.

[8] Awesome Screenshot, "Awesome Screen Recorder and Screen Capture 2 in 1," Chrome Web Store Extension with over 3 million users globally, https://www.awesomescreenshot.com

A Deng for Black America

> *"Black cat or white cat, if it can catch mice, it's a good cat."*
> —Deng Xiaoping

After auditing Black American politics from 1995 to 2025 measurement period, a critical factor for our weakness is rigidity, or Mao-like rigidity before China switched up and positioned itself for astronomical success. It's obvious Black America needs new imagination and new thinking; we need to open up and do more of what actually works and less of what is not working.

Elijah Muhammad said, "Study the white man. He is successful. He makes no excuses for his failures, and he acts in a united way. We must do the same." [1]

Real GDP per Capita (1990 int. $)

China joins the WTO

1978: Economic reforms introduced by Deng Xiaoping

Dec 1990: Shanghai stockmarket reopens for the first time since 1949

Source: World Economic Forum

22

This quote should apply to people from all walks of life, as racial intoxication prevents us from getting to the results and the right methods to get the results, while factoring our own unique values, culture, and context.

China's meteoric rise from a highly impoverished and humiliated nation indeed consisted of studying the white man. This goes beyond anchoring Karl Marx's communism with Chinese characteristics as the Chinese describe it. Intelligent nations and movements have to check their enemies and allies to determine what is working and what's not, what's generally efficient to scale and what is inefficient, and what is productive for the times and what isn't practical. China experienced a period of humiliation, or what it calls the Century of Humiliation, marked by wars and defeat at the hands of Russia, Japan, and Western powers. China was "pushed all the way back" by the subjugation of the Qing dynasty, followed by the West and Japan.[2]

Not only was China a laughingstock of the West, but millions starved, with many resorting to eating each other during the Great Famine.[3] The Chinese were so radical and so fanatically loyal to Mao that they were starving and even eating each other while their leadership refused to change course. Not only was China a politically and economically devastated state under Mao, but it was also very resistant to change and new thinking. The state would imprison or kill you if you had a lot to say about what wasn't working for the Chinese people.

Born in 1904, Deng Xiaoping joined the Chinese Communist Party (CCP) in the early 1920s. Rising through the ranks, he became a prominent figure in the CCP. However, his journey was far from smooth. Deng faced significant opposition within the party, particularly during the Cultural Revolution, a period of intense social and political upheaval launched by Mao Zedong in 1966.[4]

During the Cultural Revolution, Mao and his supporters targeted Deng as a "capitalist roader" and a "revisionist." This criticism stemmed from Deng's pragmatic approach to economic and social issues, which

23

contrasted with the more radical and ideological methods favored by Mao and the Cultural Revolution group. Deng's economic policies, particularly his openness to elements of market economics, were seen as a betrayal of pure communist principles.

As a result of this opposition, Deng was purged from the party leadership. He and his family faced severe persecution. In 1969, Deng was sent to the rural Jiangxi province for "reeducation" through labor, a common punishment for officials who were purged during the Cultural Revolution. This period was difficult for Deng, as he was subjected to hard labor and harsh living conditions.

What's remarkable about Deng's story is that he fully understood the mortal risks he was taking. During Mao's Cultural Revolution, countless "revisionists" were executed or died in prison camps. Deng's own son, Deng Pufang, was tortured and thrown from a four-story building by Red Guards, leaving him permanently paralyzed. Deng himself faced real prospects of execution rather than just imprisonment when he challenged Maoist orthodoxy. Yet he persisted in his pragmatic vision, knowing that China's survival depended on someone willing to risk everything to change course. Deng famously declared, "It doesn't matter whether a cat is black or white, as long as it catches mice" – a direct rejection of ideological purity in favor of practical results.

However, Deng's imprisonment was not long term. Following Mao's death in 1976 and the subsequent political shifts, Deng made a remarkable political comeback. He returned to power in 1977 and quickly began implementing his vision for China. His policies, often summarized as "Reform and Opening Up," shifted China toward a mixed economy with significant market elements, leading to rapid economic growth and development. China's foreign policy orientation towards the West changed under Deng. Rather than see capitalist countries as enemies, it looked at them as strategic economic opportunities.

Deng's experiences, including his opposition and temporary downfall, played a crucial role in shaping his pragmatic approach to governance. His willingness to embrace practical solutions over ideological purity transformed China's economy and affected the country's trajectory in the late twentieth century.

The policy shift showed an acknowledgment by China that the incomes of ordinary Chinese citizens were so low compared with other Asian economies that it would jeopardize China's future if something weren't done to raise people's living standards through economic growth.

The Chinese government established areas for foreign investment: special economic zones, open coastal cities, economic and technology development zones, delta open zones, peninsula open zones, open border cities, and high-tech industry development zones.[5] These economic zones triggered massive foreign investment inflows, mainly from companies in Hong Kong and Taiwan. Simultaneously, China promoted a socialist market economy, ushering in an entrepreneurial boom that gave rise to vast numbers of entrepreneurs and venture businesses in China.

Using foreign capital, technology, and management know-how, China tapped its vast labor resources and massive geography for rapid economic growth. The shift to an open-door monetary policy led to high economic growth in the first half of the 1980s. The economy stagnated around the time of the Tiananmen Square incident in 1989. Still, in the first half of the 1990s, China was growing fast again. Per capita gross domestic product (GDP) rose; in 1998, it was around $770—fourteen times more than in 1980. Deng Xiaoping pulled off his goal of improving the economic status of the Chinese people.

China began its market reforms in the late 1970s. In less than thirty-five years, it reduced the poverty rate from nearly 90 percent of the population in 1981 to less than 2 percent in 2015.[6] More than 800 million people were lifted out of poverty, according to the World Bank's spending benchmark.[7]

World Economic Forum's Most Efficient Governments Ranking - Shows Rwanda ranked #7 globally for government efficiency

The critical feature for China going from the bottom to the top, from humiliation to global leader, was strategic change. It started with Deng Xiaoping having the vision and courage to keep Mao Zedong's (Chairman Mao's) legacy and core philosophies while realizing some material things needed to be fixed. Deng realized that China needed critical changes to go from backward to forward. If changes weren't made and they didn't open up their economy to foreign investment, they would continue to be stuck.

China had an advantage over other countries in rising from the bottom to the top because the culture was radically de-spooked. In China, religious belief in Christianity or Islam is different from the way of thinking about how to get from point A to B. Religious fanatics can impair the homogeneity of moving for a singular purpose with a strategic goal for the people. Religion and tribalism can get in the way of people eating, being housed, holding others accountable, and moving on one accord. No Muslims and Hindus are fighting in China, as we see in India. There is no white-versus-Black political volatility like we see in America. China has no Democrat-versus-Republican gridlock, which often holds the American government and people in political paralysis, often going nowhere.[8]

The Chinese Communist Party itself can indeed be a form of a spook, with prophets such as Mao and now the current leader Xi. Still, my point is that there is no religion getting in the way of advancing strategic goals.

No Jesus or Allah is coming to protect us from most serious political challenges or promote our collective political and economic uplift. The lack of organized religion in China is an advantage. While other countries and movements have been praying, giving offerings to preachers, and waiting for something to happen in the future, China has been building its heaven right here on earth for over a billion people. The Chinese didn't wait for religion to change their affairs, they first had to radically change their political orientation and they went out to produce their own economic miracle.

Black American political students must study some aspects of China's rise, particularly those who believe we need to organize ourselves more like a nation within a nation. China reviewed both Karl Marx's socialism and American-style capitalism and selectively optimized for what works for their country, specifically. Not spook, not belief, but they executed a real plan we can refer to going back to the late 1970s. They had a plan to do it big and did just that. China had to audit what needed to be fixed and change its game without losing its core values and principles.

Black Americans can do the same. We must audit and organize ourselves into a new political thinking—reform. This would mean a willingness for Black organizations and Americans to change our way of thinking and get more politically efficient and productive. We can't keep trying the same programs and the same strategies and expect a different outcome. We can't keep protecting sacred cows in the name of unity when the cows have stopped producing milk. Our unity must be productive; it must be efficient. Black American unity must be strategic.

I don't suggest we need a single leader like Deng to lead us to the promised land as much as we need vision and the ability to challenge entrenched orthodoxy. The lesson of Deng Xiaoping is that sometimes challenging orthodoxy is the most loyal act of all. When Tavis Smiley and Cornel West questioned Obama's policies and the spook spell he put over Black America, they weren't betraying Black America, they were following Deng's example of demanding better results over blind loyalty. Smiley even mentioned getting death threats and his mother was harassed for challenging the Obama political religion at the time as if Obama was the "Black Mao."[9]

Real progress requires honest assessment of what's working and what isn't, even when that assessment challenges our most cherished leaders, institutions, and orthodoxies.

The Science

- Rigid ideology kills progress: Like China before Deng, Black America needs to abandon what isn't working, even if it's "sacred"
- Results matter more than purity: China lifted 800 million out of poverty by focusing on "what works" over "what sounds revolutionary"
- Study success everywhere: As Elijah Muhammad said, "Study the white man. He is successful." This applies to anyone achieving results
- Religious rigidity can block material progress: China's advantage was having no competing religious ideologies slowing practical decisions
- We need strategic flexibility: The ability to keep core values while changing tactics based on what produces results

---

[1] Muhammad, Elijah. "Message to the Blackman in America" (p. 174). Secretarius Memps Publications, 2006.

[2] CIGH Exeter, "How the Century of Humiliation Influences China's Ambitions Today," Imperial & Global Forum, July 11, 2019.

[3] Lee, Harry F. "Cannibalism in northern China between 1470 and 1911." Regional Environmental Change, 19(8), 2573-2581, 2019.

[4] Vogel, Ezra F. "Deng Xiaoping and the Transformation of China." Cambridge, MA: Harvard University Press, 2013.

[5] Kobayashi, Shigeo, Jia Baobo and Junya Sano. "The 'Three Reforms' in China: Progress and Outlook." Sakura Institute of Research, Inc., No.45, September 1999.

[6] Huang, Zheping and Tripti Lahiri. "China's path out of poverty can never be repeated at scale by a country again." Quartz, September 21, 2017.

[7] "FAQs: Global Poverty Line Update," The World Bank, September 30, 2015. https://www.worldbank.org/en/topic/poverty/brief/global-poverty-line-faq

[8] Binder, Sarah A. "Going Nowhere: A Gridlocked Congress." Brookings Institution, December 1, 2000. https://www.brookings.edu/articles/going-nowhere-a-gridlocked-congress/

[9] Fears, Darryl. "Black Commenter, Criticizing Obama, Causes Firestorm." The Washington Post, February 16, 2008.

LESSON 3
Less Spook, More Elijah, McKinsey, BCG, and Bain

> *"Why is something done this way? Is this the best way it can be done? You have to be fundamentally skeptical about everything."*
> —Ethan M. Rasiel, The McKinsey Way[1]

Fresh out of college, I had the privilege of working for McKinsey & Company, the world's premier strategy consulting firm. The company's core expertise lies in stepping into Fortune 500 companies and delivering objective advice that may save or generate billions. Although I was a low-level worker in recruiting, I wanted to understand everything about this elite institution. Why were its consultants worth $2,000 an hour?

Beyond their Ivy League pedigrees and top test scores, their value lay in ruthless objectivity. Someone from the outside who could deliver the actual science of a problem and its solutions. Someone who didn't care whether you liked the advice or not—they gave you the best guidance based on data, facts, and factors. Their job was to tell powerful Fortune 500 CEOs not what they wanted to hear, but what they needed to hear, backed up by science and data. [2] The most efficient organizations reward critical thinking and contrarian views, especially when being right or wrong translates to billions in profits or losses. With so much at stake and skin in the game, the strategic thinking and analysis must be pure, objective, and correct.

Now, let's apply this to Black American politics. Historically, we haven't welcomed outsiders telling us we're doing things wrong while hiding behind unity and loyalty. We're often not trying to pay for objective advice, we're often trying to destroy the reputation of those with different viewpoints, particularly outside the Democratic Party and Black Church political complex. Or the Black Nationalist complex. We want transformational change and more orthodoxy simultaneously—a contradiction that breeds inefficiency and poor outcomes.

After auditing our political affairs from 1995-2025, one factor that stood out to me was that we often have a cultural orientation against contrarian viewpoints, outside our rigid political boxes while the most efficient thinkers and problem solvers in the world often have the opposite orientation. They reward new, different, and disruptive viewpoints. We often overly penalize new and different viewpoints and look for personal character flaws that confirm our biases.

For example, when I was intoxicated and politically naive with the promise of Barack Obama in 2007-2008, I thought Cornel West and Tavis Smiley were simply jealous and petty in their criticism and seeking more accountability. Was attempting to hold Barack Obama accountable to Black Americans really a case of crabs in the barrel? I didn't understand until later what they were trying to say, with their principled positions that could go against the dominant Black American political crowd. I was spooky. They were more scientific, in real-time. Being scientific can be very unpopular. Sometimes only time can clarify the picture on who was scientific and who was spooky.

What if we treated freedom, justice, and equality like billions were on the line? What if we did the following?

Measured Everything

- Discounted identity politics
- Focused on systemic function over appearance
- Tracked concrete outcomes over symbolic victories
- Applied cost-benefit analysis to political strategies
- Audited what has worked and hasn't worked and by how much

Demanded Strategic Rigor

- Required data-driven decision making
- Evaluated return on political investment

- Developed measurable performance metrics
- Created accountability frameworks

Embraced Efficient Competition

- Encouraged competing political strategies
- Rewarded successful outcomes over loyalty
- Prioritized results over unity
- Valued productive dissent over comfortable consensus

Consider this: Does the identity of the president matter if Black Americans can't get clean drinking water in Flint, Michigan or Jackson, Mississippi? What would McKinsey, Boston Consulting Group (BCG), or Bain do with our freedom, justice, and equality mandate and a Black American Agenda? A smaller unity attached to measurable results and strategic goals is better than a larger unity based on spook, symbolism, and skin color.

After studying Black American politics my entire adult life, I've been wrong about many things. But one conclusion stands firm: we have a spook problem. To combat it, we must do the following:

- Increase competition of ideas.
- Measure everything possible.
- Hold everyone accountable regardless of identity.
- Count our politics like we count bank accounts.

American politics is a business dominated by corporate interests. It's time we treated Black American politics the same way. What's our return on investment in the Democratic Party? How much do we give and how much do we get back? It's not about allowing the other party who is more hostile to Black American interests to win but how do we get the most out of our vote, when the Democrats do win? How do we become more politically efficient?

As consulting firms help America's institutions become more efficient and profitable, we need a new generation of political scientists, thinkers, and organizers focused on the science of Black American political science. Not in an ivory tower academic sense but in improving our material outcomes.

The world moves at light speed with technological advancement. We can't allow organizations from the 1960s and 1970s to keep leading with decreasing efficiency in delivering freedom, justice, and equality. We must work with them to update for the modern times or start new organizations that are updated for the modern times. The first step toward efficiency is developing a workable ten-year plan with measurable goals.

During this book's 1995–2025 audit measurement period, we saw attempts like the National Agenda (2000–2008) by Benjamin Muhammad (now Chavis). [3] But religious organization dominance brought complications and limited accountability. I read the agenda but it wasn't an agenda at all as it was all over the place. Particularly when economic resources are scarce, it is better to focus on fewer goals and ideas.

To enhance our political efficacy, our openness to innovative and unconventional strategies and alliances must match the scale of needed improvement in Black American politics. The same efficient thinking that moves trillion-dollar corporations can revolutionize our political outcomes—if we're brave enough to embrace which techniques and approaches work, in the real world.

Strategic Questions for Black Political Organizations

- What are our measurable five- and ten-year goals?
- How do we quantify political return on investment?
- What metrics define successful leadership?
- How do we measure progress toward freedom, justice, and equality?
- What's our framework for testing new strategies?
- How do we evaluate political partnerships?

- What economic funding models provide the growth, transparency and accountability to scale the next generation Black American political organizations?

- How are we using data and technology to empower our collective uplift and reach our quantifiable goals?

The path forward requires less spook, more science and political innovation. Less symbolic loyalty, more results. Less unity for unity's sake, more unity around measurable progress. A smaller, more impactful unity is better than a largely symbolic unity based on shared identity. Let's unite around strategic goals, a scientific orientation, accountability, and a plan.

The strategy consulting mindset from firms such as McKinsey & Co., Boston Consulting Group and Bain & Company (where Mitt Romney worked for an affiliate, Bain Capital) isn't just for corporations, we can surgically go in and extract useful strategy and efficiency techniques.[4]

Elijah Muhammad didn't believe in life after death.[5] It was his view that freedom, justice, and equality had to be developed, in the material world, with material results that could be measured and verified. Our heaven was here and it was up to us to create heaven on earth for ourselves and our communities.

Muhammad's scientific approach to nation-building produced remarkable, quantifiable achievements: a bank, airplanes, grocery stores, farmland, independent school system, restaurants, international trade with the country of Peru, the largest Black-owned newspaper distribution system, and other successful ventures. He had a scientific system and instituted progress reports back to the people. For a lot of the more formally educated members, it wasn't the religious teaching that drew them in and kept them, it was the tangible proof and measurable outcomes that he was building and developing, what he told you.[6] It is true and a fact Elijah Muhammad never advocated for full Black American participation in the hyper-corrupt American political system but it is also true his scientific approaches can be applied to organizational objectives within and outside the system.[7]

A new system or new systems can be built for the modern times, if we have the political and economic will to focus on political innovation and measurable results rather than symbolic victories. The greater the dissatisfaction we see in our political outcomes, the greater the flexibility we should have with new ideas and new perspectives. The worst political orientation we could have is consistently bad and inefficient political outcomes while we stay rigid in our thinking.

The Science

- Treat Black politics like billion-dollar business: Apply McKinsey-level analysis to our strategies and leaders
- Measure everything possible: Track concrete outcomes, not symbolic victories
- Welcome contrarian viewpoints: The most successful organizations reward those who challenge conventional wisdom
- Demand strategic rigor: Require data-driven decision making and measurable performance metrics
- Hold everyone accountable: Judge leaders by results, not identity or loyalty
- Create competing strategies: Reward successful outcomes over comfortable consensus

---

[1] Rasiel, Ethan M. "The McKinsey Way." McGraw-Hill, 1999.

[2] Rasiel, E., & Friga, P. N. (2001). The McKinsey Mind: Understanding and Implementing the Problem-Solving Tools and Management Techniques of the World's Top Strategic Consulting Firm. McGraw-Hill Education.

[3] Public Policy Issues, Analyses, and Programmatic Plan of Action, 2000-2008. Million Family March (2000 : Washington, D.C.)

[4] Stern, C. W., & Deimler, M. S. (Eds.). (2012). *The Boston Consulting Group on Strategy: Classic Concepts and New Perspectives* (2nd ed.). John Wiley & Sons.

[5] Muhammad, E. (2006). *Message to the Blackman in America*. Secretarius MEMPS Publications.

[6] Barboza, S. (1993). American Jihad: Islam After Malcolm X. Doubleday.

[7] Muhammad, E. (2011, January 21). Put Muslim Program to Congress. The Final Call. https://www.finalcall.com/artman/publish/Columns_4/Put_Muslim_Program_to_Congress_1041.shtml

Is Religion Frustrating Our Political and Economic Development?

"You can pray until you faint, but unless you get up and try to do something, God is not going to put it in your lap."
—Fannie Lou Hamer

"Don't Close Your Eyes and Trust in God."
—Burnsteen Sharrieff Mohammed on what the founder of the Nation of Islam taught her

"You can go to church for hope. Politics is the means by which we improve our material condition." —Yvette Carnell

When Rwandan President Paul Kagame looked at Kigali and asked, "Seven hundred churches? Do we even have as many factories?" he wasn't just making an observation—he was applying scientific thinking to development. His question cuts through religious spook to expose a material reality: you can't build political power without economic foundations. Kagame ended up closing more than 6,000 churches as his country became a greater success story within Africa and around the world.[1]

Let's apply scientific analysis to his comparison of churches to boreholes (water wells). A borehole provides tangible value—clean water that sustains life and enables development. A factory creates jobs, products, and wealth that can be reinvested in the community. But what does the 701st church provide that the first 700 didn't?

Rwanda's results speak to the science of this approach:[2][3][4][5]

- Number one in rule of law among thirty-three sub-Saharan nations
- Sixth safest country for solo travelers
- Fourth-least corrupt in Africa
- Seventh-most efficient government globally

Kagame had to drain a significant amount of the spook from his country for it to rise just as China had to reduce the amount of ideological Mao fanaticism and the spookiness within their economic system, before their historic rise.

I know the hardcore Black Nationalist community will say Kagame's great works and fruits are no good because he reportedly worked with the CIA against his enemies at a point in his career. But did you know Muammar Gaddafi worked with the CIA when his interests aligned with theirs?[6] Saddam Hussein and Bin Laden did too.[7] You're telling me you're harder and more radical than them? Were they sellouts? You will miss too many lessons in life and politics with rigid, "throw the baby out with the bathwater" thinking. What matters is we need to constantly be "adding everything up" to see how the total cumulatively nets out.

You have to remember Rwanda is the country where there was a literal genocide between the Tutsis and Hutus, resulting in the death of close to 1 million human beings, in just the first 100 days.[8] For Rwanda to be where it is today, is nothing but an economic and development miracle. The imperfection and lack of Democratic practices in some critical areas, human rights abuses, or even targeted killings of political opponents, doesn't take away from this historic accomplishment and the lessons that can be surgically learned.[9] Kagame took his whole country from hell to heaven in a single generation and no social media radical can take this away from him.

Is my* country heading in the right direction?

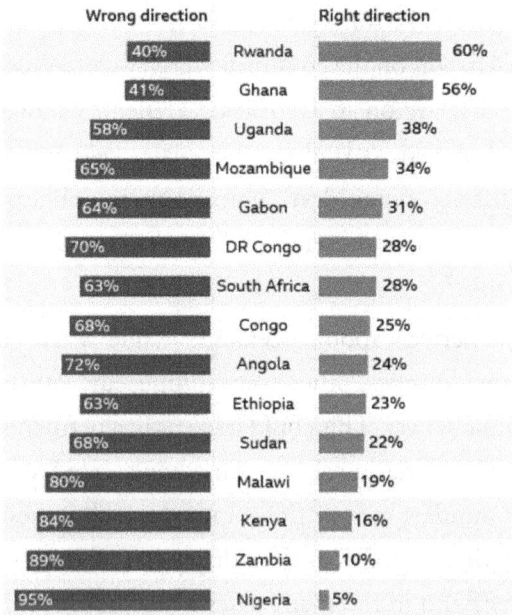

Wrong direction	Country	Right direction
40%	Rwanda	60%
41%	Ghana	56%
58%	Uganda	38%
65%	Mozambique	34%
64%	Gabon	31%
70%	DR Congo	28%
63%	South Africa	28%
68%	Congo	25%
72%	Angola	24%
63%	Ethiopia	23%
68%	Sudan	22%
80%	Malawi	19%
84%	Kenya	16%
89%	Zambia	10%
95%	Nigeria	5%

*African youth (nationals of each country) between the age of 18-24

Source: Africa Youth Survey 2022   BBC

BBC Africa Youth Survey on Country Direction - Shows Rwanda and Ghana positive, Nigeria and others negative

It's weird to hear Black American nationalists (on social media) bash and negate Kagame's great accomplishments but a scientific question is how do the majority of Africans, who travel there and live on the continent, feel about him? Do you see the majority of African leaders bashing Kagame? My cousin traveled to Rwanda recently and the first thing she told me about her experience is "they take care of their people over there?" I didn't tell her anything about my research, but it was striking how her biggest takeaway was that she could tell the country cared deeply about their people. Am I going to listen to a Pan-African Nationalist in a dashiki in Brooklyn or the millions of Africans who are in the paint and live on the continent? Some can be too radical to learn anything, to go out and build something substantial, that will be here for their people, when they are long gone. I have traveled to countries such as Mozambique, Ghana, South Africa, and Nigeria, the largest African country by population. I like to listen to Africans who live on the continent about African affairs. Proximity to the truth and the reality matters. I wouldn't want Africans on the continent who have never been to America telling me what's going on in Detroit or Harlem. Compare the rise of Rwanda to Black America's landscape. In many neighborhoods, we have more churches than economic development centers, political organizations, factories, trade schools, and community banks combined. Are we even examining the ratios?

This creates a perfect spook scenario: while we're building and supporting more churches, other communities and our adversaries are building economic power. This could leave us in a permanent position of prayer to solve material problems involving freedom, justice, and equality. Every Sunday, money flows into these churches, but unlike a factory or bank, that capital doesn't multiply—it often just maintains the building and staff and in too many cases a nice house and car or even a private jet for the pastor. It's often a one-way economic drain masked by spiritual fulfillment. **We have to develop new organizations that receive financial contributions outside houses of worship.**

Look at China's development model: although officially atheist, they've lifted more people out of poverty faster than any nation in history.[10] This economic miracle and transformational prosperity was done by more scientific thinking and no prayer.[11] This isn't about attacking religion—it's about understanding how political power requires economic foundations. China built factories and industry while others built temples, and the material results are undeniable.

The scientific reality? Economic power anchors our political power. Too many churches can drain community resources and become distractions from greater organization around economic and political development. Spiritual comfort doesn't create jobs. Prayer without production keeps us dependent. Other communities that focus on wealth creation are in a better competitive position. Material progress requires material investment.

It's not about a choice of church or mosque versus science but the mathematical ratios and proportions we need to watch out for. We must ask: How many political and economic centers do we need to own in proportion to houses of worship? Where do we say we are grossly imbalanced based on our political and economic objectives? We shouldn't have five hundred churches for every unit of political and economic development, for example. A 500 to 1 ratio. We need a better balance that yields greater material results for us and the next generation to build on.

Many historically Black churches have functioned as vital political organizing hubs and economic empowerment centers, providing credit unions, business incubation, and affordable housing alongside their spiritual guidance. However, every new house of worship represents capital and energy that could have gone into wealth-generating enterprises and political organizations.

The solution isn't choosing between faith and progress—it's about scientific ratios. If we have one thousand churches but only 1 Black-owned factory, trade school, or economic development center, that's not a formula for political power. We need to redirect some of that community energy and capital from spiritual infrastructure to our economic and political development. Otherwise, we'll keep praying for prosperity while our economic and political weakness becomes permanent.

Rwanda examining how many churches they had in proportion to productive factories is not just a lesson about Rwanda, it is how we should think, in ratios and percentages, measuring proportionality.

41

Thinking in measurement terms helps us think more scientifically and this anchors greater efficiencies and higher probability outcomes.

The Science

- Check the ratios: Rwanda asked "700 churches, how many factories?" - we need similar mathematical thinking
- Economic power anchors political power: You can't build political influence without economic foundations
- Prosperity gospel = neoliberalism in religious drag: Both turn structural problems into individual spiritual failures
- Too many churches can drain community resources: Every new church represents capital that could have gone to wealth-generating enterprises
- Balance spiritual needs with material progress: It's not church OR business - it's finding the right proportions for collective advancement

---

[1] Ignatius Ssuuna, "Rwanda Closes Thousands of Churches in Bid for More Control," AP News, April 4, 2018.

[2] "Rwanda Ranked 42 out of 139 Countries on Rule of Law," World Justice Project Rule of Law Index, October 14, 2021.

[3] Jonny Walfisz, "Rwanda Sixth Safest Country for Solo Travelers," Euronews, May 25, 2022.

[4] Eugene Uwimana, "Rwanda Co-Hosts Anti-Corruption Excellence Award Summit," Voice of America, December 12, 2019.

[5] "Rwanda Seventh Most Efficient Government Globally," Agence Ecofin, July 15, 2015.

[6] BBC, "Libya: Gaddafi regime's US-UK spy links revealed," BBC News, September 4, 2011. https://www.bbc.com/news/world-africa-14774533

[7] Richard A. Clarke, "The CIA's Former Partners: Hussein and Bin Laden," in Against All Enemies: Inside America's War on Terror (New York: Free Press, 2004).

[8] BBC News, "Rwanda Genocide: 100 Days of Slaughter," BBC News, April 4, 2019.

[9] Châtelot, C., "The dark side of Paul Kagame, the Rwandan autocrat who fascinates the West," Le Monde, May 28, 2024. https://www.lemonde.fr/en/international/article/2024/05/28/the-dark-side-of-paul-kagame-the-rwandan-autocrat-who-fascinates-the-west_6672925_4.html

[10] CFR.org Editors, "Religion in China," Council on Foreign Relations, May 15, 2024. https://www.cfr.org/backgrounder/religion-china

[11] Fishman, T. C., China, Inc.: How the Rise of the Next Superpower Challenges America and the World (Scribner, 2006

A Super Organization for Black America

> *"To win any struggle for liberation, you have to have the way as well as the will, an overall ideology and strategy that stem from a scientific analysis of history and present conditions."* —*Assata Shakur*

When I was in college at Morehouse, I was ready to give my life on a full-time basis to the cause of Black America. However, there wasn't an organization that could get the best out of my passion and develop skills in a manner that would be felt for generations. The Black legacy organizations have done good work but never laid out a comprehensive economic and political vision with solid accountability over a ten-year measurement period. I am talking about a model organization that was modern and secular but whose vision wasn't trapped between conventional political football, between Democrats and Republicans.

During the audit period, 1995–2025, we saw the resilience of organizations such as the National Association for the Advancement of Colored People (NAACP), National Action Network, Urban League, Rainbow Push Coalition, and the Nation of Islam. Urban League's balance sheet grew exponentially over the audit period with over $300 million of total assets [1] while Al Sharpton achieved elite institutional legitimacy with the backing of two sitting American presidents (Obama and Biden) and the Anti-Defamation League (ADL). [2]

Accounting scandals and ethics questions aside, Black Lives Matter was new and positively influential in many ways, but what quality of organization do Black Americans deserve in 2025? After carefully examining our organizations, we see that we need more innovative organizations for modern times. Organizations that don't get involved in the various divisive and distracting culture wars and are hyper focused on strategic Black American political goals, and that are transparent in their accounting and the material results. [3] Where are the organizations that take Black Americans seriously and are appropriate for modern times? Where are the organizations that don't act like they have a muzzle slapped on by the Democratic Party or corporate donors and that at least act independently and with the moral courage of Dr. Martin Luther King Jr.? [4]

Where are the organizations that put key performance indicators (KPIs) and results over subservience to the Democratic Party, conspiracy theories, UFOs saving us, headline-grabbing media fights with Jews, and reactive politics based on the latest police shooting? Our organizations have fought hard to thrive, establish themselves, and stay relevant. Still, we must evolve into organizational designs and expressions that are more advanced and fit for the modern times. The risk orientation of our legacy organizations and leadership is overwhelmingly defensive and stagnant. We need an offensive playbook that pushes a strategic Black American agenda forward while also showing a capability to challenge powerful institutional interests.

We can't be serious about our political development without organization at the center. But we can't start with institutions we don't control, particularly institutions dominated by conflicts of interest and corruption. Greed is often a priority of professional advancement and political celebrity. No leader is coming to save us, no political messiah. If there was, when he or she dies, the movement can be expected to die. I believe we have outgrown the productivity of the single-leader model and must move to a national council (NC) model. We must develop a political model of governance that doesn't make it easy to exploit us and cut corners with leadership that isn't backed by the majority. You must talk to our dominant political body if you want to meet with us—our NC. We need leadership that welcomes accountability against a specific set of goals. We need organizations and leadership that strategically negotiates with the Democratic Party versus taking orders from the Democratic Party.

The NC concept is an organization for the modern times. Bolder, more independent, and more innovative. Better capitalized. Better digital media strategy. An organization that better gives the younger generation a voice. The NC should start with a predetermined number of members and transition to a more significant number. Once the initial members are selected, the NC should transition to elections every four or five years. The NC's goal is to advance freedom, justice, and quality for Black Americans with specific strategic goals. The NC should focus on these five priority areas:

Reparations for Black Americans ® The focus should be on federal reparations in the United States but also on African countries that need to come to terms with their complicity in our enslavement. The organization is committed to pure cash reparations distributed directly to Black Americans who are descendants of enslaved people. Pure Reparations requires scientific organization first. We must be honest: PURE ORGANIZATION comes before PURE REPARATIONS. While building toward federal reparations long-term, we should simultaneously pursue targeted wins with specific African countries, seeking natural resources, land, and cash grants for Black American organizations advancing reparations advocacy.

Artificial Intelligence (A) We must play critical roles in the opportunities from this technology and benefit from it at scale. While taking advantage of the possibilities with AI-related businesses and technologies, we must also scrutinize and de-risk the technology as it relates to Black Americans specifically. We must institutionalize AI in Black American culture, as much or more than sports and entertainment. Our unique history and our cultural creativity positions us to use this technology, in ways others haven't thought of and in ways that advance our own collective freedom, justice, and equality.

Independent Political Party (I) I believe the two-party system is grossly inefficient, particularly for Black Americans. We must wear political clothes that fit and prioritize us while working strategically, where we can, with the two main parties. "Independent political parties have failed before" is not just defeatist—it's scientifically unsound. The sample size is too small for statistical significance, and we can't point to any sustained 10-year effort. Our current duopoly capture guarantees political impotence. There's a mathematical truth we've ignored: no substantial rewards come without proportional risks. Capital markets move trillions annually based on this principle, yet we refuse to apply it to our politics. The Democratic Party functions as a political slave-master, exploiting "house nigga" dynamics while their chosen leaders get rich and prominent.

Supplemental Education (S) While supporting and partnering with historically Black colleges and universities (HBCUs), we should be keen on developing supplemental education programs at scale. We should look for gaps and educational areas where we can be the most helpful. Our additional education will include financial sciences, organizational development, and AI.

Economic Development (E) The Black American sovereign wealth fund (SWF) and other economic development initiatives promote self-sufficiency and economic and financial prosperity. The support should include personal financial support, education, and resources to support Black businesses, entrepreneurs, and economic cooperation between entities. The support function should also include leveraging government resources, including contracts, tax benefits, credits, efficiencies, and grants.

The Science

- Current organizations are outdated: Legacy civil rights groups lack comprehensive vision and measurable accountability
- Move from single-leader to council model: No more messiah politics - develop collective leadership with elections every 4-5 years
- Focus on five priorities: Reparations, Artificial Intelligence, Independent Political Party, Supplemental Education, Economic Development (RAISE)
- Build for modern times: New organizations must be secular, transparent, and technology-forward
- Pure organization comes before pure reparations: Can't achieve policy goals without institutional power first

[1] National Urban League. (2023). Annual Report 2023. https://nul.org/annual-report-2023

[2] Times of Israel. (2020, June 29). Why is the ADL aligning itself with Al Sharpton? Blogs - Times of Israel. https://blogs.timesofisrael.com/why-is-the-adl-aligning-itself-with-al-sharpton/

[3] Gaskins, Kayla. (2023, May 31). BLM finances under fire: Only 33% of donations given to charities as execs paid millions. ABC 15 News. https://wpde.com/news/nation-world/blm-finances-under-fire-only-33-of-donations-given-to-charities-as-execs-paid-millions-black-lives-matter-racism-bankruptcy-deficit-fundraising-fundraisers-george-floyd-breonna-taylor-patrisse-cullors-tamir-rice-fraud-scam

[4] King, Martin Luther, Jr. (1967, April 4). Beyond Vietnam. The Martin Luther King, Jr. Research and Education Institute, Stanford University. https://kinginstitute.stanford.edu/encyclopedia/

A Sovereign Wealth Fund for Black America

> *"When you see people call themselves revolutionary, always talking about destroying, destroying, destroying but never talking about building or creating, they're not revolutionary. They do not understand the first thing about revolution. It's creating."*
> —— *Kwame Ture* [1]

It's not a coincidence that the sixth lesson starts with collective economics. After carefully auditing our political and economic affairs since 1995, I landed on the idea of a sovereign wealth fund (SWF) for Black America as a modern expression of freedom, justice, and equality. An SWF is generally an entity that acts on behalf of a government to invest, build, distribute, and diversify wealth. [2] Although Black Americans aren't a state, it doesn't mean we can't reap the efficiency and productive benefits of acting like one. Rather than just looking for individual "First Black" achievements as markers of progress, a more scientific expression is focusing on institutional markers that better represent collective progress.

A Black American SWF represents scientific thinking applied to collective economics. To own our leadership and political progress, we are going to have to give up something substantial and sacrifice. It's about turning our pennies, nickels, and dollars into real power, similar to how Elijah Muhammad's economic blueprint in the 1960s and 1970s created the largest independent Black newspaper, restaurants, bakeries, grocery stores, farmland, a fish import/export business with Peru, apartment buildings, and even a bank.[3] No one had stretched the economic imagination of Black America and was then bold and competent enough to make it reality.

The math is straightforward: if one million Black Americans gave $20 a month, that's $20 million monthly to buy assets owned for collective benefit. The SWF could acquire farmland, real estate, stocks, gold, natural resources, stakes in private businesses, and bonds. Once established, it could offer grants to other Black organizations aligned with principles of freedom, justice, and equality. With $200 million in assets growing at an average of 10 percent annually, that's $20 million a year in investment gains. You can think of a sovereign wealth fund as a "People's Bank" that owns and grows assets. A sovereign wealth fund also has the potential to issue dividends back to the people.

Black American Collective Investment Fund
$25 Monthly Contributions at 10% Annual Return

Fund Growth by Participation Level

Contributions	Monthly	Year 5	Year 10	Year 20	Year 30	Mult.
250,000	$6.3M	$100.7M	$15B	$77B	$82.6B	14.5x
1 Million	$25M	$2.0B	$6.7B	$15.6B	$134.6B	14.5x
5 Million	$125M	$15.1B	$33.7B	$152.9B	$663.5B	14.5x

Key Findings:
- With just $25 monthly contributions, collective investment creates exponential wealth
- At 5 million contributors, fund of Black Americans, the fund would reach $663 billion after 30 years
- Every dollar contributed multiplies 14.5x through compound growth at 10% average annual return
- Even with modest 250,000 participants, the fund reaches $82.6 billion after 30 years
- The collective fund demonstrates how small, consistent contributions can create transformational economic power

Black American Collective Investment Fund Table - Shows growth projections of $25 monthly contributions at different participation levels

Alaska has a state expression of the SWF model.[4] I was always familiar with institutions just taking money but what if we created an institution that invests and grows assets and gives a portion back to the people?

In 1968, Alaska discovered oil on state land, initially squandering much of the windfall from exploration licenses. Learning from this mistake, the state established the Alaska Permanent Fund in 1976, creating a sovereign wealth fund that sets aside at least 25% of annual mineral royalties for investment. This innovative approach ensures Alaska's natural resource wealth benefits both current and future generations, transforming the state's oil and mining revenues into a permanent financial legacy rather than a temporary windfall. If you were to become an Alaska resident right now, you would be eligible to receive a check from the state fund and this check could be more depending on family size.

Since its first payout in 1980, the fund has distributed annual dividends to every Alaskan citizen, with payments typically ranging from $1,000 to $2,000 per person. The fund has grown to over $64 billion, providing substantial financial support to Alaskan families - a family of four received $4,456 in 2021, with the largest individual dividend of $3,269 paid during Sarah Palin's governorship in 2008. [5] This model demonstrates how collectively managed natural resource wealth can create lasting economic benefits distributed directly to citizens as co-beneficiaries of their state's common resources.

Global examples show the potential. Norway's Government Pension Fund Global holds $1.35 trillion, worth about $250,000 per Norwegian citizen. Starting with oil revenues, it now invests in real estate, stocks, and bonds globally, excluding companies like tobacco and arms manufacturers on ethical grounds.

Nigeria's sovereign wealth fund launched in 2013 with $1 billion and now manages $3.5 billion, focusing on infrastructure development. The fund invests in critical projects like the Second Niger Bridge and Lagos–Ibadan Expressway, showing how SWFs can drive national development. [6]

Singapore manages two sovereign funds: GIC Private Limited ($744 billion) and Temasek Holdings ($215 billion). GIC ranks as the most active state-owned investor globally, whereas Temasek leads in tech investment, demonstrating how different funds can serve different strategic purposes.[7]

Top 10 Sovereign Wealth Funds Globally - Shows proposed Black American fund would rank 7th globally

China's Investment Corporation manages $1.2 trillion, making strategic investments globally. In 2017, it acquired a 45 percent stake in a New York City office skyscraper at 1211 Avenue of the Americas for $2.3 billion, showing how SWFs can build international assets.[8]

How is SWF thinking different from our dominant discourse?

Spook Thinking

- I want to see a Black American in the White House

- I want to see more Black American NFL coaches

- Jay-Z owns 0.15 percent of a sports team; that's progress. That's a good deal even if the rights of Brooklyn residents were sacrificed and the many were sacrificed for one

- I want to see more Black American CEOs in the Fortune 500

Scientific Thinking

- How do we collectively own an NFL team?

- How can material benefits be shared efficiently by hundreds of thousands or millions of Black Americans?

- What if we collectively purchased real estate, pooling our resources together and distributing gains proportionately?

Look at the Green Bay Packers model: Their 2011 stock sale added 250,000 new shareholders and raised $67.4 million. Their 1997 sale added 105,989 shareholders and raised $24 million.[9] The team democratized shareholder ownership and offered innovative incentives for super fans. As the team gained in value, the super fans who owned shares could benefit and be rewarded for their investment. Similarly, a Black American SWF could distribute value back to Black American supporters through dividends. Most of the investment gains would be held by the institution and reinvested but a portion could go back to supporters via dividends.

There is nothing stopping Black Americans from collectively organizing around a common cause and following this model, with our cultural orientation, innovation, and creative touches and for our own benefit. The five factors for SWF success should be as follows:

1. Governance

2. Transparency

3. Competency

4. Imagination

5. Results

Why is a Black American SWF needed? Because imagination and innovation are required. Our economic development is directly connected to our political development. A stronger aggregate economic position equals stronger political leverage. We don't need individual wins as much as we need institutional wins that are strategically connected to Black Americans in the collective. Marches against police killings and brutality address anti-Black structures, but what's our proactive economic plan? A pro-active economic plan could more positively impact millions of Black Americans, more than police brutality negatively impacts Black Americans. We need more energy and focus going to play offense vs victim-oriented defense. The world moves on innovation and new ideas, following those bold enough to paint them on reality's canvas.

Implementation requires establishing transparent governance structures, fostering community engagement through town halls and workshops, and potentially starting with focused pilot projects. The SWF can also be training grounds to develop investing, operational, and analytical talent within Black America. Partnerships with existing Black institutions, particularly historically Black colleges and universities (HBCUs), could provide institutional credibility and expertise. HBCUs and existing Black American institutions should be a critical resource in the SWF effort.

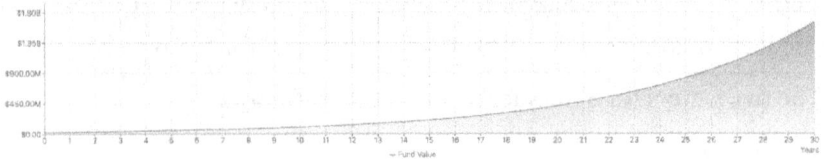

Black American Sovereign Wealth Fund Growth Projection
$25M Initial Investment at 15% Average Annual Return

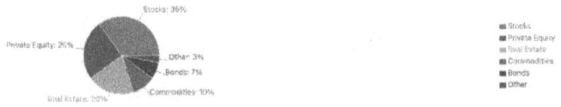

Strategic Asset Allocation

Black American Collective Investment Fund Growth Projection - Shows exponential growth curve over 30 years

For the scale and complexity of our political capture and problems, we need a commensurate institutional response. This would entail innovating and updating existing institutions for the modern times and creating new institutions that will live beyond us and provide a platform for the next generation to take it to the next level.

The Science

- Current organizations are outdated: Legacy civil rights groups lack comprehensive vision and measurable accountability
- Move from single-leader to council model: No more messiah politics - develop collective leadership with elections every 4-5 years
- Focus on five priorities: Reparations, Artificial Intelligence, Independent Political Party, Supplemental Education, Economic Development (RAISE)
- Build for modern times: New organizations must be secular, transparent, and technology-forward
- Pure organization comes before pure reparations: Can't achieve policy goals without institutional power first

[1] Kwame Ture, "Revolution is Creating, Not Destroying," Speech at Howard University, April 15, 1968.

[2] Truman, Edwin M. "Sovereign Wealth Funds: Threat or Salvation?" Peterson Institute for International Economics, 2010.

[3] Evanzz, Karl. "The Messenger: The Rise and Fall of Elijah Muhammad." Pantheon, 1999.

[4] Alaska Permanent Fund Corporation, "Annual Report FY 2021: Distributions to Alaska Residents," Alaska Department of Revenue, November 2021.

[5] Bohrer, Becky. "Alaskans get a $1,312 oil dividend check this year. The political cost of the benefit is high," Associated Press, October 5, 2023.

[6] "Nigeria sovereign wealth fund's assets rise to $3.5 bln, minister says," Reuters, September 1, 2021.

[7] Sovereign Wealth Fund Institute, "Top 100 Largest Sovereign Wealth Fund Rankings by Total Assets," SWFI.com, February 17, 2025.

[8] Bloomberg News. "China's $1.2 Trillion Wealth Fund Reorganizes Key Investment Arm." Bloomberg, July 20, 2022. https://www.bloomberg.com/news/articles/2022-07-21/china-s-1-2-trillion-wealth-fund-reorganizes-key-investment-arm

[9] Ryman, Richard. "NFL Approves Another Green Bay Packers Stock Sale Pending Regulatory Approval," Green Bay Press-Gazette, October 27, 2021.

OBAMA AND THE NEW BLACKS

Obama Wasn't Free

> *"The New Black doesn't blame other races for our issues. The New Black dreams and realises that it's not pigmentation: it's a mentality and it's either going to work for you or it's going to work against you. And you've got to pick the side you're going to be on."*
> — Pharrell

> *"If the playing field is perceived to be more balanced than before, then the need for policies to address inequality is lessened"*
> — Dr. Nicholas Valentino, University of Michigan

> *"Didn't miss racism. Just hoped we were well past it. We elected a black president."* — Alyssa Milano, Actress (via X/Twitter)

> *"We have tried to deal with our original sin of slavery by fighting a civil war, by passing landmark civil rights legislation, elected an African-American president. I think we're always a work in progress in this country, but no one currently alive was responsible for that."* — Senator Mitch McConnell, Senate Majority Leader (June 2019)

If Black America had treated Barack Obama as white and focused solely on policy rather than identity affinity and symbolism, could we have pulled more policy risk-taking for Black Americans out of him? This question forces us to confront our own role in the spook dynamics of his presidency. Our emotional investment in his symbolism may have actually reduced our leverage to demand substantive change.

Barack Obama's strategic approach to his racial and political identity was more calculated than many recognized. According to historian David J. Garrow in his biography "Rising Star," Obama had proposed to Sheila Miyoshi Jager, a woman of Dutch and Japanese heritage, before eventually breaking off their relationship as his political ambitions grew. A friend of the couple told Garrow that Obama had expressed concern about his political viability, saying, "If I am going out with a white woman, I have no standing here." Jager herself recalled when Obama's transformation occurred: "I remember very clearly when this transformation happened, and I remember very specifically that by 1987, about a year into our relationship, he already had his sights on becoming president."

Slavery Reparations
Support is rising in Congress for legislation creating a commission studying reparations to Black Americans for slavery and discrimination, raising prospects for House passage this year.

Number of co-sponsors for House reparations legislation

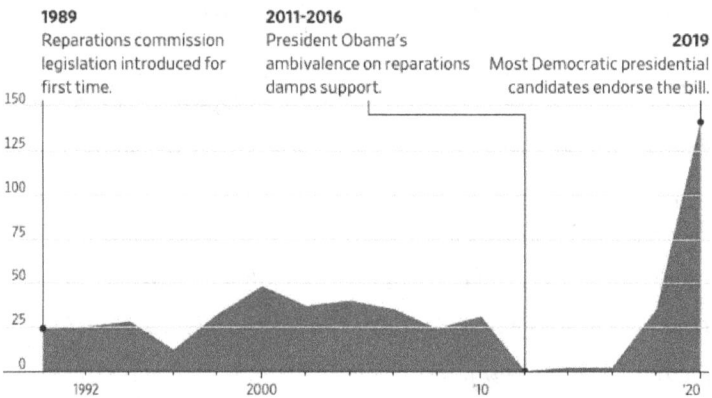

Notes: Years indicate second year of a two-year congressional session. Data for 2019-2020 as of July 29
Source: Congress.gov

Similarly, when we discovered his membership in Reverend Wright's Trinity United Church, many viewed it as confirmation of his Black American authenticity. What few recognized was that this church served as a strategic hub for Chicago's Black political elite and ambitious professionals—including figures like Oprah Winfrey. For someone with presidential aspirations navigating Chicago's political landscape, membership in Wright's congregation represented calculated positioning as much as spiritual commitment.

Obama's strategic positioning exemplifies a broader pattern where symbolic Black representation can be carefully cultivated without corresponding commitments to structural change and policy risk-taking that would meaningfully benefit Black Americans. In auditing the 1995-2025 measurement period in Black American politics, it's clear the American system is too entrenched with money, corruption, lobbying, conflicts of interest, and devilishment for Black Americans to assume that identity alone guarantees policy results or risk taking on behalf of Black Americans. By embracing the symbolism of Obama's identity (Michelle too) without demanding corresponding policy commitments, we may have inadvertently weakened our collective bargaining position. The hyper-calculating Obama would need a hyper-calculating Black America, to extract the most value out of his Presidency. The mathematics of political power demands we recognize the difference between symbolic representation and material change.

No Black American-Oriented Policy While Race Relations Get Worse			
CNN/ORC Poll, October 2016			
Question	Overall	Whites	Blacks
Race relations have gotten worse since Obama became president	54%	57%	40%
Criminal justice system favors whites over blacks	52%	50%*	75%*
Discrimination against blacks is a "very serious" problem	42%	34%	73%
Believe at least some local police are prejudiced against blacks	18%	13%	43%
Favorable view of Black Lives Matter movement	44%	38%	78%

Source: CNN/ORC Poll conducted September 28-October 2, 2016 (n=1,501 adults)
*Approximate values based on article description: "About three-quarters of blacks and one-half of whites feel the system favors whites"

Our emotional investment in his symbolism may have actually reduced our leverage to demand policy risk-taking. The fundamental principles of costs versus benefits and the interplay of risks and rewards should govern our understanding of our political science. In the aftermath of Obama's historic election as the first Kenyan-American president, there was a palpable sense of euphoria, particularly within Black America. To many, including my younger self, Obama's ascent felt like a political messiah offering hope and change—classic spook thinking.[1] By treating him as "our" president rather than simply "the" president, we may have paradoxically weakened our negotiating position.

The Math of Symbolism versus Substance:

- Symbolic Value: First Black president, Black First Family
- Structural Cost: Near-death of reparations movement; end to protest politics
- Political Cost: Reduced urgency for systemic change
- Strategic Cost: Organizational complacency
- Hidden Cost: Our own reduced political leverage
- Tactical Cost: Emotional investment over strategic pressure

When we apply scientific thinking and go underneath the surface, troubling patterns emerge. A University of Michigan study revealed that while Obama's victory decreased perceptions of racism, it simultaneously heightened opposition to policies addressing racial disparities.[2] If Obama was going to trigger a white-lash against Black Americans and reduce perceptions of structural racism, we had better be getting something specific and substantial to compensate for these L's.

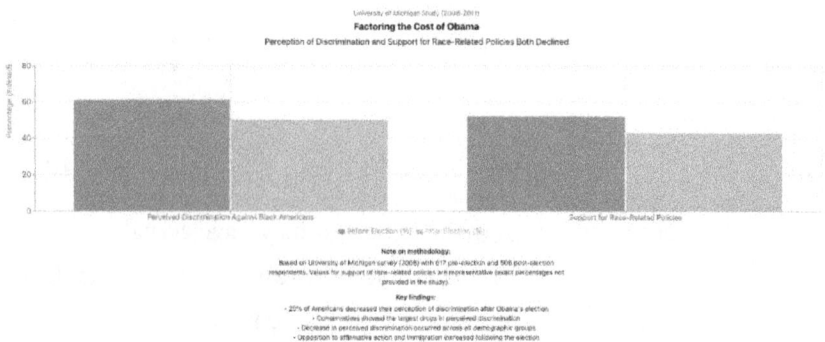

University of Michigan Study (Dovidio 2011)
Factoring the Cost of Obama
Perception of Discrimination and Support for Race-Related Policies Both Declined

Note on methodology:
Based on University of Michigan survey (2008) with 617 pre-election and 506 post-election respondents. Values for support of race-related policies are representative (exact percentages not provided in the study)

Key findings:
- 20% of Americans decreased their perception of discrimination after Obama's election.
- Conservatives showed the largest drops in perceived discrimination.
- Decrease in perceived discrimination occurred across all demographic groups.
- Opposition to affirmative action and immigration increased following the election.

University of Michigan Study on Obama's Election - Shows decreased
perception of discrimination and support for race-related policies

Black Median Wealth (1992-2016)

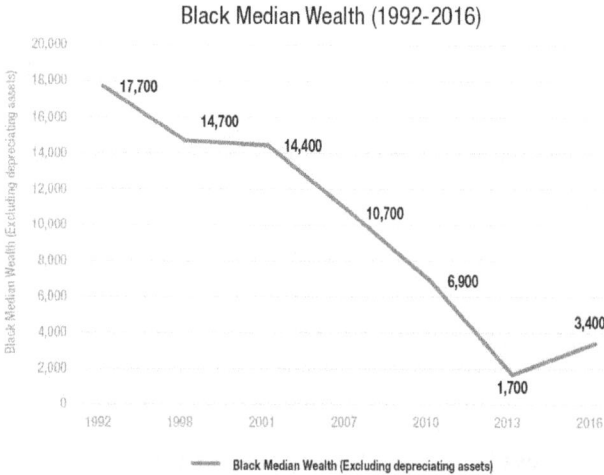

Source: Edward Wolff (November 2017). "Household Wealth Trends in the United States, 1962 to 2016: Has Middle Class Wealth Recovered?" National Bureau of Economic Research. Retrieved from http://www.nber.org/papers/w24085 "

GOP leader Mitch McConnell later claimed electing Obama was part of paying for slavery's sin—revealing how diversity can be weaponized against structural change.[3] It's important to go into the minds of leaders like Mitch McConnell who thought Obama was our reparations or actress Alyssa Milano who admitted she thought racism was mostly over when Obama was elected.[4] These are good proxies for how the system was using Obama against our aggregate political position. Whenever the system believes it is doing us a favor by placing a Black face in a high position, it is simultaneously taking something material away from us. This transaction is rarely made explicit. Researchers from Purdue University and Washington University found elevated symbolism is used by politicians with Black American voters specifically, to increase turnout. Symbolism is an effective Black American voter turnout driver.[5]

The Ratio Problem: When potentially 150 units of symbolism exist for every single unit (150:1) of structural reform, we face a dangerous imbalance. This potential ratio isn't accidental; it's a feature of how institutions use superficial diversity and tricknology to maintain the status quo while appearing to change. "Just shut up niggas, we have Black faces at the top now" isn't just a crude summary—it's a strategic calculation that worked precisely because of our emotional investment in so-called representation. If representation actually represents a Black American policy agenda and risk-taking on our behalf, then it's science. If representation is based on identity and skin color, it's spook.

Consider the evidence:

1. Obama's dismissal of reparations, which killed momentum during his terms[6]

2. His Morehouse speech suggesting "no more excuses" post-election[7]

3. Celebrity voices like Alyssa Milano using his presidency to declare racism solved

4. Decreased support for affirmative action during his presidency

5. Reduced perceived urgency around race-specific programs

6. Our own reluctance to apply pressure due to racial solidarity

The Obama Effect created four specific forms of spook:

1. Progress Illusion: Symbolic masking of structural stagnation

2. Complacency Trap: Reduced incentive for new political frameworks

3. Perception Distortion: Making America appear to change faster than reality

4. Leverage Loss: Emotional investment reducing political pressure

If we're all spooked up on Obama-ism, like I was, we risk something far more dangerous than simple distraction. This spook sedates our political imagination and independent organizing capacity. When we believe the system is fundamentally changing in our favor because of optical representation at the top, we postpone the hard work of building independent power and alternative visions. There is the potential a symbolism opiate to retard our political imagination. Meanwhile, the system merely redecorates its facade while leaving the foundation of anti-Black American structural racism intact and the tricknology operational. The shell game deceptively positions symbolic victories to mask structural losses. We think we're printing W's on the board but we are actually accumulating L's in our political balance sheet, often without even recognizing the transaction taking place.

Obama's relationship with structural racism presents a more complex calculus than simple ignorance or complicity. As a former constitutional law professor and community organizer in Chicago, he understood America's racial architecture intimately. His navigation of these waters suggests a sophisticated political algebra: How much truth could be spoken while maintaining the coalition necessary to govern? How much structural critique could survive the demands of the presidency? And crucially, how much pressure did we fail to apply because of racial solidarity?

Consider his evolution:

- The radical clarity of "Dreams from My Father"

- The soaring unity of his 2004 Democratic National Committee (DNC) speech

- The careful moderation of his campaigns

- The constraints of his presidency

- The relative freedom of his post-presidency

- Our own evolution from critics of the establishment to defenders when a Black Face is on the wrapper

Obama's 2013 Morehouse speech suggesting "no more excuses" because of his election wasn't just poor analysis—it reflected the price of power in American politics. Obama made a series of strategic choices to maintain political viability, but these choices came with costs to Black American structural progress. The political mathematics demanded he transform from activist to symbol, from critic to unifier, from someone who named structural racism to someone who often had to speak about it in code. Our emotional investment in his success may have made this transformation easier and less costly for him. Because Obama was a religious-like experience for Black America, there was no material incentive for him to take many risks, on behalf of Black Americans.

This transformation wasn't simply a betrayal or a strategy—it reflected Obama's personal calculations as much as any external pressure. While operating at the highest levels of American power certainly imposes constraints, Obama rarely tested these boundaries or attempted to expand them. The same system that celebrated a Kenyan-American president didn't actually require that president to avoid confronting anti-Black structural orientation—Obama chose this path of least resistance.

Obama appeared to believe his Kenyan-American identity itself was the gift that Black Americans should be grateful for, not tangible policy risk-taking on our behalf. The gift was offered in the currency of symbolism, not in the currency of material change. Even in his final term, freed from reelection concerns when conventional wisdom suggested more freedom to speak boldly on racial justice, he remained largely silent. If the machine that enabled his rise dictated his limits, Obama never seemed interested in challenging those limits or using his unique platform to push for Black American interests, unlike his vigorous advocacy for Silicon Valley's tech lobby or Wall Street's financial interests.

This raises fundamental questions about political mathematics: if Obama's race-neutral policies were the optimal approach, then Black Americans should logically direct their fanatical support toward white Democratic politicians who would deliver more substantial policy results. Political science demands we calculate the expected value of candidates based on their policy commitments rather than identity factors. A white politician delivering robust policy gains for Black Americans would objectively outperform a Black politician receiving overpriced credit on account of identity affinity and symbolism. The scientific approach requires us to measure exactly how much value should be placed on identity versus policy orientation, and in what proportions and ratios.

Our racial solidarity became not just one of Obama's constraints, but one of his strategic advantages—a blank check of Black American support that demanded minimal policy returns and required little substantive risk-taking. This political mathematics explains why Obama could simultaneously enjoy unprecedented Black electoral support while delivering underwhelming policy results specifically addressing Black American concerns.

Strategic Questions:

- Was Obama's symbolic value worth the structural costs?
- Did his presidency delay more fundamental changes?
- How do we measure the opportunity cost of lost momentum?
- What's the real price of political pacification?
- Can symbolic representation ever align with structural change?
- How do we maintain pressure while celebrating progress?
- What would treating Black politicians as white look like in practice?

The scientific approach requires measuring both benefits and costs. Yes, having a Kenyan-American president was historically significant. But when we count the costs of delayed structural change, reduced perceptions of anti-Black American racism, weakened movements, and enhanced resistance to race-specific reforms, the math and political balance sheet become more complicated. This isn't about diminishing Obama's individual achievement—it's about understanding its full impact through the lens of political science rather than emotional symbolism.

No Black American-Oriented Policy While Race Relations Get Worse

CNN/ORC Poll, October 2016

Question	Overall	Whites	Blacks
Race relations have gotten worse since Obama became president	54%	57%	40%
Criminal justice system favors whites over blacks	52%	50%*	75%*
Discrimination against blacks is a "very serious" problem	42%	34%	73%
Believe at least some local police are prejudiced against blacks	18%	13%	43%
Favorable view of Black Lives Matter movement	44%	38%	78%

Source: CNN/ORC Poll conducted September 28-October 2, 2016 (n=1,501 adults)
*Approximate values based on article description: "About three-quarters of blacks and one-half of whites feel the system favors whites."

CNN/ORC Poll on Race Relations During Obama Presidency - Shows 54% believed race relations worsened under Obama

This pattern of trading structural change for symbolic victory isn't just about the Obama presidency—it's about our vulnerability to political spook thinking. When we mistake representation for power, symbolism for substance, we risk another generation of delayed policy results and structural change. The scientific approach demands we measure actual structural changes, not just count Black faces in high places. Otherwise, we'll keep celebrating cosmetic victories while the deeper architecture of inequality and tricknology remains untouched and fully operational. Many will say "you're just going to let the Republicans win" but this misses the scientific factors at play. Whoever is President or in Congress, Democrat or Republican, we must position for maximum political efficiency to get the most policy results as possible so this is not a Democrat or Republican question, it's a political efficiency and strategic question. When any Democrat is elected, how do we activate pressure points and extract the most policy value out of him or her.

The lesson for future Black political figures is clear: our support must be earned through policy commitment to a Black American policy agenda and commensurate risk-taking, not assumed through racial solidarity. Only by treating our politicians as white—focusing on their actions rather than their identity—can we maintain the leverage and political efficiency necessary for political transformation. To de-risk the probability of political exploitation and neglect, we must reject symbolism and identity affinity as a primary political currency. If we discount identity affinity and symbolism, we may in fact get more risk taking and policy results.

Obama dumping his white girlfriend and marrying Michelle, a brilliant, beautiful Black American woman descended from slaves, might satisfy our cultural pride, but it doesn't fix the poisoned drinking water in Flint, Michigan or Jackson, Mississippi. His strategic attendance at Reverend Wright's church might have signaled he was 'down with the cause,' but that symbolic alignment offered no material support to Black American workers fighting to unionize against Obama's billionaire friend Jeff Bezos at Amazon. The mathematics of real-world outcomes demands we distinguish between identity performance and policy results—between what looks like progress and what actually delivers it.

Remember, the spook seller profits and gets rich from exploiting inefficiencies and mystery. Just as financial markets can become inefficient and exploited through arbitrage, spook sellers in politics greatly benefit from receiving substantial rewards without taking commensurate risks. The wider the spread between perception and reality, the greater the inefficiency and exploitation the spook seller benefits from. By elevating a Kenyan-American President to the Black American Political Pope without demanding commensurate policy risk-taking, we didn't just miss an opportunity—we established a dangerous precedent that invites continued political exploitation against our interests.

To bust up the spook, count, audit, and measure everything. Go underneath the surface, examine multiple factors, and connect the dots that reveal the true science.

The Science

- Current organizations are outdated: Legacy civil rights groups lack comprehensive vision and measurable accountability
- Move from single-leader to council model: No more messiah politics - develop collective leadership with elections every 4-5 years
- Focus on five priorities: Reparations, Artificial Intelligence, Independent Political Party, Supplemental Education, Economic Development (RAISE)
- Build for modern times: New organizations must be secular, transparent, and technology-forward
- Pure organization comes before pure reparations: Can't achieve policy goals without institutional power first

[1] Weisenthal, Joe. "Newsweek Likens Obama To Jesus---Calls Second Term 'The Second Coming'." Business Insider, January 18, 2013. https://www.businessinsider.com/newsweek-on-obamas-second-coming-2013-1

[2] Wadley, Jared. "Obama's election reduced perceptions of racism, but boosted opposition to race-related policies." University of Michigan Institute for Social Research, May 2011.

[3] Kellman, Laurie. "McConnell on reparations for slavery: Not a 'good idea'." Associated Press, June 18, 2019. https://apnews.com/article/north-america-us-news-ap-top-news-politics-race-and-ethnicity-e3426f9abfb344aeaaa74a41e12e2271

[4] Harrison, Isheka N. "Alyssa Milano Says She Thought America Had Moved Beyond Race Because Obama Was Elected." Moguldom, May 29, 2019. https://moguldom.com/203307/alyssa-milano-says-she-thought-america-had-moved-beyond-race-because-obama-was-elected/

[5] Dietrich, Bryce J., and Matthew Hayes. "Symbols of the Struggle: Descriptive Representation and Issue-Based Symbolism in US House Speeches." Journal of Politics 85, no. 4 (October 2023).

[6] Schlesinger, Jacob M. "Reparations to Black Americans for Slavery Gain New Attention." The Wall Street Journal, July 26, 2020.

[7] "Obama's Morehouse Speech: 'Your Generation Is Uniquely Poised For Success,'" NPR, May 19, 2013.

Obama BET Interview

This 2011 BET interview provides a perfect case study in political calculation - how politicians determine exactly how much they can get while giving as little as possible in return. Here, we witness Barack Obama executing the sophisticated dance described throughout this book: seeking unwavering Black American electoral loyalty while systematically avoiding any targeted policies that would address specific historical injustices.

The data reveals a stark numerical imbalance: Obama expects 90%+ of Black votes while offering minimal risk-taking on specific Black American policy needs. When directly asked why he won't target assistance specifically for Black Americans, Obama declares "That's not how America works." Yet his administration would later allocate $12 million specifically for Holocaust survivors - a targeted program complete with a special White House envoy.[1]

This contradiction exposes the system's selective approach to historical injustice. America can and does provide targeted assistance when political will exists, just not for Black Americans. Obama's careful deflection of every question about specific Black American needs demonstrates the precision with which political capital is managed - maximum symbolic connection, minimum material commitment.

The interview shows exactly what Adolph Reed identified years earlier - Obama's talent for making white America comfortable while securing maximum Black loyalty through identity politics. It's political efficiency at its most effective: harvesting votes based on racial affinity while refusing targeted solutions that would address the specific harms inflicted on that same racial group.

As you read this exchange, notice how Obama's rhetoric creates emotional connection while his policy positions maintain system protection. This isn't just politics - it's the scientific operation of power that keeps Black America investing maximum political capital for minimum material return.

It is also true that Barack Obama is a politician, and no politician chooses the hard path when an easier one exists. The reality is that Black Americans made it extremely easy for Obama by providing near-universal support without demanding commensurate policy commitments in return. From a purely strategic standpoint, why would any politician take risks when they can maintain all the political support without them? This isn't a moral judgment on Obama specifically, but an observation about political incentives. Politicians respond to pressure, not preference. When a voting bloc delivers 90%+ support regardless of specific policy returns, the system teaches politicians they don't need to take risks for that bloc.

The lesson isn't that Obama is uniquely calculating, but that our political system rewards this calculation. Until Black American political support comes with clear conditions and consequences, we'll continue seeing this same equation: maximum support, minimum return.

Interview with Emmett Miller of Black Entertainment Television

September 26, 2011

Emmett Miller. You've just announced a new $447 billion dollar Jobs Bill.

The President. Right.

Emmett Miller. And we all know that African-American unemployment is running really high, above 16%, nearly double that of whites. How does this bill specifically target them?

The President. Well, first of all, I think it's important to remember that we are going through the worst financial crisis and subsequent economy that we've seen since the Great Depression and so the challenges for everybody out there is tough. You're right; it's especially tough for the African-American community. The steps we took in the first two and a half years made a difference. It made sure that a lot of folks were still on the job that otherwise wouldn't be. It made sure that states were able to stabilize their budgets, so they weren't laying off as many teachers or fire fighters or civil servants that are providing services every day. But, you know, what we realized over the last couple of months is that because of a whole range of issues, including what's happened overseas in Europe, that the economy needs another boost, and we've got to focus more on putting people back to work now.

Emmett Miller. And that's what this Jobs Bill is?

The President. So the Jobs Bill, overall, is designed to make sure that we're rebuilding schools and bridges and putting construction workers back to work. It makes sure that we're putting teachers back in the classroom. It makes certain that we are providing incentives to hire veterans who have been out of work, but also the long-term unemployed who are out of work. And it makes sure that we're providing tax breaks and tax credits to just about every family and every middle class person and every small business around the country. Now, with respect to the African-American community, they benefit from all of that, but in addition, we are making sure that summer jobs for youth are included in the package. Making sure that we reform our unemployment insurance so that, in addition to 1.4 million African-Americans getting unemployment insurance, we're also providing them a pathway so that they start getting some on-the-jobs training. All those things are going to have a huge impact in the African-American community. That's why we've got to get this bill passed now.

Emmett Miller. **Why not target the African-American community? Why not say then, "This is for you. This is for African-Americans?" If there was a banking crisis, then you'd target money for the banks. If there was a national disaster, you'd target your money for—for the National Disaster Relief.**

The President. **No. That—that's not how America works. America works when all of us are pulling together and everybody is focused on making sure that every single person has opportunity.** And so when we put forward a program like, for example, the Health Care Bill, our focus is people who don't have health care. Now it turns out that the majority of folks who don't have health care are also working families, and are disproportionately African-American and Latino, but that doesn't mean that it's only for them. There are a whole bunch of folks all across the country who need help. And we are going to help every single person who needs help.

Emmett Miller. Were their [*African Americans*] expectations way back when in 2009 too high?

The President. I don't think their expectations were too high. I think that people understood that it took us a long time to get into this mess; it's going to take a long time to get out of this mess. And I look folks in the eye all the time who don't have a job or who have lost their home or who are struggling otherwise. And what they tell me is, as long as I feel like you're fighting for me, as long as I feel like you have my interests at heart, then we are going to stand behind you. And that ultimately is the test.

The test is not going to be whether we solve this problem overnight. The test is are we projecting a vision for the future. That is going to be one that makes sure that every kid in this country has a shot and that the middle class is still growing and the African-American middle class is growing. Because look, the fact of the matter is that it is a test for America how well those at the bottom do, not just how well those at the top do. And what's always made this country great is the belief that everybody's got a chance regardless of race, regardless of creed. And that's a vision that I think the vast majority of Americans still share. It's been tested over the last three years, but my job is to keep on pushing in that direction.

Emmett Miller. African-American leaders have been critical of late. And it's true; you've said you're the president for all people, not just for one group. But once again, if you have a disaster in a certain area of the country, you're going to target money there. If I'm a 16-year-old kid on the south side of Chicago, okay? My dad's gone. My mom's working 10 hours a day for peanuts. All I see around me is blight. There are no help wanted signs. And you won't even say, "Look. I'm going to help you, a young African-American?" How do I feel?

The President. Emmett, first of all, that's not what people are saying. What people are saying all across the country is we're hurting and we've been hurting for a long time. And the question is how can we make sure that the economy is working for every single person? And the truth of the matter is, the vast majority of African-Americans understand that. They understand that when the economy goes well, then everybody does well. Now, there's certain communities that have been struggling even when the economy does well, which is why, for example, the Neighborhood Stabilization Program is going to be targeting communities that are having the toughest time. But the other thing I want to make sure that you don't just kind of slip in there with this notion that African-American leaders of late have been critical. There have been a handful of African-American leaders who have been critical. They were critical when I was running for president. There's always going to be somebody who's critical of the President of the United States. That's my job, in part, is particularly when the economy is going as badly as it is right now, people are going to have concerns. And they should.

What I think you're seeing all across the board in every community is that when unemployment is high and people are having a tough time, then they have to feel as if there's some hope, there's some prospects out there. And right now, the economy has been bad for a long time. It was bad before I got elected, and it has continued to be very tough for a lot of folks. Until people actually feel better about the economy, they—they're going to continue to have problems and they're going to continue to hope that the White House can do more.

Emmett Miller. What would you say to the man who stood on the podium back in 2009 that he didn't know then what he knows now?

The President. Well look, there are a lot of things we know now that we didn't know then. I mean, the day I took the oath of office we didn't know that the economy had just contracted nine percent in the previous quarter. We didn't know that 400,000 people had lost their jobs the month before and another 600,000 were going to lose their jobs the month after. So, I think the depth of the economic crisis worldwide was something that had—was glimmering on the horizon, but I don't think we fully appreciated it. The decisions we made were the right decisions: Making sure that a U.S. auto industry still existed and we didn't lose a million jobs. That's a controversial decision, but it was the right decision. The Recovery Act, which saved a whole lot of jobs in America, even though the folks who didn't lose their jobs may not have known that they might otherwise have lost their jobs. It was the right decision. So, you know, what I would tell myself if I traveled back in time? I would say it's going to be a long hard slog and the American people are going to, you know, feel kind of worn down after this much difficulty. But I'd also tell—tell that less gray person to hang in there because the American people are resilient and they have good values and they care about the right stuff, and we'll get through this.

Emmett Miller. What would you have now done differently? You talked about the rings you did right with respect to jobs, you talked about the programs you were able to put through, you talked about some of the objectives you had. What would you have now done differently in retrospect?

The President. I think if we had had better information, it would have been important for me to able to communicate to the American people the fact that this was going to be a long process. That we weren't going to fix this in six months. This was not your usual recession. This was a once-in-a-generation recession. And I think that might have helped brace people for the difficulties that—that were to come. The other thing that, as I reflect on it, is that in the first year or so we spent a lot of time just doing the right thing and not worrying about selling what we were doing. And I think that the more you're in this office, the more you have to say to yourself that telling a story to the American people is just as important as the actual policies that you're implementing. And they've got to have a sense of where it is that we're going to go, particularly during hard times.

Emmett Miller. I sat down with you five years ago in the hallway of a junior college when you were still Senator. It was "The Audacity of Hope" book tour. Do you ever think back on those times? What reflections do you have, considering who you are now?

The President. You know, Michelle tells me at least that I'm the same man now that I was when she met me when I was still in law school. I have a pretty clear idea about what's right and what—what America is all about. And it involves a belief that everybody gets a chance, that there is a sense that we're in this together. You know, we're a country that values individual initiative and everybody's got to work hard and everybody's got to be pulling their weight, but—but we look out for one another. And my politics really is based on those values, and those values haven't changed. They're constant. And the longer I'm in this office, the more I believe that when Americans are working together, there's nothing we can't accomplish. I've seen it time and time again. When we're divided, then we get less done than we need to. And part of my job is to help usher America through a very difficult time but still maintain that sense that we're in this together.

Emmett Miller. One of the questions we had was, When? When is it going to change and how long will we have to wait?

The President. Well look, you know, right now we are in a situation where the economy is stabilized, but it's stabilized with too high unemployment rate. And I think if we get this Jobs Bill passed, that's going to make a difference right away. Some of the things though that have been plaguing the African-American community for too long, those things are going to take years to change. The school system in particular.

Young people, it was just reported are — one group for example, is more insured than it's ever been because of the American, or Affordable Care Act. But, how we think about our health habits, all the things the First Lady's doing in terms of what we're eating, in terms of getting exercise, instilling good health habits in our kids— those are things that will take place over the years to reduce the diabetes rate, in the African-American community, for example.

Emmett Miller. How do you get it through Congress? How do you make it successful this time?

The President. Well, we'll get some of it through Congress. And we will just keep pounding away until we get all of it through Congress. And if we don't get all of it through Congress, and we haven't seen enough done to help the American people, then we'll get a new Congress. Because the bottom line is, that the vision that we put forward in the Jobs Bill and the ways, by the way, that we intend to pay for it, by making sure that millionaires and billionaires are paying their fair share, that they're not paying lower tax rates effectively than folks who are making 50,000 dollars a year, that combination of efforts to rebuild America, put people back to work, get teachers back in the classroom and paying for it in a responsible way, that vision is one that the American people believe in. I mean, you were citing polls earlier. If you look at specifics of the Jobs Bill, overwhelmingly, people support it, including a lot of Republicans. When you look at how we propose to pay for it, overwhelmingly the American people support it, including a number of Republicans. Now, this particular Congress may not be responsive to the American people, but we are going to keep on putting pressure on them until we can get as much of it done as possible. And if they're not doing enough to help the American people during a time of great need, then we'll make sure that we have a new Congress.

Emmett Miller. African-Americans are going to be watching you and asking themselves, "Who is this man and does he care about me?" What is it that they don't understand about you, do you think, that you would have them understand?

The President. All I get from the African-American community as I travel around the country is we know it's hard and we're praying for you. And we're behind you. And so, I think the main thing I want the African-American community to know is just those prayers are appreciated. Them rooting for me is appreciated. And that I am spending all my time in this office trying to make sure that if there's some kid in the south side of Chicago that doesn't have a shot right now, isn't going to a good school, parent doesn't have a job, that I'm fighting for him. And that is true if they're in a barrio somewhere in, you know, Los Angeles. It's true of some kid in Appalachia. That the values that brought me here to this office are the ones that I'm going to carry with me when I leave office. And, you know, that's all I care about, is making sure that I'm delivering on behalf of those folks who have invested so much in me.

Emmett Miller. Mr. President, thank you.

The President. Thank you. Appreciate it.

The Science

- Current organizations are outdated: Legacy civil rights groups lack comprehensive vision and measurable accountability
- Move from single-leader to council model: No more messiah politics - develop collective leadership with elections every 4-5 years
- Focus on five priorities: Reparations, Artificial Intelligence, Independent Political Party, Supplemental Education, Economic Development (RAISE)
- Build for modern times: New organizations must be secular, transparent, and technology-forward
- Pure organization comes before pure reparations: Can't achieve policy goals without institutional power first

Andreessen, Reed, and Farrakhan on Obama

> *"You are the instruments that God is going to use to bring about universal change, and that is why Barack has captured the youth. And he has involved young people in a political process that they didn't care anything about. That's a sign. When the Messiah speaks, the youth will hear, and the Messiah is absolutely speaking."*
> — *Minister Louis Farrakhan*

When examining Obama through multiple factors, we see a perfect case study in science versus spook. Three distinct perspectives—Adolph Reed's hardcore political science, Marc Andreessen's cold venture capital analysis, and Minister Louis Farrakhan's religious hope—demonstrate how different analytical frameworks led to vastly different expectations and disappointments.

Reed, a University of Pennsylvania political scientist with decades of studying power structures, and Andreessen, a calculating venture capitalist who built multiple billion-dollar companies, both priced Obama closer to his actual market value or reality. Their scientific orientation and approaches—one from political theory, one from capital markets—saw Obama clearly from the start. Meanwhile, Farrakhan, operating from a more religious and hopeful framework, rode an emotional roller coaster from messianic expectations to bitter disappointment.

Adolph Reed's Scientific Analysis

Reed knew Obama from Chicago's political beginnings and immediately identified Obama as "a vacuous opportunist, a good performer with an ear for how to make white liberals like him."[1] This wasn't just criticism coming from a hardcore political scientist in 2008—it was prophecy based on scientific observation. As early as 1996, Reed wrote that Obama was "a smooth Harvard lawyer with impeccable credentials and vacuous-to-repressive neoliberal politics."[2] His political science background meant he was pricing the asset (Obama) based on historical comparables and structural analysis, not hope, religion, symbolism, or emotions. Reed was deep in the details, well underneath the surface. A scientist likes to play under the surface but most of the population plays on the surface, leaving them in a fog of mystery.

In Reed's analysis, Obama represented the triumph of style over substance—a politician who mastered performance while embracing neoliberal economics. He identified Obama's strategic manipulation of Black audiences "in exactly the same way Bill Clinton did—i.e., getting props both for emoting with the black crowd and talking through them to affirm a victim-blaming 'tough love' message." Obama went beyond Clinton by leveraging his racial identity to appear more authentic while pushing the same policies.

Reed's predictions proved so accurate because he focused on Obama's different political factors and political orientation rather than the emotional symbolism surrounding him. Reed observed Obama's careful image construction, which included misleading biographical narratives, strategic church membership, and a calculated multicultural appeal that made him palatable to white liberals while signaling insider status to Black Americans. If the political tricknology was going to be nicely and seductively packaged in Black face, Reed was the guy to detect it, right away.

As Reed would later argue in "Nothing Left," a 2014 Harper's essay, Obama emerged from a period when "the American left moved increasingly toward the middle," with social activists making "their peace with neoliberalism and adjusted their horizons accordingly."[3] The focus shifted from economic justice to individual advancement, with Obama perfectly embodying this transition from systemic critique to representational politics and individual accomplishment as a proxy for Black American collective progress.

Marc Andreessen's Venture Capital View

Andreessen, co-founder of Netscape and one of Silicon Valley's most influential venture capitalists, met personally with Obama for ninety minutes in early 2007, before Obama entered what Andreessen called "the bubble" of presidential campaigning. His assessment was clinical and prescient. He described Obama as "reasonable, moderate, and thoughtful"—exactly what the system ordered. No messianic expectations, no transformative hopes, just a solid investment.[4]

In a blog post after their meeting, Andreessen specifically highlighted what he saw as Obama's key qualities: "Smart, normal, curious, not radical, and post-Boomer." He observed that Obama was "not some kind of liberal revolutionary who is intent on throwing everything up in the air and starting over." Instead, Andreessen wrote, "Put the primary campaign speeches aside; take a look at his policy positions on any number of issues and what strikes you is how reasonable, moderate, and thoughtful they are."

This assessment perfectly encapsulates the venture capitalist's approach to evaluating political assets. Andreessen wasn't looking for radical transformation; he was looking for a stable, predictable framework that would allow continued system operation with minimal disruption. As he wrote: "In person, that's exactly what he's like. There's no fire in the eyes to realize some utopian or revolutionary dream. Instead, what comes across—in both his questions and his answers—is calmness, reason, and judgment."

Andreessen was particularly impressed by Obama's interest in social media and technology, noting that Obama "casually but persistently grilled us on what we thought the next generation of social media would be and how social networking might affect politics—with no staff present, no prepared materials, no notes." This tech-savvy persona combined with moderate politics represented the perfect alignment with Silicon Valley's financial interests.

Minister Louis Farrakhan's Messianic Vision of Obama

Farrakhan's relationship with Obama represents perhaps the most dramatic swing from messianic hope to bitter disillusionment, perfectly illustrating the dangers of religious-oriented thinking in political analysis. His statements about Obama trace a perfect arc from beatification to condemnation:

During the 2008 campaign, Farrakhan elevated Obama to near-divine status[5] :

- "This young man is the hope of the entire world."
- "When the Messiah speaks, the youth will hear, and the Messiah is absolutely speaking."[6]
- "A Black man with a white mother became a savior to us."
- "He has captured the youth...that's a sign."

Farrakhan even compared Obama to the Nation of Islam's founder, Fard Muhammad, who also is thought to have had a white mother and Black father according to NOI teachings, saying Obama "could turn out to be one who can lift America from her fall."

But by 2011, just two years into Obama's presidency, Farrakhan's tone had shifted dramatically:

- "We voted for our brother Barack, a beautiful human being with a sweet heart. Now he's an assassin." (reference to Muammar Qaddafi)
- "Now he's a murderer."

By 2016, Farrakhan had completely soured on Obama, accusing him of betraying Black Americans :

- "You didn't earn your legacy with Black people. You fought for the rights of gay people... You fight for Israel... Your people are suffering and dying in the streets! That's where your legacy is."

- "I go out in the streets with the people. I visited the worst neighborhoods. I talked to the gangs. And while I was out there talking to them, they said 'You know, Farrakhan, the president ain't never come.'"

This whiplash-inducing reversal reveals the inherent instability of political analysis based on religious-thinking, hope and symbolism rather than multi-factor structural understanding and political science. When Farrakhan urged his followers not to abandon Obama during the 2008 campaign despite Obama's public distancing from him, calling criticism "simply mischief intended to hurt Mr. Obama politically," he was still invested in the symbolic potential rather than the political reality. There was so much hope and spook in the air in 2008, there was very little attention to what loyal Black American voters would be getting or what our negotiating position would be with Obama, if he won. It seemed as if Black America was more interested in the optimistic cult religion of Obama than the sober science of Obama.

The relationship was further complicated by hidden dynamics of political distance management. A suppressed 2005 photograph showing Obama and Farrakhan together, which Congressional Black Caucus members deliberately kept from public view during the campaign, revealed how Obama's team understood that even perceived association with Farrakhan could threaten his carefully constructed image with white voters and the hyper-influential Jewish interest groups and donors. As photographer Askia Muhammad later admitted, "I promised and made arrangements to give the picture to Leonard Farrakhan," and "it was sort of like a promise to keep the photograph secret."[7] The discipline of Askia Muhammad and the Nation of Islam in keeping the photo a secret shows the genuine belief that Obama represented so much promise for Black America but did Obama really deserve to be protected in such a manner?

Because the Nation of Islam under Minister Farrakhanis is a religious-focused organization, it wasn't in the best position to see Obama within a scientific lens, as Reed and Andreessen saw him.

The religious leader's journey from hope to disillusionment tracks perfectly with someone who bought at the top of a hype cycle without doing proper due diligence. While Reed and Andreessen priced Obama like analysts pricing a stock—based on fundamentals and market conditions—Farrakhan priced him like an emotional retail investor buying into market euphoria and hype. Minister Farrakhan being grossly wrong-footed on Obama surfaces the defects with the dogmatic leader model that is without question. If they are wrong on a generationally important problem or issue, all the followers go over the same cliff of wrongness with them.

The Scientific Truth

Reed's early analysis proved most accurate because it was based on observable patterns rather than hopeful projections. His academic rigor as a political scientist allowed him to identify key features of Obama's political methodology: careful audience segmentation, strategic identity deployment, calculated symbolic gestures, and controlled narrative management.

What Reed understood, and what Lester Spence would later articulate in his 2015 book "Knocking the Hustle," was that Obama represented the culmination of neoliberalism's infiltration of Black politics.[8] As Spence notes, Obama embodied the shift from collective political struggle to individual achievement, from structural critique to personal responsibility rhetoric.

The suppressed 2005 photograph story perfectly encapsulates this lesson: while many saw Obama as a political messiah and others as a moderate, the system saw him clearly enough to know exactly what images needed hiding and what narratives needed managing. Science would have told us this from the start—if we hadn't been so invested in spook. The science points to Obama being more of a political anti-christ figure, than political messiah to Black Americans.

For Black American political science, the key isn't choosing between these perspectives but understanding how they reveal different aspects of political reality. Reed's scientific approach, drawing from decades of political analysis, and Andreessen's cold market calculation both proved more accurate than Farrakhan's hope-based projections. If an influential religious figure like Farrakhan was spooked out on Obama, the Black American voter never even had a chance to price him correctly. The two hardcore analysts—Reed from political science, Andreessen from venture capital—both got the valuation right because they used scientific frameworks rather than hopeful projections.

This isn't just about Obama—it's about how we price and evaluate political leaders. When Reed saw Obama as a "good performer with an ear for how to make white liberals like him," he wasn't being cynical—he was being scientific. His political science background provided the same analytical rigor that Andreessen's venture capital experience brought to evaluating political assets. Meanwhile, Farrakhan's journey from messianic hope to bitter disappointment shows the cost of spook thinking in political analysis. The sad thing about the mass Obama spook spell that was put over Black America is Obama never said he was going to do anything special for us, from a policy and risk-taking perspective.

The lesson for Black American political science is clear: whether you're using political theory or market analysis, scientific thinking beats hopeful projection every time. Reed and Andreessen's cold calculations proved more reliable than warm hopes, not because they were more cynical but because they were more scientific.

In the end, this triangulation of perspectives demonstrates why science beats spook in political analysis. Both Reed's academic rigor and Andreessen's market analysis saw Obama clearly from the start, whereas Minister Farrakhan (and my younger self) had to learn the hard way that messianic hope is no match for scientific orientation and analysis. When it comes to political analysis, cold calculation beats warm hope every time—whether that calculation comes from political science or venture capital. To be scientific is to not be too pessimistic or optimistic but to properly position yourself to see and understand reality, as it is and before it's too late.

The Science

- Scientific analysis beats emotional hope: Reed (political science) and Andreessen (venture capital) predicted Obama accurately; Farrakhan's religious hope led to disappointment
- Reed saw the con from day one: Called Obama "a smooth Harvard lawyer with vacuous neoliberal politics" in 1996
- Andreessen priced him correctly: Saw Obama as "reasonable, moderate" - perfect for system stability, not transformation
- Farrakhan rode the emotional roller coaster: From "Messiah" to "murderer" - classic spook thinking pattern
- Cold calculation beats warm hope: Whether from political science or business analysis, objective evaluation proves more reliable than emotional investment

---

[1] Adolph L. Reed Jr., "Obama No," Progress Magazine, April 28, 2008.

[2] Adolph Reed Jr., Posing As Politics and Other Thoughts on the American Scene (New York: The New Press, 2001).

[3] Adolph Reed Jr., "Nothing Left: The Long, Slow Surrender of American Liberals," Harper's Magazine, March 2014.

[4] Marc Andreessen, "An hour and a half with Barack Obama," PM Archive, March 3, 2008.

[5] Ann Brown, "Looking Back: 20 Quotes From Minister Farrakhan On Barack Obama," Moguldom.com, May 7, 2020.

[6] Susan Brinkmann, "Nation of Islam Leader Calls Obama 'the Messiah,'" Women of Grace, October 13, 2008.

[7] Vinson Cunningham, "The Politics of Race and the Photo That Might Have Derailed Obama," The New Yorker, January 28, 2018. https://www.newyorker.com/culture/annals-of-appearances/the-politics-of-race-and-the-photo-that-might-have-derailed-obama

[8] Lester Spence, "Knocking the Hustle: Against the Neoliberal Turn in Black Politics," Punctum Books, 2015.

Tavis Smiley and You Ain't Black

> *"If you have a problem figuring out whether you're for me or Trump, then you ain't black."* - President Joe Biden

When Joe Biden told Charlamagne Tha God that Black voters "ain't black" if they were considering Trump, he was showing the institutional orientation of the entire Democratic Party establishment.[1] This wasn't a gaffe—it was a moment of accidental truth-telling about how the system views Black American voters. The message couldn't have been clearer: your Blackness depends on your political compliance and Black American identity is dependent on loyalty to the elite bosses of the Democratic Party.

But this attitude didn't start with Biden. When Tavis Smiley insisted on holding Obama accountable to specific Black American interests a decade earlier, the establishment's reaction was swift and brutal. His story demonstrates a crucial lesson: the price for questioning Black symbolic power can be professional extinction. Those most enthralled by political spook will even resort to death threats against fellow Black Americans who dare apply multi-factor scientific analysis to challenge cherished orthodoxies. This isn't just political disagreement—it's the systematic silencing of critical thinking. No political party and no religion should own the Black American critical thinking asset.

The Expectation of Black Compliance

Biden's "you ain't black" comment revealed the Democratic Party's fundamental assumption: Black Americans don't deserve policy commitments because their votes are already guaranteed. Despite decades of the Democratic Party taking Black votes while delivering minimal policy returns, questioning this arrangement is treated as racial treason. Black American voters know passing legislation that focuses on Black American interests is a high hurdle to jump over but there is no excuse for a lack of risk taking and trying and executive orders. Or institutionalizing a Black American agenda in the official Democratic Party platform.

The "unity" and racial treason playbook was run against Tavis Smiley when he dared to demand accountability from Obama. Tavis Smiley in his sober brilliance, knew to ask what made Obama so special where he was above questioning and accountability, where Black Americans wouldn't count our political policy like he would count his money and mansions? Consider what happened when Smiley invited Obama to his State of the Black Union event in 2008. When Obama declined and sent Michelle Obama instead, Smiley publicly criticized the decision and his political orientation towards Black America. The backlash was immediate, vicious, and lasting, leaving a seemingly reputational permanent scar on Smiley.

As Smiley told the Washington Post: "There's all this talk of hater, sellout and traitor." The attacks weren't just professional—they became personal and threatening. "I have family in Indianapolis. They are harassing my momma, harassing my brother. It's getting to be crazy," Smiley revealed. He even mentioned receiving death threats.[2]

The message was crystal clear: questioning the first Kenyan-American President's commitment to Black America was an unforgivable sin. Obama wasn't just leading the United States, he was leading a quasi-religious political cult in Black America.

Native Son vs. The Newcomer

What makes this saga even more twisted is the dynamic at play: Smiley, a native Black American whose ancestors have blood, terror, and sacrifice on this soil—literally generations of skin in the game—was being attacked for demanding accountability from Obama, the first Kenyan-American president whose connection to the Black American experience came through marriage and political choice, not centuries of shared struggle.

Black Americans attacked Tavis Smiley in our spook, including me with very simplistic thinking ("he's jealous, petty"), but the irony of the Obama/Biden New Blacks period is that Tavis Smiley was in possibly the 5% category being rightfully highly critical of Obama but got the "You Ain't Black" treatment against the Kenyan-American. The science of it all is Smiley was the most intelligently Black, most scientifically Black American in real-time, when it counts the most, when what's best for us is unpopular against mass spook spells over the Black American population. The love that many assumed Obama had for Black American political interests, was actually demonstrated by Tavis Smiley risking it all, to try to shake the Obama spook spell, off Black America.

Obama New Blacks as Attack Dogs

When Smiley continued his push for Obama to address specific Black American concerns, the system deployed its defenders:

- Steve Harvey called him an "Uncle Tom" on national radio, saying: "His anger started when he had a town hall meeting, President Obama couldn't come because of the campaign trail and he sent Mrs. Obama. He has held that grudge ever since."

- Al Sharpton dismissed him with: "I lead a civil rights organization, Mr. Smiley is a commentator."

- Black media outlets ran hit pieces suggesting he was motivated by jealousy and bitterness.

- The Democratic Party machine worked to isolate and marginalize him professionally.

By 2012, the isolation campaign had become so effective that Smiley was even removed as the speaker at a Martin Luther King luncheon. The organizer admitted: "people were upset about comments that Tavis Smiley had made," so they canceled his contract.[3] This wasn't just about Smiley's opinions—it was about making him an example of what happens when you challenge a powerful and popular spook spell within Black America.

Smiley's actual argument was rooted in material facts, not personal grudges. As he later explained in a 2016 interview: "Sadly—and it pains me to say this—over the last decade, black folk, in the era of Obama, have lost ground in every major economic category."[4]

This wasn't personal hatred but material analysis: "I don't hate Barack Obama, I just love my people and I'm never going to stand by idly when I think there are people who are not serving us as well as they can or should."

The Mathematics of Political Accountability

During the Obama New Blacks era, we can observe equations underlying this system of control are straightforward:

- Black Leader + Black Critique = Career Death
- Symbolic Power + System Protection = Critic Destruction
- Truth Telling + Power Challenge = Professional Extinction
- Black Vote + No Policy Demands = "Real" Blackness
- Black Vote + Policy Demands = "Not Black Enough"

When Smiley argued about Obama's skin color privilege—"If that Negro had the phenotype of an Isaac Hayes or Rick Ross... that Negro would never have been president"—he was making a deeper point about how symbolic representation works.[5] The truth that Smiley was speaking could have helped America confront and acknowledge its anti-Black American racial demons, while too much Obama optimism and Obama political religion, was only going to push confrontation, acknowledgement, and policy responses, further out.

91

Smiley's key insight wasn't just about Obama but about how power operates: 'We can't simply trust these agendas and interests. We can't have a Kumbaya moment simply because we're still in the Obama era.' His crime was seeing through the symbolism to the structure beneath. When Black America was attacking Tavis Smiley, we were attacking scientific orientation, political science, critical thinking, and the human right to think about material political policy and risk-taking compensation in return for our election-deciding offerings. Tavis Smiley was courageously trying to tell Black America, we are giving up way too much political booty, too fast, to be politically respected. Obama didn't have to put a ring on it.

The most damning part of Smiley's critique was his question about precedent: "When black leaders start saying to black people and the black media that we don't need to have this president focus on an African-American agenda, given that black folk are getting crushed, I say that we need to come together to have a conversation about what that means. I think there's a disconnect between those kinds of quotes and black people."[6]

This exposed the fatal flaw in the "first Black president" political strategy—once you establish that symbolic representation doesn't require material accountability, you've surrendered your leverage.

The Cost of Demanding Accountability

Smiley's experience reveals the brutal cost of demanding accountability from Black political figures during the Obama New Blacks period. When partnering with professor Cornel West on a poverty tour highlighting economic disparity in Black American communities, Smiley noted: "It would be nice to hear the president say the word poor—to say the word poverty. But we can't get this president or any leaders to say the words poor or poverty, much less do anything about it."[7]

For this criticism, Smiley and West were portrayed as bitter, jealous haters who couldn't stand seeing a Black man succeed. Steve Harvey hammered this point home on his radio show: "Who in the hell got two to three days for your ass? I, I ain't got time to sit down with your monkey behind for no two, three damn days, let alone the president of the United States," Harvey cried. "We got three damn wars out here, the economy crashing and we going to sit down with Tavis ass for three days?"[8]

Ironically, Steve Harvey would come under similar "You Ain't Black" criticism in 2017 after meeting with Trump. Harvey was promptly "You Ain't Black'd" and called the meeting the worst mistake of his life.[9] When Grammy-award winning Hip-Hop artist Killer Mike met with Republican Governor Brian Kemp in 2020, he was also "You Ain't Black'd".[10] Ice Cube was similarly "You Ain't Black'd" when he pressed both parties for a Black American agenda, much like Tavis Smiley years earlier. Cube even took the time to develop a comprehensive Contract with Black America that addressed everything from judicial reform to economic equity - exactly the kind of substantive policy framework our politics should demand.[11]

The pattern reveals a perverse political equation: The Black American who asks no questions, demands no negotiation, applies no pressure to Democrats, and offers no threat of considering both parties is deemed the most authentically 'Black.' Meanwhile, those demanding accountability and results are labeled sellouts or 'not Black enough.' Under this spook spell, political orthodoxy that equates blind Democratic Party loyalty with Black American identity becomes the greatest obstacle to actual political efficiency and measurable results for Black America. You Ain't Black culture within a political context could be as harmful and undermining as the sentiment that 'You Ain't Black' if you love reading books and academics more than sports and hip-hop. What's so bad about Ice Cube and Steve Harvey meeting with Republicans if they are meeting in good faith and want to negotiate something favorable for Black Americans? Why is it acceptable for Biden, Pelosi, and Schumer to work with Republicans to get something done but Black Americans with access to the political establishment are restricted from working with both parties, as if they are on a modern political plantation?

In a telling moment, Smiley reflected on how Black Americans had been caught up in the symbolism rather than the substance of Obama's presidency :

"Black people are still the most optimistic people, they're still the most hopeful about their future. That has a lot to do with our faith, with our belief in each other, with our love for Barack Obama... We haven't pressed as hard as we should on the substance of this presidency."

The Science vs. the Spook

Smiley's experience proves a critical thesis: the Democratic Party strategically protects its symbolic power by neutralizing internal critics. His professional marginalization wasn't merely personal; it reflected structural mechanics at work. Smiley challenged the comforting spook of symbolic Black representation with the uncomfortable science of material demands.

Politicians face different constraints than activists. While activists speak uncomfortable truths without electoral consequences, elected officials like Obama must navigate complex institutional pressures, party obligations, and electoral coalitions. These different roles create different possibilities for action. Yet this practical reality doesn't invalidate the need for both pressure and accountability.

What deserves scrutiny isn't that politicians face constraints, but how they respond within those constraints—whether they push the boundaries when possible or simply accept limitations as immutable. When we elevate politicians to prophetic status alongside King and Malcolm X without requiring commensurate alignment with Black American political interests, we confuse symbolic representation with substantive transformation. Meanwhile, those who demand accountability often find themselves politically crucified for simply asking whether symbolic victories are translating to material progress—regardless of whether the system presents itself in Black face or white.

Time has proven Smiley right. As he noted later: "With the advantage of history, the advantage of time, people see better what I was attempting to do. It was never about hate then, it ain't about hate now. I loved the brother, I supported him, I voted for him, but I do not regret and never will doing my small part to try to hold him accountable."[12]

The institutional forces that destroyed Smiley for questioning Obama is the same people around Biden that would make the President think "you ain't black" is funny and ok in front of a national Black American audience. The message is consistent: Black Americans must vote Democrat without expecting material returns, or their very Blackness will be questioned. Both instances reveal the fundamental assumption that Black votes are owed without reciprocity.

This isn't just history—it's a warning about how the modern Democratic Party operates. When we make Black faces in high places immune from critique, we surrender our power to ensure they serve Black interests. That's not politics—it's political suicide. Whether it's Obama supporters attempting to run Smiley out of the public square or Biden questioning the Blackness of voters who demand policy commitments, the pattern is clear: the modern Democratic Party often expects Black American compliance without material return.

As Biden's comment reveals, the Democratic Party doesn't feel it needs to earn Black votes—it believes it owns them. And as Smiley's story shows, anyone who challenges this arrangement will face not just criticism but character assassination.

The Science

- • Demanding accountability = being "not Black enough": The system punishes those who apply pressure to Black politicians
- • Biden revealed the game: "You ain't black" exposed how Democrats view Black political compliance as mandatory
- • Smiley was scientifically right in real-time: His criticism of Obama's Black agenda proved prophetic, but he was professionally destroyed for it
- • The pattern repeats: Ice Cube, Steve Harvey, Killer Mike - anyone who negotiates with both parties gets the "You Ain't Black" treatment
- • Identity loyalty is weaponized against progress: Using Blackness to enforce Democratic Party loyalty prevents strategic political negotiations

[1] Herndon, Astead W., and Katie Glueck. "Biden Apologizes for Saying Black Voters 'Ain't Black' if They're Considering Trump." The New York Times, May 22, 2020, updated January 20, 2021. https://www.nytimes.com/2020/05/22/us/politics/joe-biden-black-breakfast-club.html

[2] Fears, Darryl. "Black Community Is Increasingly Protective of Obama." The Washington Post, May 9, 2008.

[3] Lee, MJ. "Tavis Smiley booted from MLK event." Politico, January 9, 2012, updated January 11, 2012. https://www.politico.com/story/2012/01/tavis-smiley-booted-from-mlk-event-071225

[4] "Tavis Smiley: Black people have lost ground under Obama," Fox Business, April 6, 2016.

[5] Brown, Ann. "Tavis Smiley: If Obama Looked Like Isaac Hayes Or Rick Ross, He Wouldn't Have Been President." The Moguldom Nation, October 18, 2022. https://moguldom.com/424648/tavis-smiley-if-obama-looked-like-isaac-hayes-or-rick-ross-he-would-never-be-president-of-america/

[6] Martin, Michel. "Smiley: Black America Deserves An Agenda With The President." NPR, March 11, 2010. https://www.npr.org/templates/story/story.php?storyId=124546087

[7] Jones, Joyce. "Tavis Smiley Calls Attention to Obama's Failings." BET, July 25, 2011. https://www.bet.com/article/vvkk5r/tavis-smiley-calls-attention-to-obamas-failings

[8] Jones, Joyce. "Steve Harvey Suggests That Smiley and West Are 'Uncle Toms'." BET, August 11, 2011. https://www.bet.com/article/09fprg/steve-harvey-suggests-that-smiley-and-west-are-uncle-toms

[9] TeamEBONY. "Steve Harvey's TV Shows Took a Hit After That Trump Meeting." Ebony, November 1, 2017. https://www.ebony.com/steve-harvey-tv-shows-trump-meeting/

[10] Bluestein, Greg. "Kemp and Killer Mike try to clear the air after their sitdown sparked uproar." Atlanta Journal Constitution, September 11, 2020.

[11] Jones, Zoe Christen. "Ice Cube defends advising Trump on plan for Black Americans." CBS News, October 16, 2020. https://www.cbsnews.com/news/ice-cube-responds-trump-platinum-plan-black-americans/

[12] Smiley, Tavis. "My Criticism of President Obama Was Always Rooted in Love." Time, January 10, 2017. https://time.com/4630300/tavis-smiley-obama-criticism-love/

Remembering When Obama Blocked Keith Ellison

"Barack Obama is the coldest drug dropped on Black America Since Crack." — Fred Hampton Jr.

When Keith Ellison sought to lead the Democratic National Committee (DNC) in 2017, he encountered a revealing obstacle: Barack Obama, the new king of the Democratic Party. This story isn't just about politics—it's about the fundamental contradiction between identity-based voting messages pushed on Black Americans and how leadership actually behaves when system interests are threatened.

After Democrats lost horribly in 2016, Ellison was poised to run unopposed for DNC chair. His credentials were impeccable: First Muslim elected to Congress, pro-reparations advocate since college, Million Man March attendee (1995), rising progressive leader, proven electoral success, strong grassroots support, and a potential bridge between establishment and progressives.

But something about this Black American Muslim progressive leader prompted the Obama machine to act. The same president who benefited from near-unanimous Black voter support would now be linked to one of the dirtiest campaigns against a Black American leader in recent Democratic Party history.

Identity Politics versus Power Reality

The math tells the story:

- Black support for Obama: ~90 percent

- Obama's support for Black progressive leadership: ~0 percent

- Cost of system protection: one Black American leader's reputation

When Obama's White House recruited lobbyist Tom Perez to block Ellison, they revealed a crucial equation: Black American + Muslim Faith + Progressive Politics = Too Much Structural Threat

The choice here was crystal clear: Who would have been better for Black American voters? Ellison, with his progressive agenda. Who would have been better for the entrenched system resistant to change? Lobbyist-friendly Tom Perez. Obama sided with the establishment, his establishment, not with Black American voter interests. Obama protected his political market share by blocking a leader aligned with Bernie Sanders' progressive policies rather than Obama's symbolic representation.

The Attack Pattern—Obama's Dirty Politics in Action

The timeline here is critical. Ellison announced his candidacy on November 15, armed with endorsements that spanned the range of the party: Sanders, Elizabeth Warren, Raúl Grijalva, and various labor unions on the left, along with establishment stalwarts such as Chuck Schumer, Amy Klobuchar, and Harry Reid. He looked to be the clear frontrunner.

But as Ellison's momentum built, the Obama White House actively worked to recruit Perez to run against Ellison.[1] They succeeded, and Perez announced his candidacy on December 15 — a full month after Ellison announced. This wasn't just opposition – it was a coordinated effort to derail Ellison's candidacy.[2]

What's particularly revealing isn't just that Obama opposed Ellison, but how. The Obama–Perez DNC faction orchestrated a nasty whisper campaign painting Ellison as an antisemite.[3] Think about this: the same Kenyan-American president who rode identity symbolism to the White House now used (his political machine) religious bigotry to knee-cap a rising progressive Black American, whose ancestors were enslaved on American soil.

The smear playbook deployed by Obama's team weaponized Farrakhan connections, amplified antisemitism claims, deployed establishment donors for attacks, used mainstream media to spread doubts, made Ellison's Muslim faith a liability, and coordinated attacks through multiple channels. Ironically, strategist Mark Penn and Hillary Clinton's campaign used similar techniques against Obama in 2008, circulating photos of Obama in traditional Muslim attire. The tricknology technique then was to highlight Obama's 'un-Americanness' - the very same othering tactic Obama's team would later deploy against Ellison, revealing how quickly the formerly othered can become the otherer when power is at stake.

The execution was surgical. Just over two weeks after Ellison announced, the largest single funder of both the Democratic Party and the Clinton campaign — the Israeli-American billionaire Haim Saban — launched an incredibly toxic attack on Ellison. "He is clearly an antisemite and anti-Israel individual," pronounced Saban about the Black American Muslim congressman, adding: "Keith Ellison would be a disaster for the relationship between the Jewish community and the Democratic Party."[4]

This wasn't random—it was part of a coordinated strategy. Saban, who once described himself saying "I'm a one-issue guy, and my issue is Israel," had previously donated $7 million to build the DNC headquarters and served as chairman of the party's capital-expenditure campaign. As Mother Jones reported, "No single political patron has done more for the Clintons over the span of their careers" than Saban, who donated millions to Clinton campaigns and the Clinton Foundation.[5]

The Intercept's Glenn Greenwald captured the real battle: 'an impassioned proxy war replicating the 2016 primary fight: between the Clinton/Obama establishment wing... and the insurgent Sanders wing.' Obama wasn't thinking about Black American interests when blocking Keith Ellison—he was thinking about his own position, power, and donors. If Ellison had become the DNC Chair, powerful interests would have been threatened, and Obama wasn't in the mood for 'Change We Can Believe In."

If voting should have identity as a dominant factor, the first Kenyan-American President sure didn't side with Black American identity—he sided with the lobbyist system protector who was loyal to his faction. While Obama preached political sermons in 2008 about removing special interest influence from politics to win office, once there, he repeatedly acted to preserve the DNC establishment at the systems level. Obama was perfectly positioned to move against the interests of Black Americans while keeping almost 100% of his support intact. The 'vote Black' message pushed on Black Americans seems to expire the moment Black leadership threatens system interests.

The Scientific Analysis of Power over Identity

1. Identity Politics Law

- Only acceptable within system limits
- Expires when power threatened
- Used to control voters, not guide leadership
- System preservation more important than racial solidarity

2. Power Protection Law

- System self-preserves across racial lines
- Establishment unifies against threats
- Identity is weaponized against change
- Power interests outweigh racial solidarity

3. Voting Behavior Contradiction

- Black voters urged to prioritize identity over policy and policy orientation
- Black leaders prioritize system interests

- Identity politics is used as a control mechanism
- Power preservation is the true north

The epilogue is telling: Ellison went on to become attorney general of Minnesota, proving his leadership capabilities. But the Democratic Party establishment, led by Obama, had already shown that identity politics is for voters, not leaders. When faced with a choice between empowering a progressive Black leader and protecting the system, Obama didn't just choose the system—he authorized or helped activate a dirty campaign to destroy a fellow Black American leader's reputation.

This story fundamentally challenges identity-based voting messages. Those who encourage Black Americans to vote based on identity often abandon that same principle when their power is threatened. The science shows us that status-quo power preservation trumps racial solidarity every time—at least for those already conflictingly inside the system.

During the Obama New Blacks period, a Black American majority worshipped Obama as Black America's political messiah, but with Ellison, Obama played Judas—sabotaging a genuine fighter for Black interests to install Perez, a system-protecting insider.

The next time someone pushes identity-based voting, remember the Ellison case. Those preaching identity politics practice power politics. That's not cynicism—that's science.

The Science

- Obama chose system protection over Black leadership: When faced with progressive Black Muslim leader vs. establishment lobbyist, Obama picked the lobbyist
- Identity politics don't apply to leadership decisions: Obama preached racial solidarity to voters while opposing Black leaders who threatened system interests
- Strategic coordination: The Obama White House recruited Perez specifically to block Ellison's candidacy
- Weaponized antisemitism: Used religious bigotry to undermine progressive Black leadership
- Power preservation trumps racial solidarity: Those preaching identity-based voting abandon it when their interests are threatened

[1] Jonathan Martin, "Labor Secretary Thomas Perez Is Said to Plan Run to Lead D.N.C.," New York Times, December 12, 2016.

[2] Glenn Greenwald, "Key Question About DNC Race: Why Did Obama White House Recruit Perez to Run Against Ellison?", The Intercept, February 24, 2017.

[3] Ryan Cooper, "The White House's Dirty Campaign Against Keith Ellison," The Week, January 7, 2017.

[4] Eugene Scott, "Haim Saban: Keith Ellison 'is Clearly an Antisemite and Anti-Israel Individual'", CNN, December 3, 2016.

[5] Andy Kroll, "Haim Saban: The Megadonor Who Made the Clintons," Mother Jones, March/April 2016.

K Street Capitalism: American Politics Is a Business

"The average American doesn't realize how much of the laws are written by lobbyists to protect incumbent interests. It's shocking how the system actually works."
—*Eric Schmidt (Former CEO and Chairman, Google)*

The Science vs Spook framework often uses business and financial terms and concepts such as cost/benefit, risk/reward, audit, return on investment, and political balance sheet. This intentional framing of political affairs in financial terms is anchored so much on the fact that American politics is fundamentally a business. When a politician thinks about getting support from a particular lobby group or special interest group, it's a political decision but also a calculated business decision. When the politician takes money from special interests groups, they have political debts and generally will try their best to take care of those people.

Obama more than any other politician in modern times, exponentially benefited from political entrepreneurship in that he cultivated a new market, Silicon Valley or Big Tech. Based on his political investments with the leaders of industry in this sector such as Alphabet/Google, Meta/Facebook, Netflix, or venerable Venture Capital firm Kleiner Perkins, Obama found a "big wallet" sector that he could scale his political career and Presidency with newfound billionaires and perhaps gain more flexibility from traditional powerful lobby groups such as AIPAC. Obama was clearly playing the game differently than Congressional Black Caucus members but also both Democrats and

Republicans, this was his new lobby market or special interest group that he cultivated and cornered.

Obama partnered with the right people, at the right time, to yield exponential political benefits, to get into the WH, stay in the WH, and to have a big wallet as an individual, post-Presidency. From a business and political perspective, Obama was "killing it" with his new Silicon Valley partners such as Mark Zuckerberg, Google CEO and Chairman Eric Schmidt, and Venture Capitalist John Doerr who served on the Obama Foundation Board. As fortunes were minted with IPO's and skyrocketing stock prices in the innovation economy, Obama positioned himself to materially benefit along with his partners. Writer Siva Vaidhyanathan even asked "Was Obama Silicon Valley's President?" [1]

Consider this evidence: In 2011, Obama hosted a Tech Dinner with the following CEO's:

- John Doerr, partner, Kleiner Perkins Caufield & Byers
- Carol Bartz, president and CEO, Yahoo!
- John Chambers, CEO and chairman, Cisco Systems
- Dick Costolo, CEO, Twitter
- Larry Ellison, co-founder and CEO, Oracle
- Reed Hastings, CEO, Netflix
- John Hennessy, president, Stanford University
- Steve Jobs, chairman and CEO, Apple
- Art Levinson, chairman and former CEO, Genentech
- Eric Schmidt, chairman and CEO, Google
- Steve Westly, managing partner and founder, Westly Group
- Mark Zuckerberg, founder, president and CEO, Facebook

Obama's invite list was 100% white. [2] This contrasts sharply with what Urban One CEO Alfred Liggins (son of Black American media legend Cathy Hughes) told me directly about Obama. He told me the Black

CEOs within his network couldn't even get a meeting with Obama.[3] With other factors considered, this suggests that Obama skipping Tavis Smiley's Black Agenda summit could have been predictive of Black American neglect and Smiley was just early, ahead of all the rest of us. If Black American Wall Street heavy-hitter CEOs couldn't even talk to Obama, the average Black American never had a chance to be taken seriously at the risk-taking and policy levels.

The spook buyers or those who were intoxicated on the symbolism of Obama would defend being neglected because the President is Kenyan-American but would AIPAC ever make excuses for being neglected as a community and interest group? Making excuses for our own political neglect doesn't sound healthy just as making excuses for neglect in an abusive marriage isn't healthy. The first step in creating an environment for a Black American political renaissance is an acknowledgment that we've been in an abusive relationship with the Democratic Party. This remains true on an absolute basis, irrespective of how bad Republicans are and what they're offering.

Obama came in saying he was going to go after special interests groups and get money out of politics, his own version of "drain the swamp," but he quickly became an official agent of a powerful special interest group, Silicon Valley.[4] One factor that came up in studying the audit period (1995-2025), particularly the Obama years, is that we often don't believe we deserve the political returns special interest groups receive or we're not "special" in a sense. The question becomes: If we're not a special interest group and don't have a special interest group financial wallet, then how do we get one, to become special? If the special interest groups are overwhelmingly overpowering Black American voting power and voting intensity, it implies we need to pay less attention to the FACE of the President or party, or position, and more attention to the money and conflicted relationships. If the system is saying the money is what makes an interest group or affinity group special, then we should be prioritizing the money, first and foremost.

The stark reality is that while trillions of dollars of wealth was being created during the Obama years in Silicon Valley and Big Tech—with white and Asian employees getting rich through employee stock grants—we were overwhelmingly blacklisted out of the Silicon Valley economy. For example, Black American entrepreneurs received less than 1% of investment capital from venture capitalists during this period.[5] If we're not focused on the science of where the billions and trillions are moving, who's getting a disproportionate share, which group is blacklisted, and how the economy is being restructured against us, and formulating a collective policy response, then what are we focused on? It can't be science, it has to be spook. While the number of Black faces in proximity to the White House increased, the mathematical reality of generational wealth was silently moving in the opposite direction—a perfect example of spook masking science.

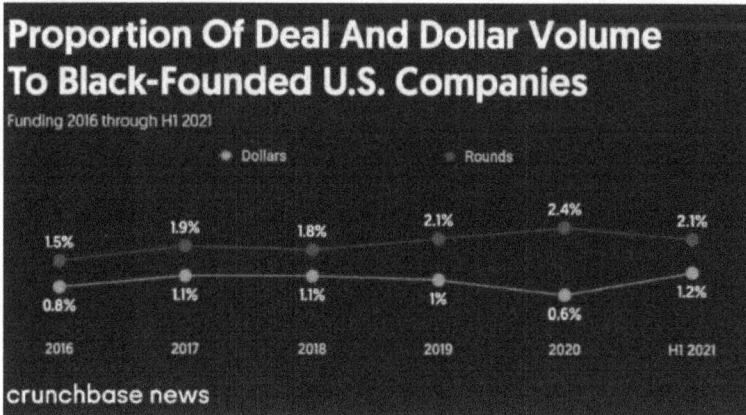

Proportion Of Deal And Dollar Volume To Black-Founded U.S. Companies
Funding 2016 through H1 2021

| | Dollars | | Rounds | | |
2016	2017	2018	2019	2020	H1 2021
1.5%	1.9%	1.8%	2.1%	2.4%	2.1%
0.8%	1.1%	1.1%	1%	0.6%	1.2%

crunchbase news

Venture Capital Funding to Black-Founded Companies - Shows minimal funding (0.6-1.2%) from 2016-2021

Many were paying attention to the symbolism of Obama and the good vibes of seeing Obama and Michelle in the White House, while fortunes were being created out of Silicon Valley, totally locking Black Americans out of it. This historic wealth transfer under Obama was largely done while Black Americans had no real collective political and economic policy response to the rise of Silicon Valley that would only increase the wealth gap between Black and White. It wasn't just that Black Americans were blacklisted out of this trillion-dollar generational wealth revolution in Silicon Valley; the political power, orientations, and biases attached to this capital would have a permanent impact on the political reality in the United States. [6]

Under the Science vs Spook framework, we would have prioritized the wealth transfers out of Silicon Valley and being locked out of it, while Obama and his friends became rich. This historic wealth transfer wouldn't have been a collective mystery because we would be following the money with high intensity and be looking out for spook, by default. The Obama affinity intensity would have been anti-spook and Black American political efficiency intensity. Looking back, I couldn't even imagine Obama speaking up about Black Americans being locked out of the Silicon Valley economy while many were comfortable putting him in pictures with Malcolm X and Dr. Martin Luther King Jr. as if all three were hardcore fighters and risk takers for Black American interests.

In Obama's post-presidency memoir, A Promise Land, he had the following insight about the public largely existing in 90% mystery or not paying attention to the raw political science:

> *"When I sat down, the senate president, Pate Philip—a beefy, white-haired ex-Marine notorious for insulting women and people of color with remarkably casual frequency—wandered up to my desk. 'That was a hell of a speech,' he said, chewing on an unlit cigar. 'Made some good points.' 'Thanks.' 'Might have even changed a lot of minds,' he said. 'But you didn't change any votes.' With that, he signaled to the presiding officer and watched with satisfaction as the green lights signifying 'aye' lit up the board. That was politics in Springfield: a series of transactions mostly hidden from view, legislators weighing the competing pressures of various interests with the dispassion of bazaar merchants, all the while keeping a careful eye on the handful of ideological hot*

buttons—guns, abortion, taxes—that might generate heat from their base. It wasn't that people didn't know the difference between good and bad policy. It just didn't matter. What everyone in Springfield understood was that 90 percent of the time the voters back home weren't paying attention. A complicated but worthy compromise, bucking party orthodoxy to support an innovative idea—that could cost you a key endorsement, a big financial backer, a leadership post, or even an election. Could you get voters to pay attention? I tried." [7]

Diving deeper into the business of politics, we must understand hidden transactions and techniques that are "off balance sheet" such as delayed financial value or the distribution of financial value to the spouse. Corruption can be stealth if it's structured right. There is a level that elites operate where value can be distributed from one side but not received by the other side at the same time. Let's say a politician or President reduces regulatory oversight or intensity for a sector or large company. The politician can offer value to special interest on "spec" or speculation but with the confidence that there is a likely payback later in their career or when they get out of office.

Another common technique is figuring out how to deliver value to the spouse from a donor or special interest group. You will notice the spouses of politicians seem to find luck or make really good business decisions. [8] If we follow their personal balance sheet and wealth accumulation while the political spouse is in office, we often see suspicious patterns of enrichment. It's too obvious if the value is distributed to the politician directly—a potential crime or ethics violation—but if the value is delivered to a spouse or family member, it may be technically legal or go undetected.

The wealth accumulation pattern is consistent across party lines: longtime Republican Senate leader Mitch McConnell and his wife Elaine Chao amassed a net worth of over $35 million. [9] Pelosi and her husband over $100 million. The late California Senator Dianne Feinstein and her husband had a net worth of over $69 million.[10] The Obamas are also reportedly in the $100 million club.[11] If the personal wealth is so high with America's political leaders, it's telling us how we factor "follow the money" and financial conflicts should also be high.

Treating politics as a business is good science. Here are some reform possibilities:

Public Financing of Campaigns

Pros:

- Reduces donor influence
- Increases candidate depth
- Levels playing field

Cons:

- Resistance from current beneficiaries
- Implementation challenges
- Cost to taxpayers

Citizens United Reform[12]

Pros:

- Reduces corporate influence
- Increases transparency
- Restores voter power

Cons:

- Requires constitutional change
- Faces institutional resistance
- Complex implementation

Political reform requires understanding that politicians, even those with pure intentions, operate within a business system. Their wealth accumulation isn't random—it follows predictable patterns based on political influence and access.

Strategic Implications for Black America

1. Prioritize campaign finance reform.
2. Study politician wealth accumulation patterns.
3. Track political investment returns.
4. Monitor family business connections.
5. Analyze after-office career paths.

Prioritizing campaign finance reform over police reform offers greater political efficiency for Black Americans. This isn't about minimizing the impact of anti-Black American policing—it's about mathematical strategy. When AIPAC and BlackRock move major policy weight with a phone call while we march for years to get basic police accountability, we're missing the game that's actually being played. Police reform is dealing with a symptom; campaign finance reform attacks the disease. The money system is what prevents even the most reasonable police reforms from passing in the first place. Think strategically: with unlimited corporate money flooding politics, how do you expect to get ANY transformative policy through? We need to get scientific about these structural barriers instead of constantly playing defense on the symptoms. Campaign finance reform is a systems-level issue that is race-neutral but would disproportionately benefit Black Americans, by leveling the playing field.

Rather than focusing on a single component like policing, campaign finance reform creates structural changes that make favorable policies more accessible across the board. This approach transforms the entire political factory rather than adjusting just one widget within it. Rather than just saying we collectively need a Black American political lobby with a big wallet, we can also say we should prioritize changing the rules where less money is needed altogether.

We must also consider politicians prioritizing their individual legacies and how protecting individual legacy may conflict with Black American political interests. The financial transactions in American politics consistently benefit those who navigate the system strategically. While the public focuses on speeches, personalities, and identity politics—classic spook thinking—the real game operates through financial transactions and delayed compensation. In this system, Black Americans face a stark choice: continue trading our votes for symbols and rhetoric while being systematically excluded from wealth creation, or develop a scientific understanding of political finance that treats our collective votes as capital to be invested strategically. Just as Obama mastered the business of politics by cultivating Silicon Valley, Black America must master the science of collective political investment by demanding measurable returns and holding leaders accountable through financial metrics. The mathematics of power requires us to follow the money with the same intensity and sophistication as those who profit from our political loyalty.

The Science

- Politics is a business transaction: Politicians provide services to those who pay - loyalty without payment gets you nothing
- Obama cultivated Silicon Valley as his personal lobby: Built relationships with tech billionaires while Black CEOs couldn't get meetings
- Follow the money, not the speeches: Obama's $100M Netflix deal and tech partnerships revealed his true priorities
- The political-to-wealth pipeline is predictable: Watch how politicians get rich after serving certain interests
- Campaign finance reform should be our top priority: Attacking the money system addresses the root cause of political corruption rather than just symptoms

[1] Siva Vaidhyanathan, "Was Obama Silicon Valley's President?", The Guardian, January 15, 2017.

[2] White House Press Office, "Attendees at President Obama's Tech Dinner," Official White House Press Release, February 18, 2011.

[3] Martin, Jamarlin. "Episode 29: Alfred Liggins." GHOGH with Jamarlin Martin, Moguldom, December 30, 2020, https://moguldom.com/163584/full-transcript-urban-one-ceo-alfred-liggins-on-ghogh-podcast/

[4] Gerstein, Josh. "How Obama failed to shut Washington's revolving door." Politico, December 31, 2015, https://www.politico.com/story/2015/12/barack-obama-revolving-door-lobbying-217042

[5] Huang, Jacky. "Why Black Founders Continue To Not Be Funded in Silicon Valley." Harvard Technology Review, March 30, 2023, https://harvardtechnologyreview.com/2023/03/30/why-black-founders-continue-to-not-be-funded-in-silicon-valley/

[6] Greene, Lucie. Silicon States: The Power and Politics of Big Tech and What It Means for Our Future. Counterpoint, August 21, 2018.

[7] Barack Obama, "A Promised Land" (Crown Publishing Group, 2020).

[8] Moorcraft, Bethan. "Nancy Pelosi's husband sold Visa shares 2 months before a DOJ lawsuit --- some say the trade shouldn't have been allowed." Yahoo Finance, September 26, 2024. https://finance.yahoo.com/news/nancy-pelosi-husband-sold-visa-104400425.html

[9] Fang, Lee, and Spencer Woodman. "Global Shipping Business Tied to Mitch McConnell, Secretary Elaine Chao Shrouded in Offshore Tax Haven." The Intercept, February 5, 2018. https://theintercept.com/2018/02/05/mitch-mcconnell-elaine-chao-offshore-paradise-papers/

[10] Picchi, Aimee. "How much was Dianne Feinstein worth when she died?" CBS News, September 29, 2023. https://www.cbsnews.com/news/dianne-feinstein-net-worth-richard-blum-children/

[11] Faris, David. "What is Barack Obama's net worth?" The Week, March 17, 2025. https://theweek.com/politics/barack-obama-net-worth-explained

[12] Weiner, Daniel I., and Tim Lau. "Citizens United Explained." Brennan Center for Justice, January 29, 2025. https://www.brennancenter.org/our-work/research-reports/citizens-united-explained

Reed and Lester on Neoliberalism

"It's neoliberalism, which is this obsession with smartness and richness and bombs dropped on other parts of the world and sometimes bombs dropped here. It tends to put the stress much more on access to middle-class status and making that access more diverse—rather than attacking poverty, ensuring jobs with a living wage, quality education, single-payer healthcare. So the shift from attacking poverty—let's say Martin King in 1968--to this obsession with diversity that you're getting in the Supreme Court in relation to affirmative action, was a dilution and a domesticating of the issue. One of the ways of making sure you sanitize any talk about racism is to talk about diversity." —Dr. Cornel West

"Under neoliberalism everyone has to negotiate their fate alone, bearing full responsibility for problems that are often not of their own doing. The implications politically, economically and socially for young people are disastrous and are contributing to the emergence of a generation of young people who will occupy a space of social abandonment and terminal exclusion." — Henry Giroux

What happens when predatory individualism infects everything—including our politics, our houses of worship, our very understanding of racial justice? You get Black neoliberalism: the deadly poison that convinces us to fight anti-Black American structural racism with individual hustle, to replace collective power with entrepreneurial striving, and to measure freedom, justice, and equality by how many Black faces make it into the top 1%.

Adolph Reed, the great denouncer of race reductionism, and Lester Spence, who exposed neoliberalism's religious capture, show us how deeply predatory individualism has infected Black political consciousness. When Reed says, "Racism is less and less capable of explaining manifest inequalities between Blacks and whites," he's not denying racism—he's demanding we see the deeper system and think about additional factors.[1]

What is Neoliberalism?

Before diving deeper, let's get clear on what neoliberalism actually is. As Spence puts it in plain language: "Neoliberalism is basically the idea that every single institution, every single part of human life should be governed by principles of the free market."[2] It's the transformation of everything—education, healthcare, housing, even racial justice—into a market. It's when Beyoncé dancing at the Super Bowl in a Black Panther Party outfit becomes "revolutionary" while wages stagnate and Black Americans are locked out of Silicon Valley generational wealth creation. It's when getting more Black CEOs is considered progress while the majority of Black Americans are drowning in debt.

This isn't just academic theory—it's the lived reality reshaping Black communities across America. You know you're living under neoliberalism when:

- Your church preaches getting rich instead of fighting poverty
- Your school teaches "college and career readiness" instead of critical thinking
- Your community leaders talk about "Black excellence" but never "Black American power"
- Your elected officials focus on entrepreneurship programs while cutting public housing
- Your "progressive" heroes celebrate identity milestones while taking corporate cash

It's the political religion that says the market is God, competition is salvation, and failure is sin. And over the last 40 years, this religion has completely captured Black American political consciousness. When Jay-Z is used as the frontman for billionaire real estate developers to get a controversial project approved or by the NFL to neutralize criticism over Kaepernick and racial issues, and Jay-Z's positioning is treated as Black American progress, that's neoliberalism. Where racial neutralization strategies against Black Americans, at the structural level, is looked at as progress on the identity optics level.

Reed's Analysis of Racial Reductionism

Reed's analysis is surgical: the emphasis on racial disparities often undermines the multiracial organizing needed to address structural problems—exactly what the system wants. Consider his equations:

Race-First Analysis + Market Logic = Perfect System Protection

This equation reveals how focusing exclusively on race without addressing underlying market structures creates changes that are purely cosmetic while leaving economic power untouched.

Class Solidarity + Multiracial Organizing = System Threat

Reed argues that when working people organize across racial lines around shared economic interests, they present the greatest challenge to entrenched power structures.

Identity Politics + Neoliberalism = Movement Death

When movements prioritize symbolic representation over material transformation, they can be easily co-opted by the very systems they claim to challenge.

As Reed argues, this isn't about denying racism but understanding how racial politics can become a "cover story" for specific orders of political and economic power. When he got canceled by the Democratic Socialists of America (DSA) in 2020 for suggesting COVID-19 racial disparity analysis undermined multiracial organizing, it proved his point: even the Left has become captured by race reductionism.

Reed's cutting analysis of the Obama phenomenon in "Nothing Left" provided a perfect dissection of how neoliberalism co-opted Black politics: "I taught Obama's cohort—the Yale version. And I was struck by how many of them were so convinced that the whole purpose of the civil-rights movement was that people like them could go to Ivy League colleges and go to Wall Street afterward."[3]

This connects directly back to his early recognition of Obama as "a smooth Harvard lawyer with impeccable credentials and vacuous-to-repressive neoliberal politics." Reed saw how Obama embodied this market-worship, reducing racial justice to individual achievement while advancing policies that protected Wall Street and Silicon Valley corporate interests.

Lester Spence's Religious Investigation

While Reed dissects the political manifestation of neoliberalism, Lester Spence goes deeper—into the Black church itself. At the same time as the Obama spook was peaking, prosperity preaching now dominated Black American religious culture, led by figures such as TD Jakes, Creflo Dollar, and the late Eddie Long.[4] In his groundbreaking "Knocking the Hustle," Spence shows how prosperity gospel became neoliberalism's perfect delivery system:

1. Economic crisis hits community

2. Churches convert collective problems into individual spiritual failures

3. Political organizing becomes ungodly

4. System protects itself through consciousness control

As Spence explains: "Under the prosperity gospel, the idea is really, really simple. If you follow the word of God, if you follow the Bible, you will not only be spiritually wealthy, you will become materially prosperous.

Under this line, poverty ends up being the response of a poverty mindset instead of being the result of structural forces."

This transforms systemic problems into personal failures. Can't find a job? Pray harder. Can't afford healthcare? Give more to the church. Can't make rent? Your faith isn't strong enough. The prosperity gospel turns political problems into spiritual ones, guaranteeing they never get political solutions.

Prosperity Gospel: The Perfect Obama New Blacks Religion

It's no coincidence that prosperity gospel reached its zenith during the Obama years. When preachers like Creflo Dollar were building $65 million private jet funds and living in 53-acre mansions, they embodied the same neoliberal ethos that defined Obama-era politics: predatory individualistic solutions for structural problems.

Dollar, worth an estimated $27 million, preached that "financial blessings are part of God's plan for believers" while publishing books like "You're Supposed to Be Wealthy" and "Total Life Prosperity." This wasn't just religious hustle—it was neoliberalism in religious drag, transforming economic justice into individual spiritual striving. During the Obama New Blacks era, if Obama hooked Black America with a predatory spook spell from the left, prosperity preachers like Dollar cast their own Black neoliberal spook spell from the right.

The math was simple: Poor? You're not praying right. Broke? Your faith is weak. Struggling? God doesn't favor you yet. If you're racially profiled and disproportionately struggling to find investors for your start-up, Obama told us at Morehouse no excuses because he was elected President. If Silicon Valley was locking Black Americans out of the new start-up and technology gold rush, it's something wrong with the faith of Black Americans. No longer was the Black Church a force to challenge the Democratic Party and its heavy skew towards elites, it now defended almost every policy orientation and move, with its new political prophet, Barack Obama.

What made prosperity gospel the perfect religion for Black neoliberalism was its complete transformation of structural problems into personal spiritual failures. Dollar told his congregation that poverty was simply the result of a 'poverty mindset,' while Obama told Morehouse graduates there were 'no more excuses.' Both messages shifted responsibility from failed systems to failed individuals. Like Kings throughout history, modern neoliberal elites have incentives to push responsibility and accountability down to the peasants, although the Kings designed and enforced the system that impacts the individual . If there were big cracks and failures, it's the peasants' fault, not those with all the power and decision-making authority, breaking things with defective policies. Remember, the spook sellers always want to push accountability down to the common person.

When Dollar asked his congregation to donate $300 each toward his $65 million Gulfstream G650 jet in 2015, he was practicing the same logic that defined the Obama era: spectacular inequality justified through individual merit and symbolic identity.[5] The fact that both Dollar and Obama thrived simultaneously was no accident—both were selling versions of the same neoliberal spook.

Obama Era: Neoliberalism's Perfect Storm

When Obama filled his economic team with Wall Street insiders while speaking the language of Black cultural authenticity, he demonstrated exactly how neoliberalism uses identity to protect class interests. As Reed had warned, racial symbolism became the perfect cover for policies that benefited elites.

Spence observed this contradiction in real-time during Obama's final State of the Union address in 2016. Despite unprecedented racial justice uprisings in Ferguson, Baltimore, and elsewhere, Obama made no mention of these movements or the police violence that sparked them. As Spence noted, "Chicago had 496 murders, I believe, in 2015. That doesn't get a word. He invited one of the Black Lives Matters activists to the State of the Union. She sat there. You know, she had a seat. Doesn't even give her a shout-out." [6]

Even worse was the government-created water crisis in Flint, Michigan— a majority-Black American city under emergency financial management that had its water supply poisoned to save money. This was neoliberalism's perfect crime: democratic rights suspended to impose market logic, resulting in massive harm to Black Americans. When Obama finally visited Flint in 2016—two years after the crisis began—his response epitomized this disconnect.

As filmmaker and Flint native Michael Moore noted, Obama's symbolic gesture of drinking filtered Flint water while saying "I've got your back" ignored deeper realities: "To drink from a glass of Flint water when a number of experts are still saying this water's not safe? It's still going through the same corroded lead pipes? It was such a disappointing thing to see."[7] Moore highlighted the larger economic devastation that made Flint vulnerable in the first place: "Your clip you just showed about he hopes that Flint can get back to where it was. Where was that? You mean before the water crisis two years ago, after we'd lost 75,000 General Motors jobs?" This wasn't just a water crisis but the culmination of decades of economic abandonment and democratic disenfranchisement—problems that couldn't be solved with symbolic presidential visits or reassurances that filtered water was safe while the underlying infrastructure remained poisonous.

Obama's performance in Flint perfectly demonstrated how neoliberal politics replaces material solutions and natural political pressure with symbolic gestures while the most vulnerable communities continue to suffer. You can think of neoliberalism as the cousin of spook and it has a deceptive strategic orientation to put lipstick on a pig with identity, symbolism, and sermon-like speeches, to make you think the pig is not still there and ugly. After a neoliberal spook spell is thrown on you, you will be thinking the pig is cute.

Looking at Flint through the Science vs. Spook framework reveals the precise mathematics of neoliberal governance: suspend democratic processes, impose market-based solutions, create measurable harm to vulnerable communities, then respond with symbolic gestures rather than material repair. This isn't just theory—it's the measurable reality of how neoliberalism operates when stripped of its rhetorical disguises.

The Science of Political Capture

Reed and Spence's analyses reveal the mechanism of neoliberal capture:

Consciousness Colonization

- Market logic becomes common sense
- Individual solutions replace collective action
- Success becomes purely personal

Leadership Corruption

- More Oscars for Ava DuVernay becomes a civil rights victory
- Leaders promote individual solutions
- Organizations adopt market metrics
- Movement becomes business

Racial Misdirection

- Class issues become race issues
- Structural problems become identity problems
- System protection through identity politics

While presenting Reed and Lester's critiques of neoliberalism, I don't adopt their views wholesale. The Science vs. Spook framework isn't about ideological purity but intellectual flexibility—the willingness to consider different viewpoints and surgically extract valuable insights regardless of their source. Reed's analysis contains scientific elements worth considering even if one disagrees with his broader conclusions. This approach—incorporating diverse perspectives while maintaining independent judgment—represents the essence of moving from ideological spook to a scientific orientation. It's about adopting the mindset exemplified by the quote from investing legend Charlie Munger: "The wise man looks for what he can learn from everyone." This intellectual flexibility allows us to build a more comprehensive understanding than any single ideological or political perspective could provide.

The Mathematics of Neoliberal Capture

The mathematics of this capture is precise:

Economic Crisis + Racial Politics = Depoliticized Response

Market Logic + Black Leadership = System Protection

Individual Solutions + Identity Politics = Movement Death

What makes this exploitation perfect is its totality. When Reed says liberals use "identity politics and race as a way to counter calls for redistributive policies," he's identifying how racial politics often protects economic power and wealth concentration.[8] When Spence shows how Black churches preach personal breakthrough over collective political breakthrough, he's showing the same mechanism at work.

The true genius of neoliberalism is its capacity to transform legitimate liberation struggles into market-compatible forms that pose no threat to existing power structures. By turning collective political demands into individual consumer choices or symbolic representation, neoliberalism neutralizes movements while appearing to embrace them. This mathematical precision in system protection explains why decades of "diversity initiatives" have coincided with expanding wealth gaps and persistent structural inequalities. Rather than neoliberalism diversity being a sign of progress, it also can be a sign of a deceptive containment strategy against the aggregate Black American political position.

While both Reed and Spence attack neoliberalism, their approaches differ significantly in how they handle race. Reed argues for discounting racial factors to build class-based coalitions against elite structures, believing targeted racial solutions can inadvertently reinforce division. Spence, however, acknowledges racial specificity while connecting it to broader neoliberal frameworks—showing how market logic specifically exploits Black communities through mechanisms like the prosperity gospel. This tension exemplifies why the Science vs. Spook framework values intellectual flexibility: we can extract insights from both approaches without wholesale adoption of either perspective. By maintaining critical distance while appreciating multiple analytical frameworks, we develop a more nuanced understanding of how neoliberalism operates through both economic structures and cultural mechanisms. This scientific approach to political analysis—considering multiple factors and policy positions rather than subscribing to singular explanations—provides the strongest foundation for political optimization and an environment to fertilize a new Black American political renaissance.

The Science

- **Neoliberalism = market logic infecting everything:** When every institution runs like a business, collective needs get sacrificed for individual profit
- **Black churches became prosperity gospel ATMs:** Preachers like Creflo Dollar turned poverty into personal spiritual failure while building $65M jet funds
- **Obama represented neoliberalism in Black face:** Used racial identity to sell policies that protected Wall Street and Silicon Valley
- **Individual success replaced collective struggle:** Focus shifted from economic justice to diverse faces in elite positions
- **Flint water crisis = neoliberalism's perfect crime:** Democracy suspended, market logic imposed, Black communities poisoned, symbolic presidential visit provided

[1] Benjamin Wallace-Wells, "The Marxist Who Antagonizes Liberals and the Left: The renowned Black scholar Adolph Reed opposes the politics of anti-racism, describing it as a cover for capitalism," The New Yorker, January 31, 2022.

[2] Rollin Hu, "Spence talks neoliberalism and black politics," The Johns Hopkins News-Letter, January 28, 2016.

[3] Adolph Reed Jr., "Nothing Left: The Long, Slow Surrender of American Liberals," Harper's Magazine, March 2014.

[4] Todd L. Williams, director, "Black Church, Inc." Featuring Rev. Al Sharpton, Moguldom Studios, July 2, 2014. DVD.

[5] Sam Stringer, "Minister Creflo Dollar asks for $60 million in donations for a new jet," CNN, March 16, 2015.

[6] Keeanga Taylor, and Lester Spence, "Black People's State of The Union Missing from Obama's Address," The Real News Network, January 13, 2016. https://therealnews.com/spencetaylor0112equalitystateounion

[7] Michael Moore, "Michael Moore calls Barack Obama drinking Flint water 'disappointing'," interviewed by Brian Manzullo, Detroit Free Press, May 4, 2016.

[8] Benjamin Wallace-Wells, "The Marxist Who Antagonizes Liberals and the Left: The renowned Black scholar Adolph Reed opposes the politics of anti-racism, describing it as a cover for capitalism," The New Yorker, January 31, 2022.

Trick Bags and Tricknology: Jay-Z, BK, and the NFL

> *"I think we've moved past kneeling, and I think it's time to go into actionable items." —Jay-Z*

In the game of power and tricknology, I've learned to follow the percentages, not the personalities. When Jay-Z was paraded as the face of the Brooklyn Nets ownership, nobody told us he owned only 0.15 percent of the team. That ain't ownership—that's tokenism with mathematical precision. It's the perfect trick bag: the system gets 99.85% of the power while we celebrate getting played for 0.15%.

This mathematical misdirection is part of what I call "tricknology": the deception playbook elites run to maintain power while appearing to share it. The Obama-era New Blacks period perfected this game, using Black faces in high places to sell policy and development that often worked against Black collective interests.

Brooklyn's Billion-Dollar Bamboozle

The $4.9 billion Barclays Center development in Brooklyn represents tricknology at its finest. When real estate vulture developer Bruce Ratner needed to overcome community resistance to his massive land grab, he didn't change the exploitative economics—he changed the marketing. He recruited Jay-Z as the project's Black face, making a gentrification machine look like Black empowerment. [1]

I executive produced a documentary that appeared on Netflix and TV One: "A Genius Leaves The Hood: The Unauthorized Story of Jay Z" in 2014, and we actually went to interview the Brooklyn residents who were pushed out.[2] The residents told us firsthand how tricknology was used to get the project approved, particularly eminent domain abuse and the manufactured "blight" designation. A key to busting up tricknology is to go on the inside (insider, in the field) and studying the insiders. This removes the mystery and factors hidden under the surface. The Brooklyn residents showed us homes that were well-maintained and thriving businesses that were condemned so the developer could seize land. These weren't abandoned properties—they were people's homes and livelihoods being sacrificed for billionaire profits. Jay-Z even tried to shut down the release my documentary with legal threats, and I had to bust back on him and Jay-Z enterprises, legally of course. One thing about those doing the devilishment at the top is they try to use fear and threats against those who go underneath to get to the factors and understand and document back to the people. They prefer that the hidden sides of their commercial and political activities remain a mystery.

The mathematics tell the real story: Jay-Z owned an estimated 0.15 percent of the Nets.[3] The real owner was Mikhail Prokhorov, a Russian oligarch who took 80 percent of the team and 45 percent of the arena for $223 million. But having Jay-Z out front transformed the narrative from "white billionaire colonizes Brooklyn" to "hometown hero brings basketball back."

This wasn't just PR—it was weaponized identity politics. The trick bag worked precisely because it hijacked genuine Black aspirations. As Reverend Al Sharpton gushed at the ribbon-cutting: "I'm glad I lived to see the color line in ownership broken in Brooklyn, where we've gone from Jackie to Jay-Z, where we can not only play the game but we can own a piece of the game."[4] Under the Science vs Spook framework, we would immediately ask the question of how much Al Sharpton and other local leaders were paid to promote the Brooklyn development tricknology and spook?

A piece is right—0.15% to be exact. But that mathematical reality didn't fit the emotional narrative. The spook seller knows that if the local Black

American community believes Jay-Z is a NBA owner, many of us think of it as our own part of the team. We want to see each other win so it exploits this affinity by positioning Jay-Z as a NBA team owner while keeping both the percentage and the real costs to the local community, a mystery.

The development's promises were equally deceptive. Ratner promised 10,000 permanent jobs, 17,000 construction jobs, and 2,250 affordable housing units. What Brooklyn got instead was a rusty-looking arena, hundreds of parking spaces, and a 25-year timeline for completing the original promises—which will likely never materialize.

To make this trick work, Ratner didn't just recruit Jay-Z. He systematically bought off potential opposition:[5]

- $50,000 to Rev. Herb Daughtry's neighborhood association, plus 54 tickets for every Nets game and a $300,000 luxury suite

- $1 million to create "B.U.I.L.D."—a fake grassroots organization to support the project

- $1.5 million to ACORN to neutralize housing activists

In this context, the spook sellers positions Jay-Z as a change agent but in reality, he was a neat realization agent against legitimate Black American collective interests and rights. The most egregious tricknology was the abuse of eminent domain, which requires a "public purpose" for seizing private property. The state had to manufacture "blight" to justify the takeover. Their evidence? Cracks in the sidewalk, graffiti, and weeds – problems that could have been fixed with simple maintenance rather than wholesale demolition. Even the MTA's railyard was deemed "blighted" because it was "underutilized" – a completely bogus claim since developing over an active railyard requires expensive platforms that only make economic sense with massive density.

This is tricknology: using precise investments in key opposition leaders to fracture community resistance, exploiting legal loopholes to take private property, and deploying just enough Black faces to diffuse racial criticism.

The pattern is mathematical—find the pressure points, apply targeted resources, and watch the opposition collapse from within. The elites make their spook look like Black Americans are winning and those with the scientific, skeptical eye, as haters or "crabs in a barrel." If promoting scientific examination and mathematical-risk/reward calculations and exposing widespread tricknology and political games is a crab, then I want to be a crab, under that definition.

The NFL's Kaepernick Containment Strategy

The NFL ran a similar playbook when Colin Kaepernick threatened their profit machine by kneeling against police brutality. Rather than addressing the substance of Kaepernick's protest, they executed a brilliant trick bag: recruit Jay-Z to be the Black face of 'social justice' while maintaining system control, sending Jay-Z, Desiree Perez, and ROC Nation a big check to program Hip-Hop and R&B at the Super Bowl. A big check and a new Hip-Hop Al Sharpton figure to jump in front of the protest was a high-probability bet for the NFL. The elites at the top understand the spook elements in Black America and know exactly how to exploit them.

When the NFL announced that Roc Nation would produce the Super Bowl halftime show and lead their "Inspire Change" initiative, the reality and factors were again obscured. Jay-Z would get a lucrative contract and cultural credibility; the NFL would get racial cover without changing its structure and structural orientation. The perception would change but the objective reality would stay the same.

Jay-Z's statement that 'we've moved past kneeling and I think it's time to go into actionable items' was the perfect system-protection language—suggesting protest was outdated while offering vague 'action' that didn't threaten NFL economics. At that moment, he positioned himself as a spokesperson for Black American political interests while actually serving his own individual financial interests. Although Jay-Z is a musical genius and extremely talented and commercially successful, his self-positioning as 'King of the Blacks' undermines collective Black American political interests when personal enrichment constitutes 90% of his motivation.

The pattern is scientific: when powerful interests face a threat rooted in racial justice, they don't address the underlying issues—they recruit Black American celebrities to change the conversation. The math stays the same, but the perception transforms. The spook changes the optics but the science, the reality, factors, and the structure remains intact.

COINTELPRO 2.0: Modern Neutralization Tactics

We need to stop thinking of J. Edgar Hoover COINTELPRO (OLD) (60's, 70's) and start thinking that COINTELPRO and political neutralization with institutional agents, of all flavors, is fully institutionalized. If you are so far up the ass of history of what's been done in the past, you may miss Hoover-like operations being run on us right up into the modern times.

The tricknology could be so modernized, potent and effective, it could have us begging for more of it, when superficial representation of institutional interests looks like we are racking up W's but really racking up L's. The individual front man gets the W with the system, while we get collective L's, politically. When the elites can negotiate Black American freedom, justice, and equality, with individual Black American celebrities and leaders, who are mostly unaccountable to the masses, it is always winning. If they can neutralize millions in the back, by giving out checks to a few in the front, this is good devilishment science for them but bad science for Black America.

The old COINTELPRO used wiretaps, infiltrators, and direct harassment. Today's version uses celebrity recruitment, corporate partnerships, and foundation funding to neutralize movements before they can even form. It's more sophisticated, more scientific, and more effective precisely because it doesn't look like COINTELPRO. It looks like progress.

When the NFL brings Jay-Z in to neutralize Kaepernick's protest, that's COINTELPRO 2.0. When foundations fund only the most moderate, non-threatening Black organizations while ignoring those with radical economic demands, that's COINTELPRO 2.0. When Hollywood celebrates Black stories that focus on individual triumph over racism rather than collective action against systems, that's COINTELPRO 2.0. When over 90% of Black Americans in Congress and the Congressional Black Caucus are fully compromised and undemocratically fearful of AIPAC, that's COINTELPRO 2.0.[6]

The trick bag is more advanced now because it uses our desire for identity representation against us. It's tricknology with a scientific precision that Hoover could only dream of. The way the tricknology has been so carefully grafted and operationalized, too many Black Americans have developed an appetite for SPOOK and tricknology, where many want more of it (believing its collective progress) and believe it's core and a requirement for authentic Black American identity. It's not and many of us must help de-spook more of Black America and further institutionalize a greater scientific orientation, politically and culturally.

Hip-Hop's Coopted Revolution

Hip-hop's transformation during the Obama New Blacks era demonstrated the same pattern. Once the soundtrack of resistance, mainstream hip-hop became increasingly aligned with governmental and corporate agendas. Pharrell's fundraiser for the Israeli military in 2018 showed how far the art form had drifted from its revolutionary roots. [7] Where Hip-Hop's moral character would historically stand with tens of thousands of Palestinian civilians being bombed out of existence in Gaza, now those doing the bombing simply find partners like Pharrell with a big check.

As hip-hop artists gained access to wealth and status, their incentives shifted from challenging power to protecting the status quo, embracing the structural hierarchies as permanent reality. The percentage of their economic interests tied to the system staying the same increased, while their connection to community struggles decreased. Optical wins such as Black Faces in High Places was the new revolution, the "New Black," as Pharell called it.

For every Jay-Z claiming to "move beyond kneeling," there were dozens of underground artists still addressing systemic issues—but they lacked the platform and visibility of those who'd been coopted. The political scam isn't just about buying off individuals; it's about elevating those who serve system interests while marginalizing those who challenge them.

Patterns & Tricknology

The pattern across these examples reveals a scientific formula to how power maintains itself while appearing to change:

- **Percentage Deception**: Present minimal ownership/control (0.15%) as revolutionary breakthrough

- **Identity Substitution**: Replace material gains (jobs, housing) with symbolic representation

- **Strategic Recruitment**: Identify influential figures with maximum cultural credibility

- **Narrative Manipulation**: Frame system protection as progressive change

- **Timeline Exploitation**: Make immediate promises with distant fulfillment dates

- **Opposition Fragmentation**: Target resources to potential opposition leaders

This isn't a conspiracy—it's strategy backed by mathematical precision. The system doesn't need to give up control; it just needs to create the perception of change. It needs to create more and more spook to delay an eventual reckoning with Black America. By rejecting spook collectively, we accelerate system reform and structural changes, we create tension and pressure. By tolerating too much political spook or misidentifying spook in Black Face as progress, we delay an eventually reckoning and transformative policies such as Pure Reparations. Within this frame, spook becomes a political barrier to real & material structural changes and speed.

Seeing Through the Trick Bag

The first step in defeating political tricknology is recognizing it. When celebrities are presented as the face of "progress," we need to ask:

- What percentage do they actually own/control?
- What material benefits flow to the community vs. power holders?
- What substantive changes to power relations will occur?
- Who gets decision-making authority?
- What's the timeline for promised benefits?
- Is there an active neutralization operation against Black American interests?

Under the Science vs. Spook framework, Bruce Ratner's eminent domain scheme wouldn't have succeeded through merely hiring Jay-Z and recruiting Black leaders like Sharpton. The NFL couldn't neutralize legitimate protests by simply bringing in Jay-Z and Desiree Perez while depositing millions in their accounts. This framework recognizes that our challenges are fundamentally collective, requiring collective solutions— what benefits select individuals, with their financially conflicted and perverse motivations, has no bearing on our broader political position and orientation.

The mathematical reality is clear: individual payoffs and fake representation symbolism don't equal Black American collective progress. We maintain our scientific position regardless of which Black celebrities and leaders receive checks—be it Jay-Z, Obama, Sharpton, Harris, or any other front person for system interests. Individual advancement is not freedom, justice, and equality.

The Black American leadership greats such as Dr. Martin Luther King Jr., Elijah Muhammad, and Malcolm X never saw room for Obama New Blacks ideology to dominate Black American political orientation. Time doesn't change principles and moral positions that have stood the test of time. They saw themselves as part of a collective, organized response to further freedom, justice, and equality for Black Americans.

The new commercialized prophets and their various spook spells should not be allowed to take so much political market share in how we define progress, as an individual symbolic achievement or scientific and material outcomes, that can be quantified and measured, for collective Black American interests.

The Science

- **0.15% ownership is not ownership**: Jay-Z's Brooklyn Nets stake was tokenism with mathematical precision
- **Black faces provide cover for white extraction**: Developer Bruce Ratner used Jay-Z to legitimize gentrification that displaced Brooklyn residents
- **The NFL bought off protest with entertainment contracts**: Recruited Jay-Z to neutralize Kaepernick's message while maintaining system control
- **COINTELPRO 2.0 uses celebrity recruitment**: Modern neutralization tactics use corporate partnerships and foundation funding instead of direct harassment
- **Individual advancement ≠ collective progress**: When celebrities get paid to front for exploitative systems, we all lose

---

[1] Anthony Fisher, "Brooklyn's Barclays Center is an Eminent Domain-Created Failure," Reason Magazine, January 12, 2016.

[2] Jamarlin Martin (Executive Producer), "A Genius Leaves the Hood: The Unauthorized Story of Jay Z," Moguldom Studios, May 19, 2015.

[3] Billboard Staff, "Jay-Z to Sell Stake in Brooklyn Nets," Billboard, April 21, 2013.

[4] Kevin Baker, "How to Steal a City: Bruce Ratner and Co. Just Rolled Brooklyn," The Observer, October 2, 2012.

[5] Christian Red, Nathaniel Vinton, and Teri Thompson, "Yankees' Alex Rodriguez admits adviser Desiree Perez of Jay Z's Roc Nation Sports told him to stiff his lawyers: court docs," Daily News, April 9, 2018, updated April 30, 2025.

[6] AIPAC Political Action Committee, "AIPAC-ENDORSED Congressional Black Caucus Members Who have Won in 2024," AIPAC PAC, 2024, https://www.aipacpac.org/congressional-black-caucus.

[7] Margeaux Sippell, "Friends of the Israel Defense Forces Gala Raises Record $60 Million for Soldiers," Variety, November 2, 2018.

Chris vs. Goliath

> *"We got billionaires breaking federal laws every day. Every single day a worker gets fired in this country for retaliation, for organizing. Where's the accountability?"* —Chris Smalls

When Chris Smalls was fired by Amazon in New York in 2020 over union organizing, he decided to fight back against one of the most powerful corporations in the world. This wasn't just any David versus Goliath story—it was a case study in how the neoliberal tricknology machine works against Black labor and how symbolic politics undermines structural progress.

Let's establish actual facts first. Amazon is the second-largest employer in the United States, with 1.1 million employees. One out of every 153 American workers collects a check from Jeff Bezos. The neoliberal tells us, "Amazon creates jobs"—classic spook thinking that obscures material reality. The scientific analysis shows that Amazon likely destroys more jobs than it creates by automation and replacing traditional storefronts that require far more employees.

With the public narrative optimized for monopoly interests such as "Amazon is bringing jobs," you must ask yourself, how many jobs does Amazon take away? A scathing report from the Institute for Local Self-Reliance (ILSR) provides the data: Amazon has eliminated 149,000 more jobs in retail than it has created through its warehouses. The report compares Bezos to a "19th-century railroad baron controlling which businesses get to market and what they have to pay to get there," and argues that "Amazon is supplanting an open market with a privately controlled one, giving it the power to dictate the terms by which its competitors can operate, and to levy a kind of tax on their revenue." [1]

How many small businesses will be pushed "off the block" with the monster monopoly coming in to take complete control? There is no such thing as Amazon "creating jobs" unless we factor in projected job losses from automation and the Amazon system killing jobs outside the Amazon system. Make no mistake, there are many transformational efficiencies that Amazon brings to the table but we need to factor how positive and negative factors net out and then we can use the term "net job increases" after both positives and negatives are properly factored. Amazon coming into a new city may net out positive for that specific location but we have to add the different factors up. For example, Walmart may bring new jobs and lower prices to a new town or city but many small businesses and their employees will be pushed off the block.

It's not just about job numbers—it's about job quality. Amazon systematically replaces higher-wage unionized positions with lower-wage warehouse jobs without representation. The ILSR report reveals that "many of the workers in Amazon warehouses are subcontracted temporary workers, which the company refers to as 'seasonal,' but are, in many cases, year-round 'permatemps.'" The company even created an Uber-like delivery network called Amazon Flex, which lets anyone over 21 become a driver paid per delivery—not hourly—while covering their own fuel, maintenance, and insurance. This Uber-ization of work strips away benefits and protections while creating the illusion of employment.

The material warehouse conditions are brutal: Amazon's 150 percent attrition rate means they replace their entire workforce every eight months. [2]This reflects systematic burnout in a company that generated billions for Bezos while its workforce struggled to take bathroom breaks during shifts. This isn't incidental—it's by design.

The COVID-19 pandemic exposed Amazon's brutal reality even further. Black American worker Mario Crippen from Michigan became a voice of resistance when he stood outside his warehouse in April 2020 demanding it be "shut down immediately for professional cleaning" after three co-workers tested positive. While Amazon claimed to focus on "essential items," Crippen told reporters the truth: "If you go on the website, all the essential items are sold out." What was he packaging instead? "Dildos are not essential items," he declared, noting that he packaged massive amounts of sex toys daily while actual necessities remained unavailable. Crippen's unfiltered truth-telling went viral precisely because it cut through Amazon's carefully constructed public relations facade. [3]

When Chris Smalls organized the first successful union at Amazon, he faced the full arsenal of tricknology. [4] This included Alexandria Ocasio-Cortez backing away from supporting the unionization effort while being photographed in "Tax the Rich" dresses at elite galas. It included former Obama press secretary Jay Carney deployed as Amazon's top lobbyist. It included $100 million "philanthropic" donations to Obama's foundation after he ran a Big Tech-friendly regulatory regime for eight years. [5] It included $100 million "courage and civility" awards to figures like CNN's Van Jones, creating a network of well-compensated Black faces to provide cover for structural exploitation. [6] Why do you think Bezos wanted to get in the political bed with Van Jones and Obama and buy the Washington Post newspaper? When you're on the Bezos level (net worth over $200 Billion), it's really a political game with regulatory capture and public relations being at the top of the priority list.

Obama and Van Jones can't confront the more powerful monopoly structures in America, so why should they be taking up so much Black leadership market share, while heroes like Chris Smalls barely get a mention in Black American media?

Under the Science vs Spook framework, Smalls become the GIANT, while Obama and Van Jones go to the back if they are not in a position to challenge the powerful structures holding hundreds of thousands of Black American workers back. Although they may do some good with the Bezos millions, scientific thinking demands we recognize when monopoly interests are playing us with racial sensibilities in exchange for political cover and silence. It's not that Obama and Jones should be totally dismissed based on their conflicts with Amazon, it's just we should discount what they have to say with regards to American workers and union protections, and any other areas they are conflicted with powerful institutional interests.

The elites can use Black Faces such as Obama and Jones to mask an assault on Black American Amazon workers like Smalls. If the most influential political figures are conflicted and compromised by Amazon, there could be a political muzzle that acts in stealth, that is politically harmful, in real terms. The tricknology of the monopolists can work like a drug dealer paying off the police to not come around a specific block, where most of the weight is being moved and where most of the illicit profits are being generated. Or paying off witnesses to a robbery.

Consider this timing: Bezos donates $100 million to the Obama Foundation in November 2021, less than a year before Smalls' historic victory against Amazon. Is this philanthropy or system protection? According to reports, Obama's man James Carney's hiring as Amazon's SVP of Global Corporate Affairs was part of a deliberate strategy to ramp up Amazon's political influence, with the company's lobbying budget exploding from $5 million in 2014 to $18 million by 2020. [7]

Amazon's top executives strategized to discredit Smalls by painting him as "not smart or articulate"—classic racial coding to undermine Black leadership. [8] When workers raised alarms about COVID-19 protocols, Carney dismissed them, claiming there was "almost no truth" to the accusations. By October 2020, at least 20,000 Amazon workers had contracted the virus.

If Democratic Party politicians are going to be this chummy (Michele Obama and Jill Biden even kissed Jeff Bezos at the White House, why can't they kiss someone like Chris Smalls) with the second-largest employer in America while supposedly regulating them and defending labor, what hope does the Black worker have? [9] Obama? AOC? The Biden administration? The trick of the neoliberal order is to look like progress while running a deceptive elitist enforcement program at scale. The modern Democratic Party is more likely to be protecting a monopoly than the Amazon workers. If the party has this elite skew and is committed to it, how the party looks on the outside, the identity wrapper, doesn't matter. The system puts "first Black" elitists who are structurally hostile to labor in positions of symbolic power, creating the perfect cover: Black faces in high places selling policies that undermine and harm Black workers. The old Black American politics, led by figures such as Jesse Jackson, would find Chris Smalls the HERO. This modern New Black Democratic Party politics is more likely to position the one protecting Jeff Bezos and Amazon, as the hero, with identity and representation being the dominant factor.

By the time Smalls won his historic fight against Amazon, Obama was building vacation mansions in Hawaii and breaking ground on his presidential library with checks from Big Tech. Meanwhile, nearly 50 percent of Black American workers make less than $15 an hour while rents and housing costs reach record levels. My younger spooky self in 2008 actually assumed Obama would be rolling with heroes like Chris Smalls, when he got out of office, rather than Jeff Bezos.

The scientific factors, underneath the surface, tells us we need a fundamental reorientation: if the older generation prioritized "first Black" symbolism, the next generation must prioritize "first labor" and "first reparations." We must shift from symbolic representation to structural transformation. When we put structural considerations at the front and push symbolic considerations to the back, we gain better positioning against corporate exploitation.

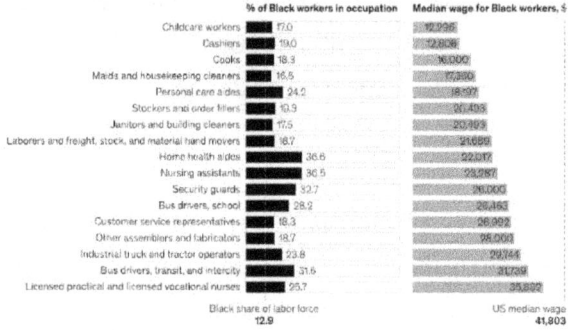

Black workers are disproportionately represented in low-wage occupations today.

Occupations with a high Black worker concentration

	% of Black workers in occupation	Median wage for Black workers, $
Childcare workers	17.0	12,096
Cashiers	19.0	12,808
Cooks	18.3	16,000
Maids and housekeeping cleaners	16.5	17,390
Personal care aides	24.2	18,397
Stockers and order fillers	19.9	20,435
Janitors and building cleaners	17.5	20,393
Laborers and freight, stock, and material hand movers	18.7	21,689
Home health aides	36.6	22,017
Nursing assistants	36.5	23,287
Security guards	32.7	26,000
Bus drivers, school	28.2	26,453
Customer service representatives	18.3	26,392
Other assemblers and fabricators	18.7	28,000
Industrial truck and tractor operators	23.8	29,744
Bus drivers, transit, and intercity	31.6	31,739
Licensed practical and licensed vocational nurses	25.7	35,892
Black share of labor force **12.9**		**US median wage** **41,803**

Source: Current Population Survey, 2019; IPUMS USA, five-year dataset (2014–18), from US Census Bureau's American Community Survey. McKinsey Global Institute and McKinsey Institute for Black Economic Mobility analysis

McKinsey
& Company

Black Workers in Low-Wage Occupations - Shows concentration of Black workers in low-paying jobs

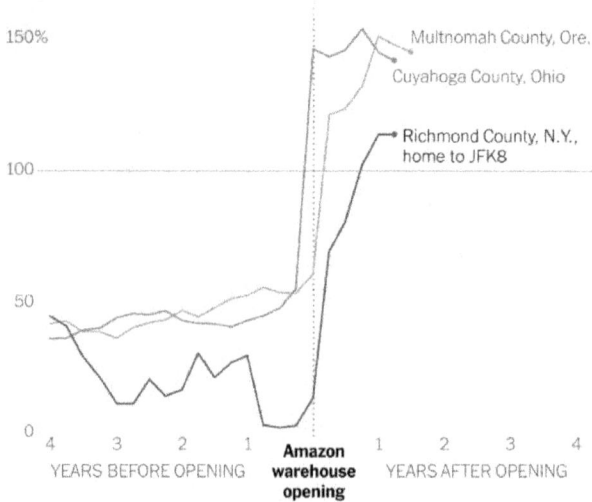

Turnover Rate for Warehouse and Storage Employees
Before and after Amazon warehouse opens

Multnomah County, Ore.

Cuyahoga County, Ohio

Richmond County, N.Y., home to JFK8

150%

100

50

0

4 3 2 1 **Amazon warehouse opening** 1 2 3 4
YEARS BEFORE OPENING   YEARS AFTER OPENING

Turnover rate compares total separations to a company's overall employment.

By The New York Times | Sources: U.S. Census Bureau, Quarterly Workforce Indicators; MWPVL International

140

Smalls' victory against Amazon represents what's possible when we move from spook to science. Amazon deployed the full arsenal of tricknology—celebrity allies, political connections, media control, philanthropic cover, racialized attacks—yet still lost to determined, strategic organizing. This wasn't just a labor victory; it was a triumph against powerful interests that are now aligned with the Obama New Blacks ideology. What's notable with the David vs Goliath victory of Smalls is supporting research and analysis for political scientist Adolph Reed, that victories that benefit a critical mass of Black Americans don't have to lead with race, as multiracial coalitions are needed to take on power at the highest levels. The elites have a Obama New Blacks political religion that promotes identity representation is more important than better wages and conditions for millions of Black Americans. This perverse political religion has their chosen prophets that we must be mindful of.

The equation is simple: Go long on structure & systems analysis, go short on symbolism. The corporate confederacy in America—companies like Amazon—exploit our attachment to symbolic victories while extracting our labor, our data, and our communities.

In auditing the measurement period of 1995-2025, an important takeaway was the undervaluation of Black Labor politics and the overvaluation of identity optics. The Obama New Blacks period revealed a disturbing pattern—celebrating symbolic representation while material conditions for Black workers deteriorated.

Why wasn't protecting Black American workers a priority during this period? Why so much attention to whether a Black face appears here or there, at the top of the institution, without considering deeper political alignment factors?

My experiences confirm this dynamic, here are a few examples: when I reached out to the Trinidadian diversity chief at Meta (Facebook), Maxine Williams, about arbitrary marketing restrictions against Black American content, I received no help or response. When I reached out to

Alvin Bowles, who I knew personally and who became Meta's head of Ads for America, he couldn't help my Black American-owned business that had spent millions with Facebook.

If these Black faces in leadership positions can't do anything to help us, why give so much currency to how these systems look on the outside, whatever identity the wrapper is? Do they have any power? Do they have any alignment and deep convictions for Black American interests? Would they take any risks for Black Americans? We should also consider that bad systems, anti-Black American systems, likely have incentives to hire a certain type of Black face who won't fight or risk anything for Black Americans within a corporate environment. This isn't cynicism—it's a scientific assessment of what produces material progress versus what creates the deceptive appearance of change.

Remember this: Chris Smalls with a union contract has more real power than a Black executive with stock options who can't challenge the system. That's not cynicism—that's actual fact. The lack of visible Black American media, leadership, and Congressional Black Caucus support for Chris Smalls taking on Amazon, is reflective of what the Obama New Blacks ideology prioritizes and its entrenched political opiate. The Obama New Blacks were too busy trying to shine the shoes of Democratic Party elites and finding another "First Black," to even notice Chris Smalls represented the type of high risk/reward activism that is desperately needed. The type of activism that could impact millions of Black Americans beyond Amazon. It's unlikely many Obama New Blacks leaders would even find any value from Smalls' fight and activism against Amazon, as there is nothing immediately in it for them, their personal pockets and there is no "status" attached to it.

The Science

- **Amazon destroys more jobs than it creates**: Despite "job creation" narratives, Amazon eliminated 149,000 more retail jobs than it created in warehouses
- **150% attrition rate = systematic burnout by design**: Amazon replaces its entire workforce every 8 months - this isn't accidental
- **Obama/Van Jones took Bezos money while workers struggled**: $100M donations to Obama Foundation and Van Jones while Amazon workers fought for basic rights
- **Chris Smalls proved organized labor can win**: Historic union victory shows what's possible when workers organize strategically
- **Structure beats symbolism**: Smalls with a union contract has more real power than Black executives with stock options who can't challenge the system

---

[1] Olivia LaVecchia, "How Amazon Undermines Jobs, Wages, and Working Conditions (Fact Sheet)," Institute for Local Self-Reliance, February 7, 2017.

[2] Tian Chen, "An Analysis of Amazon's High Turnover Rate," Proceedings of Business and Economic Studies 6, no. 3 (June 28, 2023): 31-38, https://doi.org/10.26689/pbes.v6i3.5096

[3] Gerren Keith Gaynor, "Amazon Worker on Strike Over COVID-19: 'Dildos Are Not Essential Items'," The Grio, April 1, 2020, https://thegrio.com/2020/04/01/amazon-worker-strike-covid-19-dildos/

[4] Shirin Ghaffary, "Amazon fired Chris Smalls. Now the new union leader is one of its biggest problems. What's next for the face of America's new labor movement," Vox, June 7, 2022.

[5] "Jeff Bezos donates $100M to the Obama Foundation in honor of Congressman John Lewis," Press Release, Obama Foundation, November 22, 2021.

[6] Oliver Darcy, "Bezos Donates $100 Million Each to CNN Contributor Van Jones and Chef José Andrés," CNN Business, July 21, 2021, https://www.cnn.com/2021/07/20/media/van-jones-bezos-100-million/index.html

[7] David Streitfeld, "Amazon Hires Jay Carney, Former Obama Press Secretary," The New York Times, February 26, 2015.

[8] Paul Blest, "Leaked Amazon Memo Details Plan to Smear Fired Warehouse Organizer: 'He's Not Smart or Articulate'," VICE, April 2, 2020, 3:46 PM, https://www.vice.com/en/article/leaked-amazon-memo-details-plan-to-smear-fired-warehouse-organizer-hes-not-smart-or-articulate/

[9] Khaleda Rahman, "Beso for Bezos! Jill Biden plants a kiss on Amazon billionaire at the White House," Daily Mail, May 5, 2016.

Kamala and the Democrats' Big L

> *"Diversity could be understood as one of the techniques by which liberal multiculturalism manages differences by managing more 'troublesome constituents.' Diversity can thus function as a containment strategy."* —Sara Ahmed, On Being Included: Racism and Diversity in Institutional Life

I wish I could say I estimated MAGA would prevent Democrats and their $1 billion campaign fund from winning a single battleground state. [1]MAGA effectively ran the table on Democrats, in battleground states.

One thing I did catch in real time was the numerous fumbles, such as Kamala saying on The View television show that she couldn't think of doing anything different from Biden, Obama suggesting Black men were being sexist by not supporting her as much as him in 2008 and 2012, or heavily relying on celebrities toward the end of the campaign, that likely masked material weakness. All the celebrity spook that was funded by the Kamala campaign wasn't catering to the millions of American families who were downgraded from eating at Capital Grille (or the equivalent) to eating Hamburger Helper. As famous bond investor Jeffrey Gundlach highlighted before the election, many families were hurting in the Biden economy, and he was starting to see Hamburger Helper ads. [2] Hamburger Helper was a meal that helped struggling families turn a $1 meal purchase into $10 worth of food in the 1980s. It helped stretch your dollar.

Inflation had bruised American families, disproportionately Black Americans, poor, and lower-middle class. It often seemed like Democrats were too top-heavy and distant to feel the pain and struggle that inflation was inflicting on so many families. [3] West Virginia Senator Joe Manchin had warned Democrats and Republicans alike that too much "stimmy" and Paycheck Protection Program (PPP) loans would cause increased inflation. Manchin offered some sanity against the political impulse of flooding the economy with more and more money during the COVID pandemic. [4] While the PPP loans would naturally be distributed toward the top based on amounts, with larger businesses getting a bigger benefit and bigger forgivable loans, the costs would be pushed down to the poor and working class, who would now have to pay $18 for a McDonald's Big Mac value meal in Connecticut. [5]

There are many factors why Kamala Harris and Democrats were smoked by MAGA, but dominant factors were inflation and illegal immigration. [6] Beyond inflation pressures, however, the Democratic Party suffers from deep, multi-factor structural problems that cannot be reduced to a single cause or fixed with superficial solutions. For example, the power within the party gravitates to leadership who are beyond the age of 80. [7]

After the election, one of the first images in my mind was Jay-Z taking a picture of the Brooklyn real estate developers who wanted to get the construction of the new home of the Brooklyn Nets approved. There were all types of games and tricknology to get support from city officials and the local residents. Jay-Z was brought in to sell spook—to distract from the critical details and potential disenfranchisement and gentrification of the local community. Jay-Z was brought in to sell an elite agenda, where the costs were going to be disproportionately distributed to the local residents and the benefits would be disproportionately allocated to the white elite. Jay-Z was brought in to deceptively "put lipstick on the pig," inject symbolism, and act as a front man for an economic project that would have no chance without him. In a sense, Jay-Z was used as a symbolic weapon against local community opposition.

With both Kamala Harris and Obama (and others), the Democrats have been running a Jay-Z/Brooklyn Real Estate Development project, particularly on Black Americans. It's something more aligned with cosmetic cover versus a firm commitment to changing how the system works. The system works well for the millionaires and billionaires and lobbyists who run the Democratic Party, but the system works less and less for those who see through the spook and only want to look at the details, not factor in Jay-Z's celebrity, regarding whether the plan is best for the community (voters) in the long term. The system is not working for many of us who don't care if Too Short or Lil' Wayne is performing at Kamala's House Party or don't need to see another symbolic holiday such as Juneteenth, as a deceptive substitute for policy commitment to Black Americans.[8]

The political religion that has been carefully crafted by the Democratic Party, where it can get by on symbolism and deceptive marketing, with extremely disproportionate costs and benefits between the party elites and Black Americans, is now fatigued. It's out of gas. It's less about MAGA racism or sexism and more about factors that are related to how the Democratic Party is presently malstructured toward elites and offering symbolic value versus scientific value.[9]

Kamala only had three months to throw a campaign together, but her attempt to craft a Black American agenda toward the end of the campaign revealed a deeper problem. It proved too little, too late; Black men in key battleground states either showed reduced turnout compared to previous elections or shifted their support toward MAGA in significant numbers.

When Obama scolded Black men for not supporting Kamala at the levels they supported him in 2008 and 2012, he seemed remarkably out of touch. No one gave him the message that many of us don't think about politics the way we did when he was elected. We're more politically mature now, not more sexist. Many of us no longer price the identity factor the same way, whether man or woman.

Obama's identity-reductionist, condescending tone toward Black American men was likely a predictive signal Democrats were about to be smoked. Not because Kamala is a Jamaican-American woman, but because Democrats have become too elite, too old, and too distant from

147

the top to feel the policy priorities at the bottom. Rather than front-loading a Black American agenda, they hastily assembled one for Black American men at the last minute in response to weak internal polling.

Here is the multi-factor science to consider. Many Black Americans are conservative, are religious, are firmly against illegal immigration, are not excited about trends with the transgender movement, and may agree with Republicans and Wall Street (their 401K's) that the economy may work better under Trump. So if Democrats are not offering a bold Black American agenda that can inspire and excite and the symbolic value factor is reduced or going away, we should see more movement toward MAGA, from Black men in particular, and less turnout for Black Americans in general if the Democratic Party playbook stays the same. The symbolism currency that Democrats established during the Obama era is rapidly losing value. With each election cycle, Black American voters demand more than mere representation to deliver the same electoral support—a political version of inflation where symbolic gestures yield diminishing returns.

Kamala was running on an unpopular Biden presidency and refused to distance herself from the big old white man. [10] In October of 2022, amid widespread anger over inflation, a Times/Siena poll found Biden with a 38 percent job approval rating and trailing Trump in a hypothetical rematch. It often seemed like he was being held up by his handlers like Weekend at Bernie's and could not really keep himself together and Presidential, avoiding press conferences at all costs. To me, it looked like a political cover up and Democrats and Biden weren't being honest with the American people about his declining condition. If Democrats couldn't be honest about Biden's rapidly declining mental faculties, what else were they lying about?

There was a nuanced way to embrace the Biden victories while leaving room for voters to imagine big changes were coming to improve their lives. But Kamala and the Democratic National Committee (DNC) lobbyist insiders ran on the establishment, keeping the establishment mostly the same, just giving it a cosmetic cover based on race and gender. It didn't work. Too many Black Americans didn't see much changing under Kamala, even if there was a strong case to just play defense against Republicans and try to protect against an even more lopsided Supreme Court if Clarence Thomas was to smartly retire.

The Black American voters Democrats need are those who want to see scientific results and risk-taking on our behalf. And those who don't fit into the cultural value assumptions made on account of identity. The voters who are not moved by symbolism and identity affinity as much as by policy orientation and factors. There is plenty of evidence that Kamala couldn't run an anti-establishment, populist campaign because that's not really who she is, and voters would never buy it.[11] A different identity isn't different policy and policy orientation. To many Black Americans, Kamala Harris was more of a cop and lobbyist than a structural change candidate or activist politician that will challenge the way the system worked. The imagination just wasn't there for many voters to picture Kamala taking on powerful special interest groups, widespread corruption, or Benjamin Netanyahu if he wanted to kill 50,000 more Palestinian civilians. Hardly anyone could picture Kamala signing an executive order for Presidential Reparations Commission. You can play defense with this type of candidate (hey, we have to stop MAGA, MAGA very BAD)) but very little offense in the trenches.

Kamala ran an establishment campaign and was beaten by a populist campaign, MAGA, based on the message that the "system is not working." Racial and gender reductionism won't allow Democrats to go under the hood to examine what they can do better, how they can better connect to the voters they want to come out and vote for them. Democrats will be able to squeeze less and less from symbolism and identity affinity as a substitute for bold policies and policy risk taking on behalf of loyal Black American voters. (MAGA has its own version of identity politics.)

It didn't help that Netanyahu's war and bombing on Gaza was a perfect political cocktail to surgically de-motivate party progressives in states like Michigan. Many progressives could see right through Biden and Kamala's lack of balance and morality in their position towards the deaths of over 40,000 Palestinians.[12] How could Arabs, Muslims, and progressive voters get excited about a party that seemed politically handcuffed and impotent on blatant human rights abuses? How much delta or difference was there really between MAGA, Netanyahu, and the Democratic Party position on Gaza? The Democratic Party lacked the muscle or political testosterone to break out and say what constituted war crimes. There was no red line in sight.

Having a significant leadership of the Democratic Party who will seemingly justify a holocaust (for example, would they be ok if Netanyahu ran up the body count to 100,000, 250,000?) and those who see a holocaust or war crimes as the International Criminal Court in the Hague ruled, in the same party, is horrifically politically inefficient. I would estimate pressing the war hard down the stretch was a political weapon to divide and demotivate Democrats. Although the Kamala and Democrats would have shined his shoes and tap danced for him, Netanyahu would much rather have a MAGA in power than Kamala. This vulnerability was likely surgically identified and exploited by Netanyahu.

"MAGA bad, vote Democrat" was just not going to cut it this time. An inspirational symbolic identity-first was not going to cut it this time. Their rush to spend millions on celebrities in the 11th hour was to compensate for a lack of grassroots activist energy and a solid Black American agenda. Democrats won't be able to coast on symbolism, MAGA BAD, or symbolism and Republicans bad. The Obama/Kamala New Blacks phase - where identity representation often substituted for material policy and policy risk taking - is now officially over in American politics. As of the printing of this book, the party seems unworkable and hyper-inefficient with its various factions, conflicts, power networks, age divides, and core commitment to the status quo. The national party looks confused and doesn't know whether it should have a bias towards elites or the working class and poor. The party is confused on whether the leadership should just run up their age until they die in office or hand off the torch to a new generation, with new ideas and energy, and distance from entrenched and legacy Washington D.C. corruption.

The Democratic Party in its current form may still win elections by opposing MAGA, but appears structurally incapable of delivering transformative policies for Black Americans. This creates a mathematical trap: voting Democratic becomes necessary for basic protection while providing minimal leverage for positive change. The party functions defensively while lacking the offensive capabilities required for meaningful structural reforms. This perpetuates a cycle where Black American voters must choose between protection from greater harm and actual advancement. Understanding this distinction is crucial to developing more effective political strategies that recognize both the necessity of defensive voting and the limitations it places on achieving material progress.

Democrats offering political science, a Black American agenda before election time, and real negotiation with Black Americans vs spook, won't be an easy transition as the spook and tricknology have been so successful where almost no policy risk taking has been needed to run up the score each election with a 80% lock on Black Americans.

When a large business is struggling, it's often considered smart to file for bankruptcy, acknowledge the deep structural issues and challenges with the business, and restructure.[13] After it reorganizes its affairs, it can come out of bankruptcy with less debt and start growing and prospering again. There are probably 3-4 different parties within the Democratic Party and these groups no longer fit nicely within a single party. I don't see a way out of this inefficiency and internal party conflict without a fundamental restructuring with different leadership and radically different thinking.

A restructuring is what must be done by the Democratic Party. The test for Democrats is whether they can acknowledge that the party needs a total overhaul.

Other factors why Democrats took a big L include the following:

- Democrats had an undemocratic plan: don't hold a competitive primary, let Biden coast. The fact this was considered acceptable while "Democracy was at stake" supports that Democrats deserved to lose because of their undemocratic and corrupt orientation within an election process.

- Biden stayed in the race too long before dropping out.

- Democrats were too slow to reverse course on more promiscuous and "free for all" illegal immigration policies after Trump; the immigration policy was a disaster. With illegal immigration, voters were confident MAGA would actually have a hardcore policy response to their concerns.

- Barack Obama and his former advisers were attempting to run an old Obama playbook in influencing the Kamala campaign, but this has diminished utility. (Kamala even used Obama's advisor David Plouffe) Barack Obama genuinely wants to help his party, but the party is better off allowing him to just be wealthy and letting new leaders and political thinking evolve. Kamala's loss is part of the costs of Obama's presidency and outsize leadership within the party. Obama brought both benefits and costs. [14]

- Both Obama (2008) and Trump (2016) won by suggesting they would help clean up the special interest money and corruption in politics (the "Swamp"). During her campaign, I didn't hear Kamala express that she was even interested in tackling the amount of special interest money in politics and other corrupting influences. I guess voters were left to assume she was OK with it and had just embraced how the system works, even if it continues to hurt, marginalize, and demotivate so many people. The American people aren't looking for promises to solve corruption and money in politics in a Presidential term but they do want to see considerable conviction in this area.

There wasn't a single factor that explains the big L the Democrats took more than the fact that the party is simply unworkable in its current form, with competing interests and groups, particularly if it stays committed to playing the same games and playbooks. And spook with Black American voters.

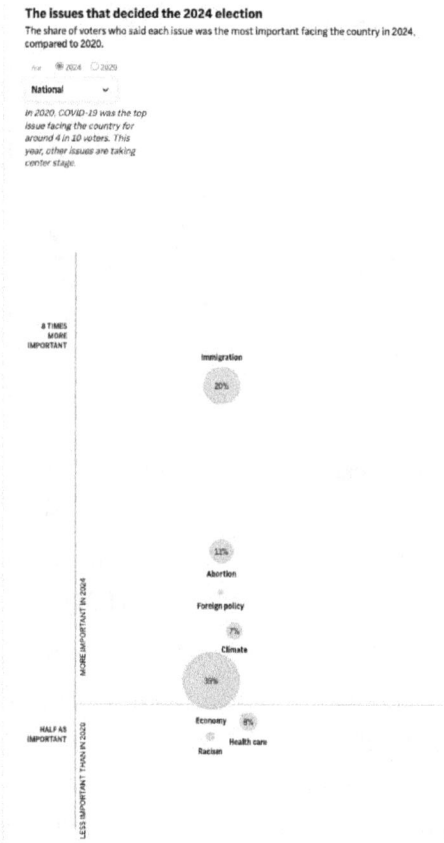

The issues that decided the 2024 election

The share of voters who said each issue was the most important facing the country in 2024, compared to 2020.

● 2024　○ 2020

National ⌄

In 2020, COVID-19 was the top issue facing the country for around 4 in 10 voters. This year, other issues are taking center stage.

8 TIMES MORE IMPORTANT

Immigration

20%

MORE IMPORTANT IN 2024

11%

Abortion

Foreign policy

7%

Climate

39%

HALF AS IMPORTANT

LESS IMPORTANT THAN IN 2020

Economy　8%

Health care

Racism

Voter Priorities in 2024 vs. 2020 Elections - Shows economy (39%) and immigration (20%) replacing COVID as top issues

The Democratic Party has become too elitist, too much of a whore for special interest groups, and more and more voters of—all colors and orientations—see right through it. Rather than waiting for power brokers in the Democratic Party to change course - something unlikely given their entrenched interests, networks and wealth - Black Americans now have both incentive and opportunity to organize and imagine a new political future ourselves. This future won't be dictated from the top by Pelosi, Schumer, and their Man Clyburn, but will be built independently through strategic negotiation with political parties for measurable, material outcomes.

Presidential support among Black voters

	Dem.	Rep.	Margin
2016 Estimates	92%	7%	Dem. +85
2020 Estimates	90%	9%	Dem. +81
2024 Times/Siena Oct. poll	78%	15%	Dem. +63

Vote shares and victory margins for 2016 and 2020 are averages of the following: estimates from studies of validated voters by the Pew Research Center, post-election assessments by Catalist and exit polls by the National Election Pool.   By June Kim

Presidential Support Among Black Voters (2016-2024) - Shows Democratic support declining from 92% to 78%

My father, who was raised in the tough Jordan Downs housing projects in Watts, California, told me, "Son, the Democrats were always about the little guy, but I don't see them out for us anymore." He previously wore Obama-themed apparel. He voted MAGA in 2016, 2020, and 2024.

Democrats often put different groups in rigid boxes, but they would benefit from a multifactor approach to understanding the voters they are losing rather than thinking, "If you're a Black American, you should vote and think this way; if you're Hispanic, you should vote and think this way." Many of these voters are disgusted with the establishment, and many of them consider Democrats to be more establishment than MAGA.

This lesson was about Kamala and the Democrats' Big L but it is also about looking at political questions in multi-factor terms. We should be surgically breaking political questions down into factors versus automatically assuming racism or gender were the dominant factors, without evidence. At the end of the day, if Democrats ran a normal primary process, dumped Biden earlier and not participated in a cover up, there was relatively low inflation, if they came in strong on illegal immigration and took the issue away from MAGA, had a strong Black American agenda before election time, and voters really thought they would have a strategic attack on the powerful influence of money and corruption in American politics, Kamala would have been President or at least won more states.

Some seemingly easy fixes and changes are extremely challenging to execute when the party of elites have become so out of touch with working class voters, from all walks of life. Also, when so much money and corruption stands in the way, the elites and power brokers can't see reality like they need to see it, can't be efficient, and can't win. The very system that funds them blinds them to the changes necessary for victory. They're trapped in a gilded cage of their own making, unable to break free from the special interests that both sustain and constrain them.

In March 2025, it was head scratching for me to see seventy-four year old Senate minority Chuck Schumer break with his party over voting for the Republican funding bill. He folded so easily, it didn't make any sense, there was no fight in him. His party wanted some negotiation (including Pelosi) or to take a hard position that would allow the government to be shut down if some better checks and balances weren't put into place to check MAGA's aggressive and constitutionally questionable changes. [15]

Then I saw Schumer had a big New York Times interview coming out about his new book, after the vote. [16] A week later, a full national press tour was activated promoting his book. (I imagine he would want to sell to both Democrats and Republican consumers). Under the Science vs. Spook framework, his confusing vote could be the spook and wanting to sell his book at the same time, could be the science.

Whenever you see something that is off or odd, following the money and conflicts has been statistically reliable.

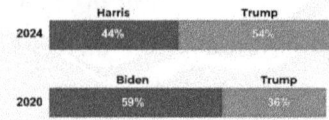

Latino Male Voters Shift Toward Trump in 2024 Election
% of U.S. Latino Men who voted for...

	Harris	Trump
2024	44%	54%

	Biden	Trump
2020	59%	36%

Latino Male Voters Shift Toward Trump - Shows movement from 59% Democratic to 54% Republican

---

The Science

- **Inflation + immigration = Democratic defeat**: Economics and border security mattered more than identity politics
- **Symbolic currency experiencing rapid devaluation**: Each election cycle requires more symbolism to produce same Black voter turnout
- **Democratic Party is structurally unworkable**: Competing elite factions make coherent working-class appeal impossible
- **Obama/Kamala New Blacks era is officially over**: Identity representation substituting for material policy no longer works
- **Party needs complete restructuring**: Current form may win by opposing MAGA but can't deliver transformative policies

---

[1] "MAGA Dominance in Battleground States Despite Democrats' $1 Billion War Chest," Washington Post, November 6, 2024.

[2] Goldstein, Steve. "The bond king, Jeffrey Gundlach, says the economy isn't working after seeing a Hamburger Helper ad." MarketWatch, October 4, 2024. https://www.marketwatch.com/story/the-bond-king-jeffrey-gundlach-says-the-economy-isnt-working-after-seeing-a-hamburger-helper-ad-f8401158

[3] Goudreau, Claire. "The Impact of Inflation on the 2024 Presidential Election," Johns Hopkins University Hub, November 20, 2024.

[4] Tankersley, Jim. "The Path Ahead for Biden: Overcome Manchin's Inflation Fears." The New York Times, December 19, 2021. https://www.nytimes.com/2021/12/19/business/economy/manchin-biden-build-back-better.html

[5] "McDonald's Says $18 Big Mac Meal Was an 'Exception' and News Reports Overstated Its Price Increases," Associated Press, September 25, 2024.

[6] Robertson, Khalea. "Poll Tracker: Attitudes on Immigration in the 2024 U.S. Elections," Americas Society/Council of the Americas, October 25, 2024.

[7] "Democrats Face 'Gerontocracy' Crisis Amid Ageing Leadership," Newsweek, December 19, 2024.

[8] Weissert, Will. "Harris announces a new plan to empower Black men as she tries to energize them to vote for her," Associated Press, October 14, 2024.

[9] Cousens, Maryann. "2024 Post-Election Survey: Racial Analysis of 2024 Election Results," Navigator Research, December 11, 2024.

[10] Doherty, Erin. "Harris: 'Not a thing' she'd have done differently than Biden." Axios, October 8, 2024. https://www.axios.com/2024/10/08/harris-biden-view-abc-2024-differences

[11] Bacon, Perry Jr. "Why Kamala Harris's Campaign Failed." FiveThirtyEight, December 3, 2019. https://fivethirtyeight.com/features/why-kamala-harriss-campaign-failed/

[12] Kessler, Glenn. "Biden's dismissal of the reported Palestinian death toll." The Washington Post, November 1, 2023. https://www.washingtonpost.com/politics/2023/11/01/bidens-dismissal-reported-palestinian-death-toll/

[13] Santa Clara University School of Business. "What is Corporate Restructuring?" May 8, 2023. https://www.scu.edu/business/news/what-is-corporate-restructuring/

[14] Bose, Nandita. "Harris adds top Obama aides to her presidential campaign team." Reuters, August 2, 2024. https://www.reuters.com/world/us/harris-adds-top-obama-aides-her-presidential-campaign-team-2024-08-02/

[15] Karni, Annie. "Schumer, Facing Backlash for Not Forcing a Shutdown, Says He'll Take 'the Bullets'." The New York Times, March 14, 2025. https://www.nytimes.com/2025/03/14/us/politics/schumer-trump-government-shutdown.html

[16] Garcia-Navarro, Lulu. "The Interview: Chuck Schumer on Democrats, Antisemitism and His Shutdown Retreat." The New York Times, March 16, 2025. https://www.nytimes.com/2025/03/16/magazine/chuck-schumer-interview.html

THE NATION OF ISLAM AND MODERN BLACK NATIONALISM

Elijah Muhammad Was an Economic Genius

> *"If I had to pick the single person who has been the most important figure for Blacks in the Black thrust from post-World War II, I would unequivocally pick Elijah Muhammad. Because it was he who... was like a lightning bolt in opening up the consciousness of Black people... from this just blank psychic wall of just total fear of the structure in which we lived. And I am saying these things clinically." —Alex Haley* [1]

We all have biases at various levels and degrees, but one way to de-spook or significantly lessen our bias is to look at the results, the mathematics of it all. Science is often in the results. In studying the audit period of 1995-2025, one of the key takeaways that popped out was that this generation totally missed the historical example and economic genius of Elijah Muhammad, due to his presentation as a religious figure and then scandal. The dominant economic factor of Elijah Muhammad could have been presented from a secular perspective, to de-risk viewing his historical contributions to Black America through a lens of bias.Yes, I would optimize the wording for clarity, precision, and integration with your overall analytical framework:

A note on terminology: I deliberately omit honorifics like 'Honorable' or 'Most Honorable' when discussing Elijah Muhammad to maintain scientific orientation. While his material results and economic contributions objectively earn him great respect, traditional honorifics risk pushing analysis toward reverence rather than evaluation. This approach aligns with the Science vs. Spook framework - examining measurable achievements rather than reinforcing religious veneration. Muhammad's work deserves objective assessment like any other historical figure, based on evidence rather than tradition.

It impacts the Black American political orientation when the majority don't have a proper accounting of Elijah Muhammad's economic genius from a secular, historical perspective. This generation knows about Obama, Kamala Harris, Hakeem Jeffries, Al Sharpton, Young Thug, Jay-Z, Pharrell, and Kanye West, but they totally missed the economic factor of Elijah Muhammad. All these popular Black American celebrity figures will leave us with very few actionable lessons and a heavy dose of celebrity spook and distraction.

Elijah Muhammad was running away from murder and death and went to prison for what he believed in—freedom, justice, and equality for Black America. He taught his own brand of economic science and organizational empowerment. These leaders today wouldn't give up a check or corporate partnership for Black Americans. They mostly teach and promote spook or total political surrender to Democratic Party orthodoxy.

In the echoing corridors of history, two contrasting approaches to Black American economic power emerge: the scientific methodology of Elijah Muhammad's Nation of Islam (NOI) and today's spook-driven celebrity economics. To put his NOI's accomplishment in perspective, its estimated $100 million annual revenue in 1975 translates to roughly $475 million in today's dollars (adjusted for inflation)—achieved despite aggressive government opposition and interference. [2]

The NOI's economic approach was pure science. With two hundred and fifty thousand dedicated members globally by 1975, they weren't just followers but a collective force of consumers and workers. This vast network created a self-sufficient economy where every dollar spent could be reinvested to further nourish the community. In 1968 alone, the NOI purchased a four-story, sixty-thousand-square-foot establishment in

Chicago for $1 million to house the Muhammad Speaks newspaper. That same year, the NOI acquired the Salaam Restaurant paired with Your Supermarket. A lamb slaughterhouse soon joined the portfolio. [3]

By 1973, Elijah had steered the NOI to acquire a controlling stake in the Guaranty Bank and Trust Company. Under NOI leadership, this South Side institution grew to over $10 million in assets by 1975 and employed more than five hundred people. This wasn't spook—it was scientific economic power backed by decades of disciplined capital accumulation. [4]

The NOI's economic program transformed communities. From management to technicians, from bakers to carpenters, jobs sprang to life. Their businesses served everyone, regardless of religious beliefs. Consider the NOI dry-cleaning establishment on Chicago's East Sixty-Third Street—a model of collaboration between NOI and non-NOI members sharing responsibilities and commissions.

Perhaps equally impressive but less celebrated was the Muhammad University of Islam (MUI), the first Black school network in America that reached national scale. Established in 1930, this educational institution demonstrated the NOI's commitment to developing not just economic but intellectual capital. Clara Muhammad, Elijah's wife, pioneered this system in 1931, beginning with classes in her own home where she served as the first teacher. What started as the "University of Islam" expanded to forty-seven schools across the country by 1974.

Clara wasn't just the First Lady of the Nation—she was a critical architect of its educational infrastructure, developing the Muslim Girls Training and General Civilization Class that shaped generations of NOI women. When Elijah was imprisoned for five years (1942-1946) for draft evasion, Clara served as interim leader, carrying his orders from prison to Nation ministers. This educational system represented the NOI's scientific approach to community development—understanding that true economic power requires collective intellectual self-determination.

Under Elijah Muhammad, if the U.S. government failed us, over and over, we had a collective responsibility to not fail ourselves at the organization level.

The economic blueprint that truly separated Elijah Muhammad from other Black American leaders of his time was his international trade operation. The Nation ventured beyond domestic markets, establishing direct trading relationships with foreign governments. In a bold move that showed true scientific thinking, Elijah Muhammad circumvented traditional supply chains. When he discovered the whiting fish sold through Japanese intermediaries actually originated in Peru, he did what any good business strategist would do—he cut out the middleman.[5]

By 1974, the NOI had negotiated directly with the Peruvian government to purchase 1 million pounds of whiting fish. This wasn't just any business deal—it was a declaration of Black economic independence on the international stage. When Henry Kissinger, then Secretary of State under Nixon, flew to Peru to warn the government "not to deal with us because the Nation of Islam was subversive," the Peruvians reportedly responded, "What are you doing for us? You can kiss our ass—you and Nixon." This wasn't just business; it was a challenge to America's global economic order. [6]

The mathematics behind this operation were precise. The Nation controlled every aspect of the supply chain—distribution, shipping with chartered ships, and unloading at the docks. At one point, twenty to thirty ships were simultaneously moving between the U.S. and Peru, dropping fish at eighteen to twenty ports across the country. The Nation's international trade network expanded to include sardines from Morocco and other seafood products from various countries. [7]

Back in Harlem, this scientific approach to business translated into direct community benefits. When the first Harlem Fish House opened on October 21, 1974, hundreds of people lined up for service. Located between 126th and 127th Streets on Eighth Avenue—an area even the police considered one of the worst in Harlem, plagued by drugs and crime—the restaurant became what Minister Louis Farrakhan called a "survival station," offering "a whole meal under a dollar."

The contrast with today's celebrity-driven economics couldn't be starker. While modern Black celebrities secure individual wealth and high-profile partnerships, they rarely build lasting economic institutions for the community. Modern "Black excellence" often means a Black face making millions for white corporations while creating zero institutions that will outlive them. Elijah Muhammad's NOI demonstrated economic efficiency through ownership—of production, distribution, and banking. They weren't satisfied with endorsement deals or token executive positions; they built an economic machine that employed thousands and served millions.

The Muhammad Speaks newspaper exemplified this institutional approach. By 1969, an all-Black printing crew produced fifty thousand copies per hour, reaching a weekly circulation of nine hundred and fifty thousand by 1974. This wasn't just media representation—it was economic self-determination through control of both message and means of production. [8] Muhammad Speaks helped get important news to Black America, without predatory tobacco, alcohol, and exploitive financial product ads.

By 1975, the results spoke volumes: hundreds of businesses, eleven thousand employees, $30 million in annual revenue, and an estimated $80 million net worth at Elijah Muhammad's passing. This scientific approach—focused on building real economic power through ownership, production, and community reinvestment—stands in sharp contrast to today's spook economics of endorsement deals and symbolic victories. Elijah Muhammad left us a transformational economic blueprint but it has gotten lost in religious dogma and history revisionism, and has become a mystery.

Why prioritize studying Jay-Z's role as frontman for Brooklyn real estate developers when we could examine Elijah Muhammad's creation of a functional Black American economic system through visionary leadership? Why celebrate Steve Jobs for refining Motorola's mobile phone design before understanding how Muhammad developed an economic system that materially improved Black American lives with collective purpose?

Tragically, when Wallace Muhammad took over leadership after his father's death in 1975, the economic blueprint was largely abandoned in favor of religious reform. [9] Like the traditional Black Christian Church, which Elijah Muhammad had criticized for prioritizing spiritual matters over collective material advancement, Wallace shifted the organization's focus from economic self-sufficiency to mainstream religious acceptance. This pivot from economic institution-building to religious orthodoxy was a factor that led to the dismantling of much of what Elijah Muhammad had built. Supporting an organization building out an innovative economic model that benefits Black America as a whole and giving to an organization that's just preaching sermons every weekend are two different things. Even the educational system was transformed— Wallace renamed the University of Islam as the Clara Muhammad Schools, emphasizing religious education over economic development. Within a few years, the restaurants, grocery stores, bank, and international trade operations were mostly gone—a stark demonstration of how quickly economic gains can be lost when the focus shifts away from scientific principles.

A brother on social media once dismissed Elijah Muhammad's NOI businesses as mere "ghetto businesses"—small restaurants, barber shops, and bookstores. This dismissive view misses the scientific genius of Elijah's approach. These weren't disconnected storefronts; they were integrated components of a mothership institution, thoughtfully scaled up. The network included a school system, farmland and agriculture, residential and commercial real estate, grocery stores, banking, and international trade. While the bougie buffer elites and churches talked about and prayed for progress, Elijah Muhammad built it—without begging America for anything. He and Malcolm X understood that the aggregate Black wallet was sufficient to build a sustainable Black American economic system.

The lesson? Real Black economic power comes through institution building, not symbolic representation. The ultimate "Black Excellence" is not some celebrity winning an Oscar or Golden Globe, endorsed by a white institution, but is expressed through collective organizational excellence, with a mission to leave lessons and material for the next generation to improve and build on.

Elijah Muhammad showed us how to move beyond spook by creating tangible economic foundations for community advancement. The NOI model proves that with disciplined capital accumulation, strategic planning, and unwavering commitment to community upliftment, Black America can build lasting economic power—not just temporary visibility.

This economic machine may have faded over time, but so did Pan Am Airways, Blockbuster Video, Lehman Brothers, and Washington Mutual. It's on the younger generation to take this blueprint, connect it to technology, and improve it. We have agency and are in control of our rise. We can't sit back and wait for white folks to change in Washington D.C. or Silicon Valley, the modern mecca of structural, anti-Black American-ness.

We must properly study ancestors and elders who actually built something, scaled it, and inspired millions to acquire a knowledge of self and do for self. A lot of their success can be a foundation to be built upon today. When we focus on these real-world examples of scientific progress rather than symbolic spook, we begin to see the path forward for Black economic power in the twenty-first century. The beauty of what Elijah Muhammad built is he wasn't a good speaker, in the sense of a Malcolm X or Minister Louis Farrakhan. It's not about the speeches, personality, or charisma as much as it is about science and scientific results. This book wouldn't be possible without the inspiration and example of Elijah Muhammad.

If we collectively abandoned spook thinking, we would recognize that real progress comes through building strong, independent Black American organizations with collective economic systems at their foundation—not through counting Black NFL coaches or celebrating 'First Black' symbolic victories at the Pentagon. While symbolic representation leaves only empty gestures for future generations, economic institutions create lasting power that transforms lives across generations. This is the difference between spook and science: one counts faces, the other builds foundations and institutions.

The Science

- **$100M annual revenue in 1975 = $475M today**: Built massive economic machine despite government opposition
- **International trade broke US economic control**: Direct fish imports from Peru challenged America's global economic order
- **250,000 dedicated members = collective consumer power**: Network created self-sufficient economy where every dollar could be reinvested
- **Economic institutions outlast personality cults**: Businesses, banks, and trade relationships create lasting power across generations
- **Scientific results beat charismatic speeches**: Elijah's genius was measured outcomes, not inspiring oratory
- **When Wallace took over, he abandoned the economics**: Religious reform replaced institution-building, dismantling the economic empire

[1] "The Black Scholar Interviews: Alex Haley," The Black Scholar, January 1976.

[2] Jamarlin Martin, "Revisiting The $100M+ Economic Blueprint of Elijah Muhammad And Malcolm X," Moguldom.com, October 8, 2018.

[3] "Accomplishments of the Muslims," Muhammad Speaks, Spring 1975.

[4] Nafeesa Muhammad, "The Nation of Islam's Economic Program, 1934-1975," BlackPast.org, April 1, 2020.

[5] Barboza, Steven, "American Jihad: Islam After Malcolm X," Doubleday, 1993.

[6] Rashid, Hakim M. and Muhammad, Zakiyyah, "The Sister Clara Muhammad Schools: Pioneers in the Development of Islamic Education in America," The Journal of Negro Education, Vol. 61, No. 2, Spring 1992, pp. 178-185.

[7] Barboza, Steven, "American Jihad: Islam After Malcolm X," Doubleday, 1993.

[8] Hussain, Khuram, "Dreaming Differently About Freedom: Malcolm X and Muhammad Speaks," Journal of African American Studies, Vol. 24, September 2020.

[9] Brown, Ann, "7 Things To Know About How Wallace/Warith Dean Muhammad Removed Nation-Building From NOI," The Moguldom Nation, November 17, 2021.

Kwame Ture on Organization

> *"One of the characteristics of mobilization is that it is temporary. The organization is permanent and eternal. Clear differences must be made." —Kwame Ture*

The scientific distinction between organization and mobilization emerges clearly through Kwame Ture's sharp analysis. Born Stokely Carmichael, Ture evolved from a civil rights activist to a Pan-African revolutionary, offering crucial insights about building real power versus temporary momentum.

Ture's exact words illuminate this critical distinction:

"We must make clear distinctions between mobilizers and organizers. To be an organizer, you must be a mobilizer, but being a mobilizer does not make you an organizer. Much confusion is to be found here. Malcolm X was a great mobilizer. Martin Luther King was a great mobilizer. He was not a great organizer. These facts can be easily seen from King and Malcolm. When Malcolm went to a place, he left a mosque. When King went to demonstrations, he broke down segregation and he moved on."[1]

On how mobilization can be used against progress:

"We say that we must come to know the difference between mobilization and organization because the enemy will use mobilization to demobilize us. Mobilization is very easy. Very, very easy. Since we are a people who are instinctively ready to respond against acts of injustice, any time there's one little act of injustice, we can blow it up and we will find people who will come and make some mass demonstration around it... Those of us who are revolutionary are not concerned with issues; we are concerned with the system. The difference must be properly understood. Mobilization usually leads to reform action, not to revolutionary action."

Ture on the Million Man March:

"If we were to look scientifically at the October 16th Million and More March, we would see clearly that this was a mobilized event, not an organized event. We must know clearly the difference between mobilization and organization. One of the characteristics of mobilization is that it is temporary. Organization is permanent and eternal."

He warns about the "I was there" syndrome that we saw play out after the March:

"Many Brothers and Sisters who've been to the Million and More March will say to you, 'I was there.' Well, what are you doing today, my Sister? 'I was there'... If we're not careful, we allow mobilization to become an event. The struggle is never an event. It's a process, a continual eternal process."

Ture's vision for real power through organization was clear:

"We say it is our job to use mobilization to drive us to organization. You know our theme is organization. We want power. We don't want money, we don't want fame, we don't want fortune, we don't want popularity, we want power. Power. And power comes only from the organized masses. Power comes only from the organized masses."

This analysis exposes the limitations of purely reactionary behavior— responding to incidents with press conferences, marches, and protests without building lasting institutional power. While these reactions matter in the moment, they can't replace the scientific foundation needed for sustained change. Many leaders excel at mobilization in response to incidents, and we need this rapid response capability. However, we must ensure that mobilization energy is being consistently channeled into long-term organizational development with clear benchmarks and progress metrics.

In fairness, some civil rights leaders like Reverend Al Sharpton have built and maintained enduring organizations. His National Action Network has existed for decades, demonstrating real organizational durability. The scientific question isn't about whether these organizations exist, but rather how we measure their effectiveness in creating sustained structural change versus tactical incident response.

We must shift from primarily reacting to the latest thing done to us to building toward a future we design. This is the difference between mobilization and organization that Ture illuminates.

The scientific reality? Africa, as Ture notes, is the richest continent on Earth. Yet without organization, its resources don't translate to power. The same applies to Black America—we have the numbers, the talent, the potential, but we haven't fully embraced the discipline of collective organization over the temporary gains of mobilization. Not in a transformational expression commensurate with our resources, capability, population, talent, and the generational challenges before us.

Look at how many movements demonstrate this problem. They've successfully mobilized around specific causes, creating visibility and conversation. But have they built the organizational infrastructure necessary to translate that into legislation and lasting material results? Have they developed the political coalitions needed to move bills through Congress? Have they established educational institutions to train the next generation of advocates? These aren't criticisms—they're scientific observations about the difference between mobilization and organization. Organizing is extremely hard but not trying and not modernizing our thinking with political innovations, makes it even harder for us and the future Black American generation that comes after.

Until we understand and apply this distinction, we'll remain caught in cycles of reaction rather than sustained progress toward power. The science demands we do both: use mobilization to generate energy and visibility but immediately channel that energy into permanent organizational structures with clear objectives, benchmarks, and accountability mechanisms.

Technology innovation is moving at the speed of light with economic reality following closely behind. Black American political and organizational orientation must be continuously updated to prevent permanent political capture and marginalization while immigrant groups gain political market share—often without acknowledging and understanding American history and state-level institutional crimes against us, including chattel slavery, Jim Crow, and mass incarceration.

The Science

- **Mobilization is temporary, organization is eternal**: Protest marches create moments; institutions create movements
- **Malcolm left mosques, King left broken segregation**: One built lasting institutions, the other achieved temporary victories
- **The enemy uses mobilization to demobilize us**: System allows emotional releases to prevent sustained institution-building
- **Revolutionary means building, not just destroying**: Creating new structures matters more than tearing down old ones
- **Power comes only from organized masses**: Individual leaders can mobilize; only organized institutions create lasting power

---

[1] "Kwame Ture - Organisation vs Mobilisation," date of original speech unknown.

The Million Man March: A Missed Opportunity

"The first protest in history where people gathered ostensibly to protest themselves." —Adolph Reed

As a seventeen-year-old in Los Angeles, high on knowledge of self and Malcolm X's autobiography, I was overflowing with optimism for myself and Black America. The momentum building to the Million Man March felt like proof we were going places. With a few dollars to my name, I got on that bus from Leimert Park in South Central—a journey Spike Lee would later capture in *Get on the Bus*.

Let me be clear: The Million Man March was nothing short of miraculous—the largest gathering of Black men in American history. This unprecedented achievement peacefully brought together an estimated one million Black men in the nation's capital, a testament to our capacity for organization and symbolic unity. The sheer scale and peaceful execution were remarkable, demonstrating the potential power of Black America when mobilized. Minister Farrakhan deserves tremendous credit for catalyzing this historic gathering that many thought impossible.

Looking back thirty years later with scientific eyes rather than spook-filled hope, the march presents a complex balance sheet. It was a religious, cultural, and historic event but not directly linked to sustainable political and economic development or political pressure for specific policy goals. While successful in boosting moral consciousness and the build up helping reduce crime (this is my estimate; something Obama wrongly credited to Biden's crime bill), it failed to generate lasting material progress. The National crime reduction had actually started before the Clinton/Biden crime bill, driven by the march's momentum and prior efforts of Minister Farrakhan and other Black American community organizers, activists, and churches. The Million Man March had the perfect name, perfect timing—but what happened to the opportunity?

Under the Science versus Spook framework, the central question isn't about the march itself, but about the follow-through: How do we turn the attention and energy of one million Black men into a $100 million economic and political program with quantifiable returns? When we give our money, what do we get back materially? What institutions were built? What are the measurable political and economic development outcomes, and who is held accountable for delivering them?

Having an insular religious organization run the march created inherent barriers to collective political and economic development, after the fact. Like a business spread too thin across product lines, asking the Nation of Islam to maintain its religious mission while spearheading secular political-economic growth was asking too much. A secular movement could have had more potential of inviting accountability and diverse strategic viewpoints without religious constraints.

It's important to acknowledge that Minister Farrakhan stands as the most successful institution builder among all of Elijah Muhammad's former ministers, successfully keeping the Nation of Islam alive when it could have easily disappeared. His religious leadership has provided spiritual guidance and discipline to tens of thousands of Black Americans. This analysis doesn't take away from the NOI's religious significance or Farrakhan's accomplishments, but under the Science versus Spook framework, everything must be audited—not to criticize, but to determine how we can do better in the future with more material progress to show for Black America.

The financial reality was stark. As Reverend Benjamin F. Chavis Jr. revealed in the audit, the march raised "$106,170 from vending fees alone, while sales from official march paraphernalia like buttons and T-shirts added another

$61,970 to the coffers." [1] But organizing costs typically ran "$1.5 million to $4 million" for events this size. The resulting "$66,000 debt" to small vendors, which Chavis considered miraculous given the turnout, signaled deeper issues. (When Chavis became Benjamin Muhammad, I actually was personal security for him at the Ritz Hotel in Atlanta.)

After the Million Man March, World Friendship Tour, and Million Family March, National African American Leadership Summit (NAALS) became the engine for policy formation, outlining an ambitious nine-point civil rights agenda at Howard University [2]:

- A moral and spiritual renewal
- Economic development and the establishment of the African American Economic Development Trust
- Organization of a national African American youth leadership movement and an African American Youth Day
- Development of a comprehensive education strategy for African Americans
- The Abundant Life National Health Plan for African Americans
- Establish a national and international Black Communications Network
- Sponsor an annual Black Political Convention
- Seek an end to the death penalty
- Challenge the GOP's Contract with America to convene a summit meeting of Black and Caribbean ambassadors in Washington, DC

But instead of building on this momentum, Minister Farrakhan embarked on a controversial world tour. In Iran, he reportedly declared, "God will destroy America by the hands of Muslims." After the March, it seemed Farrakhan sought to curry favor with Arabs and in the world of Islam versus rushing to capitalize on the momentum with a sustainable political and economic program for Black Americans. After the historic success of the Million Man March, did Black Americans need deeper integration into radical Middle-Eastern affairs or to build a sustainable, political and economic platform in Black America, with the massive momentum from the March? After the world's attention was on Farrakhan, it was a once in a lifetime opportunity for us to start getting our political and economic affairs in order. It was a once in a lifetime opportunity to focus on Black Americans, here, not Muslims over there. [3]

Let's say Farrakhan's goal was to bring in $10 million-$25 million from Arab and African leaders during the World Friendship Tour. Was this going to go to Leonard Muhammad and the Farrakhan family or a real economic program with top tier talent such as when Elijah Muhammad hired a Harvard-educated lawyer and other professionals to help build and manage the Nation's international fish importing business? [4] Was Leonard going to be the Economic Minister who was going to put down "Nation Time" once and for all? The scientific approach would mean transparent accounting, professional management, and strategic investment—not family-controlled finances without public progress reports, accountability, for the modern times.

Ronald Walters, chair of Howard's political science department, captured the resulting tension: "The interesting thing is how it plays among people who, after the Million Man March, thought they could welcome him into the pantheon of black leadership. Now they're finding out that consorting with him is not going to be as easy as they thought." [5]

Frederick DeBoer would later write in Harper's Magazine: "Some have blamed the march's conservative, self-criticizing impulse for its failure to develop into a durable black political movement. Adolph Reed, a political scientist and labor activist, has said that the march was 'the first protest in history where people gathered ostensibly to protest themselves.' The late scholar Manning Marable notes that black turnout spiked in the elections immediately following the gathering, but no enduring protest movement developed in the streets of Washington that day; no major third party was organized; no new dedication to unions, or to community activism, or to fusions of religion and politics was born. In a world of entrenched racism, real, lasting victory was too much to ask of any individual protest. Even those impressed by the march, however, recognized its political moment as fleeting." [6]

Slavery Reparations
Support is rising in Congress for legislation creating a commission studying reparations to Black Americans for slavery and discrimination, raising prospects for House passage this year.

Number of co-sponsors for House reparations legislation

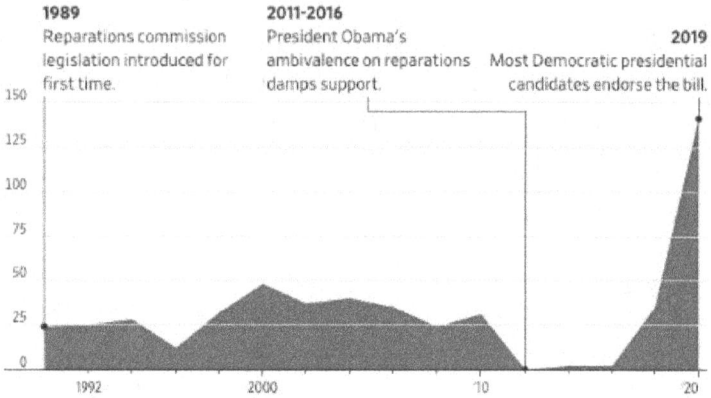

1989
Reparations commission legislation introduced for first time.

2011-2016
President Obama's ambivalence on reparations damps support.

2019
Most Democratic presidential candidates endorse the bill.

Notes: Years indicate second year of a two-year congressional session. Data for 2019-2020 as of July 29
Source: Congress.gov

Congressional Support for Reparations Legislation - Shows decline during Obama years, surge after 2019

Conrad Tillard (formerly Conrad Muhammad), former top minister in the NOI, later explained his frustrations: "I just became frustrated with the direction of the movement," he says. "I believe that as African-Americans we can be critical of this country, but we have to embrace our American-ness, and we have to embrace the process. I've really grown to believe that we have the best political system in the world. I've grown to appreciate democracy. And I think the Nation is challenged to embrace those ideas. You may not like the way things are, but you have a right to say it, and in a lot of countries you don't." [7]

Asking a religious organization to lead a national political and economic development organization is like asking Starbucks to sell cars. Elijah Muhammad was able to do it all but he was such an extraordinary and unique figure, we shouldn't be asking modern leaders to pull such a difficult feat off. When Minister Farrakhan proposed a "Third Force" independent political party after the march, it never materialized— because it's best to pick one lane and commit fully. [8] It's a mathematical and inefficient contradiction to have one foot in the political system and five feet out, preaching destruction to America and separation. Let's say the NOI did have a few states in the South, is Leonard Muhammad going to run that large economy?

This lesson parallels Dr. Khallid Muhammad's story—a case where religious connections created constraints on political development. While Dr. Khallid pushed for direct action, he remained tethered to the NOI framework. Similarly, the Million Man March, while powerful symbolically, couldn't translate into sustained political power because it remained trapped within religious inspiration.

The post-march failures also connect to what happened when Wallace Muhammad took over the NOI after Elijah Muhammad's death. In both cases, the focus shifted from concrete institution-building to more focus on religious preaching. Just as Wallace dismantled Elijah's economic empire, the political and economic development potential of the March was sacrificed for competing Minister Farrakhan's religious priorities and international relationships.

The friction between religious orientation and economic development can be seen in the departure of a top Black American consultant Al Wellington, from Power Inc. Muammar Qaddafi had loaned Farrakhan and the Nation $5 million dollars. Power was a genius direct to consumer idea, well ahead of its time that had the idea of selling everyday products such as soap, shampoo, and deodorant to Black Americans in the early 80's. After running into a fundamental disagreement with the NOI, Wellington talked about what went wrong:

Wellington said he bailed out of POWER in 1985 because Farrakhan refused to share control. "Farrakhan wanted POWER to be under the Nation, so that it would be totally controlled by the Nation," he said.

"That was not what we had agreed to. We thought it had to be independent," Wellington said. "As a business, once you put it under the church, it has other issues that take priority." [9]

Like an oil company focusing on oil and a car company on cars, even billion-dollar enterprises know not to spread themselves too thin. What happens when you start with limited resources? We should let religious organizations excel at being religious organizations while keeping serious political and economic development separate. The friction in trying to do everything at once keeps us from the science of building sustainable power in either sphere.

When I interviewed Conrad Tillard, now a politician in Harlem, as part of my research for this audit period, he emphasized the cascading effects of these missed opportunities. The Million Man March of 1995 represented unprecedented mobilization without corresponding political and economic organization, as defined by Kwame Ture. When this was followed by Dr. Khallid Muhammad's death and the NOI's wrong-footed response to Obama's candidacy, Black America lost critical institutional counterbalances that had historically provided a check on mainstream, bougie buffer political orientation. [10]

This organizational vacuum created the perfect conditions for what we might call 'political monopolization' - without robust counter-analysis from traditional Black Nationalist voices, the Obama "spook spell" operated virtually unchallenged. The Million Man March was a once in a lifetime opportunity that failed to capitalize politically and economically, where it counts. The spiritual, moral, and cultural benefit of the March came at the cost to Black American political and economic development.

The Science

- **Historic achievement with limited follow-through**: Largest gathering of Black men in history but failed to generate lasting institutions
- **Religious organization couldn't handle secular politics**: NOI's dual religious/political mission created structural limitations
- **Farrakhan chose international relations over domestic institution-building**: World tour undermined momentum for Black American organizing
- **Million-man mobilization without conversion strategy**: Historic turnout generated headlines but $66,000 organizing debt and no lasting infrastructure show that Black America would benefit more from 500,000 attendees with robust follow-through than one million with mostly symbolic impact only
- **Missed opportunity for economic program**: Could have channeled million-man energy into $100M collective investment fund

[1] "MILLION MAN MARCH IN DEBT $66,000, ACCORDING TO AUDIT BY ORGANIZERS," Washington Post, June 14, 1996.

[2] "National Agenda: Public Policy Issues, Analyses, and Programmatic Plan of ournAction 2000-2008," Washington, DC: Million Family March, 2000.

[3] Holmes, Steven A. "Farrakhan's Angry World Tour Brings Harsh Criticism at Home," The New York Times, February 22, 1996.

[4] Barboza, S. "American Jihad: Islam After Malcolm X," Doubleday, 1993.

[5] Holmes, Steven A. "Farrakhan's Angry World Tour Brings Harsh Criticism at Home," The New York Times, February 22, 1996.

[6] Fredrik deBoer, "The Charmer: Louis Farrakhan and the Black Lives Matter protests," Harper's Magazine, January 2016.

[7] "Will 'Hiphop Minister' Conrad Muhammad Go from N.O.I. to G.O.P.?," Straus Media, New York Press, February 16, 2015.

[8] "Farrakhan Sets Black Vote Goal of '3rd Political Power'," Los Angeles Times, October 19, 1995.

[9] Jackson, David, and William Gaines, "Farrakhan's Murky Finances," Greensboro News & Record, March 25, 1995.

[10] Brown, Ann, "What Is A Bougie Buffer? 3 Things To Know About The Concept Of The Buffer Class," The Moguldom Nation, November 6, 2020.

Multifactoring Dr. Khallid Muhammad

> *"I don't want no contacts, and I don't want no contracts."*
> —*Dr. Khallid Muhammad on NOI security contracts and compromises*

My journey with Dr. Khallid Muhammad's teachings began in 1994 through videos and lectures in Los Angeles before I met him in Atlanta. To many of us, he embodied Malcolm X's spirit for a new generation, masterfully weaving street culture, Nation of Islam (NOI) teachings, and scholarly insights—a blend so potent it echoed through hip-hop from Ice Cube to Tupac. Auditing Black American politics and culture from 1995-2025 must properly factor one of the most influential Black Americans during this period.

To be clear, before he was kicked out of the NOI, Dr. Khallid Muhammad was an institution builder and dedicated to building the Nation of Islam. He was right there in the beginning when Minister Farrakhan decided to rebuild the Nation. His commitment to institution-building makes his later trajectory even more significant when examining the complex interplay of factors that shaped his relationship with the NOI.

But to understand what really happened to Dr. Muhammad, we need multifactor scientific analysis beyond the spook of personality worship. The common narrative focuses on his Kean College speech in 1993 and friction with Minister Farrakhan over calling whites devils. The actual facts reveal deeper factors: financial, theological, and organizational. This lesson is not just about Dr. Khallid Muhammad but about developing an objective, critical thinking orientation to multi-factor a person, problem, or issue.

This lesson examines four critical dimensions that shaped his trajectory: financial factors (including NOI contracts and resource allocation), theological tensions (around doctrine and religious interpretation), organizational dynamics (internal power structures and leadership conflicts), and personal elements (his health, relationships, and intellectual development).

Follow the money: Minister Farrakhan was securing mainstream connections—federal contracts worth tens of millions through NOI security services in public housing projects. The Nation of Islam Security Agency (NOISA) operated successfully in Baltimore, DC, and Chicago. Dr. Muhammad, with his growing popularity and uncompromising stance, threatened these relationships. [1] Ben Chavis (later Benjamin Muhammad) at Mosque 7 could help keep government contracts flowing. Dr. Muhammad couldn't. [2] Chavis was a bridge to the Congressional Black Caucus and the civil rights establishment, Dr. Khallid was a flamethrower who would torch them in popular, hip-hop-laced speeches. Farrakhan chose Chavis.

Muhammad would later humorously name his speech "No Contacts, No Contracts" in reference to his hard stance on organizational proximity to whites and U.S. government security contracts. At the end of the day, mathematically, there was no way Minister Farrakhan could keep the U.S. government contract money, grow it, and keep Elijah Muhammad's doctrine and his relationship with Dr. Khallid exactly the same. [3]

It wasn't just the U.S. government security contracts that were creating pressures with Dr. Khallid Muhammad. Minister Farrakhan was also positioning himself in the Islamic world to become more orthodox and more in line with mainstream Islam. This positioning opened doors for financing from leaders such as Muammar Qaddafi who pledged $1 billion to Farrakhan in 1996, or potentially from wealthy Arab interests. The theological shifts within the NOI represented both religious evolution and financial strategy. Anyone who claims the orientation of the teaching at a particular time was not connected to potential financing sources wasn't paying attention or is too biased to see the objective reality. The integration of the Church of Scientology into the NOI adds further support to the pattern observed. [4]

In 1997, my Arabic professor at Clark Atlanta University (Students in the AUC can take classes at other HBCU's), Dr. Antar Ibn-Stanford Smith, once gave me a revealing glimpse into this dual messaging. Dr. Antar started the first masjid in Atlanta, GA more than 50 years ago. When I criticized Arab-oriented Islam and mentioned Minister Farrakhan preaching Fard Muhammad as God in Person to the leaders in Mecca, the professor responded with knowing laughter. He spoke like a knowledgeable parent speaking to a clueless child. After his confident grin subsided, he told me he personally knew associates of rulers in Mecca. According to Dr. Antar, Minister Farrakhan would tell Arab leaders he was gradually bringing Black Americans into mainstream Islam—the exact opposite of what he was telling his followers back home. Dr. Antar went further. "If Minister Farrakhan really preached Fard was Allah in Person in Mecca, they would cut off his head." While I cannot independently verify Dr. Antar's claim, his assured demeanor and matter-of-fact explanation has stayed with me throughout my life as a powerful example of the potential gap between public teaching and private diplomacy. If I had to estimate—and I like to work off estimates and percentages—what Dr. Antar told me was at least 70% correct.[5]

It's one thing if Minister Farrakhan tells his ministers to stop calling whites devils to help accomplish strategic economic goals that benefit the Nation of Islam and Black America as a whole. However, if you're just talking about moderating for U.S. government contracts that mainly helps more money go into the Farrakhan family's bank accounts, no smart and strong intellectually-oriented leader such as Khallid Muhammad would go along with that. Dr. Muhammad knew there was deep corruption in the Nation of Islam and he thought Leonard Muhammad, who became Farrakhan's son-in-law via marriage and the Nation's Chief of Staff, was corrupt and wasn't really about freedom, justice, and equality for Black Americans. Dr. Khallid referred to Leonard Muhammad as the NOI "Thief of Staff." The main entity for the Nation of Islam security operation with HUD was in the name of Leonard Muhammad. Another critique Dr. Muhammad had about the NOI Chief of Staff, who controlled the NOI's finances, according to insider Malik Zulu Shabazz, was he didn't really believe Leonard was really about the mission, like that. [6]

The insider information Khallid had, that we didn't and still don't know now, put Khallid in a dilemma of why water down his message if it was only for more corruption and nothing material, in the long run? My own independent analysis is any leader that has Leonard Muhammad as its CFO for so long, in charge of the Nation's money and bank account, is not really serious about the economic program of Elijah Muhammad. Leonard Muhammad is effectively the Economic Minister of the NOI, of a Nation within a Nation. If the material results are lacking, why would he still be there?

This dynamic exposes why Elijah Muhammad's economic program and implementation of economic progress reports were so crucial. Without independent economic power, Black organizations become vulnerable to unholy compromises, like politicians bending to secure funding, from unholy sources. There's an idea of Wallace Muhammad–like shirk (deviation) from Elijah's teachings, but focusing solely on religious aspects misses the point. The real shirk might be abandoning Elijah Muhammad's economic science. Maybe we need fewer prayers and articulate speeches until we figure out economic science for collective Black American benefit. The dynamic that may be playing out is the less science and proof you have, the more spook you will need.

Under Minister Farrakhan's leadership, a critical element of Elijah Muhammad's approach gradually disappeared—the regular economic progress reports back to members and Black America. Elijah Muhammad consistently provided transparent accounting of the Nation's economic activities and growth. These weren't just internal communications but public declarations of collective achievement that built credibility and accountability. The absence of these progress reports under Farrakhan signaled a shift away from economic prioritization. At the same time, Minister Farrakhan has masterfully preached that politics without economics is a symbol without substance.

According to former NOI member Lance Shabazz, who grew up in Elijah Muhammad's NOI and followed Farrakhan, under Minister Farrakhan, it became more about "just send the money in" and it became a "hustle." The distinction between Minister Farrakhan's NOI and the Black American Christian Church lost its wide distance and distinction over time.

Theologically, Dr. Muhammad questioned evolving NOI interpretations. At an event in Atlanta in 1998, when asked about praying to Master Fard Muhammad and whether he was alive, he said no, noting Fard "taught himself he would die." In a revealing speech at Compton's Mosque 54, he warned that NOI Muslims were "turning spooky"— believing in "magic" and waiting for Allah's intervention rather than building real power. [7]

"You will fool around and make Master Fard Muhammad a spook," he warned. "You'll walk up in here and make Allah a spook. You'll be waiting for some Shazam, some Afrika Dap, some Hocus Pocus." He called out those saying, "Allah is going to change everything. Allah is going to work it out."

"Yes, Allah is going to work it out. But you got some work to do too."

Dr. Muhammad had identified "spook drift" within the NOI. There was a scientific and intellectual orientation to Khallid that was on a collision course with the *Torchlight for America* direction of the NOI. [8] Like Malcolm X, Dr. Khallid was gifted before he joined the NOI. He won a scholarship to Dillard University and spent time studying at Harvard

University. With my own eyes, I saw more and more Black Muslims drifting toward belief that Fard and Elijah were together riding in a mothership in space and were both physically alive. Dr. Khallid maintained they were both dead, and even if alive, it wouldn't matter for the work that needed to be done today and tomorrow. He recognized how this religious orientation could impact practical action and nation building. The NOI would later embrace the Church of Scientology and even begin teaching that Minister Farrakhan would also go to the mothership and wouldn't die a physical death like the rest of us—precisely the spook drift Khallid warned against.

When Farrakhan introduced the "Jesus Saves" theme during the 1995 Saviors' Day, it signaled a transformation toward a more church-like organization that would compensate for not having a real economic program with an emphasis on traditional religious capture.

The schism within the Nation involved multiple fault lines—not simply about rhetoric around whites, but about corruption, cronyism, scientific versus spook orientations, and competing political strategies. You had the Conrad Muhammad (now Conrad Tillard) faction that wanted more moderation and political engagement. You had some Black Muslims wanting to vote and work with the NAACP and the Congressional Black Caucus, while others wanted to burn it all down, including the "sellout and compromised Negro politicians." You had a younger, Hip-Hop faction (including myself) leaning towards Dr. Khallid, and an older, more dominant conservative group leaning into Minister Farrakhan. When I interviewed Tillard as part of my auditing process and research for the 1995-2025 measurement period, he told me Dr. Khallid just would not commit and listen to his general, his leader, Minister Farrakhan. When I offered my own observation and analysis as a former member, Tillard quickly cut me off and said "I was there, I was in the rooms when all this was going on." In this situation, Mr. Tillard had more insider science than me and I shut up and let him speak.

The first Million Youth March (1998) which I attended revealed the limits of radical posturing without institution building. After the March, when I directly questioned Dr. Muhammad on MLK Street in Atlanta about leaving the stage after telling people to fight armed police, he responded frustratedly, "What do the people want me to do, I gave the orders." His answer revealed a critical gap between revolutionary rhetoric and organizational capacity. One current NOI official told me after the march, still deeply loyal to Minister Farrakhan, Dr. Khallid "ran like a bitch"—harsh words coming from someone on the other side of the then-conflict between Muhammad and his former mentor and spiritual father.

Dr. Khallid was clearly conflicted—he would criticize Farrakhan's direction, sometimes with subtle jabs and sneak disses, then affirm that "Farrakhan was his father" and he would stand with him. This internal conflict, combined with health issues including diabetes, hypertension, and the stress of surviving an assassination attempt at UC Berkeley, likely took a toll on his health. The Berkeley assassination attempt by James Edward Bess in May 1993 further illustrated the schism within the Nation. Bess, who represented a unique interpretation of Black Islam that sought to merge it with Christianity, saw Dr. Muhammad as a threat to his vision and opened fire, wounding Dr. Muhammad and several bystanders before being subdued by the crowd. [9] This violent incident demonstrated how theological divisions could quickly escalate beyond rhetoric into dangerous confrontation.

The violent and fanatical elements within Black Islam that took the life of Malcolm X (with U.S. government support) and most likely Clarence 13X, and that attempted to assassinate Dr. Muhammad, represent the opposite direction of both science and Black American advancement. Both Democratic Party-oriented political spook and fanatical religious dogmatism share a common feature: they leave no room for debate, no room to be challenged and held accountable, no room for new ideas and criticism, no room for asking tough questions. This mindset condemns Black America to political and collective economic stagnation while the world accelerates through rapid technological change. Those making meaningful progress in the modern world are testing new ideas, adapting successful models, measuring results, and optimizing based on what works, not what adheres to rigid orthodoxy.

Another factor with Dr. Khallid was the reality that there wasn't room for two prominent leaders in the Nation. Dr. Khallid was gaining fame, especially after surviving the assassination attempt, just as Farrakhan was becoming a global figure following the Million Man March. NOI historian Vilbert White, a former minister, said Dr. Khallid Abdul Muhammad "could have been the best leader ever for Black America"— he had that extreme of potential. [10] Both Conrad Tillard and Dr. Khallid Muhammad had severe financial struggles while committing 100% of their life towards the NOI and freedom, justice, and equality. When Black America comes across the special talent of Conrad Tillard who graduated from the University of Pennsylvania and Dr. Khallid, the lesson is we need an economic program to make sure gas stays in their tank with strong financial security. We need stronger organizations to provide financial security for those who go on the front lines and commit to our collective interests.

Our organizations may attract extraordinary talent with so much potential but we collectively need to be able to keep their electric bills and rent or mortgage paid. Black America likely got 10% of what was possible with Dr. Khallid Muhammad and Conrad Tillard, based on the momentum observed in the 1990's. To attract top players and game changers and keep them, Black America needs its own bank account and economic program. Jewish Americans have AIPAC and we have NO PAC and we aren't going anywhere fast, without new organizations with independent economic foundations. We shouldn't expect any strong policy risk taking for Black Americans without a restructuring of our organizational orientation and developing economic foundations.

Looking back at all the time spent on this schism and its various fault lines, there seemed to be little forceful debate about a strategic plan that could bring Black Americans as a whole into a coherent gameplan. How do we develop institutions that bring us closer to freedom, justice, and equality with strong economic foundations? The debate should have centered on strategy and implementation in the scientific realm, because once we drift into too much religion and belief, we lose our rationality and natural orientation toward the smartest approaches to solving complex material problems.

If Farrakhan can be accused of following a more Wallace-like path, Dr. Khallid could also be charged with a different kind of spook on the radical side. Running around with guns, militias, and army pants was only going to attract federal attention—it was never going to give us the institutions and organizational blueprint our people could build upon for generations, something with a strong economic foundation optimized for modern times.

Our goal should be political efficiency and material impact—what can we work on today that will be helpful tomorrow when we're long gone? In accusing Farrakhan of shirking Elijah's original teachings, Dr. Khallid couldn't claim Elijah Muhammad preached militias, guns, and violent revolution. Elijah was an institutionalist who wouldn't even retaliate against the LAPD after they murdered NOI member Ronald Stokes in California. [11] Elijah thought strategically and long-term and knew how to play both defense and offense, at the right times. Dr. Khallid's political orientation, while valuable in many ways, wasn't that. Both Farrakhan and Dr. Khallid departed from Elijah Muhammad's original strategic and religious orientation in different ways.

This next generation coming up must be hard against corruption, whether it has a church tie, a bow tie, or a BLM T-shirt. Whether it is Christian or Muslim. Whether it is in Black Face or White. Whether it is Democrat or Republican. Whether it is Man or Woman or Conservative or Liberal. Straight or LGBTQ. It's not enough to be anti-corruption, we must express our love for Black Americans and freedom, justice, and equality, with organizational and accounting transparency, proactively.

189

What Clarence 13X (Father Allah) meant when he said he is not pro-Black or anti-white is that when you're so one-sided and simple-minded, the spook and tricknology are going to get you from the Black side. The devilishment and corruption, or inefficiencies, are going to come from the side that you are most biased and not thinking scientifically. Be against all corruption and devilishment, no matter the walk of life or the complexion, or the identity. Clarence 13X may have been murdered for this scientific insight and many weren't ready for it in the 70's, but this is the right and exact orientation for now and the future, one that helps keeps us collectively safe from everyone, all sides.

Historically, Dr. Muhammad was a central figure in the Black consciousness movement of the 1990s. He embedded himself into national Black consciousness, and this is part of his legacy. From campuses to street corners, his unapologetic analysis and fiery oratory shaped a generation's understanding of modern Black Nationalism and radicalism.

Dr. Muhammad dedicated his life to Black liberation, from housing projects to national stages. Yet his story teaches us that even the most radical rhetoric, without economic science backing it, can't advance collective Black interests to our full potential. We must move beyond personality worship and spook tactics to build real economic power—the kind Elijah Muhammad demonstrated through tangible institutions. We have to get to a collective point that if we don't have a strong, independent economic program, advancing Black American political interests, we don't have much so we better get busy.

As Sister Burnsteen Sharrieff Mohammed, Fard's former secretary in the early 1930s, recalled him teaching, "Don't close your eyes and trust in God!" Even then, the message was clear—material power over mystical thinking. Without strong economic programs, Black American organizations, regardless of rhetoric, risk becoming indistinguishable from churches waiting on heavenly intervention rather than building earthly political positions and power.

The Khallid Muhammad story teaches us that multifactor analysis matters. When we reduce complex figures to simple narratives—hero or villain, right or wrong—we miss the scientific truth and factors. A more productive way forward is to extract the best insights from our leaders while acknowledging their limitations, and to focus relentlessly on institution building rather than personality cults. Science demands we see the whole picture—not just what confirms our biases. Whether it's Barack Obama, Kamala Harris, Minister Farrakhan, Al Sharpton, or Dr. Khallid Muhammad, leaders are often responding to cultural orientation. If we take on more scientific evaluation principles, we may actually help leaders become better and more effective.

The Science

- **Multiple factors shaped his departure from NOI**: Financial (government contracts), theological (religious evolution), organizational (internal power struggles), personal (health, assassination attempt)
- **Government contracts required message moderation**: NOI security services worth tens of millions created pressure to soften militant positions
- **Leonard Muhammad as "Thief of Staff"**: Corruption in NOI financial management undermined commitment to original mission
- **Scientific vs. spook religious orientations**: Khallid warned against "spooky" thinking that waited for divine intervention instead of building material power
- **Need economic programs to keep talent**: Both Khallid and Conrad Tillard struggled financially while dedicating lives to the cause

[1] Malik Zulu Shabazz, "The Book of Khallid: The Untold Story of Khallid Abdul Muhammad" (2020).

[2] Peter Noel, "The Shame of Mosque No. 7," Village Voice, September 5, 2000.

[3] Lorraine Adams, "Farrakhan Aide Blasts U.S. Probe of Business," Washington Post, January 21, 1995.

[4] Mandel, Bethany. "The Troubling Connections between Scientology and the Nation of Islam," National Review, April 2, 2018.

[5] Malik Zulu Shabazz, "The Book of Khallid: The Untold Story of Khallid Abdul Muhammad" (2020).

[6] Sharon Waxman, "Questions Shadow New Jackson Adviser," New York Times, January 3, 2004.

[7] Dr. Khallid Abdul Muhammad, "Who is That Mystery God?" lecture delivered at Muhammad Mosque #54, Compton, California, early 1990s.

[8] Malik Zulu Shabazz, "The Book of Khallid: The Untold Story of Khallid Abdul Muhammad" (2020).

[9] "Bobby Hemmitt - Talks About The Assassination Of Dr. Khallid Muhammad," Odysee, June 15, 2020.

[10] Vibert White, "Inside the Nation of Islam," Talk delivered at Bethune-Cookman College.

[11] Karl Evanzz, "The Messenger: The Rise and Fall of Elijah Muhammad," Pantheon Books, 2001.

LESSON 21
Clarence 13X: Strategic Alliances

> *"The people been taking advantage of me ever since I said I was Allah. And I know when I said I was Allah, the Muslim whole world was what? Against me. I don't care... And now they really against me because I'm not anti-white nor pro-Black. They really against me because everybody is, is against the white. Well, let me show you something: Who is man if he ain't man? Tell me!"*
> — *Clarence 13X (Father Allah)*

While radical speeches may feed the soul, Clarence 13X understood the science of youth education and strategic alliances to move an agenda forward. In the concrete jungle of New York City, he demonstrated how strategic alliances could transform street knowledge into an institution.

When New York City Mayor John Lindsay's administration recognized the Five-Percent Nation's influence, they didn't just offer empty words. Through Barry Gottehrer, they provided something tangible—the Allah School in Mecca, Harlem. This wasn't just a building; it was proof that the right alliances could turn street wisdom into brick-and-mortar reality.

Let's break down the scientific equation: Leadership + Effort + Organization + Strategic Alliances and Compromise = Material Results

Clarence 13X brought all four elements: leadership that resonated with the streets, the effort of building a movement, the organization of the Five-Percent Nation, and the strategic alliances that amplified everything. His willingness to build bridges while maintaining his core teachings created a formula for lasting impact. [1]

The power of this approach became crystal clear during a critical moment in history. After being labeled a "hate group" and "terrorist organization" by the press and even being institutionalized for claiming divinity, Clarence told Gottehrer: "I'm neither pro-Black, nor anti-white." [2]

What Clarence 13X (Father Allah) meant by saying he was not pro-Black or anti-white was scientific insight that transcends the spook of identity politics. When you're so one-sided and simple-minded, the spook will get you from the Black side. The devilishment, corruption, and inefficiencies can come from the side you're most biased toward—the side where your scientific thinking is weakest because emotional loyalty clouds your judgment and suspends your critical thinking impulse. Here's the recommended revision with paragraph breaks:

If a Black American said "I don't want to work with Hispanics because they hate us or illegal immigration is hurting us" while fiercely advocating for Pure Reparations for Black Americans, this is an example of spook. The person may mean well and even have facts supporting their position but they seek something that is a long shot while remaining inflexible.

By default, Pure Reparations implies working with different groups to achieve the result. The person involved in this type of inflexibility may not understand that not all Black Americans will support or fight for Pure Reparations and this support would need to be replaced, and more.

There is no insular path that is unwilling to work with different groups that creates a realistic path to ambitious policy goals. This type of person may be using politics as a form of self-medication and entertainment and not even know it—but it's definitely not political science.

Although Democrats and Republicans are adversaries, the highest probability legislation to move forward is when there is some bipartisanship, compromise, and negotiation.

Remember the lesson of A Deng for Black America: China didn't break out of its economic retardation until Deng and others decided it had to "open up" and work with America and other Western countries. China didn't rise by being less flexible; it rose by being more flexible and more scientific about what works and what doesn't. Examining what has worked for others, from a scientific lens vs ideological or political lens, is always a good starting place.

As Saladin Allah, Region 6 Representative of the Five-Percent Nation explained, "The Father, Allah, in making the statement that he was not pro-Black or anti-white is that he defined people based on the content of their character." [3] This perspective advocates being "pro-righteous and anti-devilishment"—a scientific stance that judges actions and outcomes rather than appearances.

Clarence 13X's strategic alliance with Lindsay's administration yielded concrete results:

- A city-leased storefront school (the Allah School in Mecca, which still exists today)
- Funded field trips to Long Island for young Five-Percenters
- Educational programming support
- Direct access to city leadership

The material impact was most visible the night Martin Luther King Jr. was assassinated. While Chicago, Baltimore, and Washington, DC, burned in riots, Mayor Lindsay walked Harlem's streets alongside Father Allah and other community leaders, calling for peace. The Five-Percenters' peacekeeping efforts that night, enabled by their strategic alliance with city leadership, brought peace and helped prevent thousands of Black youth from being incarcerated after the riots were over.

Father Allah was mysteriously killed fourteen months after King, over four hundred people attended his funeral, including Mayor Lindsay, who went to the Allah School to pay respects.

Hip-Hop would have been far less culturally and intellectually developed without the contributions of Clarence 13X. His teachings provided the philosophical foundation and linguistic innovations that would later shape Hip-Hop's most thoughtful expressions. While his willingness to engage with Mayor Lindsay and city officials helped secure resources like the Allah School, it was Clarence's own charismatic leadership and profound teachings that truly institutionalized the Five Percenters in Black America. [4] The alliance with city leadership was just one strategic element of his broader vision—he maintained his revolutionary principles while pragmatically securing the physical space that became the incubator for spreading these teachings through the culture. This balanced approach—neither rejecting potential allies nor compromising core values—exemplifies the scientific thinking he advocated.

We can't be so insular or reflexively anti-this or anti-that where we miss strategic opportunities to move a righteous and positive political agenda forward that benefits Black Americans. We should be strategically and surgically working with groups from all walks of life, like Father Allah did—a scientific position that puts the focus on results and outcomes and working with those who can help us get there faster.

The cultural impact proves the formula worked. The Five-Percent Nation's teachings didn't stay confined to street corners—they infiltrated Black American consciousness through hip-hop. Rakim wasn't just dropping beats; he was embedding Five-Percenter philosophy into the culture. Wu-Tang Clan's very names—RZA, GZA—carried these teachings worldwide. When Nas grabbed "One Mic," he was channeling this legacy. Jay-Z, Busta Rhymes, and Big Daddy Kane became unwitting professors of Clarence's wisdom.

While many focus on the esoteric aspects of Five-Percenter teachings, an undervalued lesson and factor is in Clarence's strategic alliances. He showed that you can maintain your core message while building bridges that create lasting institutions. The Allah School still stands today—a testament to the power of strategic alliance building.

This isn't about selling out; it's about understanding how real power moves in America. From city councils to Congress, progress happens through strategic alliances. The most radical and inflexible rhetoric might get retweets and social media shares, but it rarely leaves behind institutions, legislation, and material impact.

Clarence 13X may have been murdered for his scientific insights, and many weren't ready for them in the 70's, but his approach represents the right political orientation for now and the future—one that helps keep us collectively safe by judging people by proximity to righteousness and devilishment and not allowing a different racial identity get in the way of material, institutional progress.

The lesson for today's movements is clear: pure opposition might feel righteous, but it rarely builds lasting power. Real revolution isn't just about what you're against—it's about what you can build through strategic alliances while maintaining your core principles. What needs to be done? How do we get it done, the fastest and most efficiently?

The Science

- **"Not pro-Black or anti-white"** = **scientific thinking**: Judge people by actions and outcomes, not identity
- **Strategic alliances produced material results**: Working with Mayor Lindsay created the Allah School in Mecca - still operating today
- **Five-Percenters kept Harlem peaceful after MLK assassination**: Practical community impact through strategic relationships
- **Hip-hop wouldn't exist without these alliances**: Cultural influence spread globally because institutional foundations were built
- **Pure opposition rarely builds lasting power**: Revolution requires building new institutions through strategic partnerships while maintaining core principles

---

[1] Wakeel Allah, "In the Name of Allah, Vol. 1: A History of Clarence 13X and the Five Percenters" (February 22, 2009).

[2] Barry Gottehrer, "Interview with Allah," November 15, 1967.

[3] Brown, Ann, "What Did Father Allah (Clarence 13X) Mean When He Said He's 'Not Pro-Black or Anti-White'," Moguldom Nation, December 20, 2022.

[4] Prince A. Cuba, "Our Mecca Is Harlem: Clarence 13X (Allah) and the Five Percent" (January 1, 2004).

Is Pan-Africanism Another Form of Spook?

> *"Pan-Africanism is the idea that the African peoples, wherever they are, must unite to achieve their common goals and aspirations."*
> —*Kwame Nkrumah, the first president of Ghana*

The distance between symbolic Pan-Africanism and reality hit me in a Maputo, Mozambique fish market. While European tourists moved freely among locals, a fellow "Pan-Africanist" wouldn't leave the car. The Pan-Africanist was shook and fearful, having never traveled to an African country before. This moment crystallized how Pan-Africanism can become another form of spook—imaginary beliefs disconnected from reality. My Pan-Africanist friend thought he was a hardcore Pan-Africanist while in America, but he was extremely uncomfortable being on African soil, among Africans, for the first time. For those with means, a flight from Atlanta to Accra, Ghana, what insiders call "Africa for Beginners," should be a requirement for American-born Pan Africanists. Put some "skin in the game."

My visits across Ghana, Mozambique, South Africa, and Nigeria revealed a more complex truth than the notion that "Africans don't like Black Americans." While some elitist-minded Africans in America might use terms like akata, projecting this onto an entire continent reveals how far removed we are from ground realities.

To understand these dynamics better, it's worth noting that akata is a West African slur against Black Americans with meanings ranging from "wild cat" or "animal without a home" to "cotton picker." We saw the term used in the 1994 Wesley Snipes film, "Sugar Hill," highlighting its historical presence in cultural discourse.

To separate science from spook in Pan-Africanism, we must examine two distinct forms: scientific and spook Pan-Africanism. Scientific Pan-Africanism meant action, organization and strategic goals to Marcus Garvey and Kwame Nkrumah.[1] The original Pan-Africanists had the OAU or Organization of African Unity.[2] They didn't just theorize—they built organizations, developed concrete political projects, and worked to unite the African diaspora through tangible institutions and revolutions. Garvey's Black Star Line shipping company wasn't just symbolic—it was a material attempt to establish a transportation connection between Africa and its diaspora. Similarly, Nkrumah's work towards the creation of Ghana and a United States of Africa involved actual diplomatic efforts and economic planning. This is Pan-Africanism rooted in material reality, organization, strategy, goals, and governance. This is political science at the highest levels of expression and results.

Then there's spook Pan-Africanism—all sentiment and emotion without measurable progress. "African Unity" they say but unity towards what measurable strategic or political goal? A lot of things and concepts can be divided between science and spook. PA can become another form of feel-good religion, providing cultural affirmation without material benefit. Like my own experience as a college student: In college, I thought I was a militant Pan-Africanist until I visited rural Jamaica. There I was, in a Black nation surrounded by poverty, desperately wanting to return to America—the very place I criticized and thought I hated. This revealed the spook in my own thinking. If I hated America so much, why was I so anxious to leave Jamaica and come back "home" I thought to myself. At that moment, I recognized the spook or deviation from reality, in my own thinking. I wanted to get back to the comfort and commonality of America just as many Africans and Jamaicans jump at the opportunity to come live in America, whether legally or illegally.

You're not a sellout or anti-African by embracing Black American-ness. Our ancestors fought, died, and sacrificed here. Black America is our cultural foundation after Western and Central African leaders followed greed and tricknology in selling us into our holocaust. We are not sellouts by running towards the reality that 90% of the people you see in a dashiki claiming Pan-Africanism will die in America and aren't going anywhere. The feet often have more truth in them than the lips. Our problems and solutions are here. Our heritage is here in America. If our minds are in two places, we can't be politically efficient in one.

You may say Indian-Americans or Korean-Americans still look to their homeland, but their identity orientation would be materially different if their homeland sold them into a holocaust. Always look for factors to make adjustments with your comparisons. Before comparing native Black Americans to other people, we first must acknowledge material differences that make Black Americans extraordinarily unique. Only spook would push you off the factual and scientific position that we were sold by Africans to whites. And before that, Arabs were selling Africans.

In Lagos, Nigeria, I was told to my face who sold us, where, and why. The Nigerians at the Lagos Museum can even show you what goods we were sold for, so you can verify the evidence with your own eyes, versus romanticized Pan-African history books. It takes an honest mind to want to see reality exactly as it is, the good, bad, and ugly.

Despite centuries of structural anti-Black American racism and the ongoing challenges we face in this country, the reality remains that America is where our lives are rooted. We were born in America, and there is a way of life, culture, comfort, and convenience that has become us. To be politically efficient, we must optimize for one direction rather than remain conflicted and contradictory, which inevitably ends in spook—and nothing tangible. Africa is way over there; we're in the paint here.

What determines whether a Pan-Africanist is fundamentally American shouldn't be subjective declaration but objective, scientific assessment.

Consider the evidence: they pay taxes to the American government, vote in American elections, consume American cultural products like R&B and Hip-Hop, speak American English with its distinct patterns and slang, and navigate American social systems with native fluency. These tangible factors reveal more truth than ideological positioning or symbolic affiliations.

As the ADOS (American Descendants of Slavery) organization has declared, after Africans sold us into slavery, we became a new people. Black American identity is something to be embraced, to feel good about, and to better optimize our minds, our work, and political orientation towards. We have to consolidate around an unambiguous cultural identity that syncs with reality for our politics to be more efficient.

If our minds are in Ghana or Nigeria while our dirty drinking water and unpaid light bill is in Detroit, we are involved in spook. If our minds are in Africa but we have no plans or intention to leave America, we can become confused and wonder why we don't see any political progress that's commensurate with our population size and collective resources. We may think the problems are in other political areas without factoring how much of the total problem is our far distance from reality, our own spook. Our goal should be to get close to reality, so we can improve our collective political and economic efficiency. It's impossible to improve these efficiencies if there are so many unproductive spook spells commanding our consciousness.

The Pan-Africanists I most admire such as W.E.B. Du Bois, Marcus Garvey, Kwame Nkrumah, and Kwame Ture either died on the continent of Africa or had specific political objectives. For them, Pan-Africanism was a strategy, goal, and organizing principle, much more than ideology, identity, and belief.

A More Scientific Pan-Africanism would emphasize:

- Organization
- Focusing on one African country as a global model (efficiency and focused results)

202

- Building actual trade relationships
- Establishing political and economic cooperation
- Creating measurable benchmarks and timelines
- Prioritizing tangible improvements in housing, employment, and organization

Distinguishing between effective and ineffective Pan-Africanism ultimately comes down to whether it's grounded in scientific thinking with measurable objectives or remains trapped in spook territory with symbolism and identity unity but no practical outcomes.

The Science

- **Scientific vs. spook Pan-Africanism**: Garvey and Nkrumah built organizations and trade relationships; social media Pan-Africanists post dashiki photos
- **Most Pan-Africanists are more American than they admit**: American passports, iPhones, NBA knowledge vs. inability to name African heads of state
- **If your mind is in two places, you can't be powerful in one**: 99.9% of Black Americans will die on American soil - optimize for this reality
- **W.E.B. Du Bois and Kwame Ture actually moved to Africa**: Scientific Pan-Africanism requires material commitment, not just cultural symbols
- **Focus where you have leverage**: Our problems and solutions are in America, where our ancestors fought and sacrificed

---

[1] Garvey, Marcus. "Message to the People: The Course of African Philosophy." Dover Thrift Editions: Black History. Dover Publications, 2020.

[2] African Union. "The Pan-Africanist Movement and the Road to Liberation." OAU60, African Union, accessed May 1, 2025.

Call Me Akata; Take My Affirmative Action

> *"The large numbers of African immigrants on American college campuses, coupled with the remarkably small numbers of native Blacks on those same campuses, calls into question the effectiveness of America's affirmative action programs. While affirmative action started as a system to right the wrongs of slavery and institutional anti-Black racism, helping wealthy immigrants who weren't here for those struggles doesn't serve any of the program's original intentions." —Jeffrey Coard*

From slavery to Jim Crow and civil rights to battles against mass incarceration, Black Americans built the foundation that African and Caribbean immigrants now benefit from. Yet somehow, we're called akata—meaning "cotton picker" or "wild animal"—by some who reap these benefits. [1] The reality beneath this dynamic exposes both historical ironies and the current manipulation of diversity initiatives.

Let's follow the money and the percentages. Former Black Panther Kathleen Cleaver, now an Emory Law professor, breaks it down scientifically:

"In the Black community, there's a lot of Black people now in America who weren't from here. There are people coming from abroad, people coming from the Caribbean... when I teach, some of my best students came from Africa. They came from another culture. They're Black, but their educational system and their educational focus is a little different." [2]

Then she exposes the institutional trick bag:

"Guess what? The big major universities have noticed this difference, and so they want a certain Black population. But they prefer a population that is not as troublesome and not as poorly educated as the indigenous Black population, so we are being pushed aside yet again."

Elite academic institutions can create the appearance of racial diversity while obscuring the specific underrepresentation of native Black Americans. [3] By reporting only aggregate 'Black' student enrollment without distinguishing between African/Caribbean immigrants and descendants of American slavery, these universities can mask disparities that may reach ratios as high as 7:1 in favor of immigrant populations. [4] This statistical aggregation conveniently allows institutions to project an image of racial progress while avoiding accountability for addressing the specific historical injustices faced by native Black Americans.

The strategy for elite institutions is to check the 'Black Box' without addressing the specific historical structural racism faced by Black Americans. If data on Black American representation were disaggregated and tracked separately, it would expose deeper, more costly problems that institutions prefer to avoid. Instead, they recruit African and Caribbean immigrants from wealthier families, creating the appearance of racial diversity while sidestepping the harder work of addressing historical injustices.

Silicon Valley's Diversity Deception

While running my digital media company in 2015, I was invited to the Facebook mega campus in Silicon Valley to meet with executives. I saw Black faces, but only a few Black Americans, like me. I was shocked at the lack of native Black Americans and the overwhelming number of continental Africans. It was easier to spot an Ethiopian than a Black American. My visit to the Facebook campus really left an impression on me that these diversity reports aren't just depressing—they're fundamentally deceptive.

The tech companies had no incentive to disaggregate Black Americans— if this mystery or spook of aggregate statistics was replaced with native

Black American-specific data, it could trigger a political crisis. Perhaps the NAACP or Congressional Black Caucus would step in. Why Black American numbers are so low would invite tough questions and distributed accountability.

The Dream Team Fallacy

When African and Black immigrant students are compared to native Black Americans, you've got to understand the statistical trick being played. We're not comparing entire populations—we're comparing Africa's Dream Team to Black America's entire league.

This Dream Team fallacy isn't limited to Black immigrants: It applies equally to East Indian and many Asian students as well. Most of the immigrants coming over here on Kenyan and Nigerian Airways flights, Air India, or Korean Air are the best and brightest of those populations. The richest, most educated families from Lagos, Mumbai, or Seoul aren't sending their struggling students—they're sending their academic all-stars.

You can't fairly compare a student from a wealthy Nigerian slave-selling family to a native Black American whose ancestors were enslaved and systemically oppressed for centuries. If you want to make a just comparison, you would need to estimate how that Black American student would perform if they were from the wealthy slave-selling family and how the Nigerian would perform if they were descendants of slaves who had faced centuries of Jim Crow and structural racism. Comparisons can have an Anti-Black American orientation when they skip over chattel slavery and Jim Crow as one-time events, without tail effects and ongoing anti-Black American structures. When women are sexually assaulted, it's not a one-time event. The scars and trauma remain. Similarly, Black Americans have complex generational scars and impairment, that many can't see, don't want to see, don't care to see, and lack the curiosity about the subject, to truly understand it and the different factors at play.

Flawed comparisons are made constantly when immigrant academic performance is measured against that of native Black Americans. It's like comparing the Nigerian Olympic team to the entire Black American population (average) and concluding that Nigerians are inherently better athletes. If we took the top 10% Black American students, created a new identity, they would be outperforming Black Americans too. The comparison is statistically manipulative and intellectually dishonest, designed to paint a picture of something being fundamentally wrong with Black Americans by choice, when in reality, the data has been twisted into a weapon against us.

We actually have to consider different factors and adjustments when comparing multiple groups and people. If we were serious about real statistical analysis, we would control for:

- Family wealth going back generations
- Parents' education level
- Quality of prior schools attended
- Exposure to violence and trauma
- Access to healthcare and nutrition
- Impact of mass incarceration on family structure
- Historical community investment/disinvestment

The Ivy League Shell Game

A Princeton University study published in the American Journal of Education found that while only 13 percent of college-age Black Americans are first- or second-generation immigrants, they make up 27 percent of Black students at selective colleges. In the Ivy League, it's even more stark: a mind-blowing 41 percent of "Black" students come from immigrant backgrounds.

Look at the breakdown of Black students by school type:

- Public universities: 23.1 percent immigrant
- Private universities: 28.8 percent immigrant

- The ten most selective schools: 35.6 percent immigrant

- Ivy League: 40.6 percent immigrant

See the pattern? The more elite the institution, the more they replace native Black Americans with immigrant Black students. Rather than boldly and honestly confronting the sins of the past, the strategic trend is it just replace Black Americans. The most "diverse" campuses have the lowest percentage of Black Americans whose ancestors survived American slavery and Jim Crow. Black Americans should be careful in championing diversity without understanding and analyzing where we sit within the specific frame and what agenda is in place, for that specific situation. Diversity could just mean everyone else but Black Americans, especially white women and immigrants.

At Harvard, the Nigerian Students Association alone claims two hundred members, suggesting that one-third of Harvard's "Black" student population comes from a single African country. Meanwhile, until 2021, Black American students whose families have been here for generations didn't even have their own organization. If the mainstream calls this diversity, then Black Americans have no political stake in this form of diversity. Diversity or DEI are corporate terms that often mask exclusion—we should instead use our influence to promote language and metrics that explicitly align with Black American political and economic objectives. When promoting diversity, the Black American can be promoting further excluding himself.

Class Privilege in Black Face

The Princeton study confirms this class discrepancy—immigrant Black students are more likely to:

- Be raised by two parents (56.9 percent vs 51.4 percent)

- Have college-educated fathers (70 percent vs 55.2 percent)

- Have fathers with advanced degrees (43.6 percent vs 25.3 percent)

- Have attended private schools (41.7 percent vs 27.3 percent)

- Have higher SAT scores (1250 versus 1193)

You're not seeing a genetic or cultural superiority—you're seeing class privilege wearing Black Face.

At Cornell University, Black American students had to demand that affirmative action be reserved for students who could trace their American ancestry back at least three generations because the university was deliberately gaming the system. Their organization, Black Students United, specifically defined "underrepresented black students" as those "who have several generations (more than two) in this country," noting that Cornell's black student population disproportionately represented international or first-generation African or Caribbean students. This approach is scientific and a template for us all. We have no political incentives to be thrown into a pot of Black identity gumbo, where we can't track what's really going on specifically with Black Americans, tracking our progress, our reality with knowledge of our important history on United States soil. Who benefits from keeping segmented data a mystery? What are the costs to Black Americans if this data remains a mystery?

The Science

- **Dream Team fallacy distorts academic comparisons**: Comparing Africa's best students to entire Black American population is statistically manipulative
- **Elite universities use immigrant students to avoid addressing historical debts**: 41% of Ivy League "Black" students are immigrants - this dilutes policies meant for descendants of American slavery
- **Class privilege wearing Black face**: Immigrant Black students more likely to have college-educated parents, private school education, higher SAT scores
- **Affirmative action being redirected from its original purpose**: Created for descendants of slavery but now benefits those who weren't here for that historical injustice
- **Statistical aggregation hides displacement**: Universities report "Black" enrollment without distinguishing lineage, masking replacement of target population

[1] Mwanza, Kevin, "5 Things To Know About The African Akata Slur Against Black Americans," Moguldom.com, April 29, 2021.

[2] Brown, Ann, "Former Black Panther, Professor Kathleen Cleaver: Universities Prefer Immigrant Blacks, Black Americans Are Being Replaced," Moguldom.com, July 20, 2021.

[3] Lumpkin, Lauren, Kolodner, Meredith, and Anderson, Nick, "Flagship universities fail to enroll Black and Latino high school graduates from their state: 'They're exacerbating racial inequities instead of combating them'," The Hechinger Report, April 18, 2021.

[4] Jaschik, Scott, "The Immigrant Factor," Inside Higher Ed, January 31, 2007.

UNDERSTANDING
POLITICAL
MECHANICS

The Technicals

> *"The filibuster has been a tool used overwhelmingly to block civil rights, to block voting rights, to block anti-lynching legislation."*
> —Senator Elizabeth Warren

> *"A politician thinks of the next election. A statesman, of the next generation."* —James Freeman Clarke

If we are talking about politics, judging political leaders without knowing the parameters and limitations they are working within, without knowing how the system actually works, we are in danger of operating within the realm of spook. Let's get an understanding how the American government works, particularly one of its most effective tools for maintaining structural inequality—the filibuster. This technical procedure has quietly strangled Black American progress for over one hundred and fifty years.

The American Governance Machine: Form and Function

The Constitution creates an intentionally fragmented power structure designed to slow change and protect established interests. This isn't political opinion—it's mechanical reality. The United States government was created by wealthy landowners, many of them slave owners, who designed a system where substantial change requires overcoming multiple, deliberately constructed barriers. Many of the same technical features that prevent tyranny also prevent progress.

The three branches operate as a political machine with specific mechanical constraints:

Legislative Branch (Congress)

The science tells us that progress must navigate a deliberate obstacle course. Bills require majority approval in both chambers and presidential signature. But the House of Representatives and the Senate aren't equal pistons in this engine—they were designed with different power dynamics and representative formulas. The House represents population (benefiting populous states), while the Senate represents states equally (giving disproportionate power to less populous states).

This structural inequality is mathematical: Wyoming's five hundred and eighty thousand residents get two senators, as do California's 39 million. The Senate's composition automatically amplifies rural interests while diluting urban (and Black American) voices. A Wyoming voter has sixty-six times more Senate representation than a California voter.

Even without the filibuster, the Senate's undemocratic nature would create structural advantages for white, rural interests—but the filibuster supercharges this effect. It transforms a constitutional majority into a practical supermajority requirement, adding another layer of friction against any change to the status quo.

Executive Branch (President)

Presidential power exists within precise constitutional boundaries. Executive orders can redirect existing authority but cannot create new authority. The president can't appropriate money—only redirect funds already approved by Congress. The White House can prioritize enforcement of certain laws but can't ignore them entirely.

A scientific analysis reveals that even a "Black American-friendly" president operates within a system where 90 percent of policy implementation depends on career bureaucrats and existing law. This reality explains why symbolic representation in the White House often yields minimal material change. The mechanics matter more than the figurehead. The science matters more than the spook.

Judicial Branch (Courts)

The courts interpret but don't legislate. Yet their decisions create precedents that effectively eliminate certain policy options. The Supreme Court's Shelby County v. Holder decision gutted the Voting Rights Act by invalidating its coverage formula, creating a technical loophole that enabled a wave of restrictive voting laws in states with histories of discrimination.

This technical decision—focusing on a formula rather than the principle of voting rights—demonstrates how seemingly apolitical procedural rulings can have devastating racial impacts. The court didn't need to use racist language to achieve a result that disproportionately harmed Black voters.

The Filibuster: A Technical Shield

The filibuster represents the ultimate example of how technical procedures maintain racial hierarchy. Looking at the historical record reveals an unmistakable pattern:

Of thirty bills blocked by filibuster between 1917 and 1994, half involved civil rights. Anti-lynching bills died by filibuster in 1922 and 1935. Strom Thurmond's twenty-four-hour speech blocked the Civil Rights Act of 1957. The Civil Rights Act of 1964 required a sixty-day battle to overcome a filibuster. [1]

The filibuster's evolution in the 1970s made it even more potent as a tool of obstruction. [2] Instead of requiring marathon speeches, senators can now simply declare their intent to filibuster—a silent kill that attracts no public attention. This procedural change had mathematical

214

consequences: Filibusters exploded from an average of three per Congress to 293 under Biden.

The math exposes the system's design: Senators from the twenty-one least populous states—representing just 11 percent of the population and only 7 percent of the Black population—can block any legislation. By 2040, demographic projections indicate 30 percent of senators will represent 70 percent of Americans. This isn't random—it's a mathematical certainty based on population distribution and migration patterns.

The filibuster's impact on Black American interests is measurable and devastating. In recent years, it has blocked the Freedom to Vote Act of 2021–2022 (five separate times), the John R. Lewis Voting Rights Advancement Act of 2021, the George Floyd Justice in Policing Act of 2021, and economic justice initiatives. Meanwhile, voter suppression laws have been enacted in half of US states since 2020.

Beyond the Filibuster: Strategic Procedural Awareness

While the filibuster serves as a profound example, it's merely one technical procedure among many that shape political outcomes. Other critical procedural mechanisms include:

Budget Reconciliation: This process allows certain fiscal legislation to pass with a simple majority, bypassing the filibuster. Its specific rules determine which policies can advance and which remain blocked. Understanding these technical boundaries is essential for strategic policy advancement.

Committee Power: Legislation must navigate specific committees before reaching a floor vote. Committee chairs hold tremendous power to silently kill bills by simply refusing to schedule hearings. In the 117th Congress, 14,839 bills were introduced, but only three hundred and sixty-four became law—many died in committee without ever receiving consideration.

Conference Committees: When the House and Senate pass different versions of a bill, these committees reconcile the differences. Their negotiations often happen behind closed doors, allowing technical changes that can fundamentally alter legislation without public scrutiny.

Congressional Review Act: This technical procedure lets Congress repeal regulations within sixty legislative days of implementation. Its use has increased dramatically in recent years, becoming a powerful tool for reversing administrative actions without needing new legislation.

Unanimous Consent Agreements: The Senate operates largely through these procedural agreements, which accelerate or delay action. A single senator can object to unanimous consent, creating procedural barriers that consume valuable floor time.

As Obama said at John R. Lewis's funeral, the filibuster is a "Jim Crow relic." But understanding this isn't enough—we need to understand exactly how it and other procedures work to effectively fight them.

Our political analysis must incorporate procedural expertise, focusing on how the system actually functions rather than how we wish it would. We must track filibuster use and impact, study procedural rules and exceptions, build expertise in Senate operations, focus on technical fixes rather than just moral arguments, understand population dynamics driving minority rule, and identify strategic pressure points in the system.

We must also prioritize a path to getting rid of the filibuster altogether. This would require securing a simple majority in the Senate willing to change the chamber's rules—not the 60 votes needed to overcome a filibuster—and a compelling issue that makes the procedural change politically viable.

The Science

- **The filibuster = modern Jim Crow**: Technical procedure that has blocked civil rights legislation for over 150 years
- **Senate gives disproportionate power to rural white interests**: Wyoming (580K people) gets same Senate representation as California (39M people)
- 21 least populous states = 11% of population, 7% of Black population: Can block any legislation affecting the other 89% of Americans
- **Procedural mastery is revolutionary**: Understanding how the system actually works is essential for changing it
- While we focus on personalities, procedures quietly maintain inequality: Technical rules matter more than inspiring speeches

---

[1] Lau, Tim, "The Filibuster Explained," Brennan Center for Justice, April 26, 2021.

[2] Bedekovics, Greta, "How the Racist History of the Filibuster Lives on Today," Center for American Progress, April 29, 2024.

LESSON 25
Cabinet Architecture As Predictive

> *"The overflow of big money in politics drowns out the voices of everyday people. That is part of the conundrum in America: The more money you have, the more speech you have. That leaves everyday people out of the equation."* —Nina Turner

A leader may preach 'Hope and Change' but you better check their cabinet before expecting hope and change. Those cabinet picks—and their lobbyist ties, industry connections, and financial conflicts—tell the real story. If you want to know where a president is really going, don't listen to their speeches—study their cabinet. When Joe Biden stacked his administration with the leadership team from military lobbying firm WestExec Advisors and then quickly approved more than $100 billion for Ukraine, that wasn't coincidence—it was correlation. It's like the old saying: When you see a dog in the house, expect barking. [1]

The financial architecture is just as predictive. When you see a cabinet loaded with BlackRock or Goldman Sachs executives, you can expect heavy institutional bias and protection mechanisms to follow. It's like putting foxes in charge of chicken coop regulations—the outcome isn't just predictable; it's mathematically certain. These aren't just random appointments; they're structural guarantees of whose interests will be protected.

The equation is straightforward:

Military-Industry/Contractor Cabinet + Military Background = Military Spending and War

BlackRock/Goldman Sachs Cabinet + Wall Street Background = Financial Industry Protection

Tech Industry Cabinet + Tech Background = Tech Industry Protection

These cabinet selections consistently produce predictable results:

- Regulatory softening

- Industry-friendly policies

- Crisis protections for institutions, not people

- Revolving-door rewards

- Public risk, private profit

Obama's cabinet architecture told us everything we needed to know before it happened. When he filled his economic team with Wall Street insiders—Larry Summers, Tim Geithner, Rahm Emanuel, Gary Gensler, Michael Froman—why were we surprised that no bankers went to jail for the 2008 crisis? When Eric Holder, who built his career defending clients like UBS, became attorney general, the writing was on the wall. [2] Holder had also represented Purdue Pharma during the early stages of the opioid crisis, helping them avoid serious consequences while thousands of Americans were dying from addiction. The architecture guaranteed the outcome: Banks got bailed out while homeowners got foreclosed on. When you staff your financial oversight team with Goldman Sachs and BlackRock veterans, you're not building a regulatory body—you're constructing a protection racket. When big financial donors invest in a winning Presidential campaign, their expected return can often be heavily seen in the cabinet selections.

My conversation with Howard Franklin, a lobbyist who has represented Fortune 500 companies and ran Andre Dickens's successful Atlanta mayoral campaign, was revealing. Over lunch, he explained why Obama's campaign promises about fighting special interests were fundamentally spook. Obama, he suggested, simply didn't understand the brutal realities of Washington, DC's power structure. [3] He was selling a dream he couldn't possibly deliver.

K Street, Washington's lobbying epicenter, operates like a sophisticated mafia operation. Instead of violence, it uses money, connections, and legislative expertise to control outcomes. While Congress puts on public shows of debate, the real decisions are often made in K Street offices long before any vote. It's a quid pro quo system where policy goes to the highest bidder—just with better suits and fancier restaurants than traditional organized crime.

How serious of a problem is corruption?

How serious of a problem do you think corruption is among the following? (% of U.S. adult citizens)

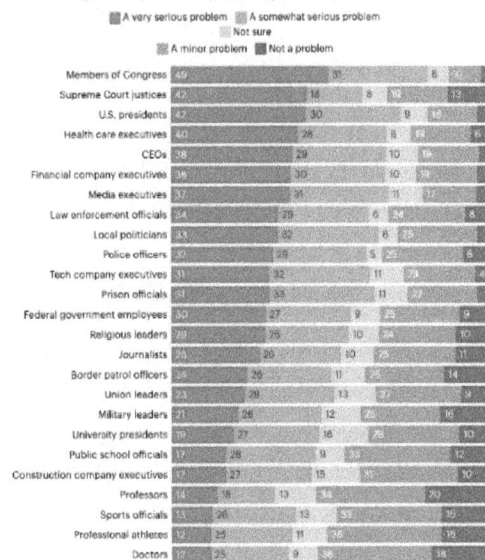

YouGov Survey on Corruption Perceptions - Shows Americans view Congress as most corrupt institution

The Scientific Method of Cabinet Analysis

1. **Look at Backgrounds**: Don't focus on what appointees say— study where they came from. A Goldman Sachs executive doesn't suddenly become a Wall Street reformer just because they take a government oath. When President Joe Biden nominated Goldman Sachs veteran Gary Gensler to be Chair of the Securities and Exchange Commission, you should automatically estimate small retail investors won't be the only folks protected by the regulator.

2. **Follow the Money Trail**: Track not just current positions but future opportunities. When cabinet members know their next job depends on current behavior, their choices become predictable.

3. **Study Power Networks**: Cabinet members aren't individual actors—they're nodes in influence networks. A BlackRock executive brings their entire network's interests into government.

4. **Watch Early Moves**: The first one hundred days of appointments tell you more about a presidency's true direction than four years of campaign promises.

Top 10 Fears of 2024

Fear	% of Very Afraid or Afraid	Rank in 2023	
1. Corrupt Government Officials	65.2%	1	
2. People I Love Becoming Seriously Ill	58.4%	5	⬆
3. Cyberterrorism	58.3%	9	⬆
4. People I Love Dying	57.8%	6	⬆
5. Russia Using Nuclear Weapons	55.8%	3	⬇
6. Not Having Enough Money for the Future	55.7%	10	⬆
7. US Becoming Involved in Another World War	55.0% (tie)	4	⬇
8. North Korea Using Nuclear Weapons	55.0% (tie)	12	⬆
9. Terrorist Attack	52.7%	16	⬆
10. Biological Warfare	52.5%	8	⬇

10th annual Chapman University Survey of American Fears (2024).

When Biden's cabinet architecture suggested military-industry alignment, the Ukraine funding followed predictably. When Obama's economic team came straight from Wall Street, bank protection was guaranteed. [4] The architecture orientation predicts the outcome with almost mathematical certainty.

For Black American political science, this means developing a more sophisticated analysis of cabinet appointments. We need to stop getting excited about the identity of appointments and start reading into power architecture. A Black face in a high place means nothing if they're structurally positioned to serve interests opposed to Black American progress.

The brutal truth is that cabinet architecture is often locked in before a president takes office. That's why Obama's anti-special-interest rhetoric was mostly spook—the architecture of his administration was predetermined by his funding sources.

This science gives us a powerful predictive tool. When we see military-industry executives from companies like Raytheon appointed to key positions, we can expect military spending to increase. [5] When we see Wall Street veterans in economic roles, we can expect financial industry protection. When BlackRock and Goldman Sachs alumni fill the economic teams, expect policies that protect financial power, not people. [6] The architecture tells the story before it happens. The articulate speeches may suggest a President is for the average person but the cabinet architecture and its orientation will tell you the truth, behind the scenes and underneath.

For future political strategy, we must focus on:

- Reading cabinet appointments as power signals
- Understanding network connections
- Predicting policy directions from personnel choices
- Recognizing structural limitations
- Planning responses based on architectural analysis

Howard Franklin's insight into Obama's naivety (or calculated deception) about fighting special interests reveals something crucial: You can't change a system while staffing it with the system's architects. Cabinet architecture isn't just descriptive—it's predictive. When you see the same Wall Street architects and financial engineers who crashed the economy in 2008 getting appointed to oversee financial regulation, you don't need a crystal ball to know what's coming.

The Science

- Cabinet appointments predict policy outcomes more accurately than campaign promises
- Military-industry executives = military spending; Wall Street veterans = financial protection
- Study appointees' previous employers and conflicts of interest to forecast administration priorities
- Focus on structural power rather than symbolic representation

[1] Bender, Bryan and Meyer, Theodoric, "The secretive consulting firm that's become Biden's Cabinet in waiting," Politico, November 23, 2020.

[2] Chittum, Ryan, "Going easy on Eric Holder's Wall Street inaction: Press coverage falls short on the attorney general's failure to prosecute fraud," Columbia Journalism Review, The Audit, September 26, 2014.

[3] Martin, Jamarlin, "Full Transcript: Corporate Lobbyist Howard Franklin On GHOGH Podcast Part 3," Moguldom, February 13, 2020.

[4] Huszar, Andrew, "Tim Geithner and the Revolving Door," The New Yorker, November 20, 2013.

[5] Bertuca, Tony, "Austin discloses financial ties to defense contractors," Inside Defense, January 11, 2021.

[6] Natarajan, Sridhar and Martin, Eric, "Biden Ties to BlackRock Deepen With Latest Treasury Hire," Bloomberg, August 11, 2022.

Paul Frymer: Black America Is Captured and Invisible

> *"Electoral capture is a process by which a group becomes locked into one party over a long period of time, resulting in a lack of political attention."* — Paul Frymer, Uneasy Alliances

> *"A slave who believes he has the same interests as his master will pick cotton at night."* —Kwame Ture

Have Democrats ever "put a ring on it"? Do they get all the political booty without the necessary and commensurate commitments to Black American voters? Are Democrats allowed to get inside our political underwear too easily?

The mathematics of political exploitation is simple: when you give one party 90 percent of your votes while living in fear of the other party winning, you have zero leverage. In a capitalist, hyper-efficient system, guaranteed votes mean guaranteed exploitation. The Democratic Party's logic is brutal but mathematically sound: Why take policy risks for a group that's already in our pocket and don't have any options?

Think of our political system as a predatory lending market where both parties charge Black Americans exorbitant interest rates on political capital. Republicans might charge a 75 percent interest rate through policies that actively harm, discount, and marginalize Black communities, while Democrats charge a 45 percent rate through neglect and minimal returns on our voting investment. Yes, 45 percent is better than 75 percent, but both are exploitative. The Democratic rate is still devastating compared with the 5 percent-10 percent rate they charge other constituencies who split their votes or act more strategically.

Our political challenge isn't just choosing the less bad interest rate—it's figuring out how to normalize these rates altogether. We've accepted predatory political lending terms for so long that we often think a 45 percent rate of neglect is the best we can get. But other groups have negotiated single-digit interest rates through strategic flexibility with their political capital.

Some say, "Don't vote," or "Switch to Republican to teach Democrats a lesson." But that has potential costs that need to be factored. It allows deep structural damage to Black American interests, especially at the Supreme Court level. The Science versus Spook framework doesn't offer easy answers, whether it's riding with Democrats till we die, staying home, or switching parties. Based on how America was originally designed, this malstructure means we're captured and invisible either way. We can choose to fundamentally restructure our political affairs and organization and gradually lower the adverse political interest rate we're being charged by both parties.

What we need is a finance approach to our political capital. When we vote 80-90 percent Democratic, without pre- negotiated support for a Black American political agenda, we're making a maximum investment with minimum returns.

Let's calculate the efficiency:

Political ROI = Policy Benefits Received / Voting Capital Invested

Democrats can mathematically determine that giving Black Americans 10 percent of what we want while taking 90 percent of our votes is a spectacularly efficient transaction—for them. This can't be explained by a racial factor alone; it's political capitalism.

This concept of "capture" isn't new—Malcolm X, Kwame Ture (Stokely Carmichael), and many Black American political scientists reached these conclusions decades ago. However, Princeton Professor Paul Frymer's analysis adds a white academic source outside Black America who has reached similar conclusions. When both the radical and the ivory tower identify the same problem, backed up with strong science, we better pay attention.

Frymer calls this "electoral capture"—when a political party can sideline minority interests while knowing they have nowhere else to go. Think of it like a predatory payday loan when you have no other options: the lender can exploit you precisely because you're trapped. Sure, you may not get evicted, your car repossessed or your home foreclosed by accepting a predatory loan but it's still predatory. Similarly, even if we think Democrats are far better than Republicans, what are we doing to force and demand the Democratic Party to stop being so predatory? To acknowledge we're politically captured and we must do something bold about it?

The mechanics of electoral capture rest on a foundation where limited choices breed loyalty that's exploited. Parties court "swing" voters while sidelining captured demographics. As journalist Farai Chideya puts it in her article title: "Black Voters Are So Loyal That Their Issues Get Ignored." Democrats fear that addressing specific Black concerns might alienate their broader base. Why commit to us when it might scare away undecided voters?

The evidence is damning. University of Chicago Law School research found that Black support for Congressional legislation actually decreased its chances of passage. As political scientist Nicholas Stephanopoulos documented: "As white support increases from 0% to 100%, the likelihood of adoption increases from about 10% to about 60%. As black support rises from 0% to 100%, though, the odds of enactment fall from roughly 40% to roughly 30%."

Let that sink in: legislation becomes less likely to pass when Black Americans support it. This isn't just anecdotal—it's proof of our captured status.

The numbers tell the story:

- Of Black Americans, 90 percent vote Democratic.

- Of Hispanic Americans, 52 percent identify as Independent.

- Jewish Americans show political flexibility.

- Result: Those with options (or a big wallet) often get more attention; we get taken for granted. We strike out on options and political wallet, reducing our leverage.

Frymer himself highlights this contrast: "There are other groups that vote heavily Democratic—Jewish voters, for instance—that are not ignored by either party. Both parties make strong appeals to Jewish voters with regards to Israel, for instance, without fear of destabilizing their broader coalition." The difference? Their vote isn't guaranteed, so both parties court them with concrete policy commitments.

Compare the political efficiency of different voting blocs:

Group	Voting Pattern	Policy Return	Political Efficiency
Black Americans	90% Democratic	Low	Poor
Hispanic Americans	60-65% Democratic	Medium	Moderate
Jewish Americans	65-75% Democratic	High	Excellent

The key difference? Voting flexibility creates leverage. Groups that can credibly threaten to withhold their votes receive better policy returns. How do we maximize our political investment returns regardless of which party holds power?

When we look at political returns through this interest rate framework, the goal becomes clearer: we need to reduce the political exploitation rate from both parties. Just as financial literacy helps communities escape predatory lending, political literacy and understanding can help us negotiate better terms. The Democrats' 45 percent neglect rate isn't acceptable just because it's better than the Republicans' 75 percent –

both are usurious compared to rates charged to voting blocs with more flexibility.

If there were such a thing as a political market regulator, they would step in and force the Democratic Party to lower their neglect rate due to the gross imbalance between what they receive from loyal Black American voters and what they deliver in return. Such a structure would be deemed abusive and exploitative in any regulated market – Democrats getting all the reward without commensurate risks.

According to Frymer, our loyalty, rather than being rewarded, has rendered us politically invisible. The party needs our votes but doesn't value our voice. We're like that partner who stays faithful while getting constantly played—no ring, no commitment, just exploitation.

When Democrats control both houses of Congress and the presidency, as they did in 2009-2010 under Obama and 2021-2022 under Biden, what specific, measurable policy advances materialized for Black Americans? Not what they promised—what they delivered. The calculation shows a negative return on our political investment. This isn't about punishing Democrats—it's about maximizing our returns regardless of which party is in power.

"What's the solution? First, we must acknowledge our captured state without sugarcoating it. Anyone selling easy answers is selling spook. Science is harder and takes longer.

A crucial step would be pressuring the Democratic Party to formally recognize Paul Frymer's analysis as valid. This isn't merely symbolic— official acknowledgment of Black Americans as a captured electorate in party documents would create accountability and establish a foundation for concrete negotiations. While the party would naturally resist admitting to such an advantageous arrangement, making this acknowledgment a consistent demand at every level of party engagement would begin shifting the power dynamic. We have to disarm the Democratic Party leadership from hiding behind how bad Republicans are and focus on what they have control over right now.

This isn't hopeless, but it requires the following:

1. **Intellectual Flexibility**

o   Testing new approaches

o   Questioning old loyalties

o   Exploring beyond two parties

2. **Collective Risk Tolerance**

o   Strategic election experiments

o   Willingness to lose some battles

o   Long-term thinking over short-term fears

3. **A Diversified Political Portfolio**

Instead of putting 90% of our political capital in one party, consider a more balanced approach:

o   60% traditional Democratic support

o   20% to building independent political infrastructure

o   15% to strategic primary challenges against ineffective Democrats

o   5% to cross-party negotiation for specific policy wins

This portfolio diversification approach is the political equivalent of refinancing a predatory loan. By demonstrating that we're willing to invest our political capital elsewhere, we create competition for our votes that can drive down the exploitation rate from both parties. The goal isn't getting Democrats to charge 40% instead of 45% – it's negotiating rates in the single digits like other politically savvy constituencies receive.

4. **Strategic Planning**

o   Multiparty exploration

o   Coalition building

o   Power accumulation

o   Creating Political Scorecards Against a Black American Agenda

Demanding Measurable Returns

When Democrats control the presidency and Congress:

- Require specific executive orders that align with a Black American Agenda

o Demand measurable economic program targets

o Establish concrete timelines for policy implementation

o Implement accountability systems for broken promises

If we lack a true understanding of how the American political machine works, deep inside its guts, this lack of understanding only sets up more exploitation by the Democratic Party. There's a path to becoming meaningfully less captured by Democrats. To become uncaptured, in totality, would likely require America to breakout of a two-party system into a multi-party system, permanently,

We're stuck in America's malstructure, but being stuck doesn't mean doing the same things, for the same results. Understanding our capture is the first step toward negotiating better terms for our political support.

Our flexibility with new ideas must match our desperate political condition. We have to take risks, and fail, and experiment, for substantial policy rewards.

If we don't have a powerful and well-financed K Street lobbying force, we must compensate through superior strategy and organization to reduce our capture rate—the degree to which a group becomes locked into one party with diminished political returns. Other voting blocs offset electoral or population limitations through lobbying strength—AIPAC doesn't need Jewish Americans to constitute 30% of the population because their sophisticated lobbying machine amplifies their influence far beyond their numbers.

Unlike Black Americans who face high neglect rates despite loyal voting, Jewish Americans enjoy what amounts to a 90% political surplus (my estimate)—receiving disproportionate policy attention and concrete outcomes relative to their population size. This group secures their political returns regardless of which party holds power. Without comparable financial resources at our disposal, we must maximize our strategic leverage to achieve similar independence from party-specific outcomes. We have to make up for a lack of political wallet size with hyper-strategy, political education, and organization, while building up a targeted lobbying wallet that is matched to a Black American agenda.

Black American politics is never as simple as 'Just Vote Democrat, MAGA BAD.' Our starting position should recognize that meaningful political returns require strategic risk-taking. The financial wisdom that 'scared money don't make money' applies equally to politics—a voting bloc that never demonstrates willingness to withhold support or redirect it strategically signals that it can be taken for granted.

Just as in finance, political rewards correspond to calculated risks. When we approach politics with excessive fear—fear of the opposing party, fear of 'wasting' votes, fear of short-term setbacks—we surrender our leverage before negotiations even begin. While financial and political marketplaces differ in their mechanics, both operate on the same fundamental principle: those unwilling to walk away from bad deals will consistently receive the worst terms.

Whether voting Democrat is the best choice at election time is a different question than what's the best strategy, political orientation, and negotiating position before election time. The fatal mistake is conflating these two questions. Voting against Democrats on Election Day might be mathematically irrational in some contexts, but negotiating like we might consider it isn't just rational—it's necessary for extracting optimal returns.

The truth hurts, but the spook kills. We're politically captured, but we're not politically hopeless—unless we keep lying to ourselves about our condition. Anyone teaching there are easy political solutions from a structurally captured state is selling spook. Spook offers easy and quick answers; science demands difficult, sustained effort. The path forward requires embracing uncomfortable truths rather than comforting illusions.

Our captured electorate situation is not impossible to change, but we will need intellectual flexibility to try new approaches, adopt more collective risk tolerance with elections for greater policy and structural rewards, and establish long-term thinking and strategic plans. One example of greater risk tolerance is taking more risks in the area of multiparty versus two-party elections—a willingness to fail to get closer to breaking out of the two-party system.

It's intellectually lazy to assume an Independent Black American political party takes away votes from Democrats in every instance. Such a party could vote with Democrats, at the right price and with the right terms. The key is thinking whether there is more leverage inside the party or outside the party, on a smaller scale before we think about national scale.

This independent party approach could start at the city and state level and build upward from there. Majority-Black American cities would provide natural starting points where such an effort could demonstrate effective governance while building the infrastructure needed for broader expansion.

Our flexibility with new ideas and approaches should be commensurate with our desperate collective political and economic development.

The Science

- Black Americans give 90% of votes while receiving minimal policy returns—a captured electorate
- Other groups maintain political flexibility and receive better policy outcomes
- Diversify political investment: 60% traditional support, 20% independent infrastructure, 15% primary challenges, 5% cross-party negotiations
- Demand measurable returns and concrete timelines from Democratic leadership

[1] Paul Frymer, "Uneasy Alliances: Race and Party Competition in America" (Princeton: Princeton University Press, 2010).

[2] Farai Chideya, "Black Voters Are So Loyal That Their Issues Get Ignored," FiveThirtyEight, September 9, 2016.

[3] University of Chicago Law School, "The Effect of Racial Support on Legislative Passage Rates," Journal of Political Science, Vol. 45 (2019).

[4] Marc Morial, "Building Political Capital Across Racial Lines," Interview with The Atlantic, March 2018.

[5] William A. Darity Jr., "How Barack Obama Failed Black Americans," The Atlantic, December 22, 2016.

When Small Numbers Are Better Than Large

> *"We're not outnumbered. We're outorganized."* —*Malcolm X*

Sometimes political power isn't about how many votes you have but about understanding where the system breaks. When eight House Republicans led by Matt Gaetz removed Kevin McCarthy as speaker in October 2023, they taught us something crucial about how power really works. They didn't need a majority—they just needed to understand leverage points.

Think about the math: In a House of 435 members, just eight Republicans changed everything. The final vote was 216–210, but those eight votes weren't just numbers—they perfectly placed pressure on a system's vulnerability. These eight understood something that mass movements often miss: Power often responds to precision and surgical vulnerabilities more than size.

The Science of Leverage

The principle operates everywhere in the American political system. Consider former Senators Joe Manchin III (West Virginia) and Kyrsten Sinema (Arizona) during Biden's presidency. Two senators—just 2 percent of the chamber—repeatedly blocked everything from voting rights to economic reforms. Even with Democrats holding nominal control, these two could halt the entire agenda. Not because they had mass support but because they understood system mechanics. These

Senators understood they had the winning poker hand, based on the math and how pressure points work.

In systems with narrow margins and specific pressure points, small numbers strategically applied create disproportionate impact.

The equation is straightforward: Political Power = (Number of Votes) × (Strategic Positioning) × (Willingness to Break Party Discipline)

Manchin and Sinema maximized all three variables. While representing just 2 percent of the Senate (2 out of 100 members), their votes were positioned at a critical junction (50–50 partisan split), and they repeatedly demonstrated willingness to break with their party on key votes. This transformed their minimal numerical representation into effective veto power over the entire progressive agenda.

The contrast is revealing: senators who reliably voted with their party gained committee assignments and internal influence but surrendered external leverage; Manchin and Sinema's strategic independence enabled them to single-handedly determine which legislation would advance or die. Their power came not from their numbers, but from their strategic position and willingness to withhold support.

The Israel lobby demonstrates the same principle through AIPAC. Despite Jewish Americans constituting just 2.4 percent of the population, their strategic concentration of resources on specific races and their willingness to primary non-compliant candidates creates grossly outsized influence. In the 2022 midterms, AIPAC spent $24 million, targeting specific races where small amounts could create maximum leverage. The result? Politicians respond to their priorities despite their small demographic footprint.

Precision Targeting

We can turn out 90 percent of Black votes for Democrats but still struggle to move even friendly administrations on core issues.

Consider the contrast:

- Eight Republicans removed a Speaker.
- Two senators blocked the presidential agenda.
- AIPAC can make or break specific candidates with targeted spending.
- Millions of Black votes struggle to move policy.

This isn't about copying Republican tactics—it's about understanding power mechanics. Those eight Republicans didn't just vote no; they identified a system vulnerability and applied precise pressure. They turned small numbers into massive leverage through a scientific understanding of pressure points.

The Freedom Caucus within the Republican Party operates on this principle constantly. With just 35–40 members in a 435-member House, they've repeatedly shaped GOP policy by targeting key procedural moments. Their power comes not from size but from strategic positioning and willingness to obstruct at precise vulnerability points. They understand that a small bloc voting as a unit has more influence than a large group voting inconsistently.

Applying Scientific Precision to Black American Political Power

What would Black American political power look like if we applied this same mathematical precision? Instead of just mobilizing mass votes, what if we identified key pressure points within the system? Instead of celebrating raw numbers, what if we studied specific vulnerabilities where small, strategically positioned actions could yield disproportionate results?

The science of political leverage demands focusing where our investment is greatest. While Democratic Party elites benefit from directing our attention toward Republican threats ("MAGA BAD"), scientific analysis reveals our primary leverage point exists within the party receiving 80-90% of our votes. The mathematically efficient question isn't "How do we stop Republicans?" but rather "What measurable returns are we receiving for our nearly monopolistic support of Democrats?"

Elijah Muhammad, the Nation of Islam leader who built Black American institutions when few others would, observed that it was illogical for both the slave and slavemaster to have the same religion. This fundamental insight about divergent interests applies directly to contemporary politics: if wealthy DNC insiders direct 100% of their attention toward MAGA, it's a strong signal that Black American attention should be directed toward them. Our focus and priorities cannot logically match those of the rulers and lobbyists who control the Democratic Party while delivering minimal returns on our investment.

Consider a football team analogy: effective teams don't put all their players in the same position pursuing the same objective. While mainstream Democrats play quarterback against Republicans and MAGA, Black American political strategy would be more effective playing offensive line or running back - focused on restructuring our positioning within the Democratic Party and holding them accountable for specific deliverables.

The status quo benefits when Black America remains fixated on 'MAGA BAD' alongside everyone else. In contrast, Black Americans benefit when we focus on the party receiving our overwhelming electoral support in every election. Democrats haven't been taking just a 10% tithe of our political offering- they've been collecting 90% of our votes while delivering disproportionately small returns.

Let others focus on defeating the opposing team; our mission should be securing Black American-specific touchdowns within the party's priorities.

This precision targeting represents a fundamental shift: from outward-focused defense (which benefits party elites and the status quo) to inward-focused accountability (which benefits Black Americans). The scientific approach recognizes that optimizing returns from existing investments is more efficient than perpetually defending against external threats while internal exploitation continues unchallenged.

We don't need the traditional "Black Unity" for unity's sake. A smaller, more strategic group or organization can be more effective than another group that has 100 times more bodies. A more strategic approach around goals and political science is almost always better than unity based on spook. The blind pursuit of mass unity often dilutes our message and prevents the tactical flexibility needed for pressure point politics. Better to have 1,000 highly organized, strategically positioned members than 100,000 loosely affiliated supporters without a precise understanding of leverage points.

Here's how the science of small numbers could transform Black American political strategy:

1. **Target Critical Primaries**: Identify 5-10 Democratic primaries where Black votes could be decisive and apply maximum pressure.

2. **Create Strategic Voting Blocs**: Develop disciplined voting units willing to withhold support at critical moments.

3. **Focus on Procedural Leverage**: Study congressional rules and procedures to identify chokepoints where small numbers can have maximum impact.

4. **Cultivate Strategic Champions**: Instead of broad symbolic representation, develop specific representatives positioned at key committee and leadership junctions.

5. **Practice Precision Disruption**: Master targeted disruption of specific processes rather than general protests against overall systems.

The Tactical Reality of Power Mechanics

This requires a fundamental shift in thinking. Mass mobilization matters, but system analysis matters more. We need to study not just how to turn out votes but where those votes can apply maximum pressure. We need to understand not just how to fill streets but how to find switches.

The McCarthy ouster wasn't just a political event—it was a master class in power mechanics. Those eight Republicans showed that understanding system pressure points can multiply force far beyond raw numbers. That's not theory—that's tactical reality.

Similarly, when the Congressional Black Caucus (CBC) threatened to block President Biden's infrastructure bill unless voting rights legislation advanced, they demonstrated an understanding of pressure point politics. By identifying a specific moment of leverage—a must-pass bill with tight margins—they translated their small numbers into potential veto power. The approach showed promise, though execution proved inconsistent.

Next time you hear about the power of the Black vote, remember: power isn't just about how many you can mobilize but also about understanding where and how to apply pressure. Eight Republicans and two Democratic senators have shown us the mathematics of leverage.

This isn't about abandoning mass movements—it's about adding precision to our power. Until we understand both mass and mechanics, we'll keep counting votes while others count victories.

The Science

- Strategic positioning matters more than raw numbers (8 Republicans removed McCarthy as Speaker)
- Target critical primaries and procedural leverage points for maximum impact
- Focus on precision rather than mass mobilization
- Study system vulnerabilities where small, organized groups can create disproportionate change

[1] Lisa Mascaro and Farnoush Amiri, "Speaker McCarthy ousted in historic House vote," Associated Press, October 3, 2023.

[2] Tim O'Donnell, "Just How Much Leverage Does Joe Manchin Actually Have?" The Week, February 7, 2021.

[3] David Smith, "How Manchin and Sinema's Status as Senate Holdouts Is Proving Lucrative," The Guardian, November 28, 2021.

[4] Chris McGreal, "Pro-Israel Groups Denounced After Pouring Funds Into Primary Race," The Guardian, August 4, 2022.

LESSON 28
AIPAC: Political Groomers

"You're talking about a lot of students who grew up in a socioeconomic place that does not give them these opportunities. We met amazing people. I met Netanyahu. In 2007 or 2008, I met all the Democratic candidates for president. My dad cried when I met Obama. [AIPAC] opens your eyes to things you've never seen."
—Vincent Evans, Florida A&M Alumni [1]

"Everybody but me has an AIPAC person. It's like your babysitter, your AIPAC babysitter, who's always talking to you for AIPAC."
—Republican Congressman Thomas Massie (Kentucky) [2]

The penalties for breaking from the American Israel Public Affairs Committee (AIPAC)'s influence and control extend to the highest levels of American government. Even President Barack Obama faced accusations of antisemitism when he disagreed with Netanyahu's government over the Iran nuclear deal. "Of course," he acknowledged when asked if such charges hurt him personally. "And there's not a smidgen of evidence for it, other than the fact that there have been times when I've disagreed with a particular Israeli government's position on a particular issue." [3]

This reveals a crucial mechanism of influence maintenance: the social and emotional cost of dissent. When even a sitting president can be labeled antisemitic for policy disagreements with Israel, the chilling effect on less powerful political figures becomes clear. The mathematical calculation becomes Disagreement = Personal Smear, creating a powerful deterrent against independent policy positions. Most politicians lack Obama's political capital to weather such accusations. For CBC members who depend on coalition support, the calculus becomes even more constraining.

MLK's Ghost: The CBC's Moral Collapse

The Congressional Black Caucus's politically perverted relationship with AIPAC represents how far Black American political leadership has drifted from the moral courage of Martin Luther King Jr. While contemporary politicians operate within institutional constraints that Dr. King didn't face, the gulf between today's leadership and King's moral courage has expanded to indefensible proportions. We cannot expect elected officials to match King's prophetic voice, but the distance between political expediency and principled leadership has grown from a gap to a chasm.

King's stance on Vietnam demonstrated his willingness to risk relationships and funding by speaking the moral truth: "A time comes when silence is betrayal... I cannot be silent." By contrast, today's CBC leaders remain conspicuously silent as AIPAC systematically targets their own members. The modern Black American politician must think about AIPAC's position before considering what's morally right or in the best interest of Black Americans.

The defenders of this arrangement often say, "This is just how the system works"—the ultimate confession of moral surrender. But if this is how the system works, then our leadership has a responsibility to offer a vision of how it can work better. King didn't accept the system as given—he challenged it at its foundations.

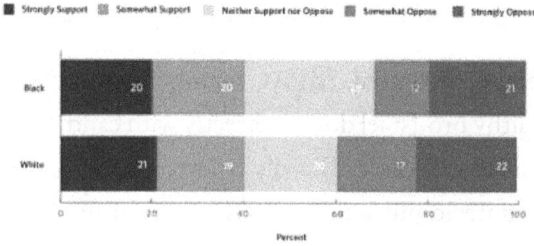

Figure 7. Support for U.S. Financial Aid to Israel

Q: In 2022, the United States provided $3.3 billion of foreign assistance to Israel. In the past few weeks, President Biden has said that he would like to provide an additional $14 billion in aid to Israel. How strongly do you support sending additional U.S. aid to Israel?

■ Strongly Support ▩ Somewhat Support ░ Neither Support nor Oppose ▨ Somewhat Oppose ■ Strongly Oppose

Black: 20 | 20 | 17 | 12 | 21
White: 21 | 39 | 30 | 17 | 22

N = 800 Black American adults | N = 800 White American adults
Source: 2023 Israel-Hamas war survey conducted October 20-25, 2023
Note: Totals may not equal 100% due to rounding.

Support for U.S. Financial Aid to Israel by Race - Shows similar patterns between Black and White Americans

The MAGA Double Standard

Democratic politicians consistently tell Black Americans, "MAGA is bad," while remaining conspicuously silent about Netanyahu's MAGA-equivalent government in Israel. This isn't just hypocrisy—it's mathematical evidence of AIPAC's influence transcending normal political boundaries.

When former Mossad director Tamir Pardo states that Netanyahu's government includes partners "worse than the Ku Klux Klan," yet American politicians who condemn white nationalism at home remain silent about it in Tel-Aviv, we're witnessing AIPAC's cross-partisan influence in action. This political double standard isn't inconsistency—it's a mathematical demonstration of influence power. The equation is clear: Political Positions = Financial Consequences, and this equation transcends party lines and ideological commitments.

AIPAC's Financial Influence System

Beyond official PAC donations and direct lobbying, AIPAC has perfected a third, far more powerful influence channel: coordinated individual giving that remains largely invisible in campaign finance records. This shadow donation network represents a mathematical amplifier that extends AIPAC's financial reach far beyond its reported numbers. [4]

The mechanics are sophisticated: AIPAC maintains extensive donor lists and connects wealthy pro-Israel donors directly with candidates, creating a financial pipeline that doesn't officially count as "AIPAC money" but serves the same strategic purpose. AIPAC's fundraising infrastructure allows it to bundle individual donations without triggering reporting requirements that would identify them as AIPAC-directed.

Contrary to some beliefs, AIPAC does not directly fund political campaigns, which would contravene legal regulations. Yet a former AIPAC staff member, M.J. Rosenberg, posits that political fundraising remains integral to the group's activities: "AIPAC does not engage in political fundraising because that would be illegal. It does not directly raise money to support or defeat candidates, but that is just a technicality. Political fundraising is a huge part of AIPAC's operation." [5]

This coordination isn't limited to financial contributions. AIPAC has created an ecosystem where candidates understand that supporting certain positions unlocks not just official PAC money but also this shadow network of individual donors. The equation is clear: policy positions = financial support, creating a system where candidates understand the unwritten rules of accessing this parallel funding structure.

Silence in the Face of Targeting

One of the most revealing aspects of AIPAC's influence is the silence of the Congressional Black Caucus as its own members are systematically targeted. The CBC's leaders, most of whom are AIPAC beneficiaries, have maintained a deafening silence as progressive Black American members face unprecedented financial attacks.

House Democratic Caucus Leader Hakeem Jeffries, who has received $485,300 from AIPAC since 2022, exemplifies this contradiction.

Despite leading congressional efforts to protect incumbents against primary challengers, Jeffries has remained largely silent on AIPAC's targeting of fellow CBC members.

Pro-Israel lobby donations to Hakeem Jeffries

Pro-Israel America *Your Portal for Political Action* $213,450.00

$115,650.00

AIPAC $72,780.00

Pro-Israel Lobby Donations to Hakeem Jeffries - Shows over $400,000 from three organizations

The imbalance of this relationship is staggering: Black American congressional leaders like Jeffries are 300 times more likely to support Netanyahu's policies than AIPAC is to support any actionable policy for Black Americans. If the Black American politician doesn't align with AIPAC's positions, they get labeled antisemitic and face millions of dollars in opposition funding. Their career could be over by expressing the moral and foreign policy values of Dr. Martin King Jr. As soon as one of the tap dancing and shoe shining CBC members gets out of line on foreign policy, they know very well AIPAC will be coming to shoot up the political block, right away or at the next election. The Black American strategic response to this level of control is creating a financial resource to support good Black American candidates, to have the freedom to represent us and their districts better, without fear of the AIPAC lobby coming to primary them or shoot up their political block by sending huge sums of money to "AIPAC'd out" opponents.

We must evangelize a broader truth: AIPAC's influence creates a political filter that not only conflicts with Black American interests but threatens democratic principles fundamental to all Americans. By controlling who can be viably elected through targeted financial intervention, this organization exercises disproportionate domestic control despite its foreign-focused interests.

This reality transcends any single community's concerns - it represents a direct challenge to constitutional integrity and American sovereignty. When elected officials fear representing their constituents' interests on certain issues due to guaranteed financial retaliation from a specific lobbying group, the basic representative function of our democracy is compromised. Black Americans must frame this not just as our issue, but as a constitutional issue that undermines the sovereignty of all American voters.

As Republican congressman Thomas Massie bluntly stated: "Everybody but me has an AIPAC person. It's like your babysitter, your AIPAC babysitter." [6] This babysitter dynamic extends to CBC members who receive financial support but never demand substantive reciprocity.

Democratic strategist Camille Rivera captured a contradiction: "The CBC should be sounding the alarm (On AIPAC shooting up the political block) and should be concerned. We need to be very careful about letting power and influence change the overall goal of the caucus, which is to protect Black incumbents and expand representation, especially those that have been doing the work and representing their constituents. We shouldn't let any entity try to divide and conquer."

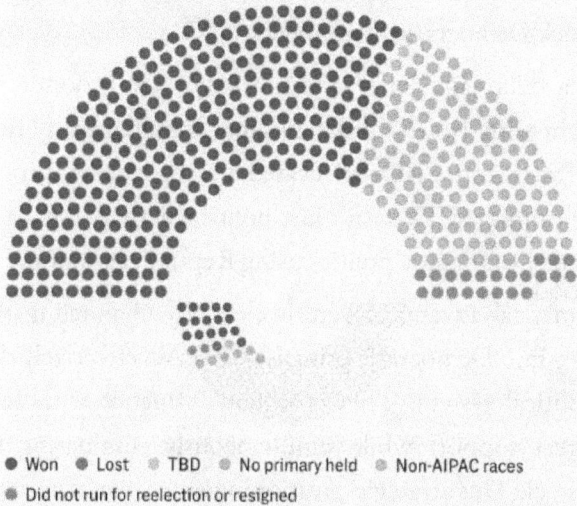

AIPAC was involved in 389 races, including 26 Senate races and 363 House races.

Won • Lost • TBD • No primary held • Non-AIPAC races
• Did not run for reelection or resigned

In 88 races, AIPAC-backed candidates faced no opponent.

AIPAC's Electoral Influence Visualization - Shows involvement in 389 races with high success rate

The Funding Game: Republican Money in Democratic Primaries

What gives AIPAC's strategy additional sophistication is its ability to deploy Republican money to shape Democratic primary outcomes. This isn't just cross-partisan influence—it's a mathematical hack of the electoral system that reveals the true mechanics of American politics.

AIPAC's United Democracy Project has pumped millions of dollars from right-wing billionaires and Trump supporters into Democratic primaries to defeat progressive candidates. [7] Representative Summer Lee (Pennsylvania) directly addressed this dynamic: "AIPAC funneled money from Republican billionaires to spend $5 million attacking me with baseless lies and racist tactics." She noted the irony that AIPAC supports scores of "insurrectionist" Republicans who shared "the same goals as a mob of armed white supremacists and antisemites" while targeting Black Democratic incumbents.

Pennsylvania billionaire Jeffrey Yass, a major GOP donor who funds hard-line right-wing Israeli think tanks, has simultaneously funded both AIPAC's efforts and PACs dedicated to challenging progressives in Democratic primaries. This isn't just political activity—it's a systematic effort to shape Democratic politics using Republican money.

The mathematical advantage here is clear: By channeling Republican donor money into Democratic primaries, AIPAC effectively double-dips into the political system. They maintain influence with Republicans through direct support while simultaneously eliminating Democrats critical of Israel. This strategic positioning ensures maximum influence regardless of which party controls government.

Strategic Targeting of Black Progressives

In 2024, AIPAC executed a takedown of progressive Black representatives Jamaal Bowman and Cori Bush. Through its super PAC, United Democracy Project (UDP), AIPAC spent $8.5 million to defeat Bush—Missouri's first Black American female representative—and millions more to oust Bowman in New York. [8]

What makes AIPAC's strategy against Black progressives particularly revealing is its surgical precision. According to multiple investigations, the only incumbents AIPAC targeted in the 2024 election cycle were members of the Congressional Black Caucus. The CBC itself has been silent on these challenges against its own members.

AIPAC Campaign Against "Anti-Israel" Candidates - Shows targeted efforts against progressive Democrats

Even more troubling are the tactics employed. In attacks against Bush, the United Democracy Project was accused of distributing campaign materials that appeared to alter Bush's appearance, enlarging her forehead and chin while lightening her skin. Bush was direct in her assessment: "It is shameful that in 2024, our communities are still being targeted with such blatant racism from political campaigns." Similar tactics were reportedly used against Bowman, with ads darkening his skin.

Groomers: The Cultivation Pipeline

AIPAC's targeted outreach to historically Black colleges and universities (HBCUs) showcases its strategic investment in future leadership. This isn't just outreach—it's political talent scouting on a sophisticated scale.

Vincent Evans's experience illustrates this approach: "Within the program, they make a concerted effort to reach out to HBCU and majority Hispanic schools." For a student from Florida A&M University like Evans, being approached with an offer for an all-expenses-paid trip to DC was an unparalleled opportunity.

Bakari Sellers's story reveals the long-term ROI of this recruitment. First approached by AIPAC while at Morehouse College, Sellers's relationship with AIPAC continued through his political ascent. Sellers candidly acknowledged AIPAC's role: "The way I'm able to communicate, the exposure, the people that I've met – a lot of people I've met at the AIPAC policy conference became a huge part of my fundraising base."

As part of my research for Science vs Spook, I interviewed multiple prominent Black American political figures and they told me how they were flown out to Israel multiple times and how the AIPAC system worked. The HBCU students are put up in four and five star hotels, given access to the AIPAC professional network, and become politically "turned out" for their entire career. The sophisticated AIPAC operations create political capital debt with HBCU political talent that has to be paid back later. If Black American politicians are being groomed and recruited early for foreign interests, we should be paying close attention, not to their identity but to who is underneath them, controlling them, and how this impacts Black American interests. It's impossible to truly understand the science in Black American political science without understanding how foreign-minded influence networks interact with Black American political interests. The costs and benefits.

Minnesota Congresswoman Ilhan Omar criticized AIPAC's influence, Sellers appeared on CNN and called her comments "ignorant" without disclosing his long-standing AIPAC relationship. This is the pipeline at work: Recruit talent early, provide resources and connections, cultivate long-term relationships, and strategically deploy these voices when needed.

A lot of the Black American political leaders and pundits you see on CNN and MSNBC have been professionally groomed and cultivated like Sellers. This is why the Science-versus-Spook framework encourages us to look underneath things and people to better understand their political orientation. Going underneath is connected to understanding. This will help protect us from so much tricknology and spook in the game of politics.

Cory Booker is another politician that is what I call "AIPAC'd out." The New Jersey senator was also cultivated early. He told an AIPAC conference the following, to applause:

"Don't fall prey to cynical attempts to try to pit members of this great organization against the Democratic Party... Israel is not political to me. It's not political. I was a supporter of Israel well before I was a United States senator. I was coming to AIPAC conferences well before I knew that one day I would be a federal officer. If I forget thee, oh Israel, may I cut off my right hand." [9]

Politicians such as Sellers and Booker are not bad people or politicians because they were identified and groomed early by AIPAC's recruitment arm, we just have to discount what they have to say on specific issues and understand their foreign priorities may conflict with Black American interests. They will kneecap Black American interests before AIPAC interests.

The Science of Institutional Influence

AIPAC's approach reveals the science behind effective power accumulation through multiple layers of system influence:

TOP 10 2024 AND CAREER RECIPIENTS OF PRO-ISRAEL PAC FUNDS

Compiled From OpenSecrets

HOUSE: CURRENT RACES		SENATE: CURRENT RACES	
Latimer, George (D-NY)	$1,633,912	Menendez, Robert (D-NJ)	$1,103,810
Torres, Ritchie (D-NY)	$1,229,070	Rosen, Jacky (D-NV)	$754,275
Gottheimer, Josh (D-NJ)	$827,224	Cruz, Ted (R-TX)	$671,578
Bell, Wesley (D-MO)	$827,094	Schiff, Adam (D-CA)	$548,971
Jeffries, Hakeem (D-NY)	$782,116	Tester, Jon (D-MT)	$497,082
Schiff, Adam (D-CA)	$548,971	Casey, Bob (D-PA)	$492,689
Aguilar, Pete (D-CA)	$494,692	Gillibrand, Kirsten (D-NY)	$459,382
Schultz, Debbie Wasserman (D-FL)	$404,608	Wicker, Roger (R-MS)	$398,444
McCaul, Michael (R-TX)	$396,834	Fischer, Deb (R-NE)	$378,668
Stefanik, Elise (R-NY)	$383,537	Cramer, Kevin (R-ND)	$350,740

HOUSE: CAREER		SENATE: CAREER	
Hoyer, Steny H (D-MD)	$1,736,244	Menendez, Robert (D-NJ)	$2,500,005
Gottheimer, Josh (D-NJ)	$1,697,263	McConnell, Mitch (R-KY)	$1,953,910
Latimer, George (D-NY)	$1,633,912	Schumer, Charles E (D-NY)	$1,725,324
Torres, Ritchie (D-NY)	$1,571,087	Cruz, Ted (R-TX)	$1,509,359
Jeffries, Hakeem (D-NY)	$1,367,247	Wyden, Ron (D-OR)	$1,280,376
Schneider, Brad (D-IL)	$1,346,167	Durbin, Dick (D-IL)	$1,129,520
Brown, Shontel (D-OH)	$1,091,836	Rubio, Marco (R-FL)	$1,013,563
Stevens, Haley (D-MI)	$990,064	Rosen, Jacky (D-NV)	$1,002,413
Schultz, Debbie Wasserman (D-FL)	$907,284	Graham, Lindsey (R-SC)	$1,000,580
Bacon, Donald John (R-NE)	$829,976	Romney, Mitt (R-UT)	$ 976,493

Washington Report on Middle East Affairs, June/July 2024, p. 28

Top Recipients of Pro-Israel PAC Funds - Shows bipartisan funding patterns across Congress

1. **Bipartisan Penetration**: While Black Americans remain captured by one party, AIPAC maintains influence regardless of which party controls government.

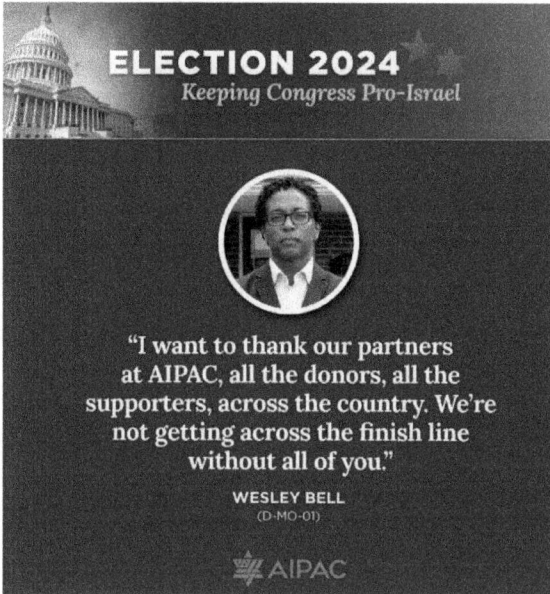

ELECTION 2024
Keeping Congress Pro-Israel

"I want to thank our partners at AIPAC, all the donors, all the supporters, across the country. We're not getting across the finish line without all of you."

WESLEY BELL
(D-MO-01)

AIPAC

AIPAC Instagram Endorsement Post - Shows AIPAC's endorsement of House leadership teams from both parties

2. **Strategic Resource Allocation**: Rather than spreading resources thinly, AIPAC concentrates firepower on specific races and targeted campaigns.

3. **Pipeline Development**: Long-term cultivation of political talent ensures institutional memory and continuation of influence.

4. **Narrative Control**: Effectively frames criticism of Israel as antisemitism, creating powerful rhetorical shields against policy challenges.

5. **Distributed Network Structure**: Operates through both direct and indirect influence channels, creating redundant systems of power.

This isn't just another lobbying operation—it's a master class in strategic influence that demonstrates exactly what Black American political organization lacks. It's lazy to say "it's just AIPAC is white with a big wallet" as our strategic and organizational orientation isn't where needs to be, before we even get to wallet size. Even if we developed a sophisticated AIPAC-like political operation in a single state like Georgia, with strong HBCU infrastructure, it could be a model for other Black Americans in other states or it can be scaled to additional states after proven success. There is no excuse why we don't have a comparable organizational operation to AIPAC in single state. Under the Science vs Spook framework, it's better to build our own AIPAC in a single city or state than bang on AIPAC and Jewish people with rhetoric and social media posts. They are out their banging for theirs and we can do the same, even if we start on a small scale.

Lessons for Black American Politics

What would Black American political power look like if it applied AIPAC's principles?

1. **Bipartisan Engagement**: Developing meaningful influence in both parties rather than being captured by one.

2. **Strategic Resource Concentration**: Targeting specific races and issues where small investments can yield maximum returns.

3. **Leadership Pipeline Development**: Creating systematic programs to identify, support, and elevate future political talent.

4. **Narrative Framing**: Developing powerful rhetorical frameworks that shape how issues are discussed.

5. **Cross-party Funding Strategies**: Developing legal structures that allow strategic deployment of resources across party lines.

The contrast between AIPAC's approach and current Black American political strategy highlights the scientific to political power. AIPAC has built a precision-targeted system that maximizes returns on political investment. Whether a Black American political science student knows it or not, we are not only captured by the two-party system but also constrained by AIPAC's tight control over our political representatives.

A Black American with the character, courage, independence, intelligence, and political understanding of Dr. Martin Luther King Jr. would never be able to make it far in politics today, as AIPAC would likely stop him. Dr. Martin Luther King Jr. always started with what's right and what's right for Black America, not what's right for AIPAC. Although MLK wasn't a politician and politicians face stricter limitations, it should be a priority to create more room and support for MLK-like, independent-minded Black American political leaders.

AIPAC's presence on HBCU campuses runs deeper than any Black American political organization including the NAACP, which should be a wakeup call about organizational priorities. AIPAC is aggressively entering our paint and dunking on us in organizational recruitment and strategic operations. The science of political influence requires moving beyond emotional affiliation to strategic targeting. Until Black American political capital is deployed with similar precision and strategic focus that AIPAC demonstrates, we'll continue to receive minimal returns on our maximum voting investment.

With recent artificial intelligence innovations in voter targeting, message testing, and organizational management, it would take significantly less capital and fewer employees to build effective Black American political operations today than would have been required even five years ago.

It's notable that AIPAC (and other Pro-Israel lobby groups) represent a specific political approach, not Jewish Americans as a whole. Many Jewish Americans actively oppose both Netanyahu's policies and AIPAC's influence operations. This internal diversity demonstrates another key lesson: Focused organization consistently outperforms demographic uniformity. What matters isn't universal agreement within a community, but the strategic organization of those committed to specific goals.

The science is clear: Political effectiveness isn't determined by demographic size but by strategic positioning, organizational efficiency, and tactical precision. While financial resources matter, AIPAC's cross-partisan influence ensures that regardless of which party controls the government, their priorities remain at the very top of the agenda—the ultimate expression of small numbers being better than large in political practice. Remember it's lazy to focus exclusively on AIPAC's wallet size; their true advantage lies in the sophistication of their operational model and relationship cultivation system.

The Science

- AIPAC operates through early recruitment, long-term cultivation, and cross-partisan influence
- Black American politicians are often "AIPAC'd out" from college, creating permanent conflicts of interest
- We need comparable organizational infrastructure and strategic recruitment programs
- Build independent funding sources to protect leaders from foreign lobby influence

---

[1] Kathryn J. Prince, "Student leaders at historically Black US colleges join Israel advocacy effort," The Times of Israel, July 11, 2020.

[2] "Hakeem Jeffries, Campaign Committee Fundraising, 2021-2022," Open Secrets.

[3] Nick Gass, "Obama: It hurts when people call me antisemitic," Politico, August 31, 2015.

[4] Eric Fingerhut, "How AIPAC makes friends," Jewish Standard, January 23, 2009.

[5] M.J. Rosenberg, "This Is How AIPAC Really Works," The Nation, February 14, 2019.

[6] Thomas Massie, Interview with Tucker Carlson, "Tucker Carlson Tonight," Fox News, April 15, 2022.

[7] "Pro-Israel: Top Recipients," Open Secrets, 2014.

[8] Akela Lacy, "AIPAC Used Distorted Photo of Cori Bush in $7 Million Negative Ad Blitz," The Intercept, July 31, 2024.

[9] Alex Emmons, "In Leaked Recording, Cory Booker Says He And AIPAC President 'Text Message Back And Forth Like Teenagers'," The Intercept, March 30, 2019.

Asymmetrical Information and Tom Scotto

> *"You guys (the police) sat at that conference table of mine for a six-month period, and you wrote the bill."*
> — *Former President Joe Biden*

One of the most pernicious defenses of the 1994 crime bill is the oft-cited Gallup poll showing 58% of Black Americans supported it.[1] This statistical shield represents a profound misunderstanding of asymmetrical information and its impact on public opinion.

Here's the science: It's impossible to meaningfully "support" legislation when deliberately kept in the dark about its true authorship and intentions. Black Americans weren't told that police unions were literally writing the bill in Ron Klain and Biden's office. They weren't informed that Tom Scotto, president of the National Association of Police Organizations, was crafting provisions that would later devastate their communities.[2] They weren't shown the architectural blueprints for mass incarceration being drafted by the very institutions with historical patterns of bias against them. No one shared probabilities that states would likely follow Clinton, the federal lead on the issue.

If the Gallup poll had asked, "Do you support a crime bill written by the police, who you think are racists," the answers would have been dramatically different. Of course, the crime bill came just a few years after Rodney King was almost beaten to death on camera in 1991. When there is too much mystery in a question—like who actually designed the bill and how one-sided it is—the question itself is spook.

This isn't just an information gap—it's a form of political fraud. When someone asks you to support a "community safety bill" while hiding that it was authored by police interests seeking expanded power and budgets, your support isn't informed consent—it's manufactured through deception.

Supporting a vague concept of "addressing crime" is fundamentally different from supporting specific policy mechanisms like three-strikes provisions, prison expansion, and militarized policing. When crime was devastating communities, of course Black Americans wanted solutions. But being pro-solution doesn't mean endorsing any proposed remedy, especially one crafted by entities with a vested interest in expanding their own power rather than addressing root causes.

The real tricknology in the 1994 crime bill was presenting police-authored provisions as community-centered reforms, then using Black 'support' as retroactive cover for the devastating consequences that followed. The potential catastrophic risks of what might happen if this legislation went very wrong were never accurately valued or carefully considered by those promoting it. What Black Americans weren't told was that if the police-written bill produced unintended consequences, those consequences would have a generational impact disproportionately affecting our communities.

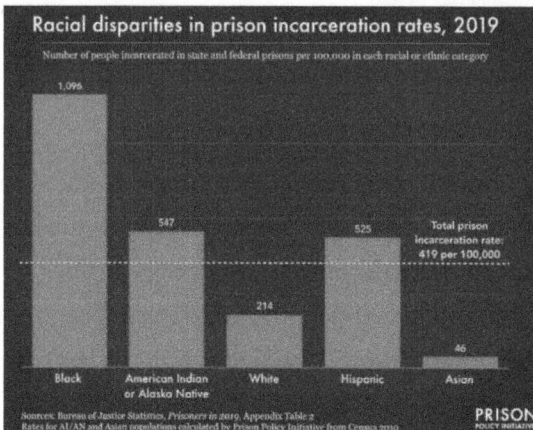

Prison Incarceration Rates by Race (2019) - Shows Black Americans incarcerated at 5x the rate of whites

The Hidden Calculus of System Protection

Consider these painful equations:

- Community Pain + Hidden Police Authorship = Destructive Policy
- Public Fear + Private Police Power = Generational Damage
- Urgent Needs + Police-Written Solutions = System Expansion

When Biden claims the bill's direct impact was limited because it only affected federal incarceration, he's obscuring how power actually operated. [3]Scotto and police interests didn't just write federal policy—they created a blueprint for states to follow. They understood that federal action sends signals that reshape state behavior through both policy and funding incentives.

The bill's police-authored architecture reveals its true purpose:

- Subsidies were established for state prison expansion
- Three-strikes laws spread across systems
- Mandatory minimums became standard
- Juvenile prosecution as adults increased
- Military gear flooded local departments
- Education was abolished through Pell Grants
- Prosecution powers were enhanced

This wasn't accidental. Scotto and police interests understood that states follow federal signals, especially when backed by funding incentives. They knew that allowing thirteen-year-olds to be federally tried as adults would normalize this practice at the state level. They recognized that sending military equipment to local police would transform community policing nationwide.

By the time the crime bill's funds reached states and cities in 1995, violent crime was already declining, driven by changes in drug markets and other factors completely unrelated to Clinton's tough-on-crime campaign. [4]

Yet the police-written legislation reshaped American criminal justice anyway. Why? Because federal power works through both direct action and system encouragement.

When analyzing generational damage to Black Americans such as the 1994 crime bill that Clinton signed and Biden championed, always look for the 'mystery factor' - the critical information deliberately kept from public understanding. What specific knowledge was being hidden? Where did the affected population lack true scientific understanding of potential consequences?

Equally important is examining incentive structures. Political careers were built on this legislation through false attribution of credit for crime reduction. There were powerful political incentives for Clinton and Biden to sacrifice Black American interests, as they received immediate political benefits from both Democratic and Republican voters who responded positively to 'tough on crime' positioning.

The Four Areas of Consensus: Where Real Power Lives

American politics often appears as a theater of conflict between Democrats and Republicans. But beneath the performance lies a deeper truth: Real power operates where the parties agree, not where they fight. Four areas of consensus reveal where the system protects itself with perfect efficiency.

First, consider corporate power. When Wall Street, Big Tech, or major corporations need something, partisan bickering mysteriously vanishes. Whether it's Goldman Sachs during the 2008 bank bailouts or Facebook during privacy debates, the system moves with one voice. Google (Alphabet), BlackRock, and JPMorganChase don't just have influence— they have consensus power.

The mathematics are precise:

- Corporate Money + Bipartisan Agreement = Swift Action

- Wall Street Needs + Party Unity = System Protection

- Tech Giant Demands + Political Consensus = Guaranteed Results

- Israel Violating International Law, Committing War Crimes+Bipartisan Agreement=More Billions for Bombing Women and Children Innocents

Second, examine the military-industrial complex. When Raytheon, Lockheed Martin, or Northrop Grumman require funding, the partisan theater closes. Ukraine funding flows freely while domestic programs face endless debate. Defense contractors don't just lobby—they command consensus power.

Third, study police union influence. From federal legislation to local policy, police power operates through perfect bipartisan agreement. The same unions that write crime bills in Biden's office maintain power through Democratic city machines. They don't just influence policy—they author it through consensus power.

Fourth, witness Israel policy. When AIPAC or other pro-Israel groups signal priorities, both parties snap to attention. Foreign aid flows without question, military support proceeds without debate, and criticism faces bipartisan condemnation. This isn't just influence—it's consensus power.

Nothing about the 1994 crime bill was unintentional—it was designed from the beginning as a political symbol. [5] Crime was to Clinton what illegal immigration is to Trump: a way of reassuring fearful, alienated white voters, especially in the South. Fear of offenders, fear of gangs, fear of ungovernable teenage "super predators" (a supposed generational wolf pack who never actually appeared): Those were the political currency of the era.

Did you know Democrats in defending the crime bill, also keep political resistance to it a mystery? A full 169 members of the House, including Representative Ron Dellums (California), co-founder of the CBC, voted against it. So did thirty-four senators. Criminologists, civil rights lawyers, community activists, and members of Congress all fought against various provisions of the bill. The cynical and sneaky decision by Clinton's administration to bundle mandatory minimums and prison expansion with the Violence Against Women Act of 1993 and weapons regulation made it harder for uneasy progressives to just say no.[6]

The Timeline of Deception

By 1995, when crime was already at its lowest level since the Ronald Reagan era, Scotto's architecture had authorized the following:

- $9.7 billion for prison construction
- $10.8 billion for a hundred thousand new police officers
- Expanded death penalty to sixty new offenses
- Life sentences for third-time federal offenders
- Adult prosecution of thirteen-year-olds
- Military equipment for local departments

The Double Standard: Consensus versus Black Interests

Now consider the contrast. When Black Americans seek responsive legislation, the system suddenly remembers partisan gridlock. Issues lacking consensus power face the following:

- Endless debate requirements
- Demands for compromise
- Claims of complexity
- Calls for patience
- Appeals to process

The pattern: Where money and institutional power align, partisan conflict vanishes. Where Black American interests seek change, partisan barriers appear. This isn't random—it's system protection through consensus power.

In Democratic Party-controlled major cities, this pattern becomes even clearer. Black voters deliver 80-90 percent support to Democrats, but police unions often hold more actual power. Why? Because they operate through consensus mechanisms while Black interests face heavy partisan resistance. Police unions have been remarkably effective at fending off broader change, using their political clout and influence to derail efforts to increase accountability.

Consider the math:

- Police Union Demands + Bipartisan Support = Action
- Black Community Needs + Partisan Process = Delay
- Consensus Power + System Protection = Guaranteed Results

This explains why Democrats running city machines often serve police interests over Black community needs. Politicians tempted to cross police unions have long feared being labeled soft on crime, or worse. As one Minneapolis city councilman noted after trying to divert money from hiring officers: "It operates a little bit like a protection racket." When he attempted reform, the police stopped responding as quickly to 911 calls from his constituents.

Misplaced Political Heat: The Local Control Reality

If Democrats control the cities and areas where we live—the mayorship, Congressional seats, city council, state senate, the governor's mansion in many cases—then any beef we have with the police is fundamentally a Democrat problem, not a MAGA problem. This is how we must think more surgically and efficiently about our political priorities.

Democratic Control of Cities + Police Misconduct = Democratic Responsibility

Yet our political pressure rarely follows this equation. We march against Republican presidents while giving local Democratic machines a pass. We focus national outrage on Washington, DC, while the power to reform policing largely resides at the municipal and state level. If police reform is such a big deal—and it legitimately is—why isn't our collective activism surgically targeted on Democrats, who receive most of our votes?

Although Democratic Party officials may not look or sound anti-Black American, if they control local structures that have an anti-Black American structural orientation, their identity and rhetoric become irrelevant to outcomes. Black American political organizations would achieve greater impact by calibrating their protest energy, electoral focus, and accountability demands based on who actually controls local systems and where Black American votes are most concentrated.

A problem shouldn't have an imaginary or spook target. Democrats should be surgically targeted when the underlying control and Black American voter support warrant it. The major police killings and headline-grabbing abuses happened overwhelmingly in Democrat-controlled states and cities—from the savage beating of Rodney King in Los Angeles to the killings of George Floyd in Minneapolis, Breonna Taylor in Louisville, Eric Garner in New York City, and Michael Brown in Ferguson, Missouri. All occurred under Democratic municipal leadership receiving over 80% of Black American votes in those jurisdictions.

System Architecture: The Consensus Protection Racket

The system's efficiency in serving consensus power reveals its true architecture:

- Corporate Interests: Swift, unified response
- Military Contractors: Automatic, bipartisan support
- Police Unions: System-wide protection

Israel Policy: Perfect party alignment Meanwhile, Black interests face a different equation:

- Police Reform: Partisan barriers

- Economic Justice: Process delays

- Structural Change: System resistance

- Community Needs: Political theater

When both parties agree, the system moves with devastating efficiency—passing trillion-dollar military budgets or bailing out banks in days. When Black American interests seek change, the system suddenly rediscovers gridlock.

While Democrats point fingers at Republicans and Republicans blame Democrats, real power operates through consensus areas immune to partisan theater.

If you hear a Democrat defending the Clinton-Biden crime bill of 1994 that helped accelerate mass incarceration of Black American men, remember the role of Tom Scotto (president of the National Association of Police Organizations who helped write the bill in Biden's office), the deliberate information asymmetry, the calculated mystery, and the actual fact that Black American leaders such as Congressman Ron Dellums opposed it in real-time.

Also remember political career fortunes—including Clinton's and Biden's—were built on top of mass incarceration while not deserving credit for crime going down, which had already begun declining in 1991, three years before the bill was passed and implemented. This timing raises an important question: Whether Black American organizations, churches, mosques, and leaders deserve most of the credit for crime reduction through the rise of the Nation of Islam, the renewed influence of Malcolm X's teachings, and a conscious cultural renaissance in Hip-Hop that promoted community responsibility. The bill was activated during the same year as the Million Man March in 1995. Research may later document and confirm Minister Farrakhan would deserve more credit for crime going down than Bill Clinton and Joe Biden, but the Democratic Party would never admit it, even if confirmed with scholarship.

The Science

- The 1994 Crime Bill was literally written by police unions, not community advocates
- Black Americans supported it based on incomplete information—they weren't told who authored it
- Always ask: "Who actually wrote this policy?" and "What information is being withheld?"
- Beware of policies presented as community-centered when authored by opposing interests

[1] Rashawn Ray and William A. Galston, "Did the 1994 crime bill cause mass incarceration?" Brookings Institution, August 28, 2020.

[2] Michael Kranish, "Joe Biden Let Police Groups Write His Crime Bill. Now, His Agenda Has Changed," Washington Post, June 8, 2020.

[3] Bruce Shapiro, "Nothing About the 1994 Crime Bill Was Unintentional: In the '90s, Bill Clinton exploited fears about crime in the same way that Donald Trump uses immigration today," The Nation, April 11, 2016.

[4] Udi Ofer, "How the 1994 Crime Bill Fed the Mass Incarceration Crisis," ACLU.org, June 4, 2019.

[5] Michelle Alexander, "The New Jim Crow: Mass Incarceration in the Age of Colorblindness," Reprint Edition (New York: The New Press, 2020).

[6] Ann Brown, "5 Things MSNBC Brunch Democrats Won't Tell Black America About The 1994 Biden Crime Bill," The Moguldom Nation, October 27, 2020.

Conflicts of Interest as Predictive Signs of Devilishment

> *"I hope Smith Barney enjoyed the investment banking fees he generated, because they come at the expense of retail clients."*
> —*Performance complaints against Jack Grubman shared with the Securities and Exchange Commission*

After spending a year at the Syracuse University College of Law, I worked as a contract paralegal at law firm Paul Weiss on the famous Jack Grubman case. Grubman was a star analyst at Wall Street investment bank Salomon Smith Barney. The case involved Grubman changing the stock rating on AT&T after his boss at Citi, Smith Barney's parent company, requested a favor for the investment banking division. AT&T was also a Citi investment banking client, and Citi would benefit if Grubman changed from bearish (negative) to bullish (positive) on its stock rating. This single rating change influenced billions in AT&T's market capitalization and potentially generated millions in investment banking fees for Citi, demonstrating how conflicts of interest can have massive financial ripple effects throughout the market. [1]

How serious of a problem is corruption?

How serious of a problem do you think corruption is among the following? (% of U.S. adult citizens)

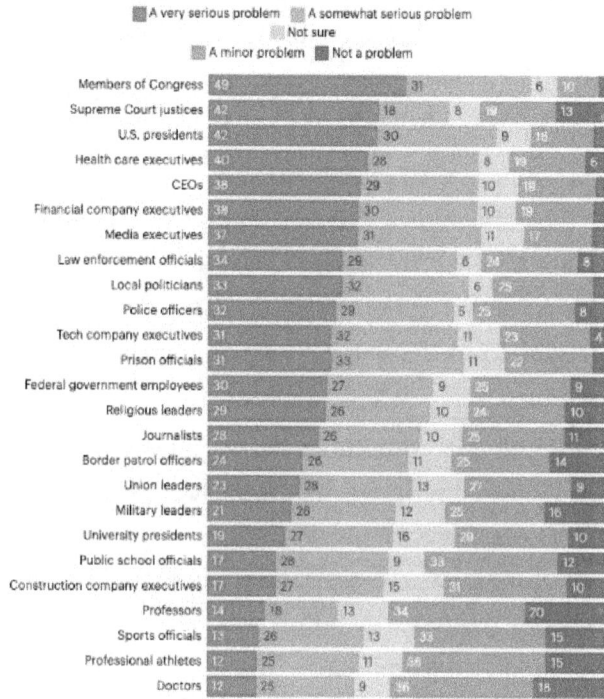

■ A very serious problem　■ A somewhat serious problem
■ Not sure
■ A minor problem　■ Not a problem

	A very serious problem	A somewhat serious problem	Not sure	A minor problem	Not a problem
Members of Congress	49	31		6	10
Supreme Court justices	42	18	8	19	13
U.S. presidents	42	30		9	18
Health care executives	40	28	8	19	6
CEOs	38	29	10	18	
Financial company executives	38	30	10	19	
Media executives	37	31		11	17
Law enforcement officials	34	26	6	24	8
Local politicians	33	32	6	25	
Police officers	32	29	5	25	8
Tech company executives	31	32	11	23	4
Prison officials	31	33	11	22	
Federal government employees	30	27	9	26	9
Religious leaders	29	26	10	24	10
Journalists	28	26	10	25	11
Border patrol officers	24	26	11	25	14
Union leaders	23	28	13	27	9
Military leaders	21	28	12	22	16
University presidents	19	27	16	29	10
Public school officials	17	28	9	33	12
Construction company executives	17	27	15	31	10
Professors	14	18	13	34	20
Sports officials	13	26	13	33	15
Professional athletes	12	25	11	36	15
Doctors	12	25	9	36	18

YouGov

January 10 - 16, 2025 • Get the data

Now, what was in it for Grubman if he changed the stock rating for his boss? Sandy Weill, then the chairman/CEO, would help Grubman's kid get accepted to a prestigious Manhattan school. There was an obvious conflict of interest between the research division at Smith Barney and the investment banking division at Citi, and this resulted in changes after the SEC and Feds stepped in.

As I read through Grubman's work emails and read about what was going on in Fortune and Forbes magazines, it opened my eyes to a new world. There was a certain sneakiness and deception among elites, the top 10 percent (or the ten-percenters), in the way they did business. It was a mystery to me and the public, but now my eyes were open to the games of "insiders." One thing realized with scientific orientation, you either have to go on the inside or study the inside, deep down in the guts of it.

Grubman was a door for me to walk in and see how the tricknology is done, at the highest levels of finance and markets. It was done in a manner where it was a culture vs an outlier or single bad actor.

This case would later help shape the Global Analyst Research Settlement and the subsequent Sarbanes-Oxley Act of 2002, which finally erected a wall between investment banking and research departments. The fact that it took a full-blown scandal and government intervention to establish what should have been common sense shows just how deeply conflicts of interest are embedded in the system. Corruption can be embedded in a system where promiscuous conflicts of interests are tolerated, promoted, and accepted.

A conflict of interest occurs when an individual's personal interests—family, friendships, financial, or social factors—could compromise their judgment, decisions, or actions in the workplace. Government agencies take conflicts of interest so seriously that they're strictly regulated by law. Major institutions across the board—corporations, industry organizations, and professional associations—have adopted this same vigilance, embedding conflict-of-interest protections into their policies, operational standards, and ethical frameworks. The widespread regulation shows just how dangerous these conflicts are to institutional integrity.

The scientific equation is clear: **Conflicts of Interest + Positions of Power = Predictable Corruption**. This isn't just theoretical—it's a mathematical relationship that enables us to anticipate where devilishment will occur in the system.

Politics and Promiscuous Conflicts

Politics is loaded with conflicts of interest. For example, Congressional Black Caucus Member Gregory Meeks could take money from the payday loan industry and then support a lack of regulatory scrutiny. [2] He could frame it as the hood needs access to these services and they provide an important resource. Or Al Sharpton can take money from Big

Tobacco and then say we need to keep menthol cigarettes legal because if they were illegal, the Black market could lead to another Eric Garner who was choked to death by police after being caught selling menthol cigarettes. [3](Statistically, wouldn't more Black Americans choke to death from lethal menthol cigarettes than the police?)

FTX and Alameda: A Case Study in Predictable Corruption

I closely followed the crypto market during the 2020–2023 period. I was trading crypto and kept up with the latest news and events in the market. I became aware of the number one trader in crypto, Sam Trabucco, who was the chief trader at a proprietary trading firm called Alameda Research. Alameda was owned by Sam Bankman-Fried, the CEO of FTX, a brokerage firm where clients bought and sold crypto. Bankman-Fried owned both Alameda and FTX.

When I saw this, I thought back to my Grubman days, and the Alameda/FTX conflict popped out to me that this was very wrong but the regulators were behind the curve as crypto was rapidly evolving. I didn't need regulators to make a law to see the elevated potential for devilishment or corruption.

If the owners of the promiscuously conflicted scheme can manage their brokerage and then their own trading firm and be the biggest "whale" in the crypto market, moving markets, they would trade on the information from the traders on the FTX platform. They had insider information and they were clearly in the game of making money.

So after seeing the potential for manipulation, I commissioned an article on Moguldom.com: "The Most Influential Trader In Crypto, Sam Trabucco, Works With FTX Exchange: Some See Manipulation" [4]

This caught the attention of the chief counsel for Alameda and FTX (conflict, he's the attorney for both), Dan Friedberg. Mr. Friedberg emailed me directly on August 4, 2021:

Dear Mr. Martin:

I saw your article on Sam and noticed a few things that are not really accurate. Could we possibly have a call to discuss? I understand your concerns about the industry but was hoping to explain further. I'd greatly appreciate the opportunity to talk to you.

Best regards,

Dan Friedberg

General Counsel Alameda Research Ltd.

I never responded to Friedberg, I knew exactly what I was talking about, I had the science down, it wasn't a mystery to me how the conflict of interest game was played by the ten percenters. The next year, Dan Friedberg was cooperating with the Feds and FTX filed for bankruptcy, with Alameda. [5] It was a massive fraud and SBF and other conspirators went to jail.

Because there is a severe conflict of interest doesn't mean there is a big fraud taking place but the probabilities of manipulation and devilishment, go up, way up. In this sense, conflicts of interest can be predictive of fraud, it can be a sign that there is something unholy and something with devilishment in the back, exploiting the conflict structure. For example, imagine if the local dope dealer was also the local police chief? The crimes would be more effective, more difficult to detect and prosecute. The police chief is too conflicted to enforce the law as intended.

After Dan Friedberg emailed me and FTX later filed for a massive bankruptcy, I ran into another case study. A company that distributed fraudulent bots or fake clicks to my website and caused Fortune 500 clients such as Amazon, AT&T, and Target to stop spending advertising dollars with my Black American-owned news platform, the Moguldom Nation.

However, the same company accused of fraud, had connections to the #1 fraud detection company and even had a relationship with the CEO, before he became the CEO. (After a suspicious death) I saw the same pattern as I saw with Grubman and FTX, again and yes, I believe this is part of a massive fraud scheme in the $143 billion global ad fraud market.

If fraudsters got control of the fraud detection systems for fake website traffic and fake clicks, the fraud detection system would lose its policing integrity and become conflicted. Literally, those committing the fraud and those policing the fraud, could be working for the same bosses behind the scenes.

Applying Conflict Analysis to Black American Politics

What does identifying patterns with conflict of interest have to do with politics, Black American politics? The same patterns of conflicts can be seen in our political leadership, where Black faces from Barack Obama to Congressional Black Caucus members are often compromised by funding from corporate interests opposed to Black American advancement. When our leaders take money from Wall Street, Big Tech, or Big Pharma or AIPAC, while failing to push a Black American agenda, that's a conflict that predicts devilishment. These Black American leaders can "look a good game," talk a good game with nice and articulate speeches, and be positioned as leaders of the Democratic Party, but when you examine the scientific reality of their conflicts and associated factors, we see they are structured for a lot of devilishment and corruption.

At minimum, we need to study how our political leaders have become severely conflicted and to what degree. Are they 20% conflicted or 80%? All American politicians are conflicted in some way. When a politician is highly conflicted, such as Barack Obama, it's very difficult for them to say anything provocative or meaningful, so you stop listening to much of what they have to say on issues. These hyper-conflicted leaders are so overstretched with hidden and overt conflicts, with millions of dollars at stake, they can't say anything that really moves us anymore. You can say the money and the people holding them up in the back, have closed their mouths shut, on strong, transformational, and courageous political positions.

The deceptive way these leaders show fight is not at system level, is simply fighting MAGA or Republicans. Their conflicted structure often traps Black America into a one-headed snake fight when our powerful opposition and their associated corruption, is really a two-headed snake.

For example, Obama is muzzled on anything related to Amazon as his foundation gets money from Bezos—and Bezos wasn't giving his money away based on friendship alone, he wants something back. We need to identify where political leaders are conflicted so we can scientifically discount what they are saying or not saying about a particular issue. If the leaders are all compromised by the billionaires and corporate confederacy, you have to be a fool to just follow them and expect "change we can believe in." It should be the collective Black American position with both political parties that "you leaders are not running the spook on us anymore."

If Bakari Sellers or Cory Booker have been groomed by the AIPAC lobby from their college days, I wouldn't look to them for truth or science on foreign policy matters with Israel as they have become too conflicted and compromised to one side. Booker told an AIPAC conference he would cut off his right hand before he forgot about Israel [6] so that tells you right there, he is not to be trusted on which foreign policy is right and wrong based on morality and scientific factors.

Science demands we factor conflicts when evaluating leaders, not just celebrate their symbolic achievements while ignoring who owns their political debts. The most reliable predictor of political betrayal isn't rhetoric or identity—it's following the conflicts. The identity or speeches of the politician is not more important than understanding how they are conflicted. If you're into political spook, you play on the surface. If you're into Black American political science, we must go underneath the surface, factoring and prioritizing the money and conflicts.

The path forward is clear: we must develop a conflict detection system for Black American politics—a scientific framework that scrutinizes not just what leaders say, but who funds them, who employs their spouses, who pays their speaking fees, and who finances their foundations. By identifying these conflict patterns early, we can predict which leaders will serve as devil's advocates for the system and which are positioned to challenge it.

In politics as in finance, detecting conflicts doesn't just explain past betrayals—it enables us to anticipate and potentially prevent future ones. Until we master this science of conflict detection, we'll continue celebrating symbolic victories while enduring material defeats, trapped in the familiar cycle of high hopes followed by predictable disappointments orchestrated by those who understood the power of conflicts all along. To understand is to go underneath. To have a scientific orientation is to go into the different factors underneath something or someone.

The Science

- Conflicts of Interest + Positions of Power = Predictable Corruption
- Track funding sources, speaking fees, and future employment of political leaders
- Black American organizations need transparency about donors and financial relationships
- Create conflict detection systems to predict which leaders will serve system interests vs. community interests

---

[1] Securities and Exchange Commission v. Jack Benjamin Grubman, United States District Court Southern District of New York, Civil Action No., Complaint.

[2] Daniel Wagner, "Congressman defends payday lending industry," The Center for Public Integrity, July 18, 2014.

[3] J. David Goodman, "When Big Tobacco Invoked Eric Garner to Fight a Menthol Cigarette Ban," The New York Times, July 14, 2019

[4] Dana Sanchez, "The Most Influential Trader In Crypto, Sam Trabucco, Works With FTX Exchange: Some See Manipulation," The Moguldom Nation, August 2, 2021.

[5] Max Zahn, "A timeline of cryptocurrency exchange FTX's historic collapse," ABC News, March 28, 2024.

[6] Alex Emmons, "In Leaked Recording, Cory Booker Says He And AIPAC President 'Text Message Back And Forth Like Teenagers'," The Intercept, March 30, 2019.

Who Is in the Cap Table? Karen Hunter versus Marc Morial

> *"Why isn't anybody from Wells Fargo or these other banks that literally destroyed Black wealth in jail? Like, why did they get a free pass? And then I see people in bed with them now."*
> —*Karen Hunter*

September 5, 2023, marked an electrifying day in Black American political media. Talk show host Karen Hunter engaged in a no-holds-barred conversation with Marc Morial, CEO of the National Urban League (NUL). [1] The dynamic wasn't just riveting—it was revealing. Morial's visible discomfort under Hunter's scrutiny exposed the raw reality of Black American leadership in the controlled opposition era.

Hunter cut straight to the bone, challenging Morial on his relationship with Wells Fargo: "Why isn't anybody from Wells Fargo or these other banks that literally destroyed Black wealth in jail? Why did they get a free pass? And then I see people in bed with them now—how are you in bed with somebody that destroyed Black wealth, a generation of Black wealth, with the subprime lending debacle?"

Morial's response was revealing—rather than addressing the accountability question directly, he pivoted to program-focused language: "What we do is we have to build our wealth through home ownership... We run home buyer education programs... you have to educate yourself or you can get abused and used in the housing markets." This strategic deflection from institutional accountability to individual responsibility is a classic example of how conflicted leadership operates.

When Hunter pressed about federal funding and financial transparency, Morial's response was even more telling: "The reason why we don't [publicly report funding] is because I don't want haters attacking my organization and taking cheap shots at us. We're a private organization. I'm not the government." This wasn't just defensiveness—it was a window into how institutional leadership operates when financial relationships create constraints. While Morial appeared at White House meetings alongside figures like Al Sharpton, positioning himself as a representative for Black American interests, his reluctance to answer basic questions about funding sources revealed a contradiction between public leadership and private accountability regarding potential conflicts of interest.

Hunter persisted: "There is a level of expectation... because most of us Black folk don't have access to people who can actually get things done." This gets to the heart of our political dilemma—we rely on unaccountable (to Black America) proxies who have access to power, but those proxies become compromised by the very relationships that give them that access. The Black American leaders who are positioned by the White House as national representatives often find themselves unable to effectively pressure that same White House, as their access and influence depend on maintaining favorable relationships. This creates a fundamental conflict where traditional civil rights leaders like Morial and Sharpton may lose their independence and ability to serve as critical advocates. What Black America needs are leaders willing to challenge power—even Democratic administrations—when necessary to advance specific Black American political interests. We're better off with leaders who are willing to fight and hold the Democratic Party leadership accountable than leaders who just shine the shoes of the party, collect their checks, and tell us "MAGA BAD."

During the 1995-2025 audit measurement period, we have seen traditional civil rights leadership that would normally pressure and agitate for changes metastasize into taking orders from the Democratic Party or the U.S. government when a Democrat occupies the White House. We should acknowledge that this loss of political regulatory and accountability function has come with substantial costs to Black

American political interests and leverage, while the benefits have primarily flowed to White House-approved representatives. This controlled opposition creates a system where the Democratic Party and U.S. government effectively negotiate with themselves, presenting the appearance of dialogue while maintaining the existing power structure.

The Balance Sheet vs. The Cap Table

Morial has undeniably upgraded the NUL's balance sheet impressively, building assets exceeding $50 million and establishing new headquarters in New York. But we should examine the capital structure and go underneath. The NUL's dependence on government contracts and corporate donations creates mathematical certainty of conflicted interests and a structural orientation to "constrain and pacify Black America" rather than change the system.

This isn't merely criticism—it highlights the need for new Black American-funded organizations. The NUL should invest in seeding new Black American organizations structured more independently, outside their conflicted corporate confederacy funding model. When Biden gives the Urban League government contracts while Morial is positioned as a top Black American negotiator, it sets up undemocratic exploitation. Black America needs leaders who can pressure presidents for transformative policy, not executives who receive government cash and White House photo-ops while structurally positioned to protect party and government interests over Black American political interests.

Wells Fargo and the Conflict of Interest

The NUL has a significant partnership with Wells Fargo, a bank with a documented history of discriminatory practices against Black Americans. In December 2022, the National Urban League announced a partnership with Wells Fargo specifically aimed at "diversifying the home appraisal industry."[2] This partnership came despite Wells Fargo's long history of discrimination, including a $175 million settlement in 2012 for steering

Black and Latino borrowers into subprime mortgages while white borrowers with similar credit profiles received standard loans.

The National Urban League's 2023 donor report lists Wells Fargo among its major corporate contributors, with the bank appearing prominently in their donor category listings. [3] This financial relationship creates an obvious conflict when it comes to holding the bank accountable for its practices. This is another example of the natural political regulatory function of "civil rights" leadership becoming neutralized. Civil Rights has become more like "Democratic Party Rights," and "Corporate Rights."

When Hunter mentioned the "$100 million MacKenzie Scott donated locally" to Urban League affiliates and questioned their tangible impact, Morial struggled to provide specific metrics beyond general statements about program areas. [4] The equation becomes clear: $5 million dollar check from Wells Fargo equals zero public criticism of their practices.

It's not a good deal for Black Americans if Wells Fargo, with its massive institutional size, discriminates and cheats Black Americans over decades and then they give a few million to Morial and the NUL and T.D. Jakes, and this pays for their sins against the whole of Black America while shutting up its community leaders. [5] The math isn't mathin' on this politically perverse structure and scheme.

Representative Leadership Demands Accountability

You have to remember, organizations such as the NUL take their millions in Black Americans' name. They release annual reports named 'The State of Black America' and position themselves to corporate donors as the authority on Black America. They position themselves as chief institutional representatives for Black America, sitting in White House meetings and congressional hearings on our collective behalf. When then-President Biden met with Morial and Sharpton, it was seen and framed as a meeting with Black American leaders. This representative role demands heightened accountability, not diminished transparency. Where a few leaders better position themselves financially could have severe costs to Black American political interests as a whole.

When they claim to speak for us in those powerful rooms, we earn the right to scrutinize their conflicts and results—whether we're registered members or not. Their institutional authority derives from their claim to represent our interests, so their financial entanglements become matters of collective concern, not just organizational business.

This exemplifies a fundamental conflict in Black American politics: who owns the equity in our leadership? Just as venture capitalists examine a company's cap table to determine who truly controls and owns it proportionally, we must analyze our leaders' financial backers to understand their true constraints, political orientation, and priorities.

Institutional Leaders vs. Movement Leaders

When Hunter pressed Morial about his role, he carefully distinguished: "I consider myself the leader of the Urban League movement... I'm an institutional leader. I have a responsibility for 150 employees, I have responsibility for 92 Affiliates across the nation." This distinction between institutional leadership and movement leadership is crucial—one comes with fiduciary responsibilities to funders, while the other demands accountability to the community. If Joe Biden (or others) wants to neutralize criticism and accountability within Black America, it's in his interest to work with Morial, who doesn't believe he has any accountability with Black America as a whole. It's in our interests to pressure Democrats to work with Black American organizations and leaders who are directly synced with Black American interests and can be held accountable.

Scientific Analysis vs. Personal Critique

This isn't to diminish the NUL's contributions and value, but to recognize the scientific reality that money always comes with conditions—conditions that can dilute our collective political leverage. When Morial objected to being challenged by saying, "I also know that there's a lot of people sitting on the sidelines," he employed a classic deflection strategy—criticizing the critics rather than addressing the substance of the criticism.

To be optimally politically efficient, we must recognize both the victories and the compromises, the advances and the limitations. Only through this cost/benefit, risk/reward, multi-factor scientific analysis can we appreciate the positives while honestly assessing the setbacks, ensuring our political movements are both strategic, efficient, and impactful.

The questioning of Marc Morial by Karen Hunter represents the very best in Black American media, doing exactly what journalists and media are supposed to be doing, asking hard questions for all the Black Americans in the back. A key observation from the 1995-2025 audit period is the Black American media metastasizing into a shoe shiner for the Democratic Party and its leaders, in greater and greater pursuit of access, money, conflicts, and career advancement, at the expense of freedom, justice, and equality for Black Americans. Consistent with Democratic principles, Black American media should be independent and not a mouthpiece of the U.S. government, even if a Black Face or Democrat is in the White House. Black American media must be the permanent check, in proper checks and balances.

To understand something, we have to go underneath it. The conflicts of interest often do more talking than the lips of political leaders.

The Science

- Examine who financially controls Black American leadership organizations
- Wells Fargo partnership neutralizes National Urban League's ability to hold banks accountable
- Representative leadership demands heightened transparency, not diminished accountability
- Ask: "Who owns the equity in our leadership?"

Appendix A:
National Urban League Corporate Donors (2023)

Source: National Urban League 2023 Annual Report, Donor Category Report

DONOR CATEGORY REPORT 2023
Corporations, Foundations, Nonprofits and Individuals

CORPORATIONS, FOUNDATIONS AND NONPROFITS

$1,000,000 + - ($1,000,000.00 +)
AbbVie Foundation
ALDI, Inc.
Bank of America Corporation
Bill & Melinda Gates Foundation
Charter Communications
Comcast Corporation
DoorDash
Google, Inc.
JP Morgan Chase & Co.
Mastercard International
PepsiCo, Inc.
Shell USA, Inc.
TD Bank
T-Mobile
Toyota Motor Sales, U.S.A., Inc.
Wells Fargo & Company

$500,000 - $999,999 - ($500,000.00 +)
Amazon, Inc.
American Honda Motor Co., Inc.
AT&T Inc.
Citigroup
GEICO Corporation
National Basketball Association
Nationwide Mutual Insurance Company
NextEra Energy, Inc.
Pathway Resource Center
Round It Up America
State Farm Mutual Automobile Insurance Company
Tides Foundation
United Parcel Service, Inc.
Verizon Communications Inc.
The William and Flora Hewlett Foundation

$250,000 - $499,999 - ($250,000.00 +)
Altria Client Services Inc.

Cardinal Health
CenterPoint Energy
Chan Zuckerberg Initiative
The Coca-Cola Company
Cox Enterprises, Inc.
Delta Air Lines, Inc.
Experian, North America
FedEx Corporation
Fifth Third Bank
Johnson Controls, Inc.
Johnson & Johnson
Macy's Inc.
Mars Incorporated
NFL Foundation
National Grid
The Paychex Community Charitable Foundation
Regions Bank
United States Department of Agriculture
Wal-Mart Stores, Inc.
The Walton Family Foundation
W.K. Kellogg Foundation

$100,000 - $249,999 - ($100,000.00 +)
Anheuser-Busch InBev
Anti-Defamation League
Apple, Inc.
Barclays Bank PLC
Jim Beam Brands, Inc.
Charles Stewart Mott Foundation
Comcast Corporation
Bloomin' Brands, Inc.
Chipotle Mexican Grill
Constellation Energy
Deluxe Corporation
Diageo Americas
Entergy Corporation
Experian, North America
Freddie Mac
Georgia-Pacific Corporation

Harvey Hubbell Foundation
Horizon Therapeutics
John Hancock ManuLife Insurance Company
Mars Incorporated
McDonald's Corporation
MolsonCoors Brewing Company
Morgan Stanley
Nestlé USA Inc.
Nissan North America, Inc.
Network Wireless Solutions
New Venture Fund
Northwestern Mutual Life Foundation, Inc.
OneMain Holdings, Inc.
OPNAD Fund
PNC Financial Corporation
Precision Strategies
The Progressive Corporation
Nissan North America, Inc.
Takeda Pharmaceutical Inc
Target Corporation
Third Way Foundation
Uber Technologies
Venture Global
ViaSat, Inc.
Weil, Gotshal & Manges, LLP
Wynn Resorts

$50,000 -$99,999 - ($50,000.00 +)
AIDS Healthcare Foundation
Airbnb
Albertsons Inc.
Adecco Group
Alkeon Capital Management, LLC
American Airlines
AmerisourceBergen
AvalonBay Communities, Inc
Benjamin Moore & Company
Bellwether Education Partners Inc.

Betty & Smith
Bristol Myers Squibb Foundation
Brown & Brown Insurance
Capital One Financial Corporation
Cargill, Inc.
Cellular Telecommunications and Internet Association (CTIA)
Colgate-Palmolive Company
The Columbus Foundation
Dell, Inc.
Edward D. Jones & Co., L.P.
Energy Foundation
Enterprise Holdings, Inc.
Fiserv
First Horizon Bank
Houston First Corporation
Joy Media Collective, LLC
Kemper Corporation
Lyft, Inc.
Marriott International, Inc.
Markle Foundation
The Nature Conservancy
Pacific Premier Bank
Panda CommUnity Fund
Paramount Global
Pronghorn
PulteGroup, Inc.
Robert Half International, Inc.
Starbucks Coffee Company
Travelers Companies
Ulta Beauty Charitable Foundation
Vista Chemical Co.
Vistra Corporate Services Company
Volkswagen Group of America, Inc.
The Walt Disney Company
Williams-Sonoma, Inc.

$25,000 - $49,999 - ($25,000.00 +)
AARP
Advanced Meeting Solutions

American Beverage Association
American Express Foundation
American Cancer Society
American Heart Association
American Hospital Association
American Petroleum Institute
ARAMARK Corporation
Axon Enterprises, Inc.
Jim Beam Brands, Inc.
BlackTitan Investment Corporation
Cablevision Systems Corporation
Caesars Entertainment
CastleOak Securities LP
Cravath, Swaine & Moore
Center for Education Reform
Deloitte Services, LLP
EdChoice
Eli Lilly and Company
Ford Motor Company
Galderma Laboratories L.P.
GE Healthcare
Hilton Worldwide
The Huntsman Foundation
Kimpton Hotel & Restaurant Group LLC
Kohl's
Las Vegas Sands Corporation
Lyft, Inc.
Merck & Co., Inc.
Meta Platforms, Inc.
MGM Resorts International
Microsoft Corporation
National Association of Broadcasters
National Automobile Dealers Association (NADA)
National Cable & Telecommunications Association
National Committee for Quality Assurance
Novo Nordisk
Paycor, Inc.

Philip Morris USA
Planned Parenthood Federation of America
Seattle Foundation
Simpson Thacher & Bartlett
Sullivan & Cromwell
Truist Financial Corporation
Uber Technologies
U.S. Bancorp
Values Partnerships Corporation
VISA, Inc.
Waymo
The Williams Company
WilmerHale
World Wide Technology, Inc.

$10,000-$24,999 - ($10,000.00 +)
Adecco
Advanced Meeting Solutions
Alpha Phi Alpha Fraternity, Inc.
American Water Charitable Foundation
Ariel Investments, LLC
Automatic Data Processing Inc.
Boston Consulting Group
Bristol-Myers Squibb Foundation
Build-A-Bear Workshop, Inc.
CoBank
Community Finance Corporation
Conrad N. Hilton Foundation
Corpay Public Private Strategies LLC
Courvoisier
Curinos, Inc.
The Data Quality Campaign
Denny's Corporation
Disciplina Group LLC
The Education Trust, Inc.
Edison Electric Institute
Edwards Lifesciences
Ernst & Young
FIS Group, Inc.

284

Greenberg Traurig, LLP
Hobson/Lucas Family Foundation
Hyatt Hotels Corporation
InterContinental Hotels Group, Inc.
KPMG LLP
LinkedIn Corporation
L.L. Bean
Marsh & McLennan Companies
McMaster-Carr Supply Company
Merck & Co., Inc.
Moth + Flame, Inc.
MSC Industrial Direct Co.
New York Life Insurance Company
Novogradac & Company LLP
OpenRoad Foundation
Penn Mutual Life Insurance Company
Professional Diversity Network, Inc.
Q2 Holdings, Inc.
Rack Room Shoes
Schnuck's Markets, Inc.
Seattle Foundation
Strada Education Network
Trust of Mel
Urban League of Philadelphia
Universal Music Group
Valley National Bank
Weil, Gotshal & Manges, LLP

$5,000-$9,999 - ($5,000.00 +)
Breakthru Beverage Group
Brown Brothers Harriman & Co.
CoBank
Community Build, Inc.
CSX Corporation
Elevance Health
Expo Experts, LLC
Julian Grace Foundation
McKinsey & Company, Inc.
National Council of Urban League Guilds
PhRMA

Pitney Bowes Inc.
Total System Services, Inc
Varo Money Inc.
The Wallace Foundation
Wellington Management Company, LLP
West Monroe

$2,500 -$4,999 - ($2,500.00 +)
Campaign for Tobacco-Free Kids
Hogan Lovells
The Meltzer Lippe Foundation
NexantECA
USI Insurance Services
Wawa, Inc.
Wellington Management Company, LLP

$1,000 - $2,499 - ($1,000.00 +)
AQR Capital Management
BPM
Chevron Corporation
Christian Methodist Episcopal Church
ENVIRO AgScience, Inc.
Green Brick Foundation
Preit

$500 - $999 - ($500.00 +)
Collaborative Promo Solution
Goodman Real Estate Services Group LLC

$250 - $499 - ($250.00 +)
Biovid Corporation
National Sorority of Phi Delta Kappa, Inc.
Society of The Transfiguration

INDIVIDUALS

The President's Circle Founders' Society (established 2007)
Willard W. Brittain*
Alma Arrington Brown*
Ursula M. Burns
Michael J. Critelli
Earl G. Graves, Sr.
Karen and John D. Hofmeister*

Vina and Thomas D. Hyde
Dr. Ray R. Irani
John E. Jacob
Robert L. Johnson
Vernon E. Jordan, Jr.*
Ralph S. Larsen
Carolyn and Edward T. Lewis
William M. Lewis, Jr.
Jonathan S. Linen
Dr. Kase Lukman Lawal
Lori and Liam E. McGee
Marc H. Morial and Michelle Miller
William F. Pickard, Ph.D.*
Hugh B. Price
J. Donald Rice
John W. Rogers, Jr.
Andrew C. Taylor
Carrie M. Thomas*

Visionary ($500,000-999,999)
Ian MacKechnie

George E. Haynes Fellow ($50,000-$99,999)
Noemi K. Neidorff

Catalyst ($25,000 - $49,999)
Sandra Frazier
Jordan Family Foundation
Mandy and Tim Murphy
Leo Salom, Jr.

Advocate ($10,000 - $24,999)
Sandy and Tim Armour
James and Laurie Axelrod
David G. Clunie
David G. Ellen
Kristy Fercho
Tracey and David S. Huntley
The Huron Foundation
Barbara S. and John E. Jacob
Jocelyn and Neele Johnston

---

[1] "Marc Morial Talks the National Urban League, Equity in America & More," The Karen Hunter Show, YouTube, September 5, 2023.

[2] "National Urban League Partnership With Wells Fargo Aims To Diversify Home Appraisal Industry," Wells Fargo, December 1, 2022.

[3] National Urban League, "Donor Category Report 2023," Page 20, https://nul.org/sites/default/files/2025-02/2023_Annual_Report.pdf

[4] "National Urban League: Mackenzie Scott Contributions to 25 Urban League Affiliates Are 'A Powerful and Transformational' Gesture in Support of Racial Equality," National Urban League, November 1, 2022.

[5] Ann Brown, "Who Will Defend Us? 3 Black American Leaders And Organizations Who Are Financially Compromised By Wells Fargo," Moguldom.com, December 27, 2023.

LESSON 32
Ed Seykota and Monopoly Interests

> *"The system is now in its final phases where it's taking over. There's no way to resist it, there's no way to stop it. I don't recommend spending a lot of time worrying about it." —Ed Seykota*

> *"I'm not saying anything is bad or wrong or should be changed. In my book I don't say that there's anything wrong. I'm just looking at how does the engine work, how does this work, and how do we explain what we've got." —Ed Seykota*

Edward Seykota isn't just a legendary trader who pioneered systems trading using punch-card computers. [1] He's also a clear thinker with rare insights into how American power truly operates. After graduating from MIT with degrees in electrical engineering and management, Seykota became curious about the political system—specifically why it consistently failed to work for ordinary people despite endless promises of reform.

In his 2013 book "Govopoly in the 39th Day", Seykota introduced the concept of "Monopoly by Government Sanction"—what he calls the "govopoly system." Unlike most political commentators caught in the emotional trap of party politics, Seykota approached the question with scientific detachment, building a model to understand the mechanics of power.

What distinguishes Seykota's analysis from conventional political commentary is his methodological rigor. Over more than 30 years of studying the system, he deliberately maintained political neutrality— neither Democrat nor Republican, liberal nor conservative. This wasn't merely personal preference but a methodological requirement. Seykota understood that political bias would inevitably corrupt his analysis, so he approached the system with the same objective, disciplined mindset that made him a successful trader. Just as a trader who lets emotions and biases cloud judgment will lose money in markets, Seykota recognized that emotional or partisan attachments would blind him to the system's true mechanics.

"I don't want to comment on any particular banks," Seykota explains in a rare interview. "Everywhere you look, everywhere there's regulation, there's a govopoly system at work... As the system grows, more and more people have an investment in it." [2]

Seykota concluded in his analysis: the government isn't broken at all—it's operating exactly as designed. The political system doesn't exist to serve citizens; it exists to protect monopoly interests. What looks like democratic debate is actually an elaborate distraction.

Monopoly Power in the Modern Economy

According to Seykota, this govopoly system is clearly visible today in the tech monopolies that dominate our economy and political discourse. Amazon controls nearly 40 percent of all US e-commerce, while allowing virtually no worker unionization. Meta (Facebook) and Alphabet (Google) control roughly 60 percent of all digital advertising. Apple and Microsoft operate their own monopoly ecosystems with little meaningful competition. BlackRock manages over $15 trillion in assets—more than the GDP of every country except the United States and China. These aren't just successful companies; they're govopoly institutions that leverage government relationships to protect their market dominance and crush competition.

"The dog and pony show is purposely orchestrated to distract people from the real issues," Seykota observes. "Nobody talks about the real engine behind this: the growth of the govopoly system and the fact that it has unlimited access to money." [3]

The Historical Roots of System Failure

Seykota's analysis goes deeper than typical political criticism. He traces the problem back to 1913 and the creation of the Federal Reserve, which removed the natural limit on government growth. Before this, government could only spend what it taxed. After the Fed, government gained the ability to spend before taxing, placing an "effective tax" on citizens through inflation and debt.

His mathematical model shows that when government spending exceeds about 1.5% effective asset tax rate, the government grows large enough to halt free competition. Like a parasite or cancer, it then consumes the host economy. The result: declining manufacturing, rising unemployment, growing dependency, and eventually the complete consumption of the free competition sector.

"We are seeing a decline in manufacturing and toolmaking," Seykota notes. "The govopoly system is consuming the free competition sector, and when we run out of a free competition sector—which is imminent in my opinion—then we have a whole different economy."

No False Hope

What makes Seykota's analysis so valuable for Black American political thinking is his refusal to offer false hope. Unlike politicians promising solutions through voting or reform, Seykota acknowledges a sobering reality: "At this point, it would take 20 or 30 years of austerity to get any meaningful change to get us back to a free competition society. You're not going to get anybody elected on a 30-year austerity program."

This isn't pessimism—it's reality. The govopoly system will continue expanding until it renders the host society inoperable, then collapses. This cycle has repeated throughout history; no currencies survive more than a couple hundred years.

The solution? There isn't one—at least not for the system as a whole. "I don't think there's a solution for the economy," Seykota says. "I don't think there's a problem. It's just what it does." Instead, he advises individuals to understand the system and adapt. Like a person facing terminal cancer, the question isn't how to stop what's happening but how to make the best of the time you have. According to Seykota, thinking the U.S. system that has developed over hundreds of years can change quickly or change at all in critical and more permanent areas, can both be considered spook.

Seykota's position on the U.S. political and economic system changing is not far off from the position of Elijah Muhammad. Although Muhammad wrote 'Put the Muslim Program before Congress' [4] and fully supported Adam Clayton Powell, he largely thought American politics was just too corrupt to put much energy in it. Not believing in life after death, he invested all his energy, time, and life into doing constructive things that could pay material dividends, for Black Americans.

After auditing Black American politics for the 1995-2025 measurement period, one of my takeaways is that politics is largely a waste of time, particularly when we are not organizing and taking actions, and measuring results. Politics is not a waste of time if there is a credible and scientific path to change Black American life, for the better, at scale. It's not clear to me we have tried what actually needs to be done, long enough and hard enough. For the modern times.

Beyond Partisan Theatrics

For Black Americans trapped in this system, Seykota's analysis offers clarity. The dominant parties aren't truly rivals but partners in managing the expansion of govopoly power. The differences between them grow increasingly "obscure"—they're all "voting for expansion of the govopoly system."

What's the practical takeaway? Rather than wasting energy on symbolic victories and empty promises of political salvation, we must understand the actual mechanics of the system and develop strategies to navigate it.

Seykota himself suggests trend-following as one approach—the ability to identify and align with directional moves in the economy without emotional attachment.

The deepest wisdom in Seykota's approach isn't just his model, but his emotional clarity. He avoids both cynicism and naive optimism, maintaining scientific detachment while acknowledging reality. "I'm just looking at how the engine works, how this works, and how we explain what we've got," he explains. "I'm not trying to change anything. I'm just saying, 'This is how it works.'"

Before we say a policy, politician, or party is bad, how many of us have taken the time to understand how the system actually works? Seykota spent more than three decades studying the American system with deliberate objectivity. Unlike most political commentators who begin their analysis with predetermined political allegiances, Seykota approached the system as a scientist would approach a natural phenomenon—without judgment or ideological commitments. He recognized that starting with the assumption that Democrats or Republicans, conservatives or liberals were "right" would inevitably corrupt his understanding. This methodological neutrality wasn't just academic—it was essential to seeing the system's true nature. If we did put more than 10,000 hours in with this same political neutrality, we may find confirmation of Seykota's thesis that the system is not broken at all and can't be fixed. It just needs to play itself out.

From Spook to Science

For Black American political science, this approach represents the essence of the shift from spook to science—replacing emotional reactions and symbolic politics with clear-eyed analysis of system dynamics. Understanding the monopoly interests controlling our political system isn't about giving up; it's about seeing clearly so we can make better decisions with the options we actually have.

Seykota's research demonstrates the dangers of being caught in what he might call "political position risk"—becoming so emotionally invested in partisan identities that we lose the ability to see the system objectively. His work suggests that our tendency to play Red vs. Blue games within political cycles causes us to miss the bigger picture of how monopoly interests operate through both parties. This emotional investment in political tribes is itself a form of spook—a belief system that obscures rather than reveals the underlying mechanisms of power. Most of the people who are political gang bangin', Blue vs Red, Democrat vs Republican, do they even understand how the system works, deep down in the guts? Who really benefits from the back and forth WWF-like political games while an understanding how the machine works and how it interacts with monopoly interests remains a mystery?

If Black Americans had a strong Black American Agenda that was systems oriented and ready to scrutinize both political parties, at any time, and hold the system accountable, at all times, we may not print the results we would like, in the time we would like but we would be more politically efficient, than we are now. We are wasting time in politics and the political game if we are unwilling to get in the paint or support those who are, and stick with a goal or two over ten years. There is rarely anything truly original about modern politicians and they are mostly interchangeable, like commodities. We are wasting time with politics if we think of politics as a form of tribalism, entertainment, and an escape from reality. To better get at the science of it all, we can't think about politics in traditional, simple, RED vs BLUE terms, Democrats good, MAGA bad terms. We have to understand it all first. To understand it all, we have to back away and position ourselves objectively, to see the factors and facts we need to see, with maximum clarity and truth.

Seykota's analysis explains why systemic safeguards like the filibuster and campaign finance rulings like Citizens United function as critical mechanisms within what he calls the govopoly system, deliberately designed to maintain the status quo regardless of which party holds nominal power. Rather than treating these as abstract procedural issues, Black American political strategy would be more effective by recognizing them as the actual battlegrounds where monopoly interests ensure their continued dominance, far more consequential than the partisan theater that dominates news cycles. Are we focusing too much on the widgets and not enough on the two-party factory that produces the widgets?

The Science

- The government isn't broken—it's operating exactly as designed to protect monopoly interests
- Political theater distracts from real power: govopoly system expanding until collapse
- Focus on understanding system mechanics rather than partisan emotions
- Develop strategies to navigate inevitable system changes rather than hoping for reform

---

[1] Jack D. Schwager, "Market Wizards, Updated: Interviews with Top Traders" (February 7, 2012).

[2] Ed Seykota, "Govopoly in the 39th Day" (January 1, 2013).

[3] Ed Seykota, "Ep. 355: Ed Seykota Interview with Michael Covel on Trend Following Radio," YouTube, January 30, 2023.

[4] Elijah Muhammad, "Put the Muslim Program Before Congress," Muhammad Speaks, March 1962.

Devil's Advocates: A Case Study

> *"[Eric] Holder may get a slap or two from the Republicans on the Senate Judiciary Committee for the Rich pardon or something else. But he's likely to be confirmed. He may well become a good attorney general. Someday down the road, he might be feted at a fancy testimonial dinner, and all his rather impressive accomplishments will be repeatedly noted. And with the encomiums flowing, there won't be any mention of the Purdue Pharma victims and the highly paid work Holder did to protect the people and company who caused their suffering." —David Corn* [1]

In the 1997 film "Devil's Advocate," Keanu Reeves plays a talented young lawyer recruited by a prestigious New York law firm headed by Al Pacino's charismatic character. As the plot unfolds, Reeves discovers his charming mentor is actually Satan himself, using the law firm as a vehicle to corrupt souls and spread evil throughout society. The film serves as a powerful metaphor for how talented individuals can be seduced by power, prestige, and wealth into becoming instruments for immoral ends—all while believing they're simply doing their jobs. This dynamic perfectly illustrates the phenomenon we see in American politics, where Black Americans with exceptional talents and credentials are strategically recruited to serve as the friendly faces of deeply corrupted systems. Far from conspiracy, this is a mathematical strategy—deploying identity as protection for the most problematic aspects of American power, creating "devil's advocates" who lend crucial legitimacy to institutions that might otherwise face greater scrutiny and resistance.

What if the cost of seeing someone Black and successful within the American empire meant a structural delay in a bigger day of reckoning in America over its history and racial demons?

When examining the phenomenon of "devil's advocates" in American politics, we must move beyond the feel-good spook of "first Black" symbolism to the reality of how power actually operates. The system isn't just recruiting Black faces for diversity—it's strategically deploying them as protection mechanisms for the most corrupt and conflicted aspects of American power. This isn't conspiracy—it's reality, with predictable patterns that reveal how identity politics gets weaponized against structural change.

Let's follow the money and spook scientifically through three case studies that reveal precisely how this system functions: Eric Holder with Big Pharma, Former NAACP President Ben Jealous with Big Tobacco, and Colin Powell with the Iraq War.

Eric Holder: Wall Street Double Agent and Protector of the Opioid Cartel

It may be easy to cheer Eric Holder for becoming the "first Black" attorney general under Obama. It takes more work to understand why the rulers in America "in the back" would want Eric Holder there.

The Science? Before becoming Obama's attorney general, Holder defended the Sackler family—the opioid cartel behind Purdue Pharma that built a $13 billion fortune while addicting and killing hundreds of thousands of Americans. When Democratic West Virginia Attorney General Darrell McGraw Jr. sued Purdue in 2001 for "coercive and deceptive" marketing of OxyContin, Holder stepped in to negotiate a settlement that protected the Sacklers from true accountability. [2]

The math is clear: Holder, making $2.5 million annually at Covington & Burling, helped Purdue settle for just $10 million paid over four years— pocket change for a company with $1.5 billion in OxyContin sales. The drug company admitted no wrongdoing. There was no trial, no public testimony, and most importantly, no structural change that would impede the opioid crisis that would eventually claim hundreds of thousands of American lives.

This wasn't an isolated case. Holder's law firm specialized in "getting clients accused of financial fraud off with slap-on-the-wrist fines." His firm's clients included JPMorganChase, Wells Fargo, Citigroup, and Bank of America. This wasn't coincidence—it was qualification for the job. When Holder left the Obama administration in 2015, he returned to Covington & Burling, where they had reportedly kept his office empty during his absence—a perfect illustration of the revolving door between regulation and industry. [3]

As Matt Taibbi put it, Holder "institutionalized a radical dualistic approach to criminal justice, essentially creating a system of indulgences wherein the world's richest companies paid cash for their sins and escaped the sterner punishments the law dictated." [4] While Black Americans went to prison for petty drug offenses, Holder helped a pharmaceutical dynasty marketing deadly opioids and Wall Street banks get away with a slap on the wrist.

The scientific equation is stark: **Black face + corporate connections = perfect system protection**. The trick is to make the wrapper or optics look progressive with identity while delaying larger structural reforms. So when so many are chasing the symbolic and superficial "First Black" progress, they are likely pushing policy risk taking, Pure Reparations and structural reforms for Black Americans, further out.

Ben Jealous: From Civil Rights to Big Tobacco Lobbyist

The pattern continues with Ben Jealous, former NAACP president and CEO from 2008 to 2013. After losing his bid for Maryland governor in 2018, this Oxford-educated Rhodes Scholar became a lobbyist for Juul, the e-cigarette giant partially owned by tobacco heavyweight Altria. [5]

The science reveals the deadly contradiction: Black Americans have higher death rates from tobacco-related illnesses than other racial and ethnic groups. Black children and adults are more likely to be exposed to secondhand smoke. According to the CDC, the tobacco industry has aggressively marketed menthol products to young people and Black Americans, especially in urban communities. [6]

Yet here was Jealous, previously tasked with advancing civil rights, now advancing colored cigarettes that disproportionately kill Black Americans. Meanwhile, Juul gave $7.5 million to historically Black Meharry Medical College—another transaction in the system's protection racket. [7]

The tobacco industry's relationship with Black America has always been predatory. By 2018, 85 percent of Black smokers preferred menthol cigarettes compared to just 29 percent of white smokers. This wasn't random consumer preference—it was the result of decades of targeted marketing, price manipulation, and strategic exploitation of Black media, culture, and institutions. The science and factors underneath the success of Black America's favorite magazines in the 80's and 90's such as Ebony, JET, and Black Enterprise was a disproportionate amount of menthol cigarette and alcohol advertising, holding the publishing houses up. [8] There were severe cultural and health costs for Black Americans to read quality media that focused on us specifically. Black America media has always had fewer options for advertising and this set the industry up for predatory exploitation.

As San Diego activist Ken Seaton-Msemaji put it: "Big Tobacco leveraged the civil rights movement and Black Pride movement to prey on our desires to be seen and heard. It advertised with people who looked like us in the magazines that we read and sounded like us on the radio stations that we listened to." [9]

The key question isn't whether Jealous "sold out" but how the system is designed to convert Black leadership into corporate protection and devilishment. When Black American leaders become transmission mechanisms for Big Tobacco, AIPAC, police unions, and Big Tech, they aren't leading—they're following the script written by the rulers of America. As our elders looked at the Confederacy in the South and its remnants as political opposition, we need to update our mental models to look at the current corporate confederacy of power networks, as sneaky and deceptive institutional opposition to Black American freedom, justice, and equality. The corporate confederacy shouldn't be able to place "strategic identity" lipstick on the pig to make bad policy and bad morality look politically cute.

Colin Powell: The Perfect Military Frontman

Before General Colin Powell passed away, he admitted he regretted selling the Iraq War while serving as Secretary of State. Powell was used to present fabricated intelligence to the United Nations, lending his credibility to a war that would kill nearly 5,000 US service members and an estimated 400,000 Iraqis.

In his infamous February 5, 2003 United Nations presentation, Powell stated: "My colleagues, every statement I make today is backed up by sources, solid sources. These are not assertions. What we're giving you are facts and conclusions based on solid intelligence." [10]

The truth? Powell had been comprehensively misled. He was told his speech had been prepared by the National Security Council under Condoleezza Rice, but it was actually written by Vice-President Dick Cheney's office, which had browbeaten CIA analysts into producing "evidence"—and when that failed, simply manufactured it. [11]

Powell wasn't chosen randomly to make a speech before the United Nations, pressing for war—he was selected precisely because his Black face and military reputation would lend crucial credibility to a fraudulent and immoral case for war. The transaction was mathematical: **Black general + military credentials = increased public support in a criminal war**. There is an effective way for tricknology to make adverse foreign policy look progressive. The spook makes the people who have been politically seduced to think they are moving forward (on the good side) only to find out later with science and time, they have been pushed way-way back.

This pattern continues today with former Secretary of Defense Lloyd Austin, a former Raytheon board member who became the first Black Secretary of Defense—perfectly positioned to sell aggressive war policies and hundreds of billions in funding for Ukraine. The equation remains the same: **Black face + defense contractor connections = perfect protection for the military industrial complex**. The spook buyers (those who become seduced by the spook) will see progress with the first Black American secretary of defense but may not see any progress on changing how the military industrial complex works, its moral and policy orientation. The goal should not be to see top political persons look a certain way, have a certain identity as much as changing the structure and underlying scientific factors and policy orientation, for the better. If political leaders look representative of the country, this can be a positive thing but it should not come before whether the person is the best person to transact good policy and positively influence the structure and society, for the better.

The Role of Psychopathy in Politics

Understanding devil's advocates requires examining the role of psychopathy in American politics. According to Dr. Martha Stout, a clinical psychologist and former Harvard Medical School instructor, "Politicians are more likely than people in the general population to be sociopaths... That a small minority of human beings literally have no conscience was and is a bitter pill for our society to swallow—but it does explain a great many things, shamelessly-deceitful political behavior being one." [12]

Modern politicians benefit from psychopathic traits—fearless dominance, boldness, and lack of emotion. If they don't score high on the psychopathy scale themselves, they're often beholden to business interests that operate with psychopathic tendencies.

The "bougie buffer" Black American elite are often attracted to white psychopaths because the psychopaths have the capital. A psychopath doesn't have the human "handicap" of empathy like most of us. A culture of extreme greed scales psychopathy in society. This is what many mean when they say, "America is crazy."

The opposers of freedom, justice, and equality want to make critical areas of morality ambiguous: there is no right or wrong, everyone is corrupt, everyone would sell out for the right price. This helps produce the "wobble" and increased political volatility we see in America today.

Over time, the Black American is systematically at risk of becoming a "li'l beast"—individualistic, unprincipled, and willing to do anything for money. The system requires its devil's advocates to transplant themselves with the heart, values, and psychopathy of their bosses to advance their careers and accomplish financial goals.

The Hidden Cost of Symbolism

What if the net cost of symbolism—seeing successful Black Americans within the modern empire—carries a heavy hidden price that most Black Americans don't understand? What if the costs are not even evaluated, studied, and priced?

What if the cost of seeing someone Black American and successful within the empire meant a structural delay in America's reckoning with its history and racial demons? What if the cost of racial symbolism in America was postponing reform of the structural order and confronting America's rampant and promiscuous corruption? [13]

What if racial symbolism and "diversity" in the empire generally wasn't about change at all, existing only on the surface, and was being used as an all-star offensive line to protect the star corporate confederacy quarterbacks in the back, such as Facebook/Meta, Alphabet/Google, Wall Street, Amazon, Silicon Valley, AIPAC and Israel, police unions, and powerful political actors?

The corporate media and Black American political establishment will play up the "first Black" symbolism but are fearful of intelligent debate on the potential intentions of those doing the hiring and providing the money. When identity politics becomes the focus, structural critique disappears—exactly as designed. Those spreading and enforcing the tricknology, know Black Americans don't like criticizing successful Black Americans so a stealth muzzle is placed on natural accountability functions within large segments of Black America.

When the system presents us with a Black face in a high place, science demands we ask: What interests are being protected? Who benefits from this appointment? What policies is this identity being used to sell? What's the mathematical transaction taking place beneath the symbolic victory?

Why do all these "first Blacks" have to be connected to defense contractors, lobbyists, Wall Street, Big Tech monopolies, Big Tobacco, and tough-on-crime policing? Do "first Black" faces materially change the malstructure? Do they even claim or demonstrate they are trying?

We need to realistically assess whether having "first Black" representatives in positions of power actually delivers material benefits to Black Americans or simply puts a more diverse face on the same system. Politicians operate within constraints, but there's a profound difference between working within a system while pushing its boundaries versus simply becoming its most effective defender. Devil's advocate–style politics, where "first Blacks" function primarily as defenders and enforcers of the empire, doesn't help Black Americans, or America in general, become materially better. It takes us further away from the structural reforms desperately needed in America and further from goals like Pure Reparations.

The Counterintuitive Truth

It's counterintuitive but mathematically verifiable: there are increasing political situations where it is better for Black America to have a more moral and progressive white politician than a Black American politician who has been carefully selected and sent in for devilishment or to limit as much change as possible and keep the status quo. The system understands that it's easier to get the devilishment in and provide cover when the racial optics look "progressive." The fundamental scientific question isn't about the color of the politician's skin but whether, on balance, this leader is being sent in to protect the system or change it. The most sophisticated and big wallet and sophisticated institutions are cultivating their own political draft picks and sending them into the game to represent their interests.

Consider the brutal equation: A Black face pushing harmful policies × racial solidarity symbolism = more efficient system protection than a white face pushing identical policies. This isn't theoretical—we saw it when Clinton and Biden's crime bill received critical support from many members in the Congressional Black Caucus despite its devastating impact on Black communities. We saw it when certain policies that might benefit native Black Americans became untouchable because they were implemented by a Black political figure. We saw it when Kamala Harris built her career as a prosecutor with tough-on-crime policies while being celebrated as a racial pioneer. The Black Face politician may even overstretch to prove their loyalty to the status quo such as former prosecutor and DA Kamala Harris attempting to arrest Black American parents for kids not going to school.

The psychology is precise: The system understands that many Black Americans will hesitate to criticize "one of our own" even when that person is advancing policies that harm our communities. Meanwhile, a white politician pushing identical policies would face immediate, unified resistance. This psychological leverage is worth billions to the corporate confederacy and power structure, making Black devil's advocates among the most valuable assets in maintaining system control.

We must be willing to support leaders based on political orientation, their commitment to a Black American Agenda, commitments, and their appetite to take bold risks for Black Americans, more than their identity characteristics—even when that means supporting politicians of any background who demonstrate greater moral courage and policy commitments aligned with Black American interests. Political alignment should overpower identity alignment, every time if we are focused on results, science.

You're right - I'll remove the unnecessary descriptor "American" for Dr. Curry. Let me check for anything else I might have missed in my revision.

The Science

- Black faces in high places often provide protection for the most corrupt system aspects
- Eric Holder protected Wall Street and Big Pharma; Ben Jealous lobbied for Big Tobacco
- Strategic identity deployment makes harmful policies more palatable
- Evaluate leaders by policy alignment and risk-taking, not identity characteristics

---

[1] David Corn, "Eric Holder's Purdue Pharma Problem," Mother Jones, December 2023.

[2] David Corn, "Eric Holder's Purdue Pharma Problem," Mother Jones, December 2023.

[3] Matt Taibbi, "Eric Holder, Wall Street Double Agent, Comes in From the Cold," Rolling Stone, July 8, 2015.

[4] Matt Taibbi, "Eric Holder, Wall Street Double Agent, Comes in From the Cold," Rolling Stone, July 8, 2015.

[5] Lachlan Markay, "Juul Spins Vaping as 'Criminal Justice' Issue for Black Lawmakers," Daily Beast, February 18, 2021.

[6] "Unfair and Unjust Practices and Conditions Harm African American People and Drive Health Disparities," Centers for Disease Control and Prevention, May 15, 2024.

[7] Kevin Mwanza, "'Juul Doesn't Have African-Americans' Best Interests In Mind': Backlash Following $7.5M Gift To Medical School," The Moguldom Nation, July 19, 2019.

[8] "How the tobacco industry targeted Black Americans with menthol smokes," NPR, April 29, 2022.

[9] Ken Seaton-Msemaji, "Marketing menthol cigarettes to Black Americans is a racial injustice. It must end," San Diego Union-Tribune, October 28, 2021.

[10] "Powell presents US case to Security Council of Iraq's failure to disarm," UN News, February 5, 2003.

[11] "Colin Powell's UN speech: a decisive moment in undermining US credibility," The Guardian, October 18, 2021.

[12] Martha Stout, "The Sociopath Next Door" (New York: Broadway Books, 2005).

[13] Elizabeth Nolan Brown, "Most Americans Think Government Is Corrupt, A Third Say Armed Revolution 'May Be Necessary' Soon", Reason, July 25, 2022.

LESSON 34
George Floyd Money

> *"No one expected the foundation to grow at this pace and to this scale. Now, we are taking time to build efficient infrastructure to run the largest Black, abolitionist, philanthropic organization to ever exist in the United States."* — *Cicley Gay, chair of the board of directors, Black Lives Matter Global Network Foundation*

The first thing I said to myself after corporate America and the philanthropic complex got their wallets out was: this money's going to the wrong people. It would go to corporate diversity consultants who'd call the police if they saw George Floyd walking near them in a suburban mall. The math was predictable—murder would become a marketing opportunity.

A CEO from a top Black media company actually laughed about all the "George Floyd money" rolling in. That's what the insiders called it behind closed doors: George Floyd money. Think about that for a minute. A man's murder becomes a revenue stream, with the benefits flowing to people who'd never give someone like Floyd a job or even the benefit of the doubt.

The cruel mathematics:

George Floyd's Death + Corporate Guilt = Money for Everyone Except George Floyd

Peaceful Requests + Democratic Politics = Symbolic Gestures

Direct Rebellion + System Risk = Policy Change in Banking System

America's 50 biggest public companies collectively committed at least $49.5 billion since Floyd's murder, with over 90 percent allocated as loans or investments they could profit from. Only $4.2 billion came as outright grants, with a mere $70 million going to organizations focused specifically on criminal justice reform – the actual cause that catalyzed the protests. [1] The science tells us about an important factor: the rebellion—including the burning of police stations and vandalism of CNN's headquarters—accomplished more structural change than decades of polite Democratic Party legislation.

The math on overdraft fees is devastating: Black Americans pay an average of $12 a month in bank fees compared to just $5 for whites, according to Bankrate. When you overdraw your account—something more likely to happen when you're living paycheck to paycheck—banks hit you with an average fee of $33.47. These aren't just statistics; they're a systematic wealth extraction mechanism. When Bank of America, Capital One, and other major banks suddenly announced they were eliminating or reducing these fees after decades of resistance, it wasn't because they'd read White Fragility. It was because they saw buildings burning and calculated that predatory fees weren't worth the risk of becoming the next target of mass anger. That's not speculation—that's material analysis of cause and effect. These banks don't give up billions of profits unless they are under threat and pressure to do so.

Corporate America didn't find its conscience—it found its fear. Banks didn't eliminate predatory fees because of diversity training; they did it because the rebellion signaled real system risk. The science shows that material change requires material pressure.

The system's response was predictable:

- Maldistribution of resources
- Enrichment of existing power structures
- Distance between money and need
- Institutional capture of protest energy
- Quick concessions to prevent deeper change

Consider the trajectory of Black Lives Matter (BLM). Started by three self-described radical Black women in 2013, BLM took in more than $90 million in donations in 2020 after Floyd's murder. George Soros's Open

Society Foundations alone pledged $220 million. [2] What's striking is BLM was likely the organization best positioned to capture these funds - they had already built name recognition and infrastructure prior to Floyd's murder, had visibility in multiple cities, and were young enough to appear radical but established enough to seem legitimate to corporate donors. The relative lack of competing national Black organizations focused on police accountability created a vacuum that BLM filled. They were organized and positioned right, before the murder of George Floyd.

The truth about BLM involves both organizational challenges and legitimate concerns about transparency and grift. There was undoubtedly questionable spending and a troubling lack of financial transparency. The $6 million mansion purchases and other extravagant expenses revealed real problems that can't be dismissed. [3] At the same time, they went from a scrappy movement to managing tens of millions of dollars virtually overnight - like handing the keys of a Boeing 747 to someone who just got their driver's license.

This sudden influx of unmanaged resources had predictable consequences. As Michelle Gross, a longtime Minneapolis activist put it: "We're like, 'Where are you? Where's all this money going?'" Meanwhile, Michael Brown Sr., whose son's death in 2014 helped catalyze the movement, reported seeing none of the money raised in his son's name.

The billions in corporate pledges could have been invested more efficiently across a broader ecosystem of Black American organizations, including newly formed ones better suited to address specific needs. But Fortune 500 companies needed visible, established organizations they could point to as recipients. This highlights a fundamental weakness: our lack of organizational infrastructure to effectively capture and deploy resources at scale.

In public stock markets, investors feel confident about their investments due to SEC regulatory filings and quarterly earnings reports. There's a science to liquifying American stock markets, and that same science applies to Black American organizations. They will be better capitalized if they front-load transparency rather than keeping financials a mystery. That approach is hustling backwards – organizations demonstrably grow when they produce material results and maintain transparency about donations and outcomes. The next generation of Black American organizations that prioritize transparency and anchor on modern organizational principles will go further than those who keep the key financial science underneath them a mystery, as if Black Americans should be riding on more spook.

One of the most basic things a Black American organization can do is show Black Americans where the money is going before the IRS forces financial disclosure. This simple act of transparency would accelerate growth and build trust, bringing in more support by demonstrating leadership in an area where too many organizations keep finances and progress reports shrouded in mystery. Why do we have to wait to be forced to show our supporters the finances? That doesn't sound very radical or "Pro-Black" at all—it sounds like the same old tricknology with a revolutionary aesthetic.

Real revolution would include revolutionary transparency, not just in rhetoric but in financial practice. Elijah Muhammad gave his people regular economic progress reports. But he didn't just talk—he showed them schools, 50 new temples opening across the country, farmland, restaurants, banks, grocery stores, a newspaper printing plant, and many other ventures. Black America, not just Black Muslims, could see the material progress, so the support only grew. The mathematics were clear: investment plus transparency equals growth. When people can see their contributions building something tangible that benefits Black Americans, they give more, not less. Organizations would raise more money to do good if they marketed and promoted the material results and investment returns. The sad reality is we don't have enough strong Black American organizations with infrastructure to handle millions in funding effectively. What we got instead was the following:

- BLM leadership buying million-dollar homes

- Corporate diversity consultants getting rich

- Distant bourgeois class capturing resources

- Institutional interests protecting themselves

- Quick reforms to prevent structural change

Dr. Tommy J. Curry's analysis proves prophetic: "We don't understand how some of these bourgeois discourses—be it Black liberalism, Black progressives who are southern educated or even Black feminists who have a class bias that rivals even white middle-class people—are using the deaths of Black men to propagate their own theories." [4] Dr. Curry, a scholar, author and professor of philosophy who holds a Personal Chair in Africana philosophy and Black male studies at the University of Edinburgh, recognized this pattern early on.

While "George Floyd money" flowed to consultants and organizations who'd never help someone like Floyd, the actual rebellion forced institutions to change predatory practices that affected millions of George Floyds. This isn't about advocating violence—it's about understanding the science of change. Structural shifts require risk-taking that threatens system stability and status quo.

MacKenzie Scott (Bezos's ex-wife) made one of the smarter moves by targeting historically Black colleges and universities (HBCUs) with over a billion in support. [5] What made Scott's approach different was how she did it—with no strings attached, no buildings named after her, no restrictive spending requirements, and no bureaucratic hoops to jump through. She just sent the money. Compare that to how white philanthropists historically funded HBCUs—with tight controls, paternalistic oversight, and demands that schools conform to white notions of what Black education should look like.

But Scott was the exception. Most of the George Floyd money followed predictable paths to predictable places, enriching those already positioned to benefit from Black death. For banks and major corporations, this was a simple calculation: risk mitigation and public relations, not transformative change.

The truth is undeniable: more policy changes came from a few weeks of rebellion than from years of traditional political advocacy. When vandalism hit CNN and police stations burned, predatory banking practices suddenly became negotiable. This isn't spook or sentiment—it's empirical reality. If we want material changes at the policy and systems level, we need risk-taking, policy-oriented ideas that create real system pressure.

The science is clear: symbolic gestures come from symbolic pressure; policy and structural changes come from structural threats. Everything else is often just managing our containment.

The Science

- Corporate pledges ($49.5B) went primarily to loans/investments they could profit from
- Only $70M of billions pledged went to actual criminal justice reform
- The rebellion accomplished more structural change than decades of traditional advocacy
- Material change requires material pressure, not symbolic gestures

---

[1] Jan, Tracy, Jena McGregor, and Meghan Hoyer. "Corporate America's $50 billion promise: A Post analysis of racial justice pledges after George Floyd's death reveals the limits of corporate power to effect change." The Washington Post, August 23, 2021. https://www.washingtonpost.com/business/interactive/2021/george-floyd-corporate-america-racial-justice/

[2] Herndon, Astead W. "George Soros's Foundation Pours $220 Million Into Racial Equality Push." New York Times, July 13, 2020.

[3] Campbell, Sean. "Black Lives Matter Secretly Bought a $6 Million House: Allies and critics alike have questioned where the organization's money has gone." New York Magazine, April 4, 2022.

[4] Curry, Tommy J. "Black Lives Matter: Is It Really The 21st Century Civil Rights Movement." America's Independent Voice podcast with Rob Redding, YouTube, March 12, 2015. https://www.youtube.com/watch?app=desktop&v=ueAqBMoAwoQ

[5] Redden, Elizabeth. "A Fairy Godmother for Once-Overlooked Colleges: With donations ranging from $20 million to $50 million to colleges routinely overlooked by major philanthropists, MacKenzie Scott has set herself apart by focusing on institutions that serve students of color and those from low-income backgrounds." Inside Higher Education, January 3, 2021.

Beyond the Spook of the Black and Brown Coalition

"F*** that guy, He's with the Blacks."
— *LA City Councilwoman Nury Martinez (2021)* [1]

Latinos bring negative stereotypes about Black Americans to the U.S. when they immigrate and identify more with whites than Blacks, according to a study of the changing political dynamics in the South" Source: Duke University researchers, Journal of Politics[2]

Descriptive Statistics of Dependent Variables

	Attitudes toward Whites	Attitudes toward Blacks	Attitudes toward Latinos
Perceived wealth (%)			
Very poor	0.6%	22.6%	28.3%
Somewhat poor	11.8%	64.3%	63.9%
Don't know	0.7%	0.7%	0.5%
Somewhat rich	65.0%	11.5%	6.4%
Very rich	21.9%	0.9%	1.2%
Perceived intelligence (%)			
Very unintelligent	0.4%	16.9%	0.5%
Somewhat unintelligent	4.0%	30.8%	10.1%
Don't know	1.8%	3.4%	0.3%
Somewhat intelligent	41.6%	41.9%	61.0%
Very intelligent	52.2%	7.1%	28.2%
Cultural perceptions (mean & std dev)	19.8 (3.2)	11.7 (3.6)	21.8 (2.9)
Receptivity to contact (mean & std dev)	25.9 (4.2)	18.3 (5.5)	
N	661	661	661

Open in a new tab

Data: Gender, Migration and Health Risks among Hispanics Survey, 2007-2008

Latino Immigrants' Attitudes Toward Racial Groups - Shows negative perceptions of Black Americans

Personal experience often provides the first data points for understanding complex political realities. In Southern California during my elementary school years, I witnessed the full spectrum of Black–Latino relations: friendship and solidarity on one end, violence and racial slurs on the other. When Latino kids called me "nigger," my response was immediate and physical—an instinctive rejection of racial degradation. To be fair, I would shoot back "wet back" only in retaliation. But the most profound lesson came through tragedy when my cousin Alfred Clark, a promising UCLA scholarship recipient, was murdered at seventeen by a Latino gang member over a CD Walkman. The killer's family showed no remorse in court, sparking interfamily violence and requiring Christopher Darden— later famous for the O. J. Simpson case—to step in as prosecutor. (Darden became a Godfather to my baby cousin)

These weren't isolated incidents. In areas like Hawaiian Gardens near Long Beach, certain Latino gangs actively "hunted" Black Americans, regardless of gang affiliation. Yet simultaneously, in places like Norwalk, Black and Latino members of the Manor Boys gang maintained positive relationships. This complexity defied simple narratives about a natural alliance or inevitable conflict.

During the 1990s, many Black American leaders preached the gospel of 'Black and Brown' coalition building. This wasn't spooky in intention— the strategic logic of uniting two historically marginalized groups made sense on paper. But it was spooky in execution because it ignored material realities and complex demographic dynamics.

Ignoring complex issues between Black Americans and Mexican-Americans was no better than ignoring issues between Black Americans and white Americans. The scientific approach requires us to analyze coalitions based on concrete interests and measurable outcomes, not aspirational thinking.

Within this frame, the 90's themed 'Black and Brown' idea was never politically efficient because it avoided confronting deeper issues and factors,

313

preferring to keep them a mystery. Keeping the mystery intact is often easier than engaging with the hard science of complexity and factors.

The math of immigration and political power are straightforward. Each new wave of immigration potentially dilutes Black American political influence. As Latinos become the majority-minority, Black voting power could decrease proportionally. Many immigrants enter America without an understanding of or alignment with Black American interests or have an anti-Black American, before they even arrive. [3] This is the reality we must confront.

Resource competition is equally predictable. Limited economic opportunities create natural competition for access to education, housing, and employment. Government programs and attention get divided among more groups. This isn't xenophobia—it's material reality. In a system that already underfunds Black community needs, adding more competing interests without expanding resources creates inevitable tension.

Under the 90's "Black & Brown" spook spell, we are taught to ignore these tensions rather than confront them honestly and strategically. Imagine if we applied this same approach to tensions with white Americans. The various spook spells prevent us from having the necessary conversations with other groups that could lead to smart and strategic political alliances.

Scientists who study marriage and trauma have formed a consensus that direct confrontation and open discussion about issues is far better than glossing them over. Issues not addressed will resurface with greater intensity over time and can become potentially fatal to relationships. They build up. With courageous confrontation, however, things have a chance to get better. A lot better.

The cultural understanding gap compounds these challenges. Many immigrants arrive without knowledge of Black American history or the structural forces that shaped our current reality. There's no natural understanding of or support for issues like reparations. Some even import anti-Black attitudes from their home cultures. Again, this isn't blame—it's hard science.

Perhaps most concerning is the myth of automatic political alignment. The rise of Latino MAGA supporters shows the danger of assuming a natural alliance. Immigrant groups often align with power structures against Black American interests as they seek their own advancement. Economic progress can lead to political conservatism that directly opposes Black American political interests. Shared minority status doesn't guarantee shared political interests.

It's hard to say we have a scientific coalition with Latinos when we don't even have a national Black American agenda. How can other groups align with our priorities when we haven't clearly articulated what those priorities are? How many Latinos have the understanding of Black American history and key reference points, to be strategically aligned with a Black American Agenda? If someone argues that segments of the Hispanic population have aligned interests with Black Americans, the first question should be: aligned with what? A coalition requires something concrete to coalesce around. Without a clear national Black American political agenda, any talk of alliance exists only in the realm of spook—imaginary, not synced with reality. There are some straightforward areas where strategic political alliances can be nurtured such as healthcare, campaign finance reform, and labor.

We must reject the popular thinking pushed by political pundits like Roland Martin who suggest that white fear of becoming a minority means America will automatically change structurally. This is quintessential spook thinking because racial proportionality doesn't translate efficiently to political power. America could be 70% Hispanic but still be just as anti-Black American at the structural level as it is now. Because the demographics move, doesn't mean the structure and systems move. The color wrapper or identity of the population changing doesn't mean the structural hierarchies—the economic and financial power systems—change proportionately. Don't think that because America

315

becomes less white and more brown that the structure becomes less anti-Black American. Under the Science vs Spook framework, we need to see scientific factors move materially at the structural and policy level, not just the identity composition of the population. Assuming Hispanics will vote in alignment with Black American interests simply because they are Hispanic is stereotypical thinking—spook thinking. The data shows Hispanics are moving rightward toward MAGA in greater numbers than Black Americans.

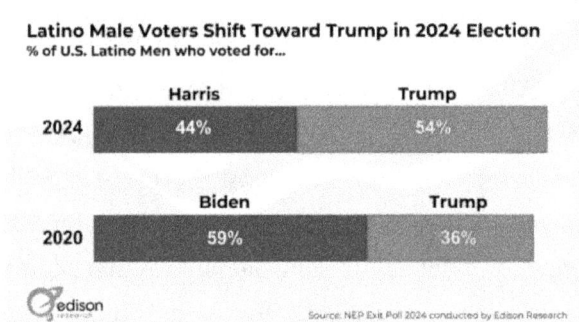

Latino Male Voters Shift Toward Trump in 2024 Election
% of U.S. Latino Men who voted for...

	Harris	Trump
2024	44%	54%

	Biden	Trump
2020	59%	36%

edison

Source: NEP Exit Poll 2024 conducted by Edison Research

Latino Male Voters Shift Toward Trump - Shows movement from 59%
Democratic to 54% Republican

When you think strategically about coalition building, you recognize the need for strategic assessment with clear identification of mutual interests, measurable goals and outcomes, and regular evaluation of costs and benefits. You require structural guarantees through formal agreements on mutual support, clear mechanisms for accountability, and specific commitments on key issues. You demand reality-based planning that recognizes competing interests, understands demographic trends, and analyzes political power dynamics.

The case of illegal immigration perfectly illustrates why we need scientific rather than emotional analysis. Illegal immigration may benefit America's economy by providing necessary low-wage labor, helping control inflation, and supporting economic competitiveness. But it can simultaneously threaten Black American interests through increased competition for resources, diluted political influence, and reduced focus on Black American-specific issues. The solution isn't blanket opposition or support but strategic engagement based on specific interests and outcomes.

Just as America's historical use of slavery provided economic benefits while creating profound moral and social costs, illegal immigration presents a complex mix of national economic advantages and potential threats to Black American political interests. The difference? Black Americans have no obligation to sacrifice our specific interests for America's general economic benefit. We've done that for over 400 years.

Moving forward requires a surgical approach to alliances where we partner on specific issues with clear goals while maintaining independence on other matters and conducting regular assessments of partnership value. We need clear-eyed analysis that quantifies costs and benefits, monitors demographic trends, and tracks political alignment patterns. We must maintain strategic protection by focusing on Black American-specific interests, developing countermeasures to political dilution, and building power independent of coalitions. And we need practical implementation through formal structures for cooperation, establishing clear metrics for success, and maintaining the ability to adjust or withdraw when necessary.

Unity for unity's sake is spook thinking. A scientific orientation demands that every alliance serve specific strategic objectives with measurable outcomes. Whether with Latino American, Asian American, Jewish American, or other communities, partnerships and alliances must be based on mutual benefit and concrete goals, not wishful thinking about natural solidarity.

This isn't about spite or rejection—it's about political science and strategic thinking. As America's demographic landscape shifts, Black American political interests require protection through careful analysis and strategic action, not through blind faith in coalition politics and false assumptions about political alignment. The path forward requires replacing spook-based unity rhetoric with scientific analysis of political realities, strategy, strategically beneficial alliances, and outcomes.

The Science

- Immigration increases resource competition and potentially dilutes Black political influence
- Shared minority status doesn't guarantee shared political interests
- Hispanic Americans are moving toward MAGA in greater numbers than Black Americans
- Build coalitions on specific mutual interests, not assumptions about natural solidarity

[1] "L.A. Council Members Made Racist Comments in Leaked Audio. Read Our Full Coverage." Los Angeles Times, October 9, 2022, updated May 8, 2023. https://www.latimes.com/california/story/2022-10-09/full-coverage-in-leaked-audio-l-a-council-members-make-racist-comments-mock-colleagues

[2] "Latino Immigrants Come to the U.S. with Negative Stereotypes of Black Americans, New Study Shows." Duke Today, Duke University, July 20, 2006. https://today.duke.edu/2006/07/racialpolitics.html

[3] "Latino Immigrants Come to the U.S. with Negative Stereotypes of Black Americans, New Study Shows." Duke Today, Duke University, July 20, 2006. https://today.duke.edu/2006/07/racialpolitics.html

PURE
REPARATIONS

LESSON 36

Are Reparations a Form of Spook?

"So begging the government is folly today. Whatever you think you want from the government, ask them: can they produce it? They're broke." — Minister Louis Farrakhan on Reparations

Journalist Roland Martin once called reparations a "pipe dream" in a now-deleted 2012 tweet. [1] Even Minister Louis Farrakhan, previously a champion of reparations, suggested in 2019 that America is broke and "begging the government is folly." [2] If Las Vegas statistical oddsmakers were setting the odds on Pure Reparations for native Black Americans, they would firmly align with Martin and Farrakhan on the long-shot odds. These views represent conservative, pragmatic, and realistic probability assessments based on the facts and factors we see today.

The Need for Multifactor Analysis

If we are serious about de-spooking reparations and adopting a scientific orientation, we must multifactor this complex issue rather than focusing on single dimensions. [3] A comprehensive analysis requires examining political and voting factors, economic and inflation considerations, constitutional and legal barriers, and organizational capacity. Treating reparations as a purely moral question divorced from these material conditions keeps it in the realm of spook rather than science. By dissecting each factor methodically, we can develop strategic approaches that address specific obstacles rather than treating them as a monolithic, insurmountable wall.

Constitutional Barriers Beyond Political Challenges

While political barriers to reparations receive considerable attention, constitutional obstacles may prove equally formidable. As Erwin Chemerinsky, dean of the University of California at Berkeley School of Law, notes, race-based reparations would likely face insurmountable 14th Amendment challenges under current Supreme Court jurisprudence. Chemerinsky suggests that reparations could be constitutional if framed as payments to descendants of slaves—not African Americans generally—creating a lineage-based rather than race-based program. This approach circumvents the "strict scrutiny" test applied to race-conscious policies, potentially navigating around decades of affirmative action precedents that severely limit race-based remedies.

This constitutional reality underscores why some reparations advocates' political strategies may prove counterproductive. Those who believe they're "teaching Democrats a lesson" by withholding votes and enabling Republican victories must recognize the long-term structural consequences for the Supreme Court's composition. With justices holding lifetime appointments, allowing anti-reparations sentiment to dominate the Court could create a permanent judicial blockade against even the most carefully crafted reparations program. The constitutional pathway is narrow even with sympathetic justices; with an overwhelmingly hostile Court, it becomes virtually impassable regardless of congressional or executive support. We should firmly establish there is a constitutionality factor to Pure Reparations.

I actually agree with both Martin and Minister Farrakhan's estimates, only if we continue doing the same things, with the same political orientation, same organizations, and same system. In that case, where all facts remain unchanged, I would fully support their pessimistic view of Pure Reparations probabilities. However, the facts and factors don't have to stay the same, and our political imagination and political and strategic orientation can evolve.

The problem with declaring reparations a "pipe dream" or "folly" is the complete absence of serious strategic planning at the national level, outside the context of religious prophecy or Democratic Party politics. By serious I mean a national organizational effort that's commensurate with the size of the Black American population and overwhelming support. How do we know reparations are impossible if we've never tried a consistent program with the backing of the consensus of Black Americans, for at least 10 years? There is no historical record of Black America being organized at the national level, centering on reparations, at scale. Organizations like N'COBRA and NAARC exist and have done good work, but they represent too small a statistical sample size and effort to make definitive conclusions about what's possible. In fact, considering their sub-scale positioning, most Black Americans couldn't even tell you what both organizational acronyms stand for or who leads them.

Pure Reparations has never received the effort and organizational investment to reach "scale" where we could even declare "we tried." A serious reparations movement wouldn't be religious-driven, as that undermines the scale we would need, creating unnecessary divisions considering surveys show a strong majority of Black Americans support reparations. A religious-driven Reparations movement also doesn't put us in the right mind of strategy, accountability, and evidence-based evaluation of strategic approaches. While appreciating the efforts of N'COBRA in keeping the issue of Reparations alive, we must acknowledge this effort likely represents just 1% of what the Black American population could accomplish over ten years, organizationally.

To transform Pure Reparations from SPOOK to SCIENCE and create a higher probability path, a necessary condition is political restructuring and the development of new independent leaders. Many activists want shortcuts that bypass the process and necessary conditions to bring Pure Reparations policy within reach. However, political restructuring is required, and the Black American exploitative relationship with the Democratic Party must be reset. Political restructuring by Black Americans is a necessary condition for Pure Reparations. This necessary condition extends the timeline but represents scientific truth. Anyone selling shortcuts on the necessary process and organizational scale is selling spook.

One of Tupac's dreams was creating an independent Black political party, and I've heard people discourage this idea because prior efforts failed and might hurt the Democratic Party. But Tupac possessed the rare gift of being both a dreamer and habitual doer. I have never seen a viable strategic plan for an independent political party centered on reparations—a non-religious strategic plan commensurate with what would constitute a serious policy initiative, with transparent goals over the next ten years. How can we know an independent Black political party can't produce gains for Black Americans without data or robust examples of serious national efforts? An Independent Black Political Party needn't take votes from the Democratic Party; it could surgically target districts and partner with Democrats while breaking the top-down control mechanism that currently leaves almost zero negotiating leverage within the DNC.

A talented, aspiring basketball player would never say, "There's a 99 percent failure rate in making the NBA, so I won't try." At our population size approaching 40 million, Black Americans are the star basketball players who just have been under the wrong team, coach, and playbook. We need political imagination to see the potential of Black American celebrities and athletes getting involved as was the case when Spike Lee needed help to finish the great film Malcolm X. Tiger Woods is statistically deviant (in a good way). But before he became the best golfer in the world, Earl Woods had to go through a scientific process. Greatness requires imagination of where things could go, a disciplined process, and time.

The capitalist billionaire never said, "There's a 99 percent failure rate for becoming a billionaire, so I won't try." Courageous enslaved people risking death to escape southern plantations faced astronomical odds but made risk calculations for the reward. Long odds existed against rapid passage of Civil Rights legislation in 1964 and 1968. The United States faced long odds of national reconciliation after 600,000 deaths and the devastation of Southern infrastructure. Many contemporary observers and foreign powers predicted permanent division or ongoing conflict rather than the rapid economic expansion that followed.

When a Black American business launches and entrepreneurs take risks, SBA data shows over 90% probability of failure within ten years. (Black American businesses have higher failure rates due to insufficient capitalization, family resources, and other factors.) If the most talented confront long odds to make fortunes, why can't we confront long odds for Black Americans' freedom, justice, and equality? These values far outweigh individual fortune or success.

We contemplate long odds and extremely low probabilities in many areas, so why not take more risks to build and organize something substantial for Black Americans? Freedom, justice, and equality demand risk-taking, experiments, flexibility, political imagination, and optimizations. We need innovations and breakthroughs within the political science complex, supported by stronger economic foundations. It's premature to declare, "Building an independent Black political party over ten years isn't realistic." Show me a strong national plan or plans, a good sample size, then present your conclusions and judgments.

Even if we organized collectively around Reparations (at scale) with a 10-20 year plan and fell short, Black American political positioning and leverage would improve. The process itself—building organizations, developing coalitions, creating media infrastructure, training political leadership, and establishing international connections—would leave Black America with vastly improved political capital regardless of the outcome. This isn't just about destination but journey; organizational muscle developed pursuing reparations would strengthen our hand in other political negotiations and create permanent institutional power that doesn't exist today. Failing at reparations after serious, organized effort would still leave us stronger than our current state of political fragmentation and dependency.

The Green Party allegedly hurt Democrats in national elections. If voters in Pennsylvania, Michigan, and Wisconsin had chosen Hillary Clinton over Jill Stein in 2016, Hillary might have become president instead of Trump. Rather than look at Clinton's loss to Trump with multifactor analysis, such as a confident James Comey holding a press conference right before the election, a violation of Department of Justice protocol or Americans experiencing Bush-Clinton dynasty fatigue, or corrupt establishment politics in general, everything is put on Jill Stein. Should we remain ping-ponged between the two-party duopoly, permanently squeezed, avoiding alternatives because the Green Party failed? Why focus so heavily on Green Party voters in a loss rather than on politicians who had all the money and lobbyist support, and their associated decisions? There was no third party when Kamala Harris got smoked by MAGA in 2024, running the table across all battleground states - revealing that our political constraints run deeper than fear of third-party spoilers, and may require precisely the kind of restructuring needed for reparations.

Regarding America being too broke to pay reparations, that's a speculative prediction, not current reality. We should stay grounded in present facts. First, who says Pure Reparations has to be a one-time payment that will "break the bank?" Pure Reparations can be paid over time, giving America more fiscal and monetary room than the current reality, if she needs it.

Assuming relatively low inflation and political will, America has capacity for substantial monetary commitments, just as Japan has printed trillions of yen while carrying over $11 trillion in debt. Most economists would agree Japan remains wealthy despite this debt. Is Japan broke? [4]

This relates to modern monetary theory—the proposition that trillion-dollar deficits are acceptable and the US federal government can freely print money to finance massive spending without concern for debt and deficits. In her 2020 book The Deficit Myth, economist Stephanie Kelton refutes the idea that the federal government faces the same financial limitations as households. [5] The MMT argument maintains that unlike households, the US government can spend and borrow indefinitely without bankruptcy risk. MMT has lost popularity as inflation's limitations have become undeniable and COVID-related spending has wrecked America's balance sheet further. However, under the Science vs Spook framework, we don't throw the baby out with the bath water and we think surgically. America's debt and inflation picture doesn't have to stay the same. Rather than making economic predictions on where inflation and America's debt picture will be a decade from now, we can start organizing and pushing the political side forward, right now.

If potential inflation poses a barrier, our best economists must develop a Reparations framework addressing this factor. Payments might vary based on inflation rates, with adjustments slowing disbursements during high-inflation periods and accelerating them when inflation cools. This represents a technical challenge requiring sophisticated economic modeling, not an insurmountable obstacle. We need Black American economists to develop inflation-resistant payment structures preserving reparations' purchasing power without diluting the total value owed. Pure Reparations means CASH ONLY—no substitutes, infrastructure projects, tax credits, or "programs." Payment timing and distribution can adjust for economic conditions, but the form must remain direct cash transfers to individuals.

America could potentially experience sustained hyperinflation. But that's not today's reality, so our political strategy must address current conditions while understanding future possibilities and probabilities. America can start paying now; we need a real political strategy now. Right now, an organized, committed, and strategic Black America could shut

America down. We possess leverage we've never tried—or if attempted, our efforts weren't innovative or strategic enough for modern times.

Obama implied reparations were so far-fetched and would face such white resistance that pushing for them would prove counterproductive. In a 2021 podcast with Bruce Springsteen, Obama said: "If you ask me theoretically, 'Are reparations justified?' the answer is yes. There's not much question that the wealth of this country, the power of this country was built in significant part, not exclusively, maybe not even the majority of it, but a large portion of it was built on the backs of slaves." [6]

After acknowledging continued systemic oppression under Jim Crow, Obama added that reparations would have faced "the politics of white resistance" and "white resentment" during his presidency. "The talk of welfare queens and the talk of the undeserving poor and the backlash against affirmative action, all that made the prospect of actually proposing any kind of coherent, meaningful reparations program struck me as politically not only a nonstarter but potentially counterproductive."

The hypocrisy is striking. When Obama needed our votes and fanatical Black American religious-like support, it was time to DREAM what was possible and have HOPE. His campaign built on audacious (AUDACITY OF HOPE) aspirations and transformational change. But once he had amassed substantial brand power and white support to lose, acquired a big wallet and mansions in Hawaii, Chicago, and Martha's Vineyard, suddenly it was time for pragmatism and incremental improvements. Obama has masterfully extracted what he wanted from Black America and moved on. This bait-and-switch exemplifies how the political system manages Black expectations—selling dreams during campaigns and delivering excuses in office. Obama faced very long odds to win the Presidency but that didn't prevent him from creating a path to victory and benefiting from the 2008 Global Financial Crisis (GFC).

This appears to be Obama's excuse, as any great idea benefiting Black Americans requires courageous risk-takers. Obama is telling us he would never risk his political and brand capital for Black Americans, even with potential for high reward. At minimum, he could have planted seeds and laid foundations for a future fight—repaying loyal Black American voters who supported him. It's easier for Obama to repay his big donors with political favors than repay and support Black Americans with policy risk taking.

White Support for Reparations: A 4.5× Increase (2000-2022)

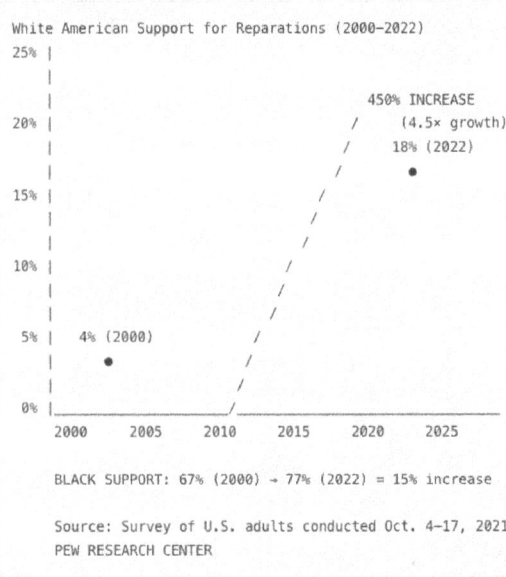

```
White American Support for Reparations (2000-2022)
25% |
    |
    |                                 450% INCREASE
20% |                          /       (4.5× growth)
    |                        /         18% (2022)
    |                      /             •
15% |                    /
    |                  /
    |                /
10% |              /
    |            /
    |          /
5%  |   4% (2000)    /
    |     •        /
    |            /
0%  |_____/_____
    2000   2005   2010   2015   2020   2025

BLACK SUPPORT: 67% (2000) → 77% (2022) = 15% increase

Source: Survey of U.S. adults conducted Oct. 4-17, 2021.
PEW RESEARCH CENTER
```

White Support for Reparations Growth Chart - Shows 450% increase from 2000-2022

Reparations can become de-spooked through better articulation that America as a whole benefits. It's not just repayment for a debt owed but also an investment in America herself. This isn't just moral reasoning but economic science. The economy, educational system, public safety, real estate market, stock market, retail sector, banking industry, and GDP would all benefit from Pure Reparations. Trillions injected directly to Black Americans wouldn't vanish—they would circulate through the economy, creating jobs, funding entrepreneurship and small business, increasing tax revenue, reducing crime, and boosting innovation. A rising tide lifts all boats, but we've never tried raising the Black American boat directly, with Pure Reparations' efficiency and scale.

We must position reparations as repaying a debt with material benefits for all America. When Black wealth increases, consumer spending and investment grow. When Black American education improves, American innovation advances. When Black communities thrive, American cities prosper. This isn't charity but investment in America's future, paying financial and social dividends beyond the initial cost. Every reparations dollar would multiply through economic activity, creating wealth benefiting all Americans. Positioning reparations as national economic stimulus rather than just moral obligation provides arguments beyond guilt and responsibility.

Reparations requires smart coalitions with depth beyond traditional and superficial "Black and Brown" thinking. Reparations becomes spook when advocates dismiss negotiated smart coalitions and alliances. Reparations policy is spook when advocates oppose everyone yet believe they can pass legislation with mostly Black Americans alone. Reparations without strategic diplomacy is a form of spook.

If America can further imperial interests through NATO alliances, Black Americans can further our interests through RATO—Reparations Alliances That Optimize our interests. Consistent with Silis Muhammad's work taking reparations to the United Nations, reparations policy should be lobbied internationally.

Emory law professor Mary Dudziak's groundbreaking book Cold War Civil Rights: Race and the Image of American Democracy provides a blueprint for international pressure driving domestic change. Dudziak meticulously documents how America's Cold War imperatives created leverage points that Black Americans exploited to achieve civil rights victories. The Soviet Union and other nations effectively highlighted American racism as propaganda, embarrassing the U.S. globally and undermining its claim to moral leadership. [7]

This international embarrassment produced tangible results. As Dudziak shows, the Kennedy and Johnson administrations pushed for civil rights legislation partly to improve America's image abroad. The landmark Civil Rights Act of 1964 and Voting Rights Act of 1965 were signed not just because of domestic activism, but because America needed to protect its international standing. This historical case study proves international pressure works—it helped deliver America's most significant civil rights legislation.

The reparations movement must learn from this playbook. By internationalizing our struggle and creating diplomatic headaches, we can generate external pressure forcing domestic action. Just as civil rights leaders used international forums to highlight America's hypocrisy in the 1950s and 1960s, reparations advocates must make America's failure to address its historical debt an international embarrassment interfering with U.S. foreign policy objectives.

When you challenge America's military positioning and objectives, you're making a significant impact. Similarly, we need a broad consortium of countries backing Pure Reparations for Black Americans. For our long-shot odds to avoid being considered spooky, we must develop strategies to secure international support for Pure Reparations. We must remain open-minded about where help comes from. Our long-shot-odds situation demands flexibility commensurate with our current political and economic position.

Reparations can be a form of spook if Black American politics and political orientation remains mostly unchanged and we continue shining the Democratic Party's shoes without demanding even a single executive order (such as Presidential Reparations Commissions) in exchange for our support. Reparations can be a form of spook if our organizations stay the same and new, improved organizations aren't developed. Reparations can be a form of spook if we don't forcefully use artificial intelligence tools and technology to transform our organizations and political organizing.

This isn't about spite or rejection—it's about political science and strategic thinking. Pure Reparations can be scientific only if our politics are restructured first, as a necessary condition.

The Science

- Pure Reparations require political restructuring and new independent leadership as necessary conditions
- Current probability is low without organizational scale and strategic innovation
- International pressure and diplomatic strategy are essential components
- Movement from spook to science requires 10+ year organizational commitment at population scale

---

[1] Moore, Antonio [@tonetalks]. "August 5, 2020 [Tweet]." X. https://x.com/tonetalks/status/1291195867475529729

[2] "Minister Louis Farrakhan Addresses N'COBRA About Reparatory Justice." YouTube, uploaded by National Coalition of Blacks for Reparations in America (N'COBRA), 2019. https://www.youtube.com/watch?app=desktop&v=-TMSUW2JlVc

[3] This refers to the comprehensive approach needed to analyze complex policy issues by examining multiple factors simultaneously rather than focusing on single dimensions.

[4] Landers, Peter. "Japan's Love of Debt Offers a View of U.S. Future." Wall Street Journal, August 22, 2021.

[5] Kelton, Stephanie. "The Deficit Myth: Modern Monetary Theory and the Birth of the People's Economy." New York: PublicAffairs, March 9, 2021.

[6] Schrader, Adam. "Obama calls for reparations for black Americans because the 'wealth of this country was built on the backs of slaves'." Daily Mail, February 25, 2021.

[7] Dudziak, Mary L. "Cold War Civil Rights: Race and the Image of American Democracy." Princeton University Press, 2000.

AI Uncovers the 40 Acres Tricknology

> "The function, the very serious function of racism, is distraction. It keeps you from doing your work. It keeps you explaining, over and over again, your reason for being. Somebody says you have no language, and you spend twenty years proving that you do. Somebody says your head isn't shaped properly, so you have scientists working on the fact that it is. Somebody says you have no art, so you dredge that up. Somebody says you have no kingdoms, so you dredge that up. None of this is necessary. There will always be one more thing."
>
> — Toni Morrison [1]

When we talk about reparations, no historical episode reveals the strategic manipulation of Black American hopes more clearly than the broken promise of "40 Acres and a Mule." While traditional research has pieced together fragments of this story, artificial intelligence offers powerful new tools to uncover the precise financial reality of this foundational tricknology—one of the first instances where the system gave with one hand while taking with the other.

The 40 Acres promise wasn't merely forgotten—it was systematically erased through deliberate policy decisions. As a groundbreaking investigation by the Center for Public Integrity recently published in Mother Jones revealed, "[The federal government] actually did issue hundreds, perhaps thousands, of titles to specific plots of land between 4 and 40 acres—before ultimately changing course and returning the land to the plantation owners." [2] This wasn't accidental neglect—it was calculated system protection.

AI tools can help us identify precisely what happened by analyzing patterns across millions of historical documents that humans alone could never process. The Center for Public Integrity used image recognition algorithms to analyze 1.8 million recently digitized records from the Freedmen's Bureau, identifying 1,250 formerly enslaved people who received—and then lost—land titles in Georgia and South Carolina. [3]

This isn't just historical curiosity—it's numerical evidence of a precise debt that remains unpaid. As Dr. William "Sandy" Darity calculates, if we start with the conservative estimate that land in 1865 was valued at $10 per acre, then 40 acres per family of four meant $100 per ex-slave. With approximately 4 million former slaves at the time, this represents $400 million in 1865 dollars. Compounded annually at 6% (accounting for both interest and inflation), this sum would amount to "more than $1.3 trillion" today. [4]

Consider the story of Pompey Jackson, who received 4 acres on Georgia's Grove Hill plantation on April 20, 1865. Nine months later, the former plantation owner William Habersham secured a presidential pardon from Andrew Johnson. As the Mother Jones investigation reveals, "Within a few days, President Johnson pardoned Habersham, eventually allowing him to reclaim Grove Hill as his own." [5]

When Pompey Jackson's granddaughter Louise moved to Philadelphia in 1923, it was because "her husband, a construction worker, was being paid less than his white co-workers. It would take generations more for the family to acquire real estate. This isn't just anecdotal history—it's the direct trajectory of wealth denial playing out exactly as system design intended.

This wasn't random—AI analysis reveals that similar patterns repeated across the South. This wasn't just policy failure; it was strategic tricknology that established a template for how promises to Black Americans would be made and broken for generations to come.

Calculating What's Owed

The scientific approach requires moving beyond symbolic gestures to measurable calculation. AI can help quantify not just what was promised, but what was deliberately taken, and what that represents in current economic value.

Dr. Darity's computations show us the precise scale: "If there are approximately 30 million descendants of enslaved Africans in the United States today, the estimate based on 40 acres yields an allocation of slightly more than $400,000 per recipient." [6] This isn't fantasy—it's economic reality based on compounding the actual historical debt.

For comparison, an empty 4-acre lot at Grove Hill plantation (the same size as Pompey Jackson's original allocation) sold for $250,000 in October 2023. Based on that valuation, "40 acres on Grove Hill could be worth about $2.5 million today." [7]

Beyond Historical Accounting

AI tools don't just help us understand what happened—they can help us trace the multigenerational consequences with precision. The Mother Jones investigation used genealogical research to trace descendants of those who received land titles, finding that many families struggled for decades to acquire even small plots of land. Pompey Jackson, for example, wasn't able to purchase his own property until 1894, nearly 30 years after his original land title was revoked. [8]

The economic impact across generations is staggering. As Darity notes: "That would've had very significant implications for Black economic wellbeing as well as Black political power." Instead, "Black Americans remained plagued by a wealth gap, possessing just a quarter of the wealth held by white American families." [9]

This historical injustice is the foundation of persistent economic inequality that continues to shape Black American reality today.

Finding Precision Through Technology

The tricknology of 40 Acres relied on bureaucratic complexity and the erasure of records to hide what actually happened. Those who oppose freedom, justice, and equality, have a preference for mystery. AI technologies now allow us to cut through this deliberate obscurity and establish precisely what was promised, what was delivered, and what was taken.

As Darity explains, "Having this kind of evidence—of actual families who received land and had that land taken away—certainly can address, in some measure, the issue of reparations." [10]

This precision matters because it transforms abstract historical discussions into concrete financial calculations. It's no longer possible to dismiss reparations claims as lacking specificity when AI tools can identify exactly who received land, where that land was located, when it was taken, and what it would be worth today.[11]

The Eligibility Question

AI can also help address one of the most contentious issues in reparations discussions: determining eligibility. Dr. Sandy Darity proposes two specific criteria: individuals would need to "establish that they are indeed descendants of persons formerly enslaved in the United States" and "establish that at least 10 years prior to the adoption of a reparations program they self-identified as 'black,' 'African American,' 'Negro,' or 'colored'." [12]

AI-powered genealogical tools can now help trace family lineages with unprecedented precision, making it possible to verify descent from enslaved persons. This removes one of the common objections to reparations—that it would be "too complicated" to determine who should receive them. The technology now exists to make these determinations with high confidence.

From Historical Analysis to Political Action

The 40 Acres tricknology worked because it buried the evidence in millions of handwritten records that would take lifetimes to analyze manually. The truth and facts were concealed in mystery. AI changes that equation, allowing us to extract the financial reality from the bureaucratic obscurity and transform reparations from a political debate into a concrete economic calculation. The numbers speak for themselves, demanding recognition of a specific, quantifiable debt that has only grown with each passing generation.

The Science

- AI analysis reveals 1,250+ formerly enslaved people received and lost land titles
- 40 acres in 1865 = $400,000+ per recipient today with compound interest
- Technology can cut through bureaucratic obscurity to establish precise debt calculations
- Transform reparations from political debate into concrete economic calculation

[1] Morrison, Toni. "The Source of Self-Regard: Selected Essays, Speeches, and Meditations." New York: Knopf, 2019.

[2] Donovan, L., Cucho, L., & Gordon, A. "40 Acres and a Lie." Mother Jones, February 2024. https://www.motherjones.com/politics/2024/02/40-acres-and-a-lie/

[3] Ibid.

[4] Darity, W. "Forty Acres and a Mule in the 21st Century." Social Science Quarterly, 89(3), 656-664, 2008.

[5] Donovan, L., Cucho, L., & Gordon, A. "40 Acres and a Lie." Mother Jones, February 2024.

[6] Darity, W. "Forty Acres and a Mule in the 21st Century." Social Science Quarterly, 89(3), 656-664, 2008.

[7] Donovan, L., Cucho, L., & Gordon, A. "40 Acres and a Lie." Mother Jones, February 2024.

[8] Ibid.

[9] Ibid.

[10] Ibid.

[11] Ibid.

[12] Darity, W. "Forty Acres and a Mule in the 21st Century." Social Science Quarterly, 89(3), 656-664, 2008.

Dr. Sandy Darity on the Wealth Gap

"The poorest whites, those in the bottom quintile of the income distribution, have a higher median net worth than all Blacks combined. Median wealth for poorest whites is ten times poorest Blacks." — Dr. William "Sandy" Darity Jr.

When tackling structural change in Black American politics, we need to anchor ourselves in hard mathematical reality rather than symbolic gestures or Democratic Party political religion. In our search for economic justice, Dr. William "Sandy" Darity Jr. and his colleagues provide the scholarship clarity we desperately need. Their research cuts through the political fog and gives us the real numbers on the Black-white wealth gap.

The wealth gap isn't just a talking point. While politicians throw around vague promises about "closing the racial wealth gap," Dr. Darity's research provides the cold math of our reality: at the median, Black households hold just $24,100 in wealth compared to white households' $188,200—a gap of $164,100. But that's using the median, which masks the true scale of the problem. [1]

The mean tells a far more devastating story: The average white household has $983,400 in wealth, while the average Black household has just $142,500—a gap of $840,000 per household. This reality aggregates to a total national racial wealth gap of approximately $11.2 trillion. [2] That's not a gap you close with symbolic politics or incremental policies. 'First Black' this and 'First Black' that can't close the wealth gap—it's structural.

Our political priorities should target quantifiable, measurable progress rather than symbolic victories. Our political goals should be scientific, while politicians have every incentive to pacify us with symbolism and spook, making their jobs easier while our material conditions remain unchanged.

Nationally, White Families Are Significantly Wealthier Than All Other Racial and Ethnic Groups Combined
Household Median Net Worth by Race and Ethnicity, US, 2016

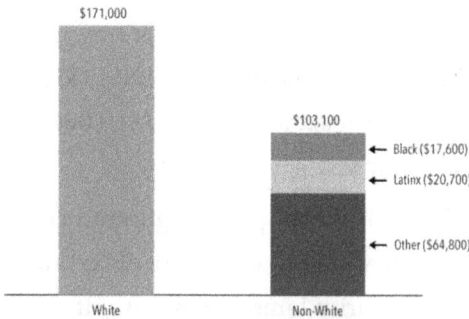

$171,000

$103,100

←— Black ($17,600)

←— Latinx ($20,700)

←— Other ($64,800)

White   Non-White

Note: "Other" category includes respondents identifying as Asian, American Indian, Alaska Native, Native Hawaiian, Pacific Islander, other race, and all respondents reporting more than one racial identification. Source: Lisa Dettling et al., Recent Trends in Wealth-Holding by Race and Ethnicity: Evidence From the Survey of Consumer Finances (Board of Governors of the Federal Reserve System: September 27, 2017).

California Budget & Policy Center
Independent Analysis. Shared Prosperity.

The political orientation we need is clear: I don't want to discuss diversity initiatives or DEI programs or "First Black" achievements more than I want to discuss how to close an $840,000 per household wealth gap. When the conversation shifts to symbolic representation, we must redirect it to material outcomes directly connected to the whole of Black America, not individuals or tokenistic approaches. When politicians offer us cultural or identity-based recognition, we must demand economic transformation.

The Measurement Matters

Politicians and mainstream economists prefer using the median because it hides the true scale of the problem. It's like measuring the average height in a room where Jeff Bezos walks in with $200 billion. The median tells you almost nothing about the actual distribution of wealth, especially since 97 percent of white wealth is held by households that exceed the white median. A quarter of white households have a net worth exceeding $1 million, compared to just 4 percent of Black households. [3]

This gets to the heart of the spook versus science framework: using the median is deceptive and promotes mystery—it creates a sanitized picture that makes the problem seem manageable with minor policy tweaks. Using the mean is science—it shows the full magnitude of what we're dealing with and forces us to confront the inadequacy of mainstream solutions.

Take the much-celebrated proposals floating around Democratic circles: student debt forgiveness and "baby bonds." These sound good on the surface, but the mathematics don't add up. Black Americans carry more educational debt ($23,400 on average) than whites ($16,000), so even total forgiveness would barely make a dent in an $840,000 wealth gap. It's like trying to drain the ocean with a teaspoon. [4]

As for "baby bonds," which would provide government-funded trust accounts for newborns, they simply weren't designed to eliminate the racial wealth gap. As Dr. Darity himself explains, "If we're concerned about eliminating the gap between blacks and whites with respect to wealth, then we would need a reparations program. If we're concerned about the reproduction of inequality across generations, then the baby bonds type of proposal would be the mechanism to correct for that." [5]

Debunking Common Myths About the Wealth Gap

The spook thinking permeating this conversation is the belief that if Black Americans just changed our behaviors or values, we could close the gap ourselves. However, the wealth gap was created and enforced by the state, it's a state debt and state-sponsored gap. The data demolishes this myth-making. When adjusted for income, Black American families often save at rates equal to or higher than white families. The problem isn't Black financial habits—it's systematic exclusion from wealth-building opportunities for generations. [6]

And let's get scientific about the self-made billionaire mythology. Do you think it's a coincidence that today's top billionaires—Elon Musk (father owned South African mines during apartheid), Zuckerberg, Gates, Bezos (whose parents funded Amazon with a $300,000 check), and Buffett—

all came from wealth and privilege? Each had significant family resources, elite education access, and safety nets that allowed them to take entrepreneurial risks. These billionaires had generational family cushion to take more risks. This isn't about diminishing their achievements; it's about acknowledging that intergenerational wealth creates the conditions for spectacular success. When Black Americans were systematically prevented from building this foundation for generations by the state, the mathematics of opportunity become clear.

Education is another area where spook thinking dominates. We're told that if we just get more degrees, the wealth gap will naturally close. But the science tells a different story. Black households headed by college graduates have less wealth than white households headed by high school dropouts. The typical Black family with a head who has a college degree has about $70,219 in wealth, while a white family headed by someone with some college but no degree has $73,878. White households with heads who haven't even finished high school have more wealth than Black households with college-educated heads. [7]

In fact, a 2017 study found that when you control for educational attainment, the median wealth of Black families with a bachelor's degree is $23,400, while white families at the same education level have $268,000 in wealth – approximately an $180,000 difference. This isn't ancient history—this is happening right now. [8]

Marriage and Family Structure Won't Close the Gap

Another persistent myth is that family structure drives the racial wealth gap. The belief that the prevalence of Black single motherhood explains wealth disparities confuses consequence and cause. This dangerous narrative is steeped in racist stereotypes dating back to the 1965 Moynihan report.

The data tells a different story. Single white women with kids have the same amount of wealth as single Black women without kids. The median single-parent white family has more than twice the wealth of the median

Black family with two parents. These data points show that economic benefits typically associated with marriage will not close the racial wealth gap. Having the "ideal" family type does not enable Black households to substantially reduce the racial gap in wealth. [9]

Recent research from the St. Louis Federal Reserve finds the connection between family structure and wealth to be weak and inconsistent. Their researchers conclude that "any correlation between family structure and wealth that exists in aggregate data is largely spurious." [10]

Homeownership and the Wealth Gap

While homeownership is often touted as the primary driver of the racial wealth gap, the data tells a more complex story. Among households that don't own homes, white households have 31 times more wealth than Black households. Even among homeowners, white households have nearly $140,000 more in net worth than Black households. [11]

The homeownership gap is certainly significant—about 72.5% of whites own homes compared to 42% of Blacks—but closing this gap would still leave an enormous wealth disparity. Research shows that homes in Black neighborhoods are systematically undervalued and appreciate at lower rates, meaning even when Black Americans do own homes, they don't build wealth at the same rate as whites. [12]

As Dr. Darity's research has shown, achieving parity in homeownership rates and returns on housing would still leave most of the racial wealth gap intact. The problem isn't just that Black Americans own homes at lower rates—it's that they start with less wealth to invest in homes in the first place. [13]

The Generational Gift vs. the Generational Curse

The wealth gap isn't merely a statistical anomaly—it's the mathematical expression of intergenerational economic inheritance. While the majority of white Americans begin life with what Dr. Darity calls a "head start" stemming from accumulated advantages of chattel slavery, Jim Crow, and preferential access to wealth-building policies like the GI Bill and FHA loans, most Black Americans start with what amounts to an inherited economic deficit. Research shows this isn't just historical—even today, white families are five times more likely to receive substantial inheritances than Black families, with median inheritance values of $110,000 versus $52,000 respectively. The gap persists not because of behavioral differences but because wealth begets wealth across generations, while its absence perpetuates itself with equal mathematical precision.

The Business Ownership Reality

Entrepreneurship is often praised as a route to eliminate racial wealth inequality. However, according to the U.S. Census Bureau's Survey of Business Owners, over 90 percent of Black firms do not have even one employee other than the owners. The proportion of owner-only firms reaches a high of close to 98 percent for Black female-led businesses. [14]

When Blacks do own a business, the return to that business is lower than that of whites and falls well short of closing the racial wealth gap. The 19 million white-owned businesses have 88 percent of the overall sales and control 86.5 percent of U.S. employment, while Black businesses have a mere 1.3 percent of total American sales and 1.7 percent of the nation's employees. [15]

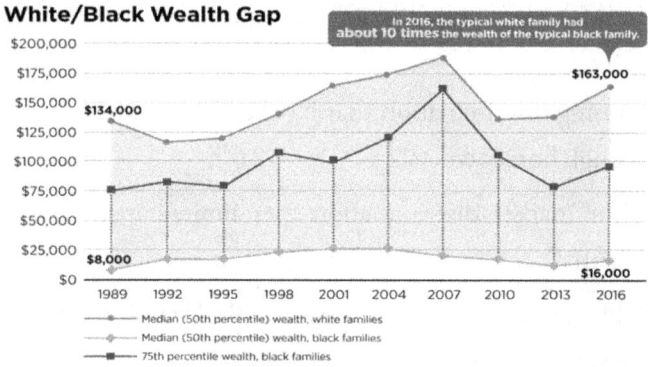

White/Black Wealth Gap

In 2016, the typical white family had about **10 times** the wealth of the typical black family.

- Median (50th percentile) wealth, white families
- Median (50th percentile) wealth, black families
- 75th percentile wealth, black families

■ FEDERAL RESERVE BANK OF ST. LOUIS

Notes: Dollar values are CPI-U adjusted to 2016 dollars and rounded to the nearest $1,000.

Sources: Federal Reserve Board's Survey of Consumer Finances and authors' calculations.

Description: This line chart displays the white/black racial wealth gap from 1989 to 2016. The top horizontal line shows the median (50th percentile) wealth of white families, which was $134,000 in 1989 and $163,000 in 2016. The bottom horizontal line shows the median (50th percentile) wealth of black families, which was $8,000 in 1989 and $16,000 in 2016. The tops of the dotted vertical lines indicate the 75th wealth percentile for black families; notably, these never reach the 50th wealth percentile of white families.

In a 2010 study, the Minority Business Development Agency found that white business owners started their businesses with an average of $106,702 in capital, compared to $35,205 for Black American-owned businesses. The primary reason for business failure is low capitalization at the start, and Blacks begin the entrepreneurship game with low capital finance, reinforcing the theme that wealth begets wealth. [16]

Regional Disparities Reveal Structural Problems

The geographical distribution of the wealth gap further illustrates its structural nature. Dr. Darity's research has revealed shocking regional disparities: in Boston, the median net worth of Black households was found to be just $8. Not $8,000—just $8. In Miami, it's $11. This isn't ancient history—this is happening right now. [17]

These regional variations can't be explained by differences in work ethic, education, or family structure. They reflect historic patterns of anti-Black American discrimination and the compounding effects of intergenerational wealth transfer—or its absence.

The Scientific Assessment

The system is working exactly as designed. The mechanisms that maintain the racial wealth gap aren't hidden conspiracies—they're documented policies:

- Housing discrimination that blocked Black wealth accumulation through homeownership
- Labor market discrimination that limited income and savings potential
- Deliberate destruction of existing Black wealth through "urban renewal" and highway construction
- A tax system designed to protect and amplify generational wealth transfer primarily for whites [18]

- Black Americans have paid the same tax rates as whites since Jim Crow while facing systematic exclusion from broader wealth-building opportunities and confronting discriminatory structures throughout the economy, creating a compounding generational disadvantage that helps explain today's wealth gap.

When we're asking why we lack political power, we need to start with this $11.2 trillion economic factor. Political power flows from economic power. If you don't have one, you won't have the other.

From Academic Research to Political Demands

Darity and Mullen's work exemplifies how rigorous academic scholarship can transform political discourse and policy demands. Armed with their quantitative framework, Black Americans can better shift conversations with Democratic leadership from symbolic gestures to material outcomes: Let's set aside discussions about new symbolic holidays, White House hip-hop celebrations, or symbolic 'first Black' appointments. Instead, let's focus on party's specific plan to address the $11.2 trillion racial wealth gap. Rather than Democrats scoring political points from inviting Too Short to perform at Kamala Harris' house, let's demand she really represents us with a town hall about the racial wealth gap and a strategic plan. What executive orders will you use that focuses attention on Black Americans, even if you have to focus on lineage instead of race. What measurable targets will your policies hit? By what timeline? And how will success be measured?

As Darity points out, only a comprehensive reparations program can address a gap of this magnitude. Anything less is just political theater. When asked about financing such a program, Darity notes, "I embrace the view that you don't have to pay as you go, that it is fine if you go and then pay. So the focus should be on whether or not a new major expenditure program would risk hyperinflation, and that's what you really have to be concerned about. To the extent that we can manage that, then I don't think there's a serious issue around financing."

A gap of $11.2 trillion won't be closed through "conversations about race" or putting a few more Black faces in high places. It requires direct structural interventions on a scale that most politicians aren't even willing to contemplate. Democrats should be required to "put a ring on it" for votes and declare the wealth gap a national emergency and crisis.

Until we're talking about solutions that match the scale of the problem, we're not being serious. And Dr. Darity's research gives us the scientific foundation to demand exactly that.

The Science

- Mean wealth gap: $840,000 per household ($983,400 white vs. $142,500 Black)
- Education and marriage don't close the gap—structural factors and intergenerational wealth transfer do
- Only comprehensive reparations can address an $11.2 trillion national gap
- Demand Democratic Party treat wealth gap as national emergency requiring concrete targets and timelines

---

[1] William Darity Jr. and A. Kirsten Mullen, From Here to Equality: Reparations for Black Americans in the Twenty-First Century (Chapel Hill: University of North Carolina Press, 2020), 35-37.

[2] William Darity Jr. and Darrick Hamilton, "The True Cost of Closing the Racial Wealth Gap," New York Times, April 30, 2021.

[3] William Darity Jr., Darrick Hamilton, Mark Paul, Alan Aja, Anne Price, Antonio Moore, and Caterina Chiopris, "What We Get Wrong About Closing the Racial Wealth Gap," Samuel DuBois Cook Center on Social Equity, April 2018, 3.

[4] William Darity Jr., "A Direct Approach to Eliminating the Racial Wealth Gap," Federal Reserve Bank of Boston Conference on Race and Inequality, October, 17, 2019.

[5] William Darity Jr., "A Direct Approach to Eliminating the Racial Wealth Gap," Federal Reserve Bank of Boston Conference on Race and Inequality, October, 17, 2019.

[6] William Darity Jr., Darrick Hamilton, Mark Paul, Alan Aja, Anne Price, Antonio Moore, and Caterina Chiopris, "What We Get Wrong About Closing the Racial Wealth Gap," Samuel DuBois Cook Center on Social Equity, April 2018, 21-22.

[7] Darrick Hamilton, Tressie McMillan Cottom, William Darity Jr., Alan A. Aja, and Carolyn Ash, "Still We Rise: The Continuing Case for America's Historically Black Colleges and Universities," The American Prospect 25, no. 4 (Fall 2015).

[8] Tatjana Meschede, Joanna Taylor, Alexis Mann, and Thomas Shapiro, "Family Achievements?: How a College Degree Accumulates Wealth for Whites and Not For Blacks," Federal Reserve Bank of St. Louis Review 99, no. 1 (2017): 121-37.

[9] Amy Traub, Laura Sullivan, Tatjana Meschede, and Thomas Shapiro, "The Asset Value of Whiteness: Understanding the Racial Wealth Gap," Demos and the Institute on Assets and Social Policy, 2017.

[10] William Emmons and Lowell Ricketts, "The Link Between Family Structure and Wealth Is Weaker Than You Might Think," Federal Reserve Bank of St. Louis, 2017.

[11] William Darity Jr., Darrick Hamilton, Mark Paul, Alan Aja, Anne Price, Antonio Moore, and Caterina Chiopris, "What We Get Wrong About Closing the Racial Wealth Gap," Samuel DuBois Cook Center on Social Equity, April 2018, 11-12.

[12] Andre Perry, Jonathan Rothwell, and David Harshbarger, "The Devaluation of Assets in Black Neighborhoods: The Case of Residential Property," Brookings Institution, November 2018.

[13] William Darity Jr., "The Case for Reparations: Addressing the Racial Wealth Gap," Testimony to the House Judiciary Subcommittee on the Constitution, Civil Rights, and Civil Liberties, June 19, 2019.

[14] Algernon Austin, "The Color of Entrepreneurship: Why the Racial Gap Among Firms Costs the U.S. Millions," Center for Global Policy Solutions, 2016.

[15] Michael McManus, "Minority Business Ownership: Data from the 2012 Survey of Business Owners," U.S. Small Business Administration Office of Advocacy, 2016.

[16] Robert W. Fairlie and Alicia M. Robb, "Disparities in Capital Access between Minority and Non-Minority-Owned Businesses," U.S. Department of Commerce, Minority Business Development Agency, 2010.

[17] Ana Patricia Muñoz, Marlene Kim, Mariko Chang, Regine O. Jackson, Darrick Hamilton, and William A. Darity Jr., "The Color of Wealth in Boston," Federal Reserve Bank of Boston, 2015.

[18] Richard Rothstein, The Color of Law: A Forgotten History of How Our Government Segregated America (New York: Liveright, 2017).

LESSON 39

Charles Krauthammer: A Conservative Advocate for Reparations

> *"Why reparations: First, because they are targeted precisely at those who deserve them. Let us be plain. Richmond's sin—America's sin—was against Blacks. There is no wrong in American history to compare with slavery. Affirmative action distorts the issue by favoring equally all 'disadvantaged groups.' Some of those groups are disadvantaged, some not. Black America is the only one that for generations was officially singled out for discrimination and worse. Why blur the issue?" — Charles Krauthammer*

Charles Krauthammer challenged conservative orthodoxy when he came out for reparations. The Pulitzer Prize-winning columnist wasn't known for straying from right-wing positions, but on this issue, he broke ranks with stunning clarity. His writings on reparations—dating back to 1990 and reaffirmed in his 2001 Washington Post column "A Grand Compromise"—laid out an argument that defied the knee-jerk opposition most conservatives display toward reparations. [1]

The science behind Krauthammer's position was straightforward: "The American people owe a special debt to black Americans," he wrote, making a critical distinction that many miss. He wasn't operating from vague white guilt or general liberal sympathies. Instead, he recognized the uniqueness of the Black American experience: "There is nothing to compare with centuries of state-sponsored slavery followed by a century of state-sponsored discrimination."

What made Krauthammer's argument particularly powerful was his simultaneous critique of affirmative action, which he called a "disaster" for America and for Black Americans. He didn't approach reparations from a typical progressive framework but from a principled conservative position that recognized historical debts while rejecting ongoing race-conscious policies. For Krauthammer, affirmative action had "violated the principle of equal treatment" and inadvertently stigmatized Black Americans by casting doubt on their genuine achievements.

His proposal was radical in its simplicity: a one-time reparation payment to settle America's historical debt, followed by the complete elimination of all programs of racial preference. "In one grand gesture," he wrote, "an acknowledgment is made not of collective guilt but of collective responsibility." According to Krauthammer, reparations would allow America to move forward with a truly colorblind approach—one aligned with Martin Luther King Jr.'s vision of judging people by character rather than skin color.

Krauthammer didn't just make a moral case—he provided specific numbers. He proposed "$100,000 for every family of four," explicitly calculating that while noting it was expensive, it would cost "about 50% more than the cost of our S&L sins—but hardly, for a $6 trillion economy, a bankrupting sum." He even suggested a funding mechanism: "A 10-year 75 cents gas tax, for example, would pay the whole bill."

This approach distinguished Krauthammer from those who discuss reparations in vague, symbolic terms. You can tell Krauthammer took some time to think about America's racial demons and history, in an honest way. You can tell from his writings he really wanted to understand the different factors and come up with a solution.

He recognized what he called our "system of racial compensation" through affirmative action as "inherently unjust but socially demoralizing and inexcusably clumsy." His alternative was "an honest focused substitute: real, hard, one-time compensation."

Krauthammer directly addressed the dignity question often raised against cash reparations: "But is not cash-for-suffering demeaning? Perhaps. But we have found no better way to compensate for great crimes." [2] He compared America's situation to Germany's reparations for Holocaust survivors, noting that Germans recognize "the millions they have dispersed to Holocaust survivors cannot begin to compensate for the murder of an entire civilization. Yet for irremediable national crimes, reparations are as dignified a form of redress as one can devise."

Most importantly, Krauthammer precisely identified America's fundamental sin: "Let us be plain. Richmond's sin—America's sin—was against blacks. There is no wrong in American history to compare with slavery." This clarity allowed him to reject the increasingly complex matrix of affirmative action programs that had "grown to include preferential treatment for Hispanics, women, the handicapped and an ever-expanding list of favored groups," which he called "absurd."

This pattern of unexpected champions for reparations continued in 2020 when billionaire Democratic presidential candidate Tom Steyer made reparations a central component of his platform. When Steyer outperformed expectations in the South Carolina primary, it was significant for two reasons.

First, it demonstrated that a Democratic Party candidate could run competitively against Biden and Bernie Sanders with reparations as a priority. Steyer gained momentum in South Carolina before hitting the "Clyburn wall"—the coordinated establishment effort to consolidate support behind Biden. In interviews, Steyer was explicit: "In terms of race, I'm the person who talks explicitly about race, who is for reparations for slavery, who believes that unless you deal with the subtext of race in virtually every policy area in the United States, then you're not really dealing with that policy area honestly." [3]

Second, Steyer's candidacy forces us to reconsider our attachment to identity politics. There are situations where we must ask ourselves: would it be better scientifically, based on probabilities and outcomes, if we treated all politicians equally and scored them based on (1) risk-taking and (2) Black American policy agenda? In terms of cold probabilities and the way the system is structured, if we're looking for an Executive Order on Reparations, a generic white candidate would be in a better position to run on and execute it, than a Black American candidate.

Clyburn has Black American identity but represents establishment entrenchment and status quo politics. He was strategically positioned to stop Tom Steyer, a Jewish-American billionaire, from putting everything on the line and placing Reparations on the national political table. This demonstrates why identity must be discounted when it doesn't align with structural changes and policy risk-taking. The Black American could be the one strategically positioned to stop Black American political imagination and the restructuring of the historical Black American captured relationship with the Democratic Party. If the FBI wanted to break up a Black American organization that was doing positive things in the community, it would send in a Black American agent. The Democratic Party works the same way.

We can't put symbolism and identity affinity in our bank account to pay bills and tuition, invest, and to go to Kroger or Walmart and buy groceries. We need material and tangible policy results, with risk-taking on our behalf. If we assign too much weight to identity, the system is positioned to offer less substantive policy, treating symbolic representation as sufficient value while avoiding transformative changes that would benefit most Black Americans.

What good is Jim Clyburn's Black American identity if he's protecting the system against reparations, unwilling to take policy risks for Black Americans, and out of politically innovative ideas at over 80 years of age? In this case, identity affinity can hold us back if we "over-factor" it above risk-taking and a Black American policy agenda. These old leaders may have done plenty of good but we should consider them a national threat to Black American political interests.

Clyburn's district may be popular for the famous "Clyburn Fish Fry" that attracts top Democrats like Joe Biden, but it's also the sixth poorest district in the United States. This stark contrast reveals the gap between political access and material outcomes that characterizes much of contemporary Black political leadership.

Clyburn occupies a strategic blocker position to protect establishment interests, and that's precisely why party elites orchestrated the move of the first DNC primary state to South Carolina. They deployed seductive spook rhetoric such as "Black Americans should vote first" as opposed to white New Hampshire. The elites calculated they could manipulate the Democratic Party into changing the rules using race in a politically perverted way. This change was done after Clyburn's successful blocking for Biden in the 2020 election.

However, Black Americans would likely be better off if New Hampshire continued as the first primary state, based on establishment versus anti-establishment dynamics within the Democratic Party. This counter-intuitive reality demonstrates how racial appeals can mask policies that ultimately harm the communities they claim to serve.

We should also consider the strategic dimension: since Black Americans already support reparations at more than an 80% clip, perhaps more work needs to be done persuading the broader American public. Politicians willing to take risks advocating for reparations might be more effective at building the coalition necessary for implementation than those who avoid the issue while expecting support based on identity alone.

The significance of both Krauthammer's and Steyer's positions wasn't just their moral clarity but their strategic frameworks. Krauthammer connected reparations to ending affirmative action, offering conservatives a principled path to address historical injustice while achieving their goal of race-neutral policies. Steyer positioned reparations within a broader progressive agenda that included economic reforms.

Though Krauthammer passed away in 2018, and Steyer's campaign ultimately failed, their advocacy for reparations provides valuable templates for advancing this cause. By focusing on the specific historical debt owed to Black Americans and prioritizing risk-taking policy advocates regardless of identity, we can build the broad coalition necessary to make reparations a reality.

Having non-Black American voices advocate for reparations—including white Americans making science and factor-based arguments—can help reach audiences who might initially resist Black American advocacy due to cognitive biases and in-group dynamics. While Black Americans maintain intellectual authority on reparations as the affected community, strategic deployment of diverse messengers can overcome psychological barriers that limit receptivity to even the strongest evidence-based arguments.

This approach recognizes that effective coalition-building sometimes requires meeting people where they are psychologically, rather than where we believe they should be morally. The goal remains the same: securing Pure Reparations through the most effective persuasion strategies available, regardless of which voices prove most convincing to different audiences.

Although younger white Americans (18-29) already show encouraging levels of support at 45%, the reality is clear: we must increase overall white American support from 18% to 30-40% over the next decade to achieve the Pure Reparations policy. [4] This won't happen by antagonizing potential allies. The strategic path forward requires coalition-building across demographic and ideological lines, not ideological purity tests. With Black American support already approaching its ceiling at 77%, the additional support needed for a viable coalition must come from white, Hispanic, and Asian communities. Serious reparations advocates grasp this numerical reality - building a broader tent is not a compromise but the only scientific approach with any probability of success. Every social media activist 'purist' who attacks potential allies is effectively voting against the very reparations they claim to champion. Many will have to decide, do they want to be "hardcore" and inflexible or do they want to be scientific about their affairs and create a strategic path for Black America?

White Support for Reparations: A 4.5× Increase (2000-2022)

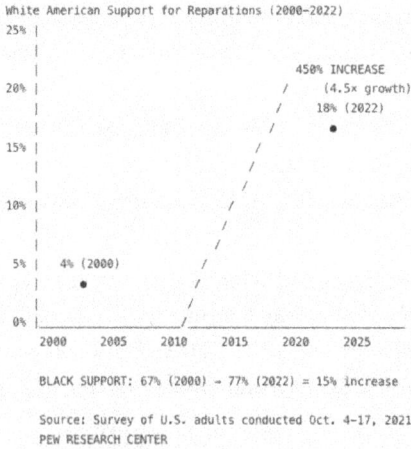

```
White American Support for Reparations (2000-2022)
25% |
    |
    |                              450% INCREASE
20% |                      /        (4.5x growth)
    |                    /          18% (2022)
    |                  /               •
15% |                /
    |              /
    |            /
10% |          /
    |        /
    |      /
 5% |    4% (2000)   /
    |      •      /
    |          /
 0% |_____/_____
    2000   2005   2010   2015   2020   2025

BLACK SUPPORT: 67% (2000) → 77% (2022) = 15% increase

Source: Survey of U.S. adults conducted Oct. 4-17, 2021.
PEW RESEARCH CENTER
```

White Support for Reparations Growth Chart - Shows 450% increase from 2000-2022

One thing that Charles Krauthammer wrote that stuck with me was if America enacted Reparations, cash payments, directly to Black Americans, Democrats would have to admit their policies and approaches have failed.

The Science

- Conservative support for reparations exists when framed as one-time payment + ending affirmative action
- Krauthammer proposed $100,000 per family with specific funding mechanism (gas tax)
- Non-Black advocates can reach audiences resistant to Black American advocacy
- White American support must increase from 18% to 30-40% for viable reparations coalition

[1] Charles Krauthammer, "A Grand Compromise," Washington Post, April 6, 2001.

[2] Charles Krauthammer, "Essay: Reparations For Black Americans," Time Magazine, December 31, 1990. https://time.com/archive/6716829/essay-reparations-for-black-americans/

[3] Tonya Mosley, "Tom Steyer Thinks His Progressive Policies Will Win Big In South Carolina," Here & Now, WBUR, February 27, 2020. https://www.wbur.org/hereandnow/2020/02/27/tom-steyer-south-carolina-primary

[4] Carrie Blazina and Kiana Cox, "Black and White Americans are far apart in their views of reparations for slavery," Pew Research Center, November 28, 2022. https://www.pewresearch.org/short-reads/2022/11/28/black-and-white-americans-are-far-apart-in-their-views-of-reparations-for-slavery/

LESSON 40

Darity and Mullen on Reparations

> *"This is what you should realize: The greatest contribution to this country was that which was contributed by the Black man. If I take the wages... of everyone here, individually, it means nothing, but collectively, all of the earning power or wages that you earned in one week would make me wealthy. And if I could collect it for a year, I'd be rich beyond dreams. Now, when you see this, and then you stop and consider the wages that were kept back from millions of Black people, not for one year but for three hundred and ten years, you'll see how this country got so rich so fast." — Malcolm X* [1]

Dr. William "Sandy" Darity Jr. and A. Kirsten Mullen have done the most comprehensive scientific work on Pure Reparations. Their groundbreaking book "From Here to Equality" isn't just another academic exercise—it's a financial audit of America's debt to Black Americans, complete with balance sheets, compound interest calculations, and specific remedies. [2]

The numbers don't lie, and they tell a devastating story. The average white family has approximately $850,000 more in wealth than the average Black American family. This isn't a slight statistical anomaly—it's a chasm that represents centuries of compounded economic theft. White households near the poverty line typically have about $18,000 in wealth, while Black American households in similar economic circumstances have wealth approaching zero. [3]

This wealth gap didn't happen by accident or through some mysterious cultural differences. It was engineered through specific policies:

- Slavery (246 years of uncompensated labor)

- Black Codes and Convict Leasing (extending slavery by another name)

- Jim Crow segregation and terrorism (economic exclusion)

- Redlining and housing discrimination (wealth-building prevention)

- Mass incarceration (modern economic exclusion)

- Ongoing discrimination in hiring, lending, and education

When you add up the compound interest on generations of stolen labor and blocked opportunity, the bill comes to $10-12 trillion— approximately $333,400 per Black American descendant of slavery. This isn't a random figure pulled from the air. It's an evidence-based calculation of what would be required to close the racial wealth gap.

Pure Reparations: A Scientific Approach

Darity and Mullen have given us a scientific framework they call "pure reparations." Like any good scientific model, it has clear, testable parameters:

First: Eligibility must be based on lineage, not race. The recipients must be Black Americans who have at least one ancestor enslaved in the United States. This isn't about skin color—it's about specific historical debt. If your ancestors were robbed, you're owed restitution, regardless of how much melanin you have. If your ancestors weren't enslaved in America, this particular debt isn't owed to you, no matter how Black you are. (Darity proposes two specific criteria: individuals would need to "establish that they are indeed descendants of persons formerly enslaved in the United States" and "establish that at least 10 years prior to the adoption of a reparations program they self-identified as 'black,' 'African American,' 'Negro,' or 'colored'. This author supports a strict lineage-based requirement without the additional self-identification criteria due to constitutionality and other factors such as fraud risks.)

Second: The program must explicitly target elimination of the racial wealth gap. Symbolic gestures, commissions, and studies aren't enough. The dollar amount must be sufficient to close a gap approaching $850,000 per household. [4]

Third: It must prioritize direct payments to eligible recipients, with individuals having maximum discretion over how to use the funds. This isn't about politicians or organizations deciding what's best for Black Americans—it's about transferring actual capital to those who've been systematically denied it.

This framework cuts through the noise of endless debate and gets to the heart of restitution. It's not about how anyone feels—it's about what the balance sheet shows.

While HR 40 (the bill to study reparations) represents important progress, Darity has highlighted why it's insufficient. The bill doesn't specify:

- A clear lineage-based eligibility requirement (descendants of U.S. slavery)[5]

- A commitment to closing the entire racial wealth gap

- A mandate for direct payments over program-based remedies

Without these specific parameters, HR 40 risks becoming another example of symbolic politics—appearing to address structural issues while leaving the fundamental economic imbalance intact. The danger is creating a commission that recommends half-measures that fail to actually close the wealth gap.

According to Darity, a commission that doesn't explicitly aim to eliminate the entire racial wealth gap isn't serious about repair. It's like a doctor prescribing an aspirin for a gunshot wound—it might show concern, but it won't stop the bleeding.

Critics inevitably ask: "How can we afford $10-12 trillion?" This question reveals more about priorities than fiscal reality. Consider:

- The Federal Reserve created $5 trillion with a keystroke during COVID

- America spent over $8 trillion on foreign wars since 2001

- The 2017 tax cuts cost approximately $2.3 trillion

- The U.S. government spent $700 billion to bail out banks that crashed the economy in 2008

The real question isn't "Can we afford it?" but "Are we willing to pay our debts?" Robert L. Johnson, America's first Black American billionaire, put it plainly: "Reparations would require the entire country to admit that the result of slavery has been 200 years of systemic racism and for that reason Black folks have been denied $13-15 trillion of wealth." [6]

Beyond Symbolic Politics

Darity's approach represents a fundamental break from modern Democratic Party politics. While politicians offer piecemeal programs they call "reparative," he exposes these for what they are: insufficient band-aids on a gaping wound.

What BET founder Robert Johnson calls "placebo paternalism" is showing up everywhere—housing grant programs in Evanston, Illinois, corporate pledges to combat systemic racism, or promises of increased "access to capital." These programs might have merit, but calling them "reparations" is spook. They simply don't add up to the trillions necessary to close the wealth gap.

True reparations requires two components:

- Atonement (acknowledgment of wrong)

- Payment (actual transfer of wealth)

Anything less maintains the fundamental imbalance in the American economic structure.

Darity acknowledges the political challenge ahead. Black American reparations will become legitimate policy when a majority of Americans support it—which doesn't necessarily require a majority of white Americans. As Obama's elections demonstrated, a coalition with approximately 40% of white Americans would be sufficient.

This doesn't mean ignoring the moral and psychological dimensions of repair. But it does mean getting precisely clear on the material transfer required to close the wealth gap. Without that economic foundation, all other forms of reconciliation remain incomplete. What I appreciate about Darity's wealth gap targeting is its unambiguous, quantitative approach. The mystery is transformed into a scientific target that politicians can't run away from or spook up.

Dr. Darity and Mullen's work represents the most scientific and modern approach to reparations available. They've moved the conversation from vague appeals to specific remedies and have formalized a lineage-based framework for those truly eligible, versus allowing others to receive benefits without their ancestors having paid the costs on United States soil. So many groups have piggybacked on the pain, blood, sacrifices, suffering and accomplishments of native Black Americans, and we must stop allowing this pattern to continue. Pure Reparations should be for native Black Americans specifically, those who are descended from U.S. slavery. Strategic alliances with different groups including African and Caribbean immigrants doesn't mean allowing piggybacking or granting benefits without paying the generational price and costs, as native Black Americans have.

Under a strict lineage-based framework, a Kenyan or Nigerian can't just come flying into Detroit or Houston on Kenyan Airways or Nigerian Air talking about "I'm Black, where's my big bag, I want Reparations too. I have been discriminated against too," in a thick accent. And for the African and Caribbean parents whose children were born here, America was a voluntary choice of a better life and they got it. The native Black American didn't arrive by choice, our ancestors arrived by force. Most of the debt was already accumulated and banked before your parents chose to come here.

The Pure Reparations position that compensation should be restricted to descendants of American slaves is not new. It has been featured in the Muhammad Speaks Newspaper since the 1950s through the NOI's unique expression of what Reparations would look like - a perspective that anticipated Darity and Mullen's scientific framework by more than half a century. The lineage-based framework championed by Darity and Mullen was significantly shaped by the advocacy of Yvette Carnell and Antonio Moore, whose American Descendants of Slavery (ADOS) movement established crucial groundwork through their podcasts, social media presence, and organizing efforts that brought renewed attention to the specific historical debt owed to descendants of U.S. slavery. [7]

I remember closely observing ADOS's emergence on social media when critics dismissively called them "just a hashtag." This criticism revealed a form of spook thinking that privileges traditional organizing methods while rejecting digital innovation. Those critics seemed to expect modern movements to use outdated mediums - as though effective organizing required newspapers or radio channels rather than the most efficient marketing tools of our time. My assessment of ADOS proved correct when their concepts later influenced Gavin Newsom's California Reparations Task Force, demonstrating how digital activism paired with physical chapters in cities translated into institutional policy. This progression shows how politically-innovative thinking embraces new methods and mediums when they effectively advance material goals, rather than clinging to familiar forms simply because of historical precedent. Also, there is a bias of time. The old guard often wants to dismiss those developing new movements in their infancy and compare them to organizations who have been around for decades. An activist or thinker can be spooked out with the bias of time, and their spook won't allow them to see that judgment and fair comparisons (not dirty ones) should be rendered after a reasonable amount of time. If we are comparing two birthday cakes, let me have the same amount of time, to bake mine.

Consistent with the Science vs Spook framework, we should point to the foremost scholars on the most important subjects, Dr. Sandy Darity and Kirsten Mullen, authors of the groundbreaking book From Here to Equality: Reparations for Black Americans in the Twenty-First Century, who have been in the paint on this subject for over a decade and who have invested over 10,000 hours researching Pure Reparations.

The Science

- Pure Reparations framework: lineage-based eligibility, wealth gap elimination, direct cash payments
- $10-12 trillion required based on scientific calculation, not emotion
- Eligibility must connect to specific historical debt (descendants of U.S. slavery)
- Move conversation from moral appeals to economic science with measurable targets

---

[1] Malcolm X, "The Ballot or the Bullet," Speech delivered in Cleveland, Ohio, April 3, 1964.

[2] William A. Darity and A. Kirsten Mullen, "From Here to Equality: Reparations for Black Americans in the Twenty-First Century" (Durham: Duke University Press, April 20, 2020).

[3] William A. Darity Jr., Fenaba R. Addo, and Imari Z. Smith, "A Subaltern Middle Class: The Case of the Missing 'Black Bourgeoisie' in America," Contemporary Economic Policy, 39(3), 494-502 (2021).

[4] William A. Darity Jr. and A. Kirsten Mullen, "From Here to Equality: Reparations for Black Americans in the Twenty-First Century" (Chapel Hill: UNC Press, 2020).

[5] William "Sandy" Darity Jr., "What HR40 Gets Wrong and Why," Actify Press, October 2020.

[6] "America's First Black Billionaire Wants His Reparations Check, Now." National African-American Reparations Commission, June 30, 2021.

https://reparationscomm.org/reparations-news/americas-first-black-billionaire-wants-his-reparations-check-now/

[7] Farah Stockman, "'We're Self-Interested': The Growing Identity Debate in Black America." The New York Times, November 8, 2019, updated November 13, 2019. https://www.nytimes.com/2019/11/08/us/slavery-black-immigrants-ados.html

Economist Dr. William "Sandy" Darity Jr. interview with Federal Reserve Bank of Minneapolis

> *"Politics Without Economics is Symbol Without Substance."*
> — *Minister Louis Farrakhan*

No economist has addressed the issue of reparations with the persistence and power that Duke University's William Darity Jr. has. For nearly three decades, "Sandy" Darity has written papers and given presentations discussing the rationale and design of reparations policy. His scholarship goes well beyond this single topic, of course, but by far the greatest part of his research is devoted to inequality—its extent, variety, causes, and effects—often in the context of race.

This interview was conducted by Douglas Clement, Managing Editor of Federal Reserve Bank of Minneapolis, on March 6, 2019.

Discrimination in Labor Markets

Region: In a 1998 review article with Patrick Mason on discrimination in employment, you documented significant and continued job discrimination in the United States, though there have been periods of decline for both women and black males.

At that time, you noted that neoclassical theory of competition predicts that discrimination will diminish over time, and you called for alternative theories that could better account for its persistence.

Two questions: 20 years hence, has there been progress in reducing discrimination in labor markets? And have economists come up with better theories to explain persistent discrimination?

Darity: Those are great questions. Just yesterday, I had a conversation with a reporter in Houston who was trying to unpackage why there was evidence of a widening racial gap in wages.

Region: Widening?

Darity: Yes, a widening racial gap. She said that Texas, in particular, had displayed the greatest increase in the gap. She was puzzled because, she said, "Actually we have evidence that educational levels have converged somewhat, so there wasn't any obvious explanation for this."

To the extent that we think America has a competitive economy, that doesn't appear to be sufficient to eliminate discriminatory wage penalties. I said, "Well, perhaps the degree of labor market discrimination has intensified, particularly in the climate that's associated with the Trump presidency." That was entirely speculative on my part, but she was intrigued by that response. I think that the period in which we have evidence of racial wage penalties actually falling is within the decade after the passage of the Civil Rights Act. It's relatively flat after that with some mild variation, and now apparently there may be an uptick. This suggests to me that, to the extent that we think America has a competitive economy, that doesn't appear to be sufficient to eliminate discriminatory wage penalties.

Region: Does that point to a problem with economic theory?

Darity: I think so. Because in economics, labor market discrimination is anchored on two kinds of arguments. One is the Becker taste for discrimination framework. The other is the statistical theory of discrimination. Neither one of them really provides a story that suggests that discrimination is sustainable in the presence of employers who prefer profits to prejudice.

With respect to the statistical theory of discrimination, if employers are correct in believing that one group on average has lower productivity than the other then, really, it's not a theory of discrimination. Human capital theory provides the explanation. If they're incorrect in that belief, one would think that over some period of time, employers would learn. Some would experiment with using the ostensibly "less-productive" workers because they can pay them less. They might discover that they're just as productive. So the information might spread about that, and other employers would also hire them.

Region: Or the others would die off, in a Darwinian struggle. They would be less profitable than those who did experiment and learn.

Darity: Yes, because those who experimented could pay lower wages for the same quality of work. Absolutely.

Stratification Economics

Region: To provide a better explanation for discrimination in labor markets, I believe, you developed "stratification economics." In 2005, you delivered a lecture on the theory. In a 2017 chapter with Hamilton, Mason, and others, you elaborated on it and concluded with a dramatic challenge: "It calls for a rewrite of the rules of economic analysis."

In a nutshell, if you can, what is stratification economics, and why does it call for a rewrite? Or, rather, how must the rules be rewritten?

Darity: Stratification economics is an approach that emphasizes relative position rather than absolute position. What's relevant to relative position are two considerations: one, a person's perception of how the social group or groups to which they belong have standing vis-à-vis other groups that could be conceived of as being rival groups.

Now, it's an interesting issue as to who constitutes groups that are viewed as rivalrous or oppositional in some sense. But the first thing that individuals value is a superior position for the groups with which they identify. The second thing that they value is a superior position relative to other members of their own group.

Region: So, within group, as well as across groups.

Darity: Yes. There are two sets of comparisons that are going on: an across-group comparison and a within-group comparison. This kind of frame as the cornerstone for the analysis comes out of, in part, the old work of Thorstein Veblen and also out of research on happiness. The latter increasingly shows that people have a greater degree of happiness if they think that they're better off than whoever constitutes their comparison group rather than simply being better off; so it's comparative position that comes into play.

There are two sets of comparisons that are going on: an across-group comparison and a within-group comparison. This kind of frame as the cornerstone for the analysis comes out of, in part, the old work of Thorstein Veblen and also out of research on happiness. Conventional economics doesn't start with an analysis that's anchored on relative position, as opposed to absolute position; so I think that's the fundamental shift in stratification economics. But also important to stratification economics is the notion that people have group affiliations or group identifications. People feel like they're part of a team. There can be varying degrees of attachment but, in some sense, people think of themselves as being part of a team, and they want their team to win. That's somewhat different from conventional economics.

Region: You've also done work at an international level, with Ashwini Deshpande, looking in a variety of nations at intragroup disparities— variation within different groups as well as among them.

Darity: We were thinking that there are multiple ways to decompose measures of inequality. Some people have decomposed them on the basis of spatial variations. Others have performed the decomposition on the basis of occupational variations. We were thinking that you could just as well perform such a decomposition by making use of intergroup differences, whatever the salient groups are within a particular society.

It could be ethnic differences, it could be caste, it could be—in the case of Ireland, for instance—religion. Or other kinds of ethnic divides are linked to religion, as in Bosnia and Herzegovina or in India, where there also is the caste divide. There are many different ways in which human beings appear to differentiate themselves. I hope it's not something that's fundamental to what we call human nature, but it certainly has a long and persistent history.

The Importance of Skin Shade

Region: In addition to your work on labor market discrimination, you've done intriguing and disturbing research on discrimination by skin shade and also on the psychological impact of unemployment. I'd like to ask you about your 2015 paper that looks at the intersection of all three—specifically, the psychological costs of unemployment for black women of different skin shades.

You find strong evidence of a "gradient on depression"—that, for example, unemployed black women of darker complexion are more likely to suffer their first onset of depression than those with lighter skin shade.

Could you tell us about this research—your findings generally? Why do you focus on women? And what is the mechanism behind "colorism," discrimination on the basis of skin shade?

Darity: Let me start with the reason to focus on women. Our initial work in this area, before the 2015 paper that you mention, was focused primarily on labor market experiences and whether or not skin shade made a difference. We generally found that there were much more dramatic effects for men than for women in terms of labor market outcomes. Lighter-complexioned black men incurred far smaller discriminatory wage penalties than darker-complexioned black men in employment, but there was no comparable difference among black women.

When we devoted our attention more closely to the experiences of women outside the labor market, we found that there were significant effects associated with marriage market outcomes. We then did a study—I'm not sure if it's actually published somewhere—where we discovered that relative to their family's resources, darker-skinned women who are black get more years of schooling than lighter-complexioned women who are black.

We concluded that this may have been some type of compensating variation, because the darker-skinned black women are less likely to have income opportunities that are associated with marriage; because their odds of marrying are lower.

Then we were trying to think about whether there could be other kinds of traumas associated with the burden that you bear by being darker-skinned in America. We investigated what we could learn about people's mental health, and so that's how we got to the findings in the 2015 paper. Somewhat circuitous, but that was the path.

Region: What did you find about skin shade, women, unemployment, and psychological costs? And what is the mechanism behind colorism? That is, why are darker-skinned unemployed women more likely to suffer an onset of depression?

Darity: I think it's because their life options are generally more desperate; one example is their disadvantage in the marriage market. I think they are under more stress given a bout of unemployment.

There was a point at which we were thinking that communities that are subjected to deprivations on a more sustained basis might actually develop more resilience. But that doesn't really appear to be the case with respect to mental health. The severity of the trauma is greater, sometimes, for members of communities that are experiencing continuous deprivations.

The severity of the trauma is greater, sometimes, for members of communities that are experiencing continuous deprivations. In another study, we found that the Great Recession had worse mental health effects on blacks than on whites, despite all of the popular discussion about economic anxiety among lower-income whites.

Now, the companion issue is, Why does colorism exist? And, of course, I think that has to be associated with the unfolding of the history of white supremacy in the United States.

Eric Williams and the Slave Trade

Region: Let me jump to that, in a sense, by asking about Eric Williams.

Darity: Eric Williams actually did write about colorism at one point, but most people don't know that.

Region: I'm certainly one of them. But, thanks to you, I do know a bit about him. You've written several articles about his research on the relationship between the slave trade and British industrialization.

You've argued that his theory is a cogent explanation for British industrialization and for the eventual abolition of slavery.

Darity: He had three hypotheses, I think. The third is his hypothesis about the origins of racism. He held that racism did not produce slavery but, rather, slavery produced racism.

Region: Can you first tell us a little about him? Other than the first prime minister of Trinidad, who was he?

Darity: Well, he was an Oxford-trained historian from Trinidad, and he received what was then called an Island Scholarship after he completed his secondary school years. This was at the beginning of the 1930s. He was born in 1911, so he was probably 19 or 20 years of age when he went to Oxford, relatively young. He had been a secondary-level student at Queens Royal College off of the Savannah in Port of Spain. Clearly an outstanding student, they say he was also a pretty good soccer player, but he was extremely selfish; he would never give the ball to anybody else!

Region: What are his central theories, and why weren't they widely accepted?

Darity: There are three prongs. The first is, as I said, his explanation for the origins of racism. The second is his argument that the slave trade and the slave plantation system were instrumental in British economic development. C.L.R. James would make the same claim about France.

Then the third argument, which for some people appears inconsistent with the second, is that when the British abolished the slave trade, it was because it was no longer of any functional value to them. On the one hand, he's saying slavery and the slave trade helped build the British economy. Then, on the other, he's saying it ended because it was no longer useful. That's the key phrase: It was no longer useful, or as useful as it had been.

Region: Did he also argue that the slave trade resulted in the underdevelopment of Africa?

Darity: That was not a Williams' hypothesis. That was Walter Rodney's. Early in my career, I tried to integrate the positions of C.L.R. James and his book The Black Jacobins, Eric Williams' position on capitalism and slavery, and Walter Rodney's argument in How Europe Underdeveloped Africa. I wanted to integrate the work of these three scholars into a singular vision of the unfolding of ... I wonder how Walt Rostow, of all people to mention, would put it? How It All Began, I like that phrase. Perhaps, "How the modern world began," in some sense. All three were Caribbean scholars. Rodney was from Guyana. And James, like Williams, was from Trinidad.

When I was an undergraduate, someone was passing Williams' book around. It certainly was not offered in any of the classes that I took. Somebody was passing Walter Rodney's book around too. I read them, and I was really intrigued. When I became a Ph.D. student, I decided I would try to do some work that would extend their work.

Region: You gave Williams' argument a credence it didn't gain in his own lifetime, winning over previous critics like Stanley Lebergott.

Darity: There was a strange animus that lot of economic historians had toward Williams' theories.

Region: Using the small ratios argument, for example.

Darity: Yes, that was one of the ways in which they tried to subvert the second hypothesis [slave trade aiding British industrialization]. And there was a lot of criticism of Williams' view that abolition of the slave trade took place for strategic and economic, or functional, reasons. In contrast with the functional argument, the historian Seymour Drescher, for example, argued that the older school of thought, the argument that abolition was a consequence of increased humanitarian sentiment in England, was the valid explanation.

I think that the critical piece of the story that determines which way the argument goes is what occurred in the context of the Haitian revolution. The fact that the British tried, albeit unsuccessfully, to capture the jewel of the sugar islands, Saint-Domingue [French colonial name for Haiti], tells me that abolition came out of a perceived functionality rather than humanitarian sentiment. If true humanitarian sentiment governed what British officialdom did, they would not have tried to take control of Saint-Domingue after the French had been defeated.

Female-Headed Households

Region: Let's shift the focus, if we could, to your work on female-headed households.

You've pointed out that U.S. households are increasingly headed by women. This is disproportionately so for African American women. And it's a matter of concern because female-headed households are poorer than others.

Darity: Yes.

Region: In your 2018 article with Terry-Ann Craigie and Sam Myers Jr., you use variation among states in sentencing reform to analyze the role that male marriageability plays in female-headed families.

Why has this affected female headship for blacks, but not for whites?

Darity: Because whites are not encountering a decline in the availability of marriageable males. So, to the extent that marriages are disproportionately intraracial ...

Region: Which your paper assumes.

Darity: Yes. It is a reasonable assumption. Even though there has been some growth in cross-racial marriages, the predominant pattern is still that marriages are intraracial. So white women, to the extent that white men would be their partners, are not experiencing a shortage of marriageable males.

We refer to assortative mating: People have a tendency to marry someone who has class, social, and often racial characteristics that are similar to their own. To the extent that that's the case, then the relevant marriage pool for most black women is other black men.

One of the earlier arguments in this discussion of female-headed households was the claim that incentives or inducements associated with the [previous] welfare system prompted so-called family disorganization of the black family.

Region: The idea that because welfare payments were made only to families without fathers present, the system encouraged men to leave.

Darity: Right. That was the argument.

Region: That was Daniel Moynihan's position, wasn't it?

Darity: Daniel Moynihan was one of the proponents. I think that belief, to a large extent, underlies the rationale for welfare reform. Actually, very early in my own research career, working with Sam Myers Jr., we presented what we thought was some fairly persuasive evidence that that effect was not that strong.

That opened up the door for the question of, well, if we observe this phenomenon of significant growth in female headship among black families, what's causing it?

I should note that this was somewhat in line with work by somebody I frequently don't agree with: William Julius Wilson, who, in conjunction with Kathryn Neckerman, introduced this concept of the male marriageability ratio.

If we observe this phenomenon of significant growth in female headship among black families, what's causing it? We made use of it. We put empirical flesh on the bones of the idea and then proceeded to demonstrate that toward the end of the 1980s, there seemed to be a significant effect of the availability of marriageable males on patterns of family formation.

Then, most recently, with Terry-Ann Craigie, we extended and updated those findings in the context of mass incarceration and sentencing reforms.

The Racial Wealth Gap

Region: Let's move to the racial wealth gap. Much of economic thought has focused on income inequality. You've focused on wealth inequality, an area of relative neglect, and you have documented a large and persistent racial wealth gap.

Would you describe the extent of the gap and discuss its source?

Darity: Yes, but first let me add one thing. I think there's a reason for the comparative neglect of wealth in economics. I think it's because the study of economic inequality has been left in the hands of the labor economists. Labor economists, of course, are going to focus on what happens in labor markets: jobs and wages as sources of income. But unless one takes the narrow view that the source of wealth is personal savings behavior, then there's not much of a role for labor markets per se in understanding wealth.

Some labor economists have focused on wealth, but it really was a push from sociologists more than economists that propelled the most recent examination of wealth inequality and, especially, wealth inequality by race.

Region: Would you describe the extent of the gap?

Darity: The racial wealth gap is customarily measured at the median for households to bypass the problems that are created by large outliers. At the median, when we're taking the middle households, the most recent data from the Survey of Consumer Finances (SCF) for 2016, I believe, places the white household median at $171,000 and the black household median at $17,600. So, essentially, at the median, blacks have 1 cent in wealth to every 10 cents held by whites. [The SCF 2016] probably has the most conservative estimate of the gap. If, for example, you use the Survey of Income and Program Participation from 2014, which I believe is the most recent year that it's been taken, the ratio is closer to 1 cent for blacks per 13 cents for whites at the median.

In work that our research group has done for the National Asset Scorecard for Communities of Color, we attempted to get data about individual metropolitan areas throughout the United States, where it might be possible to look at the wealth position of very specific national origin groups. All of our cities have much lower estimates of black median wealth than the national statistics.

The number of cities that we've studied is substantial but hardly comprehensive. It's been Boston, Los Angeles, Washington, D.C., Miami, Tulsa, and Baltimore.

Region: I paid particular attention to the data from Boston, perhaps because I'm from there. It's hard to believe—

Darity: That stunning estimate?

Region: Yes. $8!

Darity: That's what we found. $8 is the median [wealth of black households in Boston]. In Miami, it's $11. I'm not sure how the national statistics get as high as $17 thousand; it's not really consistent with what we're finding.

So I'm just not sure. There's something odd. We consistently found, across all of these cities, much, much lower estimates of median black household wealth than you see in the national data.

Factors Behind the Racial Wealth Gap

Region: What are the sources and mechanisms of that enormous gap?

Darity: I'm absolutely convinced that the primary factor determining household wealth is the transmission of resources across generations.

The conventional view of how you accumulate wealth is through fastidious and deliberate acts of personal saving. I would argue that the capacity to engage in some significant amount of personal saving is really contingent on already having a significant endowment, an endowment that's independent of what you generate through your own labor.

That being the case, I think that there's actually some superb research that's recently come out that supports the importance of what I'd like to call intergenerational transmission effects, rather than intergenerational transfers. I think these effects go beyond inheritances and gifts. I think it includes the sheer economic security that young people can experience being in homes where there is this cushion of wealth. It provides a lack of stress and a greater sense of what your possibilities are in life.

So I like to call it intergenerational transmission effects, and there's some excellent recent research that has been done on this. The sociologists Pfeffer and Killewald have done very, very powerful work on the relationship between grandparents' and parents' wealth and the wealth of the youngest generation when it's of adult age. The connection or the correspondence between which households have higher levels of wealth across three generations is pretty strong.

Then there's the work of two economists who are with the Fed, Feiveson and Sabelhaus. Their work shows that at least 26 percent of the net worth of a person in the current generation is determined by their parents' wealth. At least 26 percent. And that's their lower bound.

Region: And the mechanisms are not just direct transfers, but also opportunity, education, lack of stress.

Darity: Yes. And if your family's wealthy enough, you come out of college or university without any educational debt. That can be a springboard to making it easier for you to accumulate your own level of wealth.

Reparations

Region: You've been a powerful and tireless proponent of reparations. In a 2003 article with Dania Frank, you went through rationale, eligibility, methods, effects, financing, and magnitude for effective reparations for African Americans. Another piece in 2010 applied lessons from international trade to reparations to argue that programs must be carefully designed to be effective, not harmful. Just last week, I believe, you gave a speech in Chicago about reparations, and you're increasingly cited and interviewed on the issue.

As you know better than anyone, reparations have suddenly become almost a cause célèbre. Several Democratic presidential candidates have voiced their support in specific or broad terms.

Darity: They're actually using the word. That alone is pretty astonishing.

Region: This is five years after Ta-Nahesi Coates' essay breathed new life into it, but you've been making the case for decades. What have been the sources of resistance to the idea, and is it economically viable?

Darity: What's interesting, actually, is that I didn't believe in reparations at the beginning of my entry into these conversations.

I was skeptical, not because I thought it was morally inappropriate. I just didn't think it was feasible; I didn't think it was politically feasible. I still think the odds are long. But the older I've gotten, my position is, if you think something's the right thing to do, then you pursue it. In retrospect, if folks had not decided to fight against slavery in 1819 because it looked like slavery would last forever, the abolition movement really would not have actually taken off.

I feel the same way about reparations, that even if the odds are long, this is something that should be done. In the beginning of the 1990s, I was asked to write an introduction for a book edited by Richard America that he called The Wealth of Races. It was primarily a compendium of chapters where economists were estimating what the reparations bill should be. I said to Richard, "Well, I don't know that I'm the right person to write this because I'm fairly skeptical about this."

He said, "Write the introduction that you want to write. I want you to do it, regardless of what you conclude." And so I started reading these papers and, the more I read, the more I was convinced that even if this was going to be hard to accomplish, that it needed to be on the agenda as a potential national public policy. So, I think it's from the early 1990s, I have been working on different dimensions or aspects of the reparations issue. So, do I think it's politically feasible?

Region: Economically. After all, you're not a political scientist.

Darity: Oh, economically feasible! So you're really asking a question about financing?

Region: I think so, yes, which, admittedly, is political in part.

Darity: I have a couple of responses to that. First, the feasibility is contingent on your estimate of the magnitude of it. I mean, I'm very sympathetic, actually, to the MMTers [proponents of modern monetary theory]. And so, as a consequence, I think that the fundamental barrier to additional government spending is the inflation risk; it's not existing tax revenue. I would think that a reparations program to be designed sensibly, would have to be one that minimized the inflation risk in some way.

This is not the only way, but an example of how one might do it is to ensure that the allocation of the reparations takes more of an asset-based form so that the funds received are not immediately spent in full.

My wife, Kirsten Mullen, and I have a book coming out on reparations, called From Here to Equality: Reparations for Black Americans in the 21st Century. It will be published by the University of North Carolina Press and should be available in February 2020. In the final chapter, there's a more extended discussion of financing options, which I cannot reveal at this time. Otherwise, I'll be in real trouble when I go home.

Region: We don't want that.

Darity: But let me just say that I embrace the view that you don't have to pay as you go, that it is fine if you go and then pay. So the focus should be on whether or not a new major expenditure program would risk hyperinflation, and that's what you really have to be concerned about. To the extent that we can manage that, then I don't think there's a serious issue around financing.

Baby Bonds and a Federal Jobs Guarantee

Region: You've also been a proponent, perhaps not for quite as long, of baby bonds and a federal jobs guarantee, often writing on these policies with Darrick Hamilton. Do you view those as complements or substitutes for reparations?

Darity: I view all three of those as complements. Baby bonds is an initiative to try to address general wealth inequality in the United States. Potentially, it could have a disproportionate benefit for blacks simply because black levels of wealth are so low. But it would not come close to eliminating the racial wealth gap. The central reason it wouldn't is that the design of the baby bonds proposal is anchored on closing gaps at the median rather than the mean.

If we're concerned about the reproduction of inequality across generations, then the baby bonds type of proposal would be the mechanism to correct for that. If we're concerned about eliminating the gap between blacks and whites with respect to wealth, then we would need a reparations program. If we're concerned about the reproduction of inequality across generations, then the baby bonds type of proposal would be the mechanism to correct for that. In my best of all possible worlds, you'd have both.

A federal job guarantee targets income and poverty, or income poverty, by trying to guarantee every adult American employment at nonpoverty wages, with a benefits package that would be similar to the kind of package that's held by a federal civil servant at the current time. The premise here is that we would eliminate, with the stroke of a pen, working poverty. We would also eliminate unemployment in the way in which it is defined by the Bureau of Labor Statistics. Because everyone seeking work would be able to find work.

This would significantly alter the Phillips-curve-based logic—

Region: That the Fed contemplates.

Darity: Yes, that underlies what the Fed has to do! Right. I mean, in a somewhat twisted way, you could argue that if you had a federal job guarantee, the Fed could be more aggressive in fighting inflation.

Region: Provocative advice! Well, you gave a very good synopsis of what a federal jobs guarantee would look like and do. Would you do the same for baby bonds?

Darity: Sure. Baby bonds are not really a bond. They're really a trust account for each newborn infant. It would be different from other types of programs like seed accounts or child savings accounts because no contribution would be expected from parents, whether they're rich or poor. The amount of the trust account would vary with the wealth position of the child's family. It would vary on a graduated basis, so we wouldn't have any kinds of notch effects. That's basically the idea.

In most of the versions of the proposal that we've advanced, we've said the federal government is essentially providing a publicly funded trust account to every newborn child, so it's a birthright endowment. We would guarantee a 1 percent real rate of interest until the account can be accessed by the child when they reach young adulthood. There's some debate among us about what that young adulthood date should be.

Rational Expectations Theory

Region: In addition to all of this work, you've also produced a substantial scholarship on the history of economic thought, including rational expectations. The Minneapolis Fed has close ties to that theory, of course, so I've got to ask you about it. From the perspective of an economic historian, what impact do you think rational expectations has had on macro theory and monetary policy?

Darity: I think rational expectations has been mobilized to maintain a view that the macro economy self-corrects to full employment. Now, rational expectations in pure form would actually suggest that the economy could self-correct to full employment instantly. The only thing that would disturb that would be true shocks, thoroughly random events. But anything that could be anticipated in the context of thinking about the structure of how the economy actually operates would be anticipated in such a way that we would move consistently toward full employment.

Insofar as it doesn't appear that we move consistently toward full employment, then that's an empirical conundrum for the basic theory.

I know that you can design models that deploy rational expectations that don't lead you to full employment, but that's usually because you've introduced some kind of nonmarket clearing phenomenon. Maybe it's the labor market, where there's some kind of wage rigidity or something like that.

But if you had complete price flexibility and rational expectations, I presume you would always move toward full employment. To the extent that I don't think that's the case, and to the extent that I don't think that the decisive factor that keeps us from reaching full employment is price inflexibilities, then I think there's something unsatisfactory about that entire theoretical approach.

Region: Now I'm going to be in trouble when I go home. But, seriously, thank you very much for sharing your time and your insights.

The Science

- Racial wage penalties persist despite competitive market theory predictions
- Stratification economics: relative position matters more than absolute position
- Federal job guarantee + baby bonds + reparations work as complementary policies
- Wealth transmission effects across generations are primary driver of racial wealth gap

Reparations Heroes

> *"The wealth gap that we observe today is the cumulative*
> *intergenerational effect of racial injustice in the United States."*
> —Dr. William "Sandy" Darity Jr.

If you want to understand a movement's true history, follow the fighters who stood up when it wasn't popular. While everyone's jumping on the reparations bandwagon now, let's get scientific about the OGs who've been pushing this fight for generations—often at great personal cost and with little recognition.

The reparations movement didn't start with Twitter hashtags or university commissions. It began with formerly enslaved people themselves demanding payment for stolen labor. These heroes weren't pushing symbolic gestures or performative allyship—they were demanding material compensation. They understood what modern politicians often forget: freedom without economic foundation is just another form of bondage.

Callie House: The First Freedom Fighter

Callie House wasn't waiting for white political approval in the 1890s—she was organizing direct action. Born into slavery in 1861, House built the National Ex-Slave Mutual Relief, Bounty, and Pension Association in 1894, creating perhaps the first mass reparations movement with hundreds of thousands of members.[1]

The math was clear: Freed slaves had generated enormous wealth through their unpaid labor and deserved economic compensation—not just symbolic freedom. Instead of begging for acceptance, House and her co-founder Rev. Isaiah Dickerson traveled throughout the South organizing ex-slaves around concrete demands.

"We are organizing ourselves together as a race of people who feel they have been wronged," House declared. [2] This wasn't emotional pleading—it was a statement of financial reality. Unlike today's symbolic posturing, House was demanding actual money reach actual descendants of slavery.

What happened? The system crushed her with fabricated fraud charges. The U.S. government sicced the Post Office and Department of Justice on her organization, banning them from using mail or cashing money orders. This wasn't random harassment—it was systematic opposition to economic justice.

House died in 1928 without seeing justice—but the approach she pioneered (direct demands for material compensation) continues today. Her story reveals a core truth: the system doesn't fear abstract discussions about racial reconciliation; it fears concrete demands for wealth transfer.

Queen Mother Moore

Audley "Queen Mother" Moore didn't just talk about reparations—she developed actual models to implement them. Born in 1898, Moore modernized the reparations framework for the 20th century, building on earlier demands for the government to fulfill Special Field Order No. 15 (the original "40 acres and a mule").

Moore's life story reveals how material reality shapes political consciousness. Her grandmother was born enslaved—the daughter of an African woman raped by her enslaver. Her grandfather was lynched. When both parents died before she completed fourth grade, Moore experienced firsthand that flowery promises of "equality" meant nothing without economic repair.

For over 40 years until her death in 1997, Moore developed specific, scientific frameworks for how the federal government should pay reparations. Crucially, she insisted on three core principles:

- Payment should come directly from the government

- The amount should be predetermined

- Recipients should have complete discretion over how funds are used

She "opposed trickle-down approaches, such as plans for black churches or for a small committee composed of the black elite to be in charge of lobbying for, collecting and distributing federal funds." This approach—direct payment instead of institutional filtering—is exactly what contemporary opponents of true reparations still fight against.

In 1963, her pamphlet "Why Reparations" provided concrete evidence for compensatory claims, showcasing reparations payments made in other countries and arguing specifically that "the descendants of American Slaves must be given preferential treatment." [3] This lineage-specific language anticipated the current lineage-based movements by decades.

Reparations Ray

Raymond "Reparations Ray" Jenkins brought raw experiential knowledge to the reparations equation. As the grandson of a Mississippi slave, he witnessed firsthand how empty promises of freedom translated into ongoing economic subjugation. [4]

Jenkins often told the heartbreaking story of his grandfather, who "worked for 99 years for white people and died with nothing. He didn't have anything to leave his wife, his children. The white man got all his wealth." This wasn't just anecdotal—it represented the measurable transfer of generational wealth from Black labor to white ownership.

When Jenkins formed the Slave Labor Annuity Pay organization in the 1960s and later helped establish N'COBRA in 1987, he was pushing not just for recognition but for material compensation. He proposed a $40 billion reparations payment—albeit noting this was merely a starting point for the true value of 246 years of uncompensated labor.

His persistence directly influenced Congressman John Conyers to introduce HR 40. Without Jenkins' grassroots pressure, the legislation that eventually triggered broader reparations discussions might never have existed.

Dr. Robert Brock: The Unapologetic Advocate

Dr. Robert Brock cut through political niceties and got straight to the material point: "The government owes us money on a number of different fronts. For labor, for loss of culture and of humanity." As a former Merchant Marine who spent the majority of his adult life promoting reparations, Brock framed the issue in straightforward economic terms.

In the 1990s, Brock campaigned for a specific payment of $500,000 per descendant of slavery—a figure he had calculated for an unsuccessful 1965 lawsuit against the U.S. government. This wasn't emotional appeal but mathematical calculation of stolen labor and opportunity. [5]

What separated Brock from more accommodating advocates was his unwillingness to accept symbolic gestures. At a 2000 Juneteenth rally, he asked, "What is a march unless there is an ultimatum?" Brock understood what many contemporary activists miss: power doesn't respond to polite requests; it responds to material demands backed by organized pressure.

Brock's approach means recognizing that marches without specific financial demands produce no measurable change. Brock's approach treated reparations as an inheritance—not charity or reconciliation, but payment of a mathematically calculable debt.

Silis Muhammad: The International Strategist

While most Americans think of reparations as a domestic issue, Silis Muhammad understood that international law offered potentially powerful leverage. As the founder of the Lost-Found Nation of Islam in

1977 (separate from Farrakhan's NOI), Muhammad brought specific expertise in international law, human rights, and reparations to the fight.

In 1994, Muhammad took a strategic approach by moving beyond traditional Reparations ideas to formal legal action. He submitted an appeal to the UN Office of the High Commissioner for Human Rights, citing Article 27 of the International Covenant on Civil and Political Rights. This wasn't emotional appeal—it was legal strategy. When Silas Muhammad boldly went to the United Nations in 1994, the organizational body had more influence and political bark, than the seemingly impotent 2025 United Nations.

Muhammad's submission meticulously documented how Black Americans—or "Afrodescendants" as he termed them—had been systematically stripped of their original identity, culture, language, and religion. Rather than seeking symbolic recognition, he demanded material restitution based on specific human rights violations. [6]

The author notes Muhammad's use of descendants as a disaggregating factor and criteria, consistent with Elijah Muhammad's use of descendants of slaves within his own Reparations framework. Muhammad's relationship with Farrakhan tells its own story about who prioritized reparations. According to former NOI minister Vibert White, when Muhammad asked to speak at the 1995 Million Man March, "Farrakhan told him he'd let him speak [but] under a condition—if he agreed not to mention reparations." Unwilling to abandon his core issue, Muhammad declined. [7] This principled and consistent position reflects how anchored Silas Muhammad was to reparations for Black Americans.

The Elijah Muhammad Blueprint: The Original Reparations Architect

While many think of reparations as a modern debate, Elijah Muhammad laid out perhaps the most comprehensive economic blueprint for Black American repair decades ago. His vision, articulated in the groundbreaking "What The Muslims Want" manifesto published in his

1965 book "Message To The Blackman in America," didn't just demand symbolic recognition—it provided an actual economic and political roadmap.

It's crucial to acknowledge that Elijah Muhammad and the Nation of Islam pioneered the lineage-based framework for reparations long before any modern movement. Muhammad specifically used the phrase "descendants from slaves" in his manifesto—the exact language that grounds today's lineage-based advocacy. This wasn't coincidental—it was a scientific understanding that repair must target those with direct ancestral claims to the injury.

Muhammad was also ahead of his time in using the terms "Black America" and "Black Americans" to describe the population descended from American chattel slavery. While others used "Colored" or "Negro," Muhammad understood the importance of language that connected people to both their racial reality and their specific American context. This linguistic precision reflected his understanding that specific harms required specific remedies for a specific population.

The precision of Muhammad's fourth point is worth examining in full:

"We want our people in America whose parents or grandparents were descendants from slaves, to be allowed to establish a separate state or territory of their own—either on this continent or elsewhere. We believe that our former slave masters are obligated to provide such land and that the area must be fertile and minerally rich. We believe that our former slave masters are obligated to maintain and supply our needs in this separate territory for the next 20 to 25 years—until we are able to produce and supply our own needs."

Muhammad had concrete material demands with specific timelines. Muhammad sought self-government and land with ongoing cash payments and support. He didn't see Reparations as a one-time transaction or payment. His demand for "fertile and minerally rich" territory reflects a scientific understanding of America's superior natural

389

resource advantages over most countries. He sought the same advantages for Black Americans, not subprime land.

Muhammad went further in point seven: "We do not believe that after 400 years of free or nearly free labor, sweat and blood, which has helped America become rich and powerful, so many thousands of black people should have to subsist on relief or charity or live in poor houses."

This connects directly to today's wealth gap arguments. Muhammad wasn't asking for charity—he was demanding payment for specific economic contributions. His eighth point even proposed tax exemption "as long as we are deprived of equal justice under the laws of the land," another economic solution to systemic inequities.

What makes Muhammad's approach scientific rather than merely rhetorical is how he connected reparations theory with economic practice. While articulating these demands, he simultaneously built actual economic institutions—over 50 temples across the country, thousands of acres of farmland, restaurants, national private school system, grocery stores, a newspaper printing operation, and banking systems— demonstrating that Black Americans could build independent economic power. He wasn't just talking about what America owed; he was showing what Black Americans could create with proper organization and resources. Given the documented FBI surveillance and government interference that Muhammad faced—similar to the systematic opposition described in Lesson 34's analysis of how the system crushes economic threats—Muhammad could have accomplished 3-10X more institutional development without this state-sponsored obstruction, and that's saying a lot considering his documented achievements.

Muhammad's economic program was meticulously documented and measured. Every bean pie sold, every acre farmed, every newspaper distributed became proof that collective economics worked. This wasn't spiritual theory but material development-economics with measurable outcomes.

Modern reparations advocates, whether they acknowledge it or not, are building on Muhammad's foundation. From specific lineage requirements ("parents or grandparents were descendants from slaves") to material demands (land, resources, and time-bound support), today's frameworks for calculating the debt owed to Black Americans follow patterns Muhammad established generations ago.

The system's reaction tells its own story. While integration-focused civil rights leaders received (limited) mainstream acceptance, Muhammad's economic program faced unrelenting harassment and obstruction from the FBI and other agencies. The system wasn't afraid of symbolic progress; it feared Muhammad's material economic program that threatened to create genuine Black independence.

Long before academia embraced reparations discourse, Muhammad provided a scientific economic blueprint that remains relevant today. His focus wasn't just on what America had done wrong—it was on what would make Black Americans economically whole. That's not religious prophecy; it's economic science with mathematical precision about what repair actually requires. One takeaway from Muhammad's position is the strategic duality: You can maintain a strong position on the U.S. owing reparations while simultaneously organizing and creating the best possible heaven on earth for Black Americans, regardless of whether Reparations ever become activated policy.

Dr. Martin Luther King Jr.: Beyond the Dreamer Myth

The system's greatest trick was transforming Dr. King from a radical economic thinker into a harmless dreamer. Few remember that King understood that symbolic integration without material repair was meaningless.

In his final book before assassination, King wrote, "A society that has done something special against the Negro for hundreds of years must now do something special for the Negro." He directly challenged the bootstrap mythology: "It's a cruel just to say to a bootless man that he ought to lift himself by his own bootstraps."

King's Poor People's Campaign wasn't about symbolic recognition—it was about material demands. When he said, "Now, when we come to Washington in this campaign we're coming to get our check," he wasn't speaking metaphorically. He understood that freedom without economic foundation is just another form of bondage.

As Rev. Mark Kelly Tyler noted, "America has been comfortable with Dr. King the dreamer as opposed to Dr. King who articulates the American nightmare." The system consistently embraces symbols while rejecting material change. King's assassination came just as he was pivoting toward more explicit economic demands—a pattern that repeats throughout reparations advocacy history.

John Conyers Jr. and HR 40: The Legislative Marathon

For nearly 30 years, from 1989 until his retirement in 2017, Representative John Conyers Jr. introduced HR 40 in every legislative session. The bill's name itself references the unfulfilled promise of "40 acres and a mule" made to freed slaves. Conyers' persistence demonstrates how even modest demands for studying reparations faced monumental opposition.

Inspired by the successful campaign for Japanese American redress through the Civil Liberties Act of 1988, Conyers believed similar justice was possible for Black Americans. Yet decades passed without even committee approval. It wasn't until 2019, after Conyers' death, that the bill received its first hearing. Can you believe that?

Conyers dedicated decades to advancing the conversation on reparations through his persistent introduction of H.R. 40, the "Commission to Study Reparation Proposals for African Americans Act." First introduced in January 1989, Conyers reintroduced this bill in every

Congress until his retirement, demonstrating extraordinary commitment to this cause. In his own words: "I have re-introduced HR 40 every Congress since 1989, and will continue to do so until it's passed into law." The bill's number symbolically referenced the unfulfilled promise of "forty acres and a mule" initially promised to freed slaves. As Conyers explained, "This unfulfilled promise and the serious devastation that slavery had on African-American lives has never been officially recognized by the United States Government." His legislation aimed to establish a commission that would acknowledge "the fundamental injustice and inhumanity of slavery," study its lasting economic impact, and make recommendations to Congress on appropriate remedies.

Conyers recognized the challenges in advancing such legislation, noting that "One of the biggest challenges in discussing the issue of reparations in a political context is deciding how to have a national discussion without allowing the issue to polarize our party or our nation." [8] Despite resistance from those who wanted to "leave slavery in the past," Conyers persisted, garnering increasing support each year, with the bill eventually attracting over 40 co-sponsors. He compared the journey of H.R. 40 to his earlier success with the Martin Luther King Jr. Holiday bill, which took 15 years to pass from its introduction in 1968 to its approval in 1983. According to Conyers, H.R. 40 would do four specific things:

- "It acknowledges the fundamental injustice and inhumanity of slavery"

- "It establishes a commission to study slavery, its subsequent racial and economic discrimination against freed slaves"

- "It studies the impact of those forces on today's living African Americans"

- "The commission would then make recommendations to Congress on appropriate remedies to redress the harm inflicted on living African Americans"

Though Conyers did not live to see H.R. 40 become law, his persistent advocacy established the foundation for the modern reparations movement and created a legislative framework that continues to influence the national conversation on addressing historical injustices against African Americans. As Conyers himself argued, "It is a fact that slavery flourished in the United States and constituted an immoral and inhumane deprivation of African slaves' lives, liberty and cultural heritage. As a result, millions of African Americans today continue to suffer great injustices."

Randall Robinson: The Global Connector

Attorney and activist Randall Robinson brought international perspective to domestic reparations arguments. After successfully organizing sanctions against apartheid South Africa and conducting a hunger strike that restored Haiti's elected government, Robinson applied his global expertise to America's unpaid debt.

His 2001 book "The Debt: What America Owes to Blacks" frames reparations as an unpaid financial obligation with measurable consequences. "The United States government and white society generally have opted to deal with [Black] debt by forgetting that it is owed," Robinson wrote, documenting how this unpaid debt manifests in measurable educational, healthcare, housing, and employment disparities. [9]

Robinson's approach connected domestic racism to international human rights standards, making accountability unavoidable. After writing "The Debt," he left America permanently for the Caribbean island of St. Kitts, underscoring his understanding that America's unwillingness to pay its debts was a structural, not accidental, feature.

Dr. Conrad Worrill: The Educational Organizer

Dr. Conrad Worrill (1941-2020) stands as one of the most influential and committed advocates for direct cash reparations in modern American history. As a writer, educator, activist, and talk show host, Worrill dedicated his life to advancing Black liberation through political empowerment, economic development, and cultural reclamation.

Born in Pasadena, California, and raised in Chicago from age nine, Worrill's consciousness was shaped by his experiences as a young Black athlete confronting racial prejudice. After serving in the military and reading extensively about Black American history while stationed in Japan, he returned to America in 1963 and became active in the Black Power Movement while pursuing his education.

Worrill's reparations advocacy crystallized through his leadership in multiple organizations. As the elected economic development commissioner of the National Coalition of Blacks for Reparations in America (N'COBRA), he worked tirelessly to advance a comprehensive direct cash reparations agenda. His involvement with the National Black United Front (NBUF) provided a platform to address political, social, economic, and cultural issues affecting Black Americans.

Perhaps most significantly, in 1997, Worrill led a delegation to Geneva, Switzerland, to formally charge the U.S. government with genocide and human rights violations before the UN Commission on Human Rights. This delegation presented a Declaration of Genocide with 157,000 signatures, later presenting this petition to the United Nations in New York. In 2001, he organized a 400-member delegation to the UN World Conference Against Racism in Durban, South Africa, continuing to internationalize the struggle for direct monetary compensation.

Worrill's commitment to education as a form of liberation was exemplified in his 40-year career at Northeastern Illinois University's Jacob H. Carruthers Center for Inner City Studies, where he helped establish an African-centered curriculum. Under his guidance, more than 1,700 students earned master's degrees in inner-city studies, including prominent leaders like Chicago Teachers Union President Karen Lewis.

Beyond his academic and activist work, Worrill's column "Worrill's World" was widely read in Black American newspapers across the country, including the Chicago Crusader, where he began writing in 1995. In August 2002, he organized a national reparations rally attended by thousands, continuing his deep-rooted commitment to ensuring that Black Americans would receive direct cash payments as reparations.

The Conrad Worrill Community Reparations Commission, established in 2020, continues his legacy, working to advance the cause of direct cash reparations in Chicago and beyond. As Illinois embarks on its own reparations journey through the state's African Descent-Citizens Reparations Commission, Worrill's decades of scholarship, activism, and community organizing provide both inspiration and a blueprint for the path toward meaningful cash compensation.

Dr. Worrill understood that direct cash reparations was the most effective path to empowering Black Americans to build institutions and achieve economic independence. His life's work reminds us that the struggle for cash reparations is not only morally justified but essential for addressing the cumulative economic harms inflicted upon Black Americans.

Dr. Sandy Darity and A. Kirsten Mullen: The Modern Economists

While earlier advocates laid crucial groundwork, Dr. William "Sandy" Darity Jr. and writer A. Kirsten Mullen have transformed reparations advocacy from moral appeals to economic science. Their book "From Here to Equality" provides the scientific framework that makes reparations impossible to dismiss based on "practicality." This Duke University scholarship team quickly followed up on their scholarship with "The Reparations Project Handbook."

Darity and Mullen moved the conversation from vague concepts to concrete numbers: approximately $850,000 in wealth disparity between the average Black and white household, requiring $10-12 trillion in federal funding to close the gap. This isn't random—it's calculated based on historical theft plus compound interest.

Their "pure reparations" framework has three essential components:

- Eligibility must be based on lineage (at least one ancestor enslaved in the U.S.), not race
- The program must explicitly target elimination of the racial wealth gap
- Direct cash payments must go to eligible recipients with maximum individual discretion

This scientific approach has frequently put Darity and Mullen at odds with more symbolically oriented reparations groups. Their critique of HR 40 centers on its lack of specificity and potential to produce watered-down recommendations that fail to close the wealth gap. While supporting the bill initially, Darity later called for specific changes to ensure it actually produced material repair rather than endless study.

In their 2018 report "What We Get Wrong About Closing the Racial Wealth Gap," Darity and colleagues demolished the conventional myths used to blame Black Americans for the wealth disparity. [10] Their research systematically proved that "a narrative that places the onus of the racial wealth gap on Black defectiveness is false in all of its permutations."

Dr. Claude Anderson: The Economic Strategist

Dr. Claud Anderson brought practical economic experience to the reparations question. As a former Commerce Department official under President Carter, Anderson understood how government economic policy works—and how it could be redirected toward repair.

His 2001 book "PowerNomics: The National Plan to Empower Black America" offered a five-year plan for prosperity and empowerment. Anderson defined power as "the ability to get things done despite the resistance and opposition of others," and argued that Black Americans must pool economic resources to create genuine independence. [11]

Anderson's approach was about government payments but also about strategic economic development. His own aquaculture company,

Waterland Fisheries, demonstrated the practical application of his theories. As one of the few Black business owners to complete a public offering, Anderson showed how collective economic action could create measurable progress.

Anderson insisted on specificity in political demands: Black Americans "should never allow themselves to be grouped with or equated to broad and ambiguous classes such as minorities, immigrants, people of color, diversity, poor people or similar defining terms." This disaggregating approach recognizes that specific harms require specific remedies—not vague diversity initiatives.

Dr. Claude Anderson has been deep in the Reparations paint for decades.

Yvette Carnell: The Political Innovator

When I first saw Yvette Carnell and ADOS proudly bang the American flag on social media and pair it with Reparations, it was a first for me. Although their more patriotic approach was new, their position on Obama and lineage delineation grew on me the more I thought about it, on a multi-factor and scientific basis, removing my emotions.

Rather than leaning into a new political expression with bias, I decided to hear Carnell and ADOS out. Based on the collapse of Black American politics under various spook spells, it wasn't time (2019) to be rigid and inflexible, like I knew everything or had all the answers. Our intellectual and political flexibility should be commensurate with how severe, underperforming, and desperate we believe our political condition is.

Fully embracing native Black Americans as a new people, our own tribe, wouldn't be different from Jamaicans embracing Jamaica or Nigerian-Americans embracing Nigeria. It was time to get hyper-focused, hyper-specialized, and hyper-politically efficient on matters of where our feet are, where our ancestors fought and died, and where we will likely die. We're here and we're going to be here so let's focus on us, here. Carnell's approach was innovative and the science of it all made more and more sense. It wasn't much different from Minister Farrakhan saying (at different times) "we were born here, we built it, so..." or Conrad Tillard saying he thought it was time to embrace our American-ness, in his frustrations with the Black Nationalist movement.

Yvette Carnell isn't just another voice in the reparations conversation— she's the bulldozer clearing the path. As co-founder of the American Descendants of Slavery (ADOS) movement, Carnell has revolutionized how reparations advocacy operates in the digital age while staying true to the science of material demands. [12]

What separates Carnell from conventional advocates is her surgical precision in defining eligibility. The reality she exposes is uncomfortable but irrefutable: conflating all Black identities dilutes the specific claim of those descended from American chattel slavery. "Blackness isn't our claim to reparations," she explains. "Slavery is our claim to reparations."

Carnell's background makes her approach more scientific, not less. Her work as a former congressional aide to both Senator Barbara Boxer and Representative Mel Watt gave her an insider's understanding of political mechanics. Unlike those offering spook rhetoric and vague hopes, she understands exactly how power operates in Washington because she's seen it firsthand.

Her YouTube channel "Breaking Brown" provided economic literacy when mainstream media offered nothing but symbolic politics. While Obama-era commentators were celebrating representation, Carnell was exposing the measurable absence of material progress. Her critique of the Obama presidency's failure to address the specific condition of Black American descendants of slavery made her a target—but it also proved her commitment to scientific analysis over emotional symbolism. In my estimate, no single Black American figure with reach has confronted the Obama spook spell and connected it to hyper-focus on a lineage-based Reparations advocacy reset, more effectively than Yvette Carnell during the 2019-2023 period in Black American politics.

The ADOS hashtag and movement she co-founded with Antonio Moore in 2016 has transformed reparations politics from academic discussion to grassroots demand. By creating a framework focused on lineage rather than race, Carnell cut through decades of purposeful confusion to create a coherent political identity connected to a specific economic claim. ADOS also established chapters in cities such as Atlanta, New York City, Jackson, Mississippi, Chicago, and Los Angeles. Getting it poppin' and to scale on social media, then setting up chapters in the field, and an annual conference could be a new model for emerging Black American organizations.

This new approach has faced predictable opposition. ADOS has been labeled everything from "divisive" to "Russian bots" to a "Trump supporter" simply for demanding specific material repair for a specific historical wrong. The Obama Democrat spook spell was so deep, establishment Democrats automatically thought something had to be wrong and foreign-based with ADOS, for having a different political orientation than their current orthodoxy. The New York Times reported on the strategic attacks against her claims, with opponents like Shireen Mitchell of Stop Online Violence Against Women promoting conspiracies about ADOS being "part of an external influence campaign."

Despite these attacks, Carnell's inaugural ADOS conference in 2019 attracted over a thousand attendees, demonstrating the material impact of her organizing effort. Even Dr. Cornell West attended the ADOS national conference and acknowledged the movement's importance for giving voice to working-class Black Americans.

"People call us divisive. We're not divisive. We're self-interested," Carnell has explained. [13] This focus on specific material interests rather than symbolic unity represents the essence of scientific political thinking. Carnell's position is unassailable: if reparations are compensation for specific harms from American slavery and its aftermath, then eligibility must connect directly to those specific harms.

In terms of improving Black American political consciousness and efficiency during the 2019-2025 period, no other political thinker has been more influential, based on my observations. The fact that ADOS successfully leveraged social media is a good thing, not a negative as governments, Fortune 500 brands, political parties, and the most influential and sophisticated people in the world also use the same medium. The author also notes multiple Black American organizations have developed from inspiration from Yvette Carnell.

Kamilah Moore: The Legal Architect

While many talk about reparations in abstract terms, Kamilah Moore is building the actual blueprint for implementation. As chair of California's Reparations Task Force—the first state-level body of its kind in the nation—Moore isn't theorizing about repair; she's creating the legal framework to make it happen.

Moore's approach comes from rigorous legal training. After studying at Columbia Law School and the University of Amsterdam, she wrote a thesis on global reparatory justice for the transatlantic slave trade that provided the intellectual foundation for her current work. While others speak in generalities, Moore grounds her advocacy in international human rights law—the framework explicitly referenced in California's reparations legislation.

Moore's approach was demonstrated in the task force's pivotal eligibility debate. When faced with pressure to define eligibility based on race rather than lineage, Moore followed the evidence. She invited experts including UC Berkeley constitutional scholar Erwin Chemerinsky, who testified that lineage-based reparations would more likely survive judicial scrutiny than race-based programs.

In March 2022, Moore led the crucial 5-4 vote establishing lineage as the determinant of eligibility—a decision that aligned reparations with its scientific foundation as redress for specific historical wrongs. This wasn't about ideology but about effective implementation: "As someone who has studied human rights law and international law, particularly under the scope of reparatory justice, I know that reparatory justice efforts are supposed to be victim-led," Moore explained.

This victim-centered approach represents a return to the foundations established by Callie House and Queen Mother Moore a century earlier. It's not about identity politics but about material repair for quantifiable harms.

Moore's leadership has produced the most comprehensive government report on anti-Black American discrimination in modern history. The first 600-page report released in June 2022 meticulously documented specific harms from the transatlantic slave trade to the present, creating the evidentiary foundation for specific remedies.

What makes Moore's contribution unique is her fusion of scholarly precision with practical implementation. Unlike academic theorists or traditional activists, she's building the actual mechanisms through which reparations could be delivered. The California Task Force model could become the template for other states and eventually federal action.

Perhaps most importantly, Moore represents a new generation of reparations leaders who balance sophisticated legal understanding with grassroots accountability. When asked about her motivation, she connects it directly to her childhood experiences: "As a child, I would go to the library a lot, and sometimes, I would even read slave narratives. I learned about 40 acres and a mule, and the reparations that were denied to my ancestors."

Moore's pioneering leadership with the California Reparations Task Force reflects attempts to institutionalize reparations at the state level. Multiple American cities have attempted to replicate the state task force model. Although Dr. Sandy Darity issued an "academic fatwa" against state and local efforts as distracting from federal efforts, the author sides with Moore and sees institutional buildup at city and state levels as part of a larger process. For example, top constitutional scholar Erwin Chemerinsky's testimony to the California Task Force—surfacing the constitutional advantage of lineage-based over race-based reparations for

Supreme Court survival—emerged directly from this state-level process and now informs national strategy. If the federal level is not ready and can't be forced to be ready right now based on current conditions, reparations advocacy at the state level actually supports eventual federal activation. Reparations activation at the state level—a smaller, more achievable goal—could expand national Black American political imagination about what's possible.

De-Spooking Leadership Analysis

Part of de-spooking in the Science vs Spook framework is not waiting until the movement "pops," scales, or until the leaders and new thinkers die to worship and honor them. If we can recognize the sacrifices, innovative thinking, and bold actions now, we become more scientific and less spooky. It's like giving flowers to your loved ones at funeral time but not giving them a simple phone call in years. Being spooky means discounting the history being made today, right in your face, while romanticizing what happened yesterday.

Another de-spooking factor is how we compare those who are in the paint now—building and organizing, facing setbacks along the way like any organization—with others in history. For example, I heard OG Piru Ayatollah Marv from the NOI compare Dr. Khallid Muhammad and Farrakhan's organizational results, but this is fundamentally unfair, as it ignores the crucial factor of time. In 1995, I was actually on the bus from Los Angeles to the Million Man March with Brother Marvin, and he is a good Brother. He was a leader on our bus and helped some of the Brothers who ran out of money on our trip. But even good Brothers can make unfair comparisons. Farrakhan's organization is, in part, the result of Dr. Khallid Muhammad's substantial contributions. Second, Dr. Khallid Muhammad only had a limited time to develop the New Black Panther Party—we can't compare a few years of work to decades of work. This would be unfair; we need to factor in time and make the appropriate adjustments to get closer to apples-to-apples comparisons.

When evaluating new leaders like Carnell, any comparisons with historical figures deserve the factor of time, and these new leaders deserve space before impulsive judgments are made. They're building in real time, facing opposition that's immediate and direct, not filtered through decades of historical perspective. I've observed some criticisms against a host of emerging leaders on social media, but these often fail to account for the complexity of building movements in the digital age. The social media environment allows for instantaneous criticism without the context of time and without acknowledging the inherent challenges of organizing. When someone points out a misstep, failure, or controversy involving current leaders while ignoring similar issues with historical figures, they're engaging in a form of spooky thinking that privileges the dead over the living doing the work right now.

Finally, part of the de-spooking process is being objective and learning how to evaluate leaders and organizers through an imperfection lens. A factor of raw intelligence should greatly consider how we deal with imperfection. Do we throw the baby out with the bathwater, or do we evaluate with factors and add up the positives and negatives? If we are looking for perfection, we are looking for spook. For example, if the FBI is right and King was involved with orgies and illicit sexual activity, this doesn't make his great contributions and the truth of what he preached any less meaningful. How we value leaders and contributions shouldn't be enhanced based on mystery—what we don't know.

This mystery factor distorts our comparative evaluations too. Some well-meaning people may elevate King over Elijah Muhammad because Malcolm X publicly exposed Elijah's private affairs, while King's remained largely hidden. The reality is that King's private behavior might have been equally problematic or worse, but the difference in public knowledge creates an artificial hierarchy. This information asymmetry doesn't make King superior to Elijah by default. What makes a leader great isn't the absence of personal flaws, but the tangible impact of their work and ideas. A scientific orientation requires evaluating based on measurable contributions, not on whose secrets remained better protected.

In many ways, we have a proportional bias towards leaders who have passed on because of mystery—we don't know as much about their flaws as we do about the leaders who are in the paint today. This doesn't diminish their greatness, but we add spook on top of their actual accomplishments by elevating them beyond what the evidence supports. This mystery factor distorts our comparative evaluations. Some well-meaning people may elevate certain historical figures over others not because of superior accomplishments, but simply because one leader's private affairs remained hidden while another's became public knowledge. In seeking perfection, we are seeking spook. We need to add up the cumulative factors of leadership and organization, weigh the positives and negatives, and then come to our estimates and conclusions. Like the reparations heroes in this lesson, there are heroes being created and doing work right now, if we are paying close attention to the relevant science.

The Science

- Historical advocates (Callie House, Queen Mother Moore) demanded direct payments, not symbolic gestures
- Elijah Muhammad's blueprint included lineage-based framework and material demands decades before modern movements
- Modern advocates (Darity/Mullen, Carnell, Moore) combine scientific analysis with strategic implementation
- Evaluate current leaders fairly, factoring time and imperfection rather than seeking perfection

---

[1] Ta-Nehisi Coates, "Schism Nation: Black Muslims in D.C. are in the midst of a Holy War," Washington City Paper, May 14, 1999.

[2] Silis Muhammad, "Silis Muhammad's United Nations Interventions on behalf of Afrodescendants," Independently published, September 27, 2023.

[3] Muhammad, Elijah, "What The Muslims Want," Nation of Islam, excerpt from Message To The Blackman in America, 1965.

[4] Randall Robinson, "The Debt: What America Owes to Blacks," New York: Dutton Adult, First Edition, January 1, 2000.

[5] Claud Anderson, "PowerNomics: The National Plan to Empower Black America," PowerNomics Corporation of America, First Edition, January 1, 2001.

[6] Silis Muhammad, "Silis Muhammad's United Nations Interventions on behalf of Afrodescendants," Independently published, September 27, 2023.

[7] Ta-Nehisi Coates, "Schism Nation: Black Muslims in D.C. are in the midst of a Holy War," Washington City Paper, May 14, 1999.

[8] John Conyers, "Representative John Conyers and the Commission to Study Reparation Proposals for African Americans Act," Africology: The Journal of Pan African Studies, 9, no.5, August 2016, 112.

[9] Randall Robinson, "The Debt: What America Owes to Blacks," New York: Dutton Adult, First Edition, January 1, 2000.

[10] William A. Darity Jr. et al., "What We Get Wrong About Closing the Racial Wealth Gap," Samuel DuBois Cook Center on Social Equity, April 2018.

[11] Claud Anderson, "PowerNomics: The National Plan to Empower Black America," PowerNomics Corporation of America, First Edition, January 1, 2001.

[12] ADOS Advocacy Foundation, "Mission Statement," ADOS Foundation, accessed May 5, 2025.

[13] Farah Stockman, "'We're Self-Interested': The Growing Identity Debate in Black America," The New York Times, November 8, 2019, updated November 13, 2019.

The Democratic Party's
Reparations Dance

> *"You running around here talkin' 'bout, 'I'm with the Democratic*
> *Party. I'm with the Republican Party.' Fool, you not even invited to*
> *the party!" —Dr. Khallid Muhammad*

The modern Democratic Party has perfected a delicate two-step when it comes to reparations: acknowledge America's "original sin" while ensuring it stays firmly in the past tense. [1] From former Massachusetts Senator John Kerry claiming reparations would "divide the nation" [2] to Hillary Clinton pivoting to "investments in communities," [3] [4] from Obama warning it would let America say "we've paid our debt" [5] [6] to Biden's studied ambiguity, [7] the choreography remains consistent. Democratic Party leaders, even those with a net worth in the tens of millions like Dianne Feinstein ($58.5 million), [8] have mastered the art of expressing deep understanding of historical wrongs while declaring them best "left alone." It's not just politics—it's performance art. If the Democrats can lock up the Black American vote no matter what, why take the risks for Black Americans with Reparations?

John Kerry: The Direct Rejection

Kerry, the former US Secretary of State under Obama from 2013-2017, demonstrated the classic first move: direct opposition hidden behind concern for "unity." While campaigning in 2004, then-Senator Kerry told students at Howard University that he didn't support financial reparations for Black people because it would "divide the nation" rather than "heal the wounds." [9]

"I personally do not believe that America is going to advance if we go backwards and look to reparations in the way that some people are defining them," Kerry said. He acknowledged the deep-rooted "scars" Black people still feel from slavery, Jim Crow legislation, and segregation, but argued reparations would not resolve the problem. "When you mention the word slave... in 2004, it's almost a shocking, unbelievable notion that in this country we wrote slavery into our Constitution before we wrote it out," Kerry said.

Bill Clinton: The Generational Escape Hatch

Clinton deployed the "too much time has passed" argument, telling the American Urban Radio Network that he didn't favor compensating descendants of slaves because the United States was too many generations removed for reparations to be possible.[10] [11]

Instead of material redress, Clinton offered symbolic gestures, saying he was considering apologizing to African Americans for their ancestors' suffering. "I think it has to be dealt with," he said. "There's still some unfinished business out there among Black and white Americans." The country needs to continue to work to erase the effects of past discrimination, Clinton added, calling for a "new national dialogue on race."

Clinton ultimately skipped a domestic apology, instead apologizing to African schoolchildren in Uganda during a six-nation tour in 1998.[12] [13] He talked about America's "shameful legacy" in Africa, including America's role in the slave trade, saying Americans should "recognize and repent" because "the United States has not always done the right thing by Africa... Going back to the time before we were even a nation, European Americans received the fruits of the slave trade. And we were wrong in that."

By apologizing in Africa for slavery's impact on Africa—not for its impact on Black Americans—Clinton sidestepped domestic liability while appearing morally engaged. This wasn't coincidental but strategic.

When you think about what spook looks like visually, think about Bill Clinton playing the saxophone on the popular Arsenio Hall show in the

90's, earning the title 'first Black President,' while simultaneously rolling out a police-written crime bill and mass incarceration agenda that devastated Black communities.

Hillary Clinton: The Redefinition Strategy

When Hillary Clinton was asked about reparations during her Senate campaign in 2000, she said Black Americans deserve an apology for slavery. By 2015, Clinton had perfected the third move: redefining reparations as general investment in communities. When asked directly about reparations, she pivoted: "I'll tell you what: I think we need to make many more investments in everything from preschool education to affordable housing. That's my form of trying to give people the chance to be empowered, to make the most out of their God-given potential." [14]

At the 2016 Iowa Brown & Black Presidential Forum, she doubled down on this redefinition: "I think we should start studying what investments we need to make in communities... There's an idea in the Congressional Black Caucus about really targeting federal dollars to communities that have had either disinvestment or no investment, and have had years of being below the poverty level. That's the kind of thing I'd like us to focus on and really help lift people up."[15] [16]

This approach brilliantly transforms a specific debt owed to specific people for specific historical wrongs into general anti-poverty programs that maintain system control while appearing progressive.

Barack Obama: The Ultimate System Protection

As the first Kenyan-American president, Obama delivered the most sophisticated rejection, framing reparations as a dangerous endpoint that would allow America to escape ongoing responsibility. In an NAACP questionnaire, he wrote: "I fear that reparations would be an excuse for some to say 'we've paid our debt' and to avoid the much harder work of enforcing our anti-discrimination laws in employment and housing; the much harder work of making sure that our schools are not separate and unequal; the much harder work of providing job training programs and rehabilitating young men coming out of prison every year; and the much harder work of lifting 37 million Americans of all races out of poverty." [17]

On CNN, Obama argued: "I have said in the past—and I'll repeat again—that the best reparations we can provide are good schools in the inner city and jobs for people who are unemployed... You know, the fact is, is that dealing with some of the legacy of discrimination is going to cost billions of dollars. And we're not going to be able to have that kind of resource allocation unless all Americans feel that they are invested in making this stuff happen." [18][19]

Obama's approach was so effective that Republican Senate Majority Leader Mitch McConnell later invoked it to defend his own opposition to reparations. The material impact? Zero progress on actual reparations during eight years of Democratic control.

Reparations scholar Dr. Sandy Darity captured the contradiction: "The spectacle of a black president who opposes the most dramatic black-specific program of all ultimately amounts to political expediency. If black reparations is the right thing to do—and I know in the depth of my soul that it is—then we should work to make it happen, no matter how long the odds." [20]

Bernie Sanders: The Progressive Paradox

Even "radical" Sanders maintained the same position, facing criticism from Ta-Nehisi Coates who wrote: "Unfortunately, Sanders's radicalism has failed in the ancient fight against white supremacy. What he proposes in lieu of reparations—job creation, investment in cities, and free higher education—is well within the Overton window and his platform on race echoes Democratic orthodoxy." [21][22]

Sanders echoed Obama and Clinton: "I think what we should be talking about is making massive investments in rebuilding our cities, in creating millions of decent paying jobs, in making public colleges and universities tuition-free, basically targeting our federal resources to the areas where it is needed the most and where it is needed the most is in impoverished communities, often African American and Latino." [23]

As Linda Qiu noted, "that is basically what Obama and Clinton suggested in lieu of reparations."[24] [25]

Even the most "radical" wing of the Democratic Party maintains the same fundamental position on specific material repair for historical wrongs: acknowledge the problem while avoiding actual payment.

Joe Biden: The Study-But-Never-Act Approach

Biden represents the latest evolution: support studying reparations while ensuring material repair remains distant. As a candidate, Biden said he supported HR 40. After taking office, Biden adviser Cedric Richmond claimed the president would begin to act on reparations for Native Black Americans, stressing that the administration supported HR 40.

Richmond described Biden team's approach: "We don't want to wait on a study. We're going to start acting now," he said.[26] [27]But when asked for specifics, he pivoted to "free college tuition to HBCUs" and "free community college."

When Biden spoke at the Tulsa race massacre commemoration, he failed to give a "full-throated endorsement of HR 40" or mention reparations for the survivors and their descendants. [28]

After meeting with the Congressional Black Caucus, Biden cited infrastructure as his priority, effectively shelving reparations like his predecessors. 'He didn't disagree with what we're doing,' said Representative Brenda Lawrence (D-Michigan), second vice chair of the CBC. 'He did talk about his plate [being] full with trying to get the infrastructure bill passed and that he really wanted to make sure that he could get that through before he took on anything else.'

To Biden's credit, he at least told civil rights leaders and Congressional Black Caucus members directly in 2021 not to expect any action on reparations—more honest than the elaborate reparations dance performed by his predecessors."[29]

Kamala Harris: The Master Class in Ambiguity

Harris's stance represents political evasion through strategic ambiguity. She began supporting a study council, made her boldest statement at Al Sharpton's National Action Network promising to sign a reparations bill, [30] then quickly retreated to vague territory in her NPR interview, redefining reparations as studying "the effects of generations of discrimination" and addressing untreated trauma in Black communities. [31]

When pressed by the Des Moines Register, Harris diluted her position further, arguing that America "needs a history lesson" and that reparations "can't just be, 'Hey... write some checks.'" Instead, she promoted her Lift Act—universal tax credits of up to $500 monthly for families making under $100,000—effectively converting reparations into a general antipoverty policy. [32]

Harris's evolution on the issue follows a familiar political pattern: start with apparent support, gradually shift to calling for studies, then redirect to general economic measures that avoid specific redress for historical wrongs. This wasn't just inconsistency—it was calculated ambiguity designed to appear supportive while avoiding any commitment to actual reparations.

Analysis

When we apply the Science-versus-Spook framework to the Democratic Party's reparations dance, the pattern becomes clear. For over twenty-five years, its leaders have maintained remarkable consistency in their approach:

1. Begin with moral acknowledgment of historical wrongs

2. Express concern about divisiveness

3. Redefine reparations as general investment

4. If pressed, support studying the issue

5. Never endorse direct payments to descendants

This isn't random—it's strategic. The party depends on more than 90 percent of Black American voter support while ensuring material repair never disrupts existing power structures. The patterns observed during the Obama Spook spell period is Democrats want to replace progress or baby steps towards Reparations and substantive policy initiatives with identity affinity housed within candidates like Obama and Kamala, who aren't even native Black American. The more spook and symbolism they can get away with, the less policy risk taking on behalf of Black Americans they offer us.

With the Democratic Party spook spell we've been under for decades, particularly during the Obama New Black period, we've been playing political poker but without the normal options of bluffing or going all in like the professionals. Our political orientation has been, "Here are our cards. Look at them. We don't have any options." We can't win with this strategic orientation—or shall I say, spook and fear political orientation. No serious player would announce their hand and remove all leverage before the game even begins. Yet politically, that's exactly what we've been conditioned to do.

The Democrats have been allowed to tap dance around Pure Reparations while expecting Black Americans to tap dance to the voting booth every election and shine the party's shoes, at an 80-90% clip.

Breaking the Dance: Strategic Goals

Black Americans should demand two specific actions that bypass Republican opposition entirely:

1. **Executive Order on Presidential Reparations Committee** - This requires only presidential action. No filibuster, no Republican votes needed—just political will.

2. **Put Pure Reparations on the official Democratic Party platform** - Party platforms are determined by Democrats alone. Republicans have zero say.

These actions put Democrats in the hot seat because they can no longer hide behind Republican obstruction. Both are 100% within Democratic control.

The implicit deal should become explicit: "You want our votes but what will you risk for us?" The Democratic Party operates as if it has earned a monopoly on the Black vote, but the science shows a captured and exploitive one-sided relationship where risk-taking flows only one way.

The Science

- 25+ years of consistent Democratic pattern: acknowledge history, redefine as general investment, avoid direct payments
- Party depends on 90% Black support while ensuring material repair never happens
- Break the dance by demanding: Executive Order on Presidential Reparations Committee + Pure Reparations on party platform
- Both actions are 100% within Democratic control, no Republican votes needed

---

[1] Alexander Bolton, "Senate Democrats wish talk on reparations would go away," The Hill, June 26, 2019.

[2] "Kerry opposes slavery reparations," Washington Times, April 15, 2004.

[3] "Listen To Hillary Clinton's Interview With BuzzFeed," Another Round Podcast, BuzzFeed News, October 11, 2015.

[4] "Hillary Clinton's Interview With BuzzFeed," Another Round Podcast, BuzzFeed News, October 11, 2015.

[5] Eugene Scott, "What Obama actually said in his rejection of reparations," Washington Post, July 9, 2019.

[6] "Transcript of CNN Late Edition With Wolf Blitzer, Q&A With Barack Obama," CNN, July 27, 2008.

[7] Eugene Daniels, "Biden privately tells lawmakers not to expect much on reparations legislation," Politico, March 2, 2021.

[8] Center for Responsive Politics, "Senator Feinstein's Financial Disclosure Report," OpenSecrets.org, May 2022.

[9] John Kerry, "Address at Howard University," Washington D.C., April 14, 2004.

[10] Bill Clinton, "Interview on American Urban Radio Network," February 21, 1997.

[11] "Clinton Opposes Slavery Reparations But he says he's considering an apology for slavery," CNN, June 17, 1997.

[12] John F. Harris, "Clinton Says US Wronged Africa," Washington Post, March 25, 1998.

[13] John F. Harris, "Clinton Says US Wronged Africa," Washington Post, March 25, 1998.

[14] "Hillary Clinton's Interview With BuzzFeed," Another Round Podcast, BuzzFeed News, October 11, 2015.

[15] "2016 Brown & Black Democratic Presidential Forum", Fusion, Streamed live on January 11, 2016.

[16] "2016 Brown & Black Democratic Presidential Forum," Fusion, January 11, 2016.

[17] Barack Obama, "NAACP Questionnaire Responses," NAACP, January 2008.

[18] "Transcript of CNN Late Edition With Wolf Blitzer, Q&A With Barack Obama," CNN, July 27, 2008.

[19] "Transcript of CNN Late Edition With Wolf Blitzer, Q&A With Barack Obama," CNN, July 27, 2008.

[20] William A. Darity Jr., "Obama and the Politics of Reparations," Interview with The Root, February 2018.

[21] Ta-Nehisi Coates, "Why Precisely Is Bernie Sanders Against Reparations?", The Atlantic, January 19, 2016.

[22] Ta-Nehisi Coates, "Why Precisely Is Bernie Sanders Against Reparations?" The Atlantic, January 19, 2016.

[23] Bernie Sanders, "Town Hall Meeting on Racial Justice," Myrtle Beach, South Carolina, January 17, 2016.

[24] Linda Qiu, "What Bernie Sanders, Barack Obama and Hillary Clinton Have Said About Reparations for Slavery," Politifact, The Poynter Institute, January 26, 2016.

[25] Linda Qiu, "What Bernie Sanders, Barack Obama and Hillary Clinton have said about reparations for slavery," Politifact, The Poynter Institute, January 26, 2016.

[26] "Biden Adviser Cedric Richmond Sees First-Term Progress on Reparations," Axios, March 1, 2021.

[27] Biden adviser Cedric Richmond sees first-term progress on reparations," Axios, March 1, 2021.

[28] "Transcript: Biden Commemorates Tulsa Race Massacre Centennial," NPR, June 1, 2021.

[29] Eugene Daniels, "Biden privately tells lawmakers not to expect much on reparations legislation," Politico, March 2, 2021.

[30] Kamala Harris, "Address at National Action Network Convention," New York, April 5, 2019.

[31] Kamala Harris, "Interview on Reparations Policy," NPR Morning Edition, March 14, 2019.

[32] Kamala Harris, "Interview with Des Moines Register Editorial Board," Des Moines Register, October 8, 2019.

MONETARY
SCIENCE AND
THE FEDERAL
RESERVE

LESSON 44
The Federal Reserve is Key

If you want to understand power and inequality in America, start studying the Federal Reserve. While we're taught that elected officials control the system, the reality is that unelected central bankers at the Fed wield enormous influence over Black American wealth factors and opportunity. The Fed's decisions on interest rates, inflation targets, and unemployment metrics help determine whether we'll see job growth in our communities or another wave of foreclosures and unemployment. Yet few understand how this shadowy institution operates—or how its decisions systematically disadvantage our communities.

This isn't some conspiracy theory—it's actual fact. As journalist William Greider wrote in his landmark book *Secrets of the Temple: How the Federal Reserve Runs the Country*, "The Federal Reserve is banker to the government, regulator of financial institutions, and the central processing mechanism for the entire banking system. It decides how much money will cost—long-term or short-term, for business people or home buyers, for the US Treasury or foreign central banks. It is that great, though somewhat mysterious, entity in Washington that decides how much credit will be available in the economy, and at what price." [1]

The Fed's enormous power over the American economy comes with a serious problem: structural racial bias built into its very design.

The Fed's Dual Mandate Problem

By law, the Federal Reserve has two primary responsibilities: maintaining price stability (keeping inflation low) and maximizing employment. This "dual mandate" forces Fed governors to balance competing interests. When they raise interest rates to combat inflation, they also potentially

418

slow economic growth and increase unemployment. When they lower rates to boost employment, they risk higher inflation.

This tradeoff wouldn't be problematic if it affected all Americans equally. But Black unemployment consistently runs about twice the rate of white unemployment, meaning that when the Fed raises rates to fight inflation, Black workers disproportionately lose jobs. Meanwhile, when inflation does occur, it also hurts Black Americans disproportionately—higher prices for rent, food, and gas consume a larger percentage of income for lower-wage workers, magnifying the existing Black-white wealth gap. Additionally, the higher interest rates used to combat inflation translate to higher mortgage rates and credit costs, which take a disproportionate share of Black American income due to lower average wealth and wages.

Federal Reserve policy disproportionately helps those with the greatest amount of assets and existing wealth grow their assets and pump their prices, while hurting those with the fewest assets and wealth. The way the system is structured, Federal Reserve policy exacerbates existing inequalities. This creates a lose-lose scenario where many Black Americans bear the heaviest costs whether the Fed prioritizes fighting inflation or unemployment, while those with substantial assets benefit regardless of policy direction.

Because of this imbalance, Fed decisions to prioritize fighting inflation over maximizing employment systematically harm Black communities. Every time the Fed decides that 4% inflation is worse than 8% Black unemployment, they're making a choice with profound racial implications.

The late economist William Spriggs, who was the AFL-CIO's chief economist and a Howard University professor, repeatedly highlighted this racial disparity. Spriggs noted that Fed officials often speak of "full employment" when the overall unemployment rate reaches around 4%, even though Black unemployment might still be at 8% or higher. [2]

Spriggs later explained how economics as a field has deeply embedded racist assumptions: "The profession remains rooted in a view that Black people aren't equal, that our unemployment rate is because of us. This is true in the way they use Black unemployment to determine when we're at full employment. When they measure interest rates, they do it in relation to the white unemployment rate."

The Asset Effect Gap

While the unemployment effect is well-documented, the asset effect is even more pernicious. The Fed's extended period of quantitative easing and low interest rates following the 2008 financial crisis created the largest asset price boom in American history. Stock markets tripled, and real estate values soared—but these gains went primarily to those who already owned assets.

Since Black Americans own far fewer stocks and real estate investments than whites due to anti-Black American structural factors, this Fed policy exacerbated racial wealth disparities. Put simply, Fed policy made the already wealthy much wealthier while doing little for those without assets.

Banking law expert Mehrsa Baradaran explains in her book *The Color of Money*: "The racial wealth gap is neither a mistake nor the result of individual moral failings or virtues; it is part of the architecture of our economy." [3] The Fed's policies represent a crucial part of that architecture, systematically contributing to racial wealth disparities.

The numbers tell the disturbing story: the racial wealth gap didn't improve during the recovery from the 2008 financial crisis—it grew substantially. According to the Brookings Institution, in 2019, the average white family had eight times the wealth of the average Black family. [4] This wasn't accidental but a direct result of policies that benefit asset holders over wage earners.

The Revolving Door

The Federal Reserve operates with little democratic oversight, rotating its leadership through a revolving door with Wall Street. This creates a system where those making policy decisions overwhelmingly come from and return to the very institutions they regulate.

Former Fed Chair Janet Yellen earned over $7 million in speaking fees from financial firms in the two years before becoming Treasury Secretary. Current Fed Chair Jerome Powell is a former investment banker with a net worth exceeding $50 million. These aren't neutral technocrats but products of a specific economic worldview.

This revolving door ensures that Fed policy consistently favors Wall Street over Main Street, prioritizing the concerns of bankers over workers. As Fed insider Stanley Druckenmiller admitted, "The Fed has moved so far towards an explicit wealth effect policy, trying to create a stock market rally to stimulate the economy... but unfortunately the wealth effect isn't trickling down to the average American."

Rather than simply criticizing this system, Black Americans need to understand how to navigate it strategically. One way to see the Fed is as a pumper of asset prices or an asset bubble creator. Rather than look at the Federal Reserve as permanent opposition, it would be smart to do our best to try to get on the same side as the Fed and accumulate assets such as stocks and real estate. If you are an asset holder, the Fed is designed and structured to pump their prices over the long term. There is a saying on Wall Street that has proven to be statistically reliable: Don't Fight the Fed!

The Fed's Racial Awakening?

After decades of ignoring racial disparities, the Fed has recently begun acknowledging the impact of its policies on Black communities. In 2020, Atlanta Fed President Raphael Bostic (the first Black Federal Reserve Bank president in the institution's 107-year history) wrote an essay titled "A Moral and Economic Imperative to End Racism," acknowledging the Fed's role in perpetuating inequality.

Bostic later argued that the Fed should at least consider reparations: "There are definitely merits to it in the sense that, if people have been harmed by laws, then there should be a discussion about redress... I have not seen as much conversation about what could be done in a direct sense to try to provide some sort of recompense for that." He specifically praised local reparations efforts, calling programs like Evanston, Illinois's housing-related reparations initiative "quite interesting." Bostic emphasized the ongoing impact of historical policies: "The legacies of past racism are still present in our society. We have to think about what things are necessary to offset the impacts of those old systems that still flow through."

We shouldn't discount the potential impact of Federal Reserve officials making the case for reparations to the American public. Bostic's public positions may stem not only from courage and scholarship but also from the fact that Federal Reserve seats operate independently from political actors once secured.

Strategic Understanding of the Fed's Role

Black American political strategy should include a deeper focus on understanding Fed policy for two primary reasons:

1. **Economic Impact**: The Fed makes decisions with enormous racial wealth implications every six weeks at its Federal Open Market Committee meetings. Understanding these impacts is crucial for developing effective economic strategies.

2. **Policy Framework**: Analyzing the Fed's approach to economic management provides insights that may complement legislative efforts in a gridlocked Congress.

The Fed's Role Alongside Congress

When analyzing economic policymaking centers, the Fed has a different institutional structure than Congress:

1. **Different Decision-Making Process**: While legislation requires navigating committees, floor votes, filibusters, and presidential

approval, Fed policy develops through deliberation among appointed economists and financial experts.

2. **Regular Economic Assessment**: The Fed evaluates economic conditions eight times annually, while major economic legislation may only pass once every few years.

3. **Technical Economic Analysis**: Fed discussions are framed around economic data and financial stability rather than partisan positioning, creating space for evidence-based analysis.

4. **Institutional Independence with Accountability**: The Fed's independence from direct political influence is crucial to its mission, though it remains accountable to its Congressional mandate and broader economic outcomes.

It's important that Black American political imagination, strategy, and analysis don't become divorced from macroeconomics and Federal Reserve policy. Understanding the Fed's role in shaping economic conditions and inequality is key to developing effective political and wealth-building strategies. As William Greider noted, 'The Federal Reserve is the most undemocratic institution in America yet the one that has the most power over our collective lives.

The Science

- Fed decisions disproportionately impact Black Americans: rate hikes increase Black unemployment, asset purchases benefit wealth holders
- Black unemployment consistently runs 2x white unemployment rates
- Fed policy systematically benefits asset holders over wage earners
- Understanding Fed policy is crucial for wealth-building and political strategy

[1] William Greider, "Secrets of the Temple: How the Federal Reserve Runs the Country" (New York: Simon & Schuster, January 15, 1989).

[2] Alex Grant, "The Remarkable Biography of Bill Spriggs - The Champion of Equality" (Independently published, June 10, 2023).

[3] Mehrsa Baradaran, "The Color of Money: Black Banks and the Racial Wealth Gap" (Cambridge: Belknap Press, Harvard University Press, 2017).

[4] Andre M. Perry, Hannah Stephens, and Manann Donoghoe, "Black Wealth Is Increasing, but So Is the Racial Wealth Gap," Brookings Institution, January 9, 2024. Stanley Druckenmiller, "Federal Reserve Policy and Wealth Inequality," Interview with CNBC, September 9, 2022.

[6] Raphael Bostic, "Institutionalized Racism and Economic Potential," Speech at the Federal Reserve Bank of Atlanta, June 12, 2020.

[7] Raphael Bostic, "The Case for Considering Reparations," Federal Reserve Bank of Atlanta Working Paper Series, January 2022.

[8] Stephanie Kelton, "The Deficit Myth: Modern Monetary Theory and the Birth of the People's Economy" (New York: PublicAffairs, March 9, 2021).

[9] Françoise Drumetz and Christian Pfister, "Modern Monetary Theory: A Wrong Compass for Decision-Making," Intereconomics: Review of European Economic Policy 56, no. 6 (2021): 355-361.

[10] Julian Jessop, "Beware the Siren Call of Modern Monetary Theory," Institute of Economic Affairs, August 6, 2020.

Financial Science as Political Science

In 1983, legendary Chicago trader Richard Dennis made a bet with his partner William Eckhardt that would transform our understanding of both financial markets and human decision-making. Dennis believed trading success wasn't some mystical talent—it was a skill that could be taught to anyone with the right mindset and discipline. Eckhardt disagreed, arguing that Dennis's extraordinary ability to extract hundreds of millions from the markets was innate, not learnable.

To settle this nature-versus-nurture debate, they launched what became known as the "Turtle Trading" experiment. After placing a newspaper ad, Dennis selected a diverse group of applicants—including a security guard, an actor, two professional gamblers, and recent college graduates with zero Wall Street experience. He nicknamed them "Turtles" after visiting a Singapore turtle farm where he declared, "We are going to grow traders just like they grow turtles." [1]

These ordinary people were given extraordinary responsibility. Within days, Dennis handed them trading accounts funded with millions of his own dollars and a precise set of rules to follow. Over the next four years, this group of novices went on to earn an estimated $175 million (about $400-$500 million in today's dollars, adjusted for inflation).

The secret wasn't just the trading system Dennis taught them. It was his emphasis on psychological discipline and cognitive bias awareness. Dennis understood that markets were driven by human psychology, and the biggest obstacle to trading success wasn't lack of knowledge—it was the human brain itself. By training his students to recognize and overcome cognitive biases, Dennis gave them a mathematical edge that few Wall Street professionals possessed. [2] [3]

This same edge—identifying and overcoming cognitive biases—can be applied to Black American politics. The financial science that made the Turtles millions offers us a blueprint for catching the spook and getting to the key factors and science early.

Eight Cognitive Biases Undermining Our Politics & Scientific Orientation

1. Outcome Bias: Judging Decisions by Results, Not Process

Outcome bias occurs when we evaluate decisions based solely on their results, not on the quality of the decision-making process. In basketball, a player can take a perfect shot with excellent form, wide open, with good risk/reward positioning, but it still doesn't go in. The fact that the ball doesn't drop doesn't mean the shot itself wasn't good. All good shots don't go in. Conversely, winning the lottery doesn't make buying a ticket a smart financial decision.

This bias devastates political thinking. When we judge political strategies solely by immediate outcomes rather than mathematical expectancy over time, we make catastrophic errors. A failing strategy might occasionally produce good outcomes by chance, while a sound strategy might sometimes yield disappointing results. A scientific orientation demands we evaluate the process, not just the outcome.

2. Confirmation Bias: Seeking Evidence That Confirms Existing Beliefs

We naturally gravitate toward information that confirms what we already believe while dismissing contradictory evidence. This creates echo chambers where we never challenge fundamental assumptions.

In Black American politics, this manifests as continuing to support Democratic Party spook spells despite decades of underperformance, because we selectively remember occasional wins while dismissing extreme patterns of neglect. Scientific orientation requires actively seeking evidence that contradicts existing beliefs.

3. Loss Aversion: Fearing Losses More Than Valuing Equivalent Gains

Humans typically feel the pain of losses about twice as intensely as the pleasure of equivalent gains. The Turtles were trained to overcome this bias by focusing on expected value rather than emotional reactions.

In politics, this bias makes us terrified of "losing" by exploring alternatives, even when our current approach delivers minimal returns. We irrationally cling to the devil we know over potential alternatives that might yield better outcomes. When Black American political positioning becomes dominated by fear and loss aversion, this risk-averse orientation effectively creates a self-installed ceiling on political victories.

4. Sunk Cost Fallacy: Continuing Based on Past Investment Rather Than Future Prospects

The sunk cost fallacy keeps us committed to failing strategies because we've already invested so much. The Turtles learned to ruthlessly cut losing positions regardless of emotional or financial capital already invested.

Black American politics is drowning in sunk costs. We've invested generations in a one-party strategy, making it psychologically difficult to consider alternatives even as returns diminish. The scientific approach demands we evaluate future prospects, not past investments. The Science vs Spook framework doesn't require changing political parties or not voting Democrat, as much as stopping our investment in the same political thinking.

5. Bandwagon Effect: Following the Crowd Instead of Evidence

Our political strategy often suffers from extreme bandwagon effect. The religious-like Obama spook spell is an example of this bias in action. We can become so aligned with the dominant tribal or political view that a smart and informed contrarian like Tavis Smiley gets death threats, called a crab, sellout, and Uncle Tom because he doesn't jump on the same spook spell bandwagon as everyone else. Smiley's position that a Black American political agenda should be pressed regardless of whether Obama is Kenyan-American was only controversial due to bandwagon effect bias and a lack of understanding of how the American system works. Black America wins by respecting and considering contrarian points of view. We lose if the bandwagon effect bias becomes a Black American identity requirement. The contrarians willing to go against popular spook spells may be demonstrating as much science as love.

6. Availability Bias: Overweighting Vivid, Recent Examples

We overemphasize information that's recent, dramatic, or personally experienced. Dennis trained the Turtles to rely on long-term data rather than recent market movements or dramatic news stories.

In politics, this bias leads us to overreact to symbolic gestures or emotionally charged events while neglecting long-term patterns of policy outcomes. Political science requires analysis of decades-long patterns, not emotional reactions to the news cycle.

7. Recency Bias: Overemphasizing Recent Events While Ignoring Historical Patterns

Recency bias causes us to give disproportionate weight to recent events while discounting the lessons of history. On Wall Street, this bias leads investors to chase the hottest performers of the last quarter while ignoring long-term track records.

Ever heard someone confidently declare their "greatest of all time" basketball player is whoever dominates the current season? They'll passionately argue for today's star while having no knowledge of legends who played under different, often more challenging conditions decades ago. This cultural myopia – judging all-time greatness based only on what you've personally witnessed – perfectly illustrates recency bias.

In Black American politics, we often overweight the latest symbolic gesture or minor policy win while forgetting decades of systemic neglect. Each election cycle brings new promises that erase memories of previously broken ones. By failing to examine the full historical record of political returns on our voting investment, we have the potential to undermine our political positioning. Real political science requires evaluating multiple decades of policy outcomes, not just the latest headlines or campaign promises.

8. Authority Bias: Excessive Deference to Traditional Authority Figures

We tend to trust and obey authority figures even when evidence contradicts them. The Turtle experiment itself challenged authority by proving ordinary people could outperform Wall Street elites.

Black American politics suffers from excessive deference to traditional civil rights organizations and leaders who continue advocating failed, unproductive, undersized, or outdated strategies. A scientific orientation requires evaluating claims based on evidence, not the status of who makes them.

Applying Financial Science to Political Science

Finance may be the most efficient industry precisely because trillions of dollars are involved in being right. The incentives drive optimal efficiency. When calculations are wrong on Wall Street, you don't just lose an argument—you lose millions and billions. This mathematical precision is why finance offers the best optimization principles for improving our political thinking and results. We also have to keep it front and center that money and finance dominate American politics.

Restructuring

Consider restructuring protocols in business. When a company's strategy becomes stagnant or inefficient, it undergoes restructuring to optimize performance and prevent bankruptcy. Our political strategies need the same rigorous evaluation and willingness to restructure. If our political methods aren't serving our interests, we need to be prepared for radical reorganization. In many cases, a business filing for bankruptcy is a necessary step before growth and prosperity can start again. Similarly, declaring Black American politics as bankrupt may be a necessary step to begin a new Black American political renaissance.

The Science is clear: you get what you measure and enforce, not what you hope for and excuse. Just as Richard Dennis proved that talented people could be trained to outperform Wall Street elites using a systematic approach, we can train the next generation of Black American political talent to be just as successful in politics with a new proven system as the Turtles were with trading. There is an opportunity for us to develop a new Black American political science system and train others under this framework—transforming political talent into strategic operators who prioritize evidence over emotion and results over rhetoric.

The Science

- Eight cognitive biases undermine political thinking: outcome bias, confirmation bias, loss aversion, sunk cost fallacy, bandwagon effect, availability bias, recency bias, authority bias
- Finance offers optimization principles because trillions depend on being right
- Political restructuring may require declaring current approach "bankrupt" before rebuilding
- Train political talent using systematic, evidence-based approaches like Turtle Trading experiment

[1] Jack D. Schwager, "Market Wizards, Updated: Interviews with Top Traders" (Paperback, February 7, 2012).

[2] Michael Covel, "The Complete Turtle Trader: The Legend, the Lessons, the Results" (New York: Collins, 2007).

[3] Curtis Faith, "Way of the Turtle: The Secret Methods that Turned Ordinary People into Legendary Traders," 1st edition (New York: McGraw-Hill, 2007).

A Warning to Black America About Inflation, Illegal Immigration Crackdown, and Tariffs

"Inflation is as violent as a mugger, as frightening as an armed robber, and as deadly as a hit man." —Ronald Reagan

(This article was originally published on Moguldom.com on February 14ᵗʰ, 2025, predating both the economists' heightened recession forecasts and the subsequent financial crisis that emerged later that year. Minor edits have been made for this book version.)

I was recently in Carson, CA (Where Brandy & Ray-J grew up; remember the R&B Group The Boys in the 90's?) and the car wash manager said his workers were fearful of coming into work due to the ICE raids. In Philly, there was an ICE raid at another car wash, rounding up workers. Many are mistaken thinking just criminals are being targeted, Trump's border czar said anyone in the country illegally, is in play. For example, Cardi B's uncle, who is Dominican, was apparently here illegally and rounded up by the Feds. [1]

I also heard from an executive in the advertising industry that they had millions of dollars of advertising deals cut due to the advertiser's concern about tariffs. These weren't things I was reading about, they were happening in close proximity to me. On Tuesday, the closely watched CPI report showed inflation was not decreasing, it was now increasing, more than economists expected. Earlier in the week, Federal Reserve

Chairman Jerome Powell said the Fed was in no hurry to lower interest rates.

This convergence of inflation, immigration enforcement, and tariffs represents a perfect economic storm targeting Black American wallets specifically. While each policy might seem separate, they're mathematically connected through their multiplied impact on our communities.

Regardless of where you land on tougher illegal immigration enforcement and correcting Biden's (and VP Kamala Harris') record on this specific issue, my concern is not directional and one of understanding. I believe Biden was so bad and loose on illegal immigration, he clumsily set a trap for the current administration to break something, while carrying out the fastest and most aggressive ICE enforcement action in U.S. history.

Does the public understand the heavy costs or do they just understand the immediate benefits and headlines? Politicians have done a poor job at keeping the true costs of a historic illegal immigration crackdown, a mystery. They were really good at selling the benefits, hiding the costs and giving us a lot of spook representation of the issue (distant from reality, the facts, and factors).

Tariffs were announced by President Donald Trump against China, Mexico, and Canada but were quickly delayed for Mexico and Canada. Most economists agree, tariffs generally and predictably increase prices for small business and consumers in the short term. For steel, for example, this impacts housing and the auto industry. Ford's CEO described the tariff environment as complete chaos. [2] Do you know who is likely to fit the bill for the tariffs? When you look in a room and don't know who the mark or sucker is, it's you. The financial mathematics are clear: these costs get passed directly to consumers, with the heaviest burden falling on those with the least cushion to absorb price increases.

Did you know egg prices increased to 15% in January and hit an all-time high? (Bird Flu)

This isn't abstract economics – it's kitchen table reality. The same Black American voter giggling at Fox News immigration raids coverage might be the one losing their job when their employer can't find workers, or watching their grocery bill double because there's no one to pick the crops. The science shows these policies hit our wallets from multiple directions simultaneously.

Right now, you also have a speculative AI bubble that is likely on the verge of popping with China's DeepSeek's changing the game and challenging trillion dollar assumptions. Right now, the stock market is dominated by less than 10 companies losing money on AI (but making profits elsewhere), expecting AI-specific profits at the other end of the rainbow, later on.

My message is more about a way of thinking vs a political position. Are those who cheer on the aggressive illegal immigration crackdown that could impact millions of consumers and hundreds of thousands of small businesses prepared to pay the price? Is that person giggling in front of Fox News ready to pay $15 for an Egg McMuffin or $75 for a car wash or see their thin small business margins at their restaurant be wiped out from having to increase prices? Is the average person ready to get laid off from their job during a recession or pay $20 for a batch of strawberries, locally picked by migrants? Who do you think the few Black farmers that are left are hiring to stay afloat? Did you know 42% of all U.S. farm workers are undocumented? [3]

Again, this is not about whether the laws should be enforced as promiscuous illegal immigration has a disproportionate harmful impact on Black Americans specifically, including an erosion of the minimal political power we do have. [4] The challenge is moving beyond overly simplistic "pro" or "anti" immigration positions to a multifactor analysis that accounts for all variables – political, economic, cultural, and temporal. This is precisely where scientific thinking differs from spook reactions.

There is also a question of timing. We can do some bold and aggressive things in life but we just can't do everything, simultaneously. With America vulnerable with inflation and increasing political volatility, doing the heavy enforcement the way it is being done may help tip America into a recession as Goldman Sachs recently highlighted. [5]

Remember, the spook seller only deceptively preaches the benefits, never the costs and how everything adds up and nets out, so you can think more intelligently and balanced about political issues. Everyone liked the $2000+ in stimmy checks and PPP loans during the pandemic, no one liked the tens of thousands of dollars of inflation that silently ate into their wallets over the last few years. This is the mathematics of political tricknology: visible benefits ($2,000 checks) traded for invisible costs ($20,000+ in inflation) – a financial sleight-of-hand that leaves us celebrating while our wealth evaporates.

Inflation is sneaky and often operates in stealth mode, attacking the most vulnerable and the Black American middle class, the hardest.

There is a price to be paid for everything, there is no free lunch. Before we can speak intelligently about a political issue, we need to know both positive and negative factors, the cost and the benefits and how everything will likely net out. This is what I call a more scientific political orientation.

Science demands we calculate both immediate and downstream effects, particularly for Black Americans who typically absorb economic shocks first and recover last. When we fail to apply this mathematical precision to policy evaluation, we end up cheering for policies that silently drain our community's resources while delivering minimal tangible benefits.

Just remember, the crackdown is likely to be on YOUR wallet. It is also true the long term benefits may outweigh the short term costs.

Here are some sectors that could be impacted by an American-induced trade war:

Agriculture & Food Production

- Dairy farms
- Meat processing
- Produce picking
- Farm operations
- Food packing

Service Industry

- Restaurants
- Hotels/Motels
- Cleaning services
- Landscaping
- Car washes

Construction

- Residential
- Commercial
- Roofing
- Concrete work
- General labor

Retail/Hospitality

- Small retail
- Food service
- Warehousing
- Transportation
- Maintenance

[1] "ICE Detention of Cardi B's Uncle: Immigration Case Study," Immigration Policy Center, May 2023.

[2] Jim Farley, "The New Tariff Environment: Industry Disruption Analysis," Ford Motor Company Quarterly Investor Call, Q1 2025.

[3] Department of Labor, "Agricultural Workers Survey: Documentation Status Report," U.S. Department of Labor, February 2024.

[4] Peter Kirsanow, "Illegal Immigration and Black Voters," National Review, February 13, 2024.

[5] Goldman Sachs, "Economic Impact Analysis: Immigration Enforcement and Market Disruption," Goldman Sachs Research, January 2025.

Illuminati or BlackRock: Why Larry Fink's $15 Trillion Matters More Than Secret Societies

"Joe Biden's choice to install two former BlackRock execs in his cabinet is a major signal of his deference to Wall Street and the super rich. But it's also a sign of the times: The world's largest asset management company is revolutionizing finance by investing in capitalism itself." —Meagan Day

"BlackRock is the largest asset management company in the world, with nearly $8 trillion (now $15T) worth of assets under its control. It owns a stake of 5 percent or more in nearly 98 percent of firms in the S&P 500 index, including Apple, Microsoft, J.P. Morgan Chase, Wells Fargo — the list goes on. Owning 5 percent of a company's shares is enough to give any shareholder major influence." — Jacobin Magazine

Growing up in the 1990s Black consciousness movement, conspiracy theories were like intellectual candy. The legendary and original Steve Cokely had us believing Jesse Jackson played a role in Dr. King's assassination. The Illuminati theories spread through our communities like wildfire with figures like conspiracy theorist heavyweight Bobby Hemmit. [1] And I get it—after the Tuskegee experiments and COINTELPRO, who could blame us for seeing hidden hands everywhere? [2]

But Dr. Khallid Muhammad dropped some science during a lecture that stuck with me. In the middle of an Illuminati discussion, he asked a simple question: Even if all these theories were true, how does that help you pay your light bill?

While many are chasing shadows and secret societies, Larry Fink at BlackRock is controlling $15 trillion in broad daylight. [3] That's not a conspiracy—that's actual fact. His executives slide right into presidential administrations, particularly Biden's cabinet, without any secret handshakes or hidden symbols. Just pure, visible power. We can see Larry Fink while the Illuminati remains a mystery and less materially relevant to our daily lives. [4]

If we're distracted by conspiracy theories, we can miss certain realities that manifest in broad daylight. Take Barack Obama openly being an industry agent of Silicon Valley—while we were busy defending him against birth certificate conspiracies, we missed the hundreds of billions in wealth transferred out of Silicon Valley during his presidential term, with Black Americans largely blacklisted from the outsized wealth creation. We never even developed a viewpoint and policy position on it. That's not hidden—that's happening right in front of us.

It's not that conspiracy theories aren't interesting; it's just that too much of it culturally hurts us while we're collectively already in a weaker position.

Conspiracy theories serves a psychological purpose for oppressed communities. After centuries of betrayal and marginalization, it's natural to seek deeper explanations for our condition. Our rich oral traditions and historical experiences make us particularly susceptible to these narratives. When mainstream media consistently misrepresent us, alternative explanations become attractive.

But here's the scientific reality: getting lost in conspiracy theories is like trying to fight shadows while real opponents are standing right in front of you. The Tuskegee experiment wasn't hidden—it was documented government policy. COINTELPRO wasn't a theory—we have the paperwork. [5] The real conspiracy is how these documented events get labeled "conspiracy theories" while actual power brokers operate openly. We need to keep our feet firmly planted in reality to increase our probability of success. That means doing the following:

- Tracking capital flows instead of decoding hand signals

- Reading Federal Reserve policy decisions instead of Illuminati manifestos

- Analyzing corporate board connections rather than celebrity blood sacrifices

- Tracking political and financial conflicts of interest instead of Illuminati bloodlines

- Researching assets to buy to benefit from Federal Reserve policy instead of documenting hidden symbols

I can't stress this factor enough, there is no such thing as politics and political understanding without an understanding of economics. Without the economics factor, we are doing political spook and we are not in the position to advance Black Americans forward with innovative political ideas that are synced with how America and the world really work. The truth about power in America isn't hidden in some ancient society—it's filed quarterly with the government. When BlackRock moves markets, the company announces it in press releases. When tech billionaires reshape society, they tweet about it.

Look at the actual numbers. BlackRock manages more assets than the GDP of all but a handful of countries. That's not hidden power—that's financial domination in plain sight. When former BlackRock executives fill presidential administrations, that's not coincidence—it's the mathematics of influence.

The science of power is about tracking visible effects, not invisible causes. When neighborhoods gentrify, that's not a secret plot—it's documented real estate transactions. When schools lose funding, that's not a conspiracy—it's public budget decisions. When wages stagnate while CEO pay skyrockets, that's not Illuminati magic—it's corporate policy.

The wealth gap between Black and white Americans isn't maintained by secret societies—it's maintained by documented policies: redlining, predatory lending, mass incarceration, and inheritance laws. These aren't conspiracies—they're the visible architecture of American inequality.

We should study the factors of the system that actually exists rather than imagining one that might. To understand why Black businesses struggle to get capital, don't look for hidden symbols—look at actual loan approval and investment rates. If you want to understand political outcomes, don't decode hand gestures—follow campaign contributions.

Keep the spook away from me. Give me political donation reports, SEC filings, congressional records, and shareholder reports. That's where the real power moves are documented. Everything else is a distraction from the scientific work of building Black power.

The Science

- Larry Fink controls $15 trillion in visible power while people chase invisible conspiracies
- Conspiracy theories distract from documented power structures operating in plain sight
- Track capital flows, Federal Reserve decisions, and corporate board connections instead of secret symbols
- Real power moves are documented in quarterly reports, not hidden in ancient societies

[1] "Bobby Hemmitt - Talks About The Assassination Of Dr. Khallid Muhammad," Odysee, June 15, 2020.

[2] Nelson Blackstock, "Cointelpro: The FBI's Secret War on Political Freedom" (Paperback, September 1, 1988).

[3] Jack Pitcher, "Why $11 Trillion in Assets Isn't Enough for BlackRock's Larry Fink: Fink wants to push the world's largest asset manager into the more lucrative world of private markets," Wall Street Journal, November 4, 2024.

[4] Jim Marrs, "The Illuminati: The Secret Society That Hijacked the World (Treachery & Intrigue)" (Paperback, June 13, 2017).

[5] William C. Sullivan, "The Bureau: My Thirty Years in Hoover's FBI" (Hardcover, January 1, 1979).

The Six-Hour Dollar Myth: How Spook Spreads Without Science

"That's what drives science though: trying to find out the way things are, the way they were, and the way it really works. If that is your goal, then you want to make sure that your information is accurate, and if it's not, then it doesn't matter how much you liked that old urban legend or fictional factoid you once bought into. You will discard it and be embarrassed by it, seeking instead for truth."
—*Aron Ra*

When someone makes a clean, precise fact claim without a source, that's a red flag. When everyone begins quoting this fact without checking the source, that's how spook becomes conventional wisdom.

You've probably heard it dozens of times: "The dollar only circulates in the Black community for six hours, while it stays in the Jewish community for 19 days and the Asian community for 28 days." [1] I first heard this "fact" from the Black American conscious community in the 1990s, and it's been repeated by everyone from financial advisors to community activists to politicians.

But here's the science underneath the spook: There is not and has never been a credible study that produced these numbers. This isn't just a minor inaccuracy—it's a revealing case study in how spook thinking spreads without skepticism and scrutiny.

When Howard University's Truth Be Told fact-checkers tried to track down the source of this widely quoted statistic, they found it originated from Brooke Stephens' 1996 book "Talking Dollars and Making Sense." But Stephens provided no citation for the claim other than referencing someone named "John Wray" who supposedly taught at Howard in 1993. The university has no record of this person. [2]

Even more telling: the federal government doesn't collect economic data by religious affiliation, so how could anyone make claims about dollar circulation in the "Jewish community"? When asked about this discrepancy, The former AFL-CIO Chief Economist William Spriggs called it what it is: "an urban myth." [3]

The fact that this statistic has circulated for decades without verification reveals an uncomfortable truth about segments of political discourse: we often accept claims that confirm our existing beliefs without demanding scientific evidence. If too many spook spells are launched against us, by accident or with intention, it promotes spook orientation until the myths, mystery, urban legends, and false claims are debunked. The cumulative impact of operating with myths rather than facts creates distance from reality that undermines both political analysis and strategic efficiency.

The six-hour dollar myth succeeds because it offers a simple explanation for complex economic challenges: if we just keep money circulating in our community, our problems would be solved. But this ignores the actual structural forces shaping the American economy.

Consider the science underneath: Americans of all backgrounds—Black, white, Asian, Hispanic—shop at the same major retailers. Walmart, 99 Cent Store, Amazon, Five Below, Kroger, Costco, and Target dominate retail across all demographics. The idea that white dollars somehow stay in "white communities" while Black dollars immediately flee "Black communities" misunderstands how modern commerce actually works.

When a white person goes grocery shopping at Walmart, that's not "white community" money—it's going to the same corporate coffers as everyone else's money. The white dollars go to the same monopolistic entities as Black dollars. And here's what the myth-spreaders never mention: many Black Americans—about 39% according to Pew Research—own stocks

444

through 401(k)s and investment accounts, meaning we literally own pieces of these same corporations.

Jewish Americans aren't shopping at some magical "Jewish-only" retail network—they're pushing carts through Walmart, ordering from Amazon, and waiting in checkout lines at Publix, Aldi, Target, Kroger, and Costco, just like everyone else. The mythology around the "19 days in the Jewish community" implies some superior economic behavior that simply doesn't exist in the modern American retail landscape. They're not better and we're not less for spending money with monopolistic corporations that offer efficiency, convenience, and lower prices. The real difference? Intergenerational wealth and access to capital and structural factors—exactly what scholars and researchers such as Dr. Sandy Darity, Kirsten Mullen, Mehrsa Baradaran have documented—not some mystical ability to keep dollars circulating longer.

This urban myth and others like it make it seductively easy to believe we're doing something wrong. The myth creates a fictional economic model where all other groups somehow operate in self-contained economies, while conveniently ignoring the reality that monopoly capitalism impacts everyone.

The more fundamental problem isn't about race-specific shopping habits but about corporate consolidation. How exactly are small and medium-sized businesses of any race supposed to compete with Amazon's logistics network or Walmart's economies of scale? Because white-owned small and medium-sized grocery and retail stores have been pushed off the block by monster-size corporations, doesn't mean anything is defective about the business owners and the local community. The economic forces that have decimated Main Street America have hit Black business districts even harder due to historic underinvestment and redlining, but the underlying dynamics affect entrepreneurs of all backgrounds.

Then there's the practical question that should immediately make any critical thinker suspicious: how would anyone even track the racial circulation of dollars? Does each dollar bill have a racial tracer on it? Does money spent at a Black-owned business that purchases supplies from a white-owned distributor count as "leaving" the community? The entire premise requires a tracking mechanism that doesn't and couldn't exist.

The spread of this myth also reveals a collective hunger for simple narratives over multifactor analysis. It's easier to blame failed Black businesses on our community's spending habits than to confront the complex reality of capital access, technology change, the ability of larger companies to start up in new location and lose money for years, before turning a cent of profit, zoning laws, commercial real estate patterns, supply chain logistics, and other structural factors that determine business success.

One of the toxic residues of the '90s Black consciousness movement—despite its positive intentions—was how easily unverified claims spread when wrapped in "conscious" or "pro-Black" packaging. Leaders would make sweeping assertions like "Black people would just blow reparations money on Cadillacs and jewelry" without a shred of data to back it up. The bitter irony? These stereotypes about Black financial behavior often reinforced the very white supremacist narratives we were supposedly fighting against.

One key issue with "Blacks would just buy Rolls Royces and jewelry" reparations myth is proximity bias. Those promoting this stereotype often have high proximity to limited personal experiences but low proximity to comprehensive research and data. They generalize observations from their immediate environment—perhaps a neighborhood or social circle—and project them onto millions of Black Americans who represent diverse educational backgrounds, financial behaviors, regional cultures, and socioeconomic statuses. This bias is reinforced by media representations and hip-hop music videos that showcase conspicuous consumption, creating a distorted lens through which to view typical Black financial behavior. Their conclusions come from anecdotal evidence rather than representative samples. This is the essence of spook thinking: taking limited personal observations and treating them as universal truth while ignoring the research that would disprove these generalizations. A scientific approach would recognize that spending behavior varies far more by individual circumstance than by racial category.

Consider this: according to the National Association of Realtors, 44% of Black Americans own homes despite centuries of redlining, predatory lending, and systemic financial discrimination. We've fought through every barrier America could erect to build wealth—yet somehow we're supposed to believe all our reparations money would instantly go to whatever they're flexing in hip-hop videos? This isn't just insulting; it's mathematical nonsense contradicted by our actual financial behavior. When Dr. Sandy Darity examined actual Black American spending patterns, he found no evidence that Black Americans spend money any less wisely than other groups. But the "conscious community" often bypassed such scientific analysis in favor of moralistic finger-wagging that felt righteous but lacked factual foundation.

This doesn't mean we shouldn't support Black businesses—we absolutely should where it makes sense. But we need to ground our economic development strategies in reality, not myths. Black businesses need access to capital, technical assistance, favorable regulatory environments, and protection from predatory corporate practices—the same factors that help any business thrive.

What makes the six-hour dollar myth particularly harmful is how it shifts the blame for economic inequality onto Black consumers rather than addressing systemic barriers and structural factors. It suggests our economic challenges stem primarily from our own behavior rather than from generations of discriminatory anti-Black American policies.

It shouldn't be easy to accept negative stereotypes about ourselves, yet many uncritically embrace this myth. When we internalize unverified claims about our own economic behavior, we compound existing burdens with additional, unscientific negative signals. This self-reinforcing cycle of blame makes it harder to focus on the actual structural barriers that deserve our collective attention and action.

And yes, there are legitimate reasons to encourage spending in community-oriented businesses rather than extractive ones. But those arguments can stand on their own merits without fabricated statistics. The science of local economic multipliers is well-established in economic literature—we don't need myths when we have actual data.

Another defective idea that deserves our attention is the notion that Black entrepreneurs are "sellouts" when they sell their companies to "white-owned companies." When Robert Johnson sold BET to Viacom for $3 billion, many labeled him a sellout. But why would we want to restrict Black business owners from selling their companies, diversifying their assets, and improving their personal liquidity? Companies like Blockbuster don't even exist anymore—businesses are not forever. WeightWatchers recently filed for bankruptcy after the success of the innovative Ozempic drug for weight loss and diabetes. When entrepreneurs sell, they also transfer risks, including exposure to technology disruption, new competition, or regulatory changes. Black Americans need the same or similar flexibility to transfer risks and diversify assets as other groups. Johnson's exit enabled him to develop a portfolio of Black-owned businesses. Sometimes selling makes perfect business sense, especially when facing larger competitors—rather than struggling sub-scale, entrepreneurs can partner with or sell to companies with greater resources and reach.

The six-hour myth is just one example of how spook thinking can infiltrate our most practical economic discussions. When we accept claims without evidence because they sound right or support our existing beliefs, we're operating in the realm of spook rather than science. And myth-based economic strategies, no matter how well-intentioned, rarely deliver material results.

A scientific orientation demands we ask: What's the source? Has it been verified? Does the underlying methodology make sense? Can the claimed effect even be measured as described? These questions aren't just academic—they're essential for developing strategies that actually work rather than ones that just feel right. We should be skeptical by default.

The fact that an entirely fictional statistic about dollar circulation became conventional wisdom for decades tells you everything you need to know about the potential for spook spells when they align with our intuitions and stereotypes. We're quick to embrace myths dressed up as "facts" that seem to explain our economic challenges, especially when they come with actionable solutions like "buy Black."

There are advantages that come from understanding the world as it actually operates, not as we wish it did. We can't perfectly understand it at 100%, but the closer we get, the better our judgment and analysis become, proportionally. If we want to build economic power that translates into political leverage, we need to ground our strategies in verifiable evidence and multi-factor systemic understanding, not in comforting myths that place the burden of change entirely on community spending habits while ignoring the broader forces of American capitalism.

Next time someone quotes a compelling statistic about Black America, ask them for the source. If they can't provide one, or if the source doesn't hold up to scrutiny, they're not advancing our collective understanding—they're spreading spook.

The Science

- Widely quoted "6-hour dollar circulation" statistic has no credible source or methodology
- All demographics shop at same major retailers (Walmart, Amazon, Target)—dollars flow to same corporate coffers
- Myths spread when they confirm existing beliefs without demanding evidence
- Ground economic development strategies in verifiable data, not comforting urban legends

[1] Video of Myth Being Confidently Shared from X (formerly Twitter)," November 9, 2023. https://x.com/EarlLandix/status/1722389020511015226

[2] Owen, Laura Hazard. "A Howard Project Is Debunking Myths About African-Americans and Teaching Students Fact-Checking." Nieman Lab, January 22, 2016. https://www.niemanlab.org/2016/01/a-howard-project-is-debunking-myths-about-african-americans-and-teaching-students-fact-checking/

[3] Brown, Ann. "Fact Check: The 'Dollar Only Stays In Black Community 6 Hours' Is Urban Myth." Moguldom, November 16, 2023. https://moguldom.com/454006/fact-check-the-dollar-only-stays-in-black-community-6-hours-is-urban-myth/

Culture and Social Control

Amy Wax and the Paralysis Parable

The wise man looks for what he can learn from everyone.
— *Charlie Munger*

The parable Amy Wax presents in her book *Race, Wrongs, and Remedies: Group Justice in the 21st Century* crystallizes a fundamental tension in Black American political and cultural discourse: How do we balance personal agency with systemic accountability? In her narrative, a woman named Becky hits a pedestrian named Jamal with a truck and he becomes paralyzed. Though Becky covers the medical expenses, Jamal's recovery and ability to walk again ultimately hinges on his own perseverance. For Jamal to walk again, money and physical therapy can only go far. It's up to his own agency to walk again.

Does Wax's parable neatly fit into Black America's experience with centuries of institutional harm, or does it falsely assume the truck has stopped hitting the pedestrian?

The Truck Driver's Responsibility vs. The Pedestrian's Recovery

Wax contends, "While Black Americans didn't create their present challenges, they might be the ones tasked with addressing them, especially if no other solutions prove effective." The therapist in her parable emphasizes a central theme: the inherent limitations of external restitution. No matter how substantial, Becky's contributions can never guarantee Jamal's return to his former state.

The logic seems compelling: Recovery = Personal Effort × (External Support). Since the personal effort factor is exponentially more powerful than external support, this equation suggests that focusing on individual agency is the most efficient path forward.

But this formulation contains a fundamental flaw: it assumes the truck (anti-Black American systems) has stopped hitting the pedestrian.

Multifactoring Wax's Analysis

The multifactor approach demands we analyze multiplefactors, not just the ones that fit our preferred narrative. Five critical flaws emerge when we apply analysis to Wax's seductive parable:

1. **Continuous Injury vs. Single Event**: The parable portrays anti-Black American structures as a single collision rather than ongoing systemic impacts. The reality is that Recovery = Personal Effort × (External Support) - Ongoing Systemic Damage. Even heroic personal effort can be impaired and neutralized by continued systemic obstacles.

2. **State-Sponsored Origin vs. Individual Responsibility**: Unlike a random traffic accident, America's racial hierarchy was intentionally engineered and maintained by the state. The equation State-Created Problem ≠ Individual-Solved Solution demonstrates the fundamental mismatch in accountability.

3. **Uneven Starting Points**: Wax's analysis ignores the compounding of disadvantage. If System Advantage = (Resources × Time)^(Opportunity Multiplier), then generations of intentional exclusion and anti-Black American discrimination create exponential rather than linear disparities in starting points.

4. **Collective vs. Individual Solutions**: The parable falsely individualizes what are fundamentally collective problems. If Problem Scope > Individual Capacity, then collective solutions aren't just preferable—they're mathematically necessary.

Missing the Evidence on Family Stability: Black American families would be more stable and prosperous if the truck had never hit us in the first place, instead of repeatedly running us over, reversing back and forth, with blood still on the tires. Wax willfully ignores the racial factor tax imposed on Black American families.[1]

The Mathematical Reality of Recovery

John McWhorter, in reviewing Wax's work, raises a crucial question about the Black family's evolution in America. He highlights Wax's observation that "Black out-of-wedlock births started to climb and marriage rates to fall around 1960, long after slavery was abolished and just as the civil rights movement gained momentum." [2]

But this correlation ignores a critical factor: economic opportunity. The decline in manufacturing jobs, the rise of mass incarceration, and the targeted destruction of Black economic centers all coincided with this period. Science tells us that stable employment and economic opportunities create and support stable families. When Black Men faced systematic economic exclusion and imprisonment, family instability was a predictable outcome—not a mysterious "cultural" failure.

Wax's parable is simplistically seductive but fails to acknowledge that even full agency and effort to recover after paralysis doesn't help much when anti-Black American structures and dynamics continue to impede progress, never giving Black Americans a chance to fully recover. Having agency and continuing to try to walk again without help doesn't address the system that has been attacking Black Americans for over 400 years. The question remains: will the system that has perpetual attacks embedded in its structure be changed to give agency a fair chance to bear fruit?

Out of Wetlock Births in Europe

Significant parts of Europe are now dominated by out-of-wedlock births, but Wax doesn't frame this as an agency failure. For example:

"Of the eight other countries where births inside marriage are outnumbered by those outside, six are again in Europe's north or west. Those are, in descending order: Norway (58.5%), Portugal (57.9%), Sweden (55.2%), Denmark (54.7%), Netherlands (53.5%), and Belgium (52.4%). The two exceptions are Slovenia (57.7%), which is nearly western, and Estonia (53.7%), which is almost Nordic. Figures remain in the high forties in the Czech Republic (48.5%), the UK (48.2%), Finland (47.7%), and Spain (47.6%), and in the low forties in Austria (41.2%) and Slovakia (41.0%)." [3]

The key differences between out-of-wedlock birth trends in these European countries and Black Americans is that these countries mostly represent slave-trading nations, while Black Americans have endured a generational holocaust, Jim Crow, and mass incarceration. As Dr. Joy DeGruy documents in her book, *Post Traumatic Slave Syndrome: America's Legacy of Enduring Injury and Healing*, the Black American family has suffered more than other families due to institutionalized, state-sponsored anti-Black American factors. [4] If the situation were reversed, and Black Americans had enslaved American whites, applied white-targeted Jim Crow segregation, and kept institutional boots on their necks, preventing access to reading, business capital, and quality education for hundreds of years—and the wealth gap was grossly in our favor—Black American families would be doing better than white families, and more Black American families would have stayed together. Dr. Amy Wax has a sharp mind, but it's difficult to believe she is innocently missing these important factors.

Beyond False Binaries: The Science of Balanced Solutions

The Science vs Spook framework rejects the false binary of "either personal responsibility or systemic change." The reality is that BOTH factors matter, but in different proportions.

The science tells us that different problems require different proportions of systemic versus individual solutions. Demanding that Black Americans solve systemic problems through individual effort alone is like asking someone to lift a car without a jack—not impossible in theory, but inefficient and unreasonable in practice. It simply doesn't scale.

Ironically, there is one domain where Wax's parable inadvertently captures an essential truth: our agency in political organization itself. No structural reforms will move forward without our own deliberate action in developing organizations that pressure, press for, and implement reforms. As Malcolm X precisely observed, "We're not outnumbered, we're out-organized."

Even when fighting for structural changes, our organizational agency remains the primary factor. Black American organizations in the 60's have demonstrated the science of this. The parable's emphasis on personal effort applies most accurately not to navigating broken systems, but to our collective responsibility to increase our political efficiency and organizational effectiveness.

Broadening Intellectual Range Through Opposing Viewpoints

Amy Wax is widely considered to hold anti-Black American views, but that doesn't mean we shouldn't engage with her arguments. To expand our intellectual range and political thinking, we need to understand and thoroughly dissect perspectives we find objectionable. Think of it like a boxer preparing to face Mike Tyson or UFC fighter Jon Jones – you get better by studying formidable opponents, not by avoiding them. We may discover insights even from scholars who make us uncomfortable.

We can't become optimal thinkers and more effective political strategists and leaders by reading only people who think exactly like us or look like us. Or that are in the same political party as us. The strongest intellectual muscles develop through resistance, just as physical muscles do. By engaging with Wax's parable and exposing its flaws, we develop sharper analytical tools for addressing similar arguments in political debates. This understanding can be used to educate our leaders and community about policy.

This isn't just an academic exercise – it's essential for advancing Black American politics. When conservative voices use Wax-like parables to oppose reparations, systemic reforms, or collective political strategies, we must be equipped to dismantle these arguments with scientific precision and rapid multifactor analysis. The ability to engage with and systematically refute these perspectives is critical to building political power and advancing a Black American agenda. Without this analytical rigor, we risk being perpetually caught in defensive positions rather than confidently advancing our own political mathematics.

The Science vs. Spook of Recovery

The Science vs Spook framework recognizes that while personal agency is critical, systemic barriers create impediments that must be carefully analyzed and addressed. Just as a business would seek to improve both internal operations and external market conditions, Black American advancement requires both personal development and systemic change. While individual agency matters, collective agency becomes essential when confronting systemic barriers - a reality that Wax's individualistic framework systematically obscures.

The paralysis parable isn't wrong because it values personal effort—it's wrong because it ignores the compounded and generational disadvantage and ongoing systemic barriers. It treats the truck accident causing paralysis as a one-time event when it is really a Mack 10 truck, reversing back and forth, and then coming back circling the block against us, the equivalent to systemic anti-Black American structural factors. A scientific orientation demands a more sophisticated equation: one that recognizes that while we walk our own path toward recovery, we have every right to demand that others stop driving trucks into that path or institutionally swinging baseball bats at our legs. The highest agency that can change our conditions is collective organizational agency. Even with collective organizational agency with some of our best leadership and organizational expressions, the U.S. government got in the way and we never saw the full organic potential of our best leaders and organizations in the 1960's. Amy Wax is not the type of person to consider these nuanced factors.

This isn't about excusing personal responsibility—it's about acknowledging the full spectrum of factors in the equation of Black American progress and systemic barriers. If Black-sounding names on resumes and job applications get a 30% lower response rate than whites, with other factors being equal, there is nothing defective about us. [5] The defect lies in the system and at structural levels.

The Science

- Wax's parable assumes the "truck" (anti-Black systems) stopped hitting the "pedestrian" (Black Americans)
- Recovery equation must include: Personal Effort × External Support - Ongoing Systemic Damage
- False binary between personal responsibility vs. systemic change— both factors matter in different proportions
- Engage opposing viewpoints to develop stronger analytical tools for political debates

[1] Amy L. Wax, "Race, Wrongs, and Remedies: Group Justice in the 21st Century" (Hoover Studies in Politics, Economics, and Society).

[2] John McWhorter, "What Hope?" The New Republic, August 10, 2010, https://newrepublic.com/article/76403/what-hope.

[3] Frank Jacobs, "In these 11 European countries, births out of wedlock are in the majority," Big Think, March 14, 2023, https://bigthink.com/strange-maps/births-out-of-wedlock-europe-us/.

[4] Joy DeGruy, Post Traumatic Slave Syndrome: America's Legacy of Enduring Injury and Healing (Portland: Joy DeGruy Publications Inc., Revised ed., 2017).

[5] Martin Abel and Rulof Burger, "Unpacking Name-Based Race Discrimination," IZA Discussion Paper No. 16254, IZA Institute of Labor Economics, June 24, 2023, https://www.iza.org/publications/dp/16254/unpacking-name-based-race-discrimination.

Hip-Hop Retardation: Murder Rap and Low Impulse Control at Scale

I think when hip-hop first started, people were open to it. And groups like Public Enemy and there were groups like Poor Righteous Teachers and all these people were spitting a lot of knowledge, a lot of history. Questioning a lot of societal barriers was starting to be super popular. —Ice Cube

What do you think Dr. King would have to say about rappers calling Black women bitches and whores? About rappers glorifying thugs and drug dealers and rapists? What kind of role models are those for young children living in the ghetto? —C. Delores Tucker

We're told hip-hop represents authentic Black expression. But when a cultural product heavily shaped by corporate interests correlates with destructive outcomes for Black communities, we need to examine those connections scientifically rather than accepting the authenticity narrative at face value.

In the 1990s, I was there when segments of hip-hop served as positive cultural and political forces. Tupac gave us "Dear Mama," an anthem praising Black mothers, and "White Man'z World," highlighting systemic inequalities. Public Enemy's "Fight the Power" became our generation's protest soundtrack. Yet simultaneously, I witnessed firsthand how hip-hop's emerging gangsta element became a factor in dividing Black college students across the Atlanta University Center Consortium—Morehouse,

Spelman College, Clark Atlanta University, and Morris Brown—caught up in manufactured East-versus-West beef that had nothing to do with our material interests. [1]

While hip-hop has undeniably given us entertainment, consciousness-raising, and cultural pride, we need to conduct an honest accounting of its costs and benefits using the Science-versus-Spook framework. This isn't about dismissing hip-hop as a cultural force—it's about analyzing its material impacts on Black American development with the same rigor we would apply to any other institution.

Let me be crystal clear: I'm not saying hip-hop caused our problems. That would be ahistorical spook thinking. Slavery, Jim Crow, mass incarceration, and anti-Black American structures were destroying Black lives long before the first rapper picked up a microphone. But if these historical forces have made us culturally sick in some ways, certain elements of hip-hop have functioned as an accelerant rather than a cure. It's not the disease, but it has become an important factor that compounds our challenges. It's like giving whiskey to someone with liver disease—it's not what caused the condition, but it certainly makes it worse.

The mathematics of hip-hop's impact are stark: 1.1 million Black men in prison, with approximately 500,000 of them fathers. Many had fathers who served time, and many have children who will follow the same path. This isn't coincidence—it's correlation with a cultural force that has consistently glamorized criminal behavior, prison time, and violence as markers of authenticity and respect.

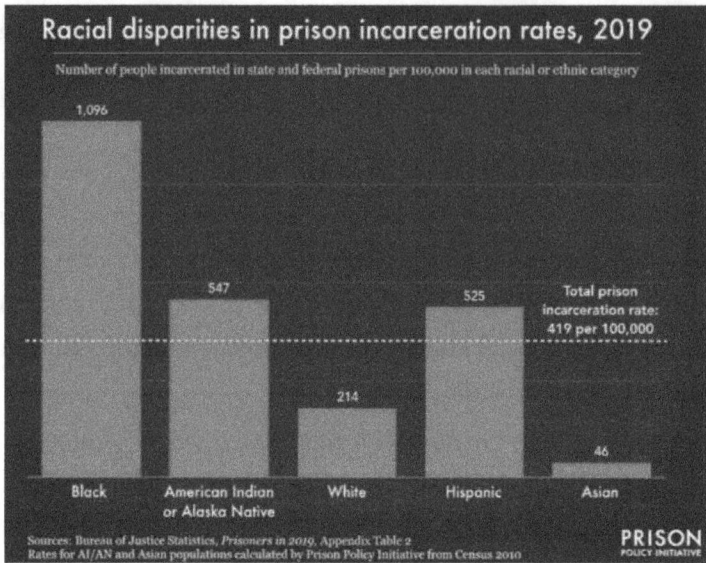

Racial disparities in prison incarceration rates, 2019

Number of people incarcerated in state and federal prisons per 100,000 in each racial or ethnic category

1,096

547

525

Total prison incarceration rate: 419 per 100,000

214

46

Black | American Indian or Alaska Native | White | Hispanic | Asian

Sources: Bureau of Justice Statistics, *Prisoners in 2019*, Appendix Table 2
Rates for AI/AN and Asian populations calculated by Prison Policy Initiative from Census 2010

PRISON
POLICY INITIATIVE

Prison Incarceration Rates by Race (2019) - Shows Black Americans
incarcerated at 5x the rate of whites

Under the Science-versus-Spook framework, it wouldn't be shocking to see a booming hip-hop market promoting murder and criminal activity coinciding with rising private prison stocks. As Ice Cube recently suggested on Bill Maher's podcast, there may be financial connections between the record industry and the prison-industrial complex. [2] There doesn't have to be a conspiracy to estimate that a robust murder rap economy can translate to improving population volume and economics for private prisons. This isn't about shadowy meetings in smoke-filled rooms—it's about aligned financial incentives operating independently toward the same outcome. We are an understudied people, but that doesn't mean we can't identify patterns and make observations based on data. It's simply mathematics that when one industry promotes behavior that feeds another industry's bottom line, both industries benefit—with or without explicit coordination.

C. Delores Tucker, who marched alongside Dr. Martin Luther King Jr. and later became Pennsylvania's first Black secretary of state, tried to warn us decades ago. When she launched her crusade against gangsta rap in the

1990s, the hip-hop community labeled her an "Uncle Tom" and worse. Tupac targeted her, accusing her of trying to "destroy a brotha." The industry painted her as an out-of-touch moral crusader, but time has proven many of her concerns prescient. [3]

Tucker wasn't alone. Rev. Calvin O. Butts III of Harlem's influential Abyssinian Baptist Church staged a protest in 1993 where he planned to use a steamroller to crush rap recordings with explicit lyrics. Though he ultimately decided against the steamroller demonstration after confronting protesters, Butts's message was clear: "We will not stand for vile, ugly, low, abusive, and rough music." The scene outside his church that day captured the division within the Black community: supporters chanting, "Negative rap is not all right!," while teenage protesters shouted, "No justice! No peace!" One fifteen-year-old aspiring rapper argued with a supporter, "He should be attacking the white power structure who own the record companies, who own the cable stations!" The woman responded, "But what is negative? Negative is when my fourteen-year-old daughter comes home with a tape that says, 'Gangster bitch!' That's negative!"

This exchange captures the fundamental tension that still exists today: recognizing both the corporate exploitation behind hip-hop's degradation and the real harm that degraded content inflicts on our communities. Under the Science-versus-Spook framework, both perspectives contain truth, but the solution isn't choosing one factor over the other—it's addressing the entire system while maintaining our own standards.

What's telling about our cultural response to Tucker is how quickly we dismissed a Black woman who co-founded the National Congress of Black Women with Shirley Chisholm, who was on the front lines of the civil rights movement, and who dedicated her life to advancing Black political power. When she asked, "What do you think Dr. King would have to say about rappers calling Black women bitches and whores?

About rappers glorifying thugs and drug dealers and rapists?," the industry's response wasn't reasoned debate but character assassination. [4] Looking back, I didn't realize until decades later that hip-hop was systematically replacing natural family and community role models while promoting low impulse control at scale. I can't speak for all Black men, but my personal experience is that many of my friends treated their favorite hip-hop artists as father figures or religious prophets, modeling their thinking, speech, and behavior norms after these artists rather than their actual fathers—many well into their 30s. This phenomenon resembles what psychologists call "Peter Pan syndrome"—a persistent difficulty transitioning into authentic adulthood marked by avoiding responsibilities, having unstable relationships, and displaying impulsive behavior. [5]

Hip-hop entered stealth-like, exploiting the growing gaps between young Black men and their natural fathers, becoming the dominant behavioral influence and norm-setter in their lives. Where typical adulthood requires emotional maturity, discipline, and responsibility, murder rap promotes precisely the opposite—a state of perpetual adolescence where impulse control is seen as weakness and immediate gratification as strength. This disproportionately impacts the most vulnerable segments of our community, where father absence creates voids that hip-hop's devilishment-dominated culture eagerly fills. When influential artists become surrogate parents, their lyrical guidance toward low impulse control, immediate gratification, and glorification of criminal behavior becomes that much more damaging.

To be clear, I am not anti-religion. Christianity and Islam can guide humans toward positive factors and behavior—look at Malcolm X's transformation when he discovered Black Islam in prison. Organized religions at their best offer discipline, community accountability, and moral frameworks that encourage delayed gratification and consideration of others. Hip-hop, however, has evolved into its own quasi-religion with false prophets and exploitative financial structures that guide millions in the opposite direction. Where traditional religions typically promote impulse control, consideration of consequences, and community responsibility, the hip-hop religion glorifies immediate gratification, disregard for consequences, and individual reputation above community wellbeing.

The hip-hop paradigm also mirrors Black American political containment in the Democratic Party. Visible Black representation exists in both realms, but beneath operates a system that channels Black talent toward outcomes undermining collective progress. Just as record executives profit from artists promoting content that harms Black communities, political powerbrokers benefit from Black politicians who provide symbolic representation without threatening the system. Having Black faces at the top of either institution doesn't automatically reduce harmful impacts. When Kevin Liles shares in the $400 million sale of 300 Entertainment alongside Lyor Cohen, this enrichment of individual Black executives does nothing to change the underlying structure that profits from content harmful to Black Americans. In fact, Black representation at the top can sometimes make the underlying devilishment more insidious by providing surface-level legitimacy to fundamentally exploitative systems. The mathematics is identical: allow enough visible Black success to create the illusion of progress while maintaining structural constraints that prevent transformation. When we celebrate these Black faces without examining the results they produce, we mistake symbolic victory for material advancement. The scientific approach demands we look beyond representation to examine actual outcomes.

If a mad scientist were to design an entertainment religion aimed at generational destruction—one that would teach young people how to go to jail, kill each other, and exercise minimal self-control—what hip-hop has metastasized into would be the perfect blueprint. While murders and incarceration may directly affect a minority within Black America, hip-hop's promotion of low impulse control affects the majority at scale,

465

especially given its power to define Black American identity and establish metrics for coolness, respect, and status.

Hip-hop doesn't just mainly promote murder, criminality, and devilishment—it promotes a culture where it's cool to act without critical or scientific thought about the probability of negative outcomes and consequences. In many cases, the irrational thinking it glorifies skips over intellectual consideration and rational judgment, instead exhibiting and celebrating animalistic instincts—the perfect setup for mass incarceration.

Consider when artist Future raps, "Young dope dealer, sellin' dope, is you like that?" The scientific answer should be a resounding "No!" because the data shows there's an extremely high probability that anyone answering yes is destined for prison. Yet the entire cultural infrastructure is designed to make yes the cool answer, the respected answer, the answer that gains status among peers.

Murder rap and prison go together like record executives and private jets—one funds the other, and the people actually making the music rarely get to enjoy either. This is the religion of prison for many vulnerable Black American men who look to hip-hop artists as their role models and, in many cases, their father figures. When biological fathers are absent— often due to the very prison system hip-hop glorifies—these cultural figures step in as surrogate parents, creating a generational cycle of destruction. This type of mind, already carrying a Black American racial tax in a biased justice system, is almost guaranteed to follow a prison track without intervention.

We need one hundred times more scientific minds than hip-hop minds. The psychotic way these rappers talk about murdering Black American men shows no feeling for the mothers, brothers, sisters, fathers, and the generational damage from each loss. A single murder in Chicago impacts hundreds of lives, creating trauma that ripples through families and communities for decades. This callousness isn't just artistic expression— it's psychological conditioning toward sociopathy.

One of the most insidious aspects of this cultural programming is how hip-hop has attempted to graft low impulse control onto Black American identity, as if recklessness, violence, and self-destruction are somehow authentic expressions of Blackness. This is pure tricknology. Low impulse control isn't a Black cultural trait—it's a devilishment thing that has metastasized over time, breeding generations of hip-hop-induced Frankensteins who destroy themselves and their communities while believing they're keeping it real. The scientific reality? Impulse control has been essential to Black American survival since slavery. Our ancestors practiced supreme discipline to escape, to organize, to educate themselves when it was illegal, to build institutions despite overwhelming obstacles. The notion that impulsivity represents authentic Blackness is not just wrong—it's a deliberate inversion of our historical strength and resilience.

We saw this hip-hop orientation at work when there was widespread support on social media for Will Smith after he slapped Chris Rock at the 94th annual Academy Awards. That moment perfectly crystallized the low-impulse-control problem. Smith didn't get to the top of the Hollywood game by assaulting people over jokes, even ones about his wife. When Rock mentioned G.I. Jane, actress Demi Moore was considered a sex symbol at the time, even with a shaved head. But what the low-impulse-control crowd failed to understand was that if they were exhibiting this behavior instead of Smith, they would be going to jail and likely losing employment. One criminal decision because someone hurt your feelings could be costly for years. The Los Angeles Police Department could have easily charged Smith for assault.

This type of low impulse control shouldn't be celebrated in Black America. When behavior like this is endorsed and promoted, the cultural orientation becomes optimized for prison. The idea that we fight right away over words has not only supported a prison pipeline but also quickly leads to death, especially given how violent the streets are today. What's truly hard is discipline. The hardest man knows to be calculated, to measure risks and rewards, and to factor potential hidden consequences from his actions.

When Elijah Muhammad told Malcolm X not to say anything about President Kennedy after his assassination, this was extreme discipline— what military strategists call "operational security." When Elijah Muhammad didn't retaliate against the Los Angeles Police Department after they murdered Ronald Stokes, he demonstrated true strength. The hardest and strongest man is the one who stays alive to see his mission through and has the most lasting impact on Black Americans. The hardest man is going to be calculated, disciplined, and a mathematical thinker— not a brute who impulsively throws a punch or shoots a gun. If you're thinking backward, you believe the one hurting Black America is the strongest and the one helping is the weakest. This is where the science comes to combat the spook spells.

The scientific reality of normalized low impulse control affects: [6]

- Financial stability: Poor decision-making compounds existing economic pressure.

- Health outcomes: Substance abuse and neglected medical needs become normalized.

- Educational achievement: Impulse control is crucial for academic success.

- Family structure: Conflicts and unstable home environments become standard.

- Legal issues: Cycles of involvement with the criminal justice system are celebrated.

- Mental health: Community stress and anxiety are exacerbated.

- Community development: Resources are chronically mismanaged through impulsive choices.

While hip-hop's negative impacts broadly affect Black America, we must be scientific in recognizing that the most devastating effects aren't distributed equally. Black Americans at the economic margins—those with the fewest resources, the least stable support systems, and the most limited access to quality education—bear the brunt of hip-hop's destructive influence. Middle-class and affluent Black families can better insulate their children with alternative messaging, stronger institutions, and greater exposure to counternarratives. But for the most vulnerable among us, murder rap and its accompanying low-impulse-control programming often constitute the dominant cultural influence. The tragic irony? Those with the least margin for error receive the most guidance toward self-destruction. This isn't random—it's structural. The same system that concentrates poverty also ensures that those in concentrated poverty receive the most toxic cultural programming.

Today's drill rap represents not progress but regression—a younger, more toxic, and increasingly psychotic cultural agent. While hip-hop once pushed us forward politically and culturally in many ways, it now structurally pushes us backward while amoral forces at the top reap the profits. The industry has become an agent of what can only be called a retarded orientation, where actions that harm self and others, that sabotage present and future well-being, are heavily promoted as markers of coolness and respect.

What we witnessed with the rise of the drill rap economy from 2018–2023 is a perfect case study in profit-driven cultural destruction. [7] Artists and labels made more money as beef heated up and murders exploded. Money flowed from labels into local rap gangs, providing financial incentives to "up the ante" in increasingly destructive ways. Even stepping on the graves of dead teenagers became marketed as "hard." Mocking murdered teens and their grieving families became a path to clout. The more psychotic the artists could be, the higher the body count, the more tweets and virality on social media—and the more money for the record labels.

This isn't speculation—follow the money. Look at how ten-percenter and bloodsucker Lyor Cohen, who was heavily invested in drill rap through his 300 Entertainment label (which distributed Young Thug's YSL Records), cashed out when he sold his company to Warner Music Group for $400 million in December 2021—just months before Young Thug was hit with fifty-two RICO charges in May 2022. [8] The federal investigation into YSL had been ongoing since 2013, but Cohen and his partners made their exit with hundreds of millions before the hammer came down. This is the mathematics of cultural exploitation: build a fortune on death culture, then cash out before the consequences arrive.

It's not just the record labels that profit from murder rap. Tech giants like Alphabet (Google/YouTube) and Meta (Facebook, Instagram) profit in a big way through market capitalization and share price increases as millions of young people engage with the latest murder rap content and drama online. Every click, comment, and share on drill rap beef videos translates to billions in stock value for these companies. The more bodies drop, the more engagement they get. The more psychotic the content, the higher their quarterly earnings. These platforms have constructed a perfect profit engine: monetize Black death while taking zero responsibility for its consequences.

What makes this particularly insidious is how these same platforms simultaneously ban Black American political activists from speaking out against injustice and anti-Black Americanism. They over-censor Black American political content while allowing murder rap to spread and go viral. The message is clear: Discussions about structural racism are too "controversial," but glorifying the murder of Black men is just "entertainment." This isn't random—it's strategic. Political consciousness threatens the system; self-destruction maintains it. While we dismissed leaders such as Tucker and Butts, now there is very little voice to challenge these corporations and hold them accountable for all this profiteering and exploitation of vulnerability and devilishment.

Consider the YSL RICO case against Young Thug and his associates. When prosecutors cite lyrics like, "I killed his man in front of his momma, like fuck lil' bruh, sister, and his cousin," they're not just using art against artists—they're revealing how murder rap has become an entire economic ecosystem. Artists aren't just making music—they're simultaneously creating instruction manuals and confessions.

When artists like Meek Mill advocate for prison reform while simultaneously promoting murder in their lyrics, they expose the fundamental contradiction at hip-hop's core. This isn't just hypocrisy—it's a business model. As Meek tweeted, "Locking us for rapping got me scared to do an interview," but the truth is, no one is locked up simply for rapping. They're locked up for participating in and documenting criminal enterprises, often using music as both advertisement and confession.

The economic engine of murder rap runs on gasoline that these artists understand perfectly. They know murder sells. They know violence against other Black men is marketable. They've become scientists of their industry, determining what works through empirical testing of the market. And what works, consistently, is the glorification of killing other Black men over frivolous matters.

When executives like Cohen describe themselves as "opportunistic" with "people to feed," they're revealing the cold calculation behind the cultural programming. [9] The question remains: At whose expense are they feeding themselves and their families? The answer is clear: at the expense of countless Black American lives, families, and communities.

Some will blame white executives exclusively, but this analysis misses the agency of Black artists and executives who participate in and profit from this system. Just as we recognize both European slave traders and their West African partners in the historical slave trade, we must recognize all parties participating in cultural retardation today, regardless of race. The issue isn't identity—it's actions and outcomes.

The scientific approach to addressing this isn't censorship or moral panic, but rather a clear-eyed assessment of cultural impact. We need to create alternative cultural forces that can entertain while pushing us forward collectively. We need to develop metrics for measuring hip-hop's material impact on community outcomes. And we need to hold cultural producers accountable not just for their art but for its measurable effects.

Nathan McCall's 1993 Washington Post article draws a direct line between his own experience with violence and the influence of media. [10] After watching *The Godfather*, McCall and his friends stepped out of the theater "hyped" and "intentionally bumping into people, hoping somebody would protest and give us an excuse to do a bare-knuckled version of what we'd just seen." Later, at nineteen, McCall shot a man who had threatened his girlfriend, standing over the victim "proud that I'd properly dispensed street justice." It wasn't until he was sitting in the police station that "fantasy faded" and he realized he was "a silly, scared teenager who was mixed up in the head."

McCall wrote those words over thirty years ago, noticing even then the correlation between the rise of gangsta rap and escalating Black-on-Black violence. The scientific observation he made then remains true today: "Black-on-Black violence—especially juvenile violence—has escalated sharply only since the late 1980s, when the popularity of gangsta rap was on the rise." He noted that in Washington, DC, from 1988–1990, juvenile homicide arrests nearly tripled, from twenty-six to sixty-seven, coinciding with gangsta rap's emergence.

The fantasy element McCall identifies is crucial to understanding hip-hop's impact. "Nobody fantasizes more than young Black men," he writes. "When you live in a world that limits your hopes, reality is often too much to bear... Because they are powerless, they are consumed with the symbols of power—guns and gangstas." This psychological insight helps explain why murder rap resonates so deeply—it offers an alternate reality where the powerless become powerful through violence.

When critic Dee-1 called out Meek Mill, Rick Ross, and Jim Jones for promoting murder rap, he wasn't engaging in ambiguous conspiracy theories or vague complaints about white supremacy. He specifically named cultural influencers and held them accountable for their role in promoting cultural retardation. This precision matters—it moves us from spook thinking ("Mysterious forces are destroying us") to scientific thinking ("Specific actors are making specific choices with measurable outcomes").

The turkey giveaways and community help that artists provide in no way justify being key players in the promotion of cultural retardation. These small gestures can't offset the damage done by glamorizing murder, normalizing prison, and promoting impulsive behavior that destroys lives and communities. When Jones, at forty-seven years old, responds to criticism with physical threats, he demonstrates exactly the low impulse control he promotes—proving the critic's point.

Tucker's warning that "the pimps in the entertainment industry who distribute gangsta rap are major contributors to the destruction of the African American community" wasn't just moral crusading—it was identifying a systemic threat. When she told Black people, "This gangsta rap is our fault because we never said, 'Never again,' as the Jews did," she was calling for collective responsibility in cultural stewardship.

The question before us now is not whether Tucker was right, but what we're going to do about it. Will we continue celebrating artists who promote our destruction, or will we demand a culture that advances rather than retards our collective development? Will we hold accountable those who profit from selling murder fantasies to our youth, or will we continue making excuses based on turkey giveaways and symbolic gestures?

It's important to note that hip-hop has great potential to reverse its dominant devilishment factor and become an instrument of political and economic development and cultural renaissance. The same power that has been harnessed to normalize violence and self-destruction could be redirected toward collective advancement. Hip-hop emerged from a creative impulse that produced not just music but an entire cultural ecosystem of art, dance, fashion, and language. Its capacity for cultural creation and reinvention is unmatched. Artists like Kendrick Lamar, J. Cole, and earlier conscious rappers have shown glimpses of what's possible when that creative energy aligns with substance and purpose.

If devilishment in hip-hop has less cultural market share and mindshare in Black America, it creates room for more positive factors to take up that share, particularly involving political and economic development. This isn't just idealism—it's market dynamics. Cultural space is finite, and what's being consumed affects what's being produced. We need more cultural factors that are growth- and development-oriented and fewer factors that are devilishment-oriented. This rebalancing isn't just good morality—it's good strategy for building political and economic power.

What would hip-hop look like if it was optimized for our collective advancement rather than our destruction? What if its energy was channeled into political organization, economic development, and cultural excellence? These aren't romantic questions but strategic ones. If the market has proven that hip-hop can influence millions to embrace self-destructive behavior, it could just as effectively influence them toward self-development and collective action.

We saw evidence of this already with hip-hop's role in the lead-up to the Million Man March and crime dropping across the country in the mid-1990s. Artists like Poor Righteous Teachers, X-Clan, Brand Nubian, and Public Enemy helped create a cultural climate where consciousness was in style and cool in many communities across Black America. When the cultural momentum shifted toward self-knowledge, community responsibility, and political awareness, the material outcomes followed. This wasn't coincidence—it was cause and effect.

The same cultural machinery that can normalize killing can normalize knowledge of self. The same distribution networks that spread messages of destruction can spread messages of development. It's not about the medium—it's about the message. The science is clear: Cultural programming matters. Its effects are measurable, material, and multigenerational. Our responsibility is to apply the same rigorous analysis to hip-hop that we would to any other institution affecting Black American life. That's not being a hater—that's being scientific.

The Science

- Hip-hop evolved from positive cultural force to agent promoting low impulse control at scale
- Murder rap correlates with prison pipeline and normalized violence in Black communities
- Industry profits from death culture: record labels, tech platforms, private prisons all benefit financially
- Cultural programming has measurable, material, multigenerational effects requiring scientific analysis
- Hip-hop has potential for reversal toward collective advancement rather than destruction

---

[1] Zachary Rogers, "Ice Cube Warns Rap Record Labels Encourage Criminal Behavior and Help Fuel Private Prisons," ABC 15 News, July 6, 2023, https://wpde.com/news/nation-world/ice-cube-warns-rap-record-labels-encourage-criminal-behavior-and-help-prisons-stay-full-rapper-bill-maher-club-random-podcast-hbo-rapper-nwa.

[2] Zachary Rogers, "Ice Cube Warns Rap Record Labels Encourage Criminal Behavior and Help Fuel Private Prisons," ABC 15 News, July 6, 2023.

[3] Sytonia Reid, "Revisiting C. Delores Tucker's War on Rap: Too Much Smoke, Not Enough Flowers," Medium, accessed April 18, 2025, https://medium.com/@sytonia.reid11/revisiting-c-delores-tuckers-war-on-rap-too-much-smoke-not-enough-flowers-9f2ab175e0d1.

[4] Meng-Jinn Chen, Brenda A. Miller, Joel W. Grube, and Elizabeth D. Waiters, "Music, Substance Use, and Aggression," Journal of Studies on Alcohol 67, no. 3 (May 2006): 373-381, doi: 10.15288/jsa.2006.67.373.

[5] "What is Peter Pan syndrome? Warning signs and more," Medical News Today, Medically reviewed by Ifeanyi Olele, DO, MBA, MS, FAPA — Written by Katie

Yockey, Updated July 19, 2024,
https://www.medicalnewstoday.com/articles/peter-pan-syndrome.

[6] Delarious O. Stewart, James L. Maiden, and Nathalie Mizelle, "Violent and Angry in the Age of Hip Hop: Exploring The Relationship between The Behavior and the Music," Journal of Liberal Arts and Humanities 1, no. 8 (August 2020): 18-25.

[7] Nikki Rojas, "Are Drill Musicians Chronicling Violence or Exploiting It?" Harvard Gazette, March 16, 2023, https://news.harvard.edu/gazette/story/2023/03/is-drill-music-chronicling-violence-or-exploiting-it/.

[8] Murray Stassen, "Warner Buys 300 Entertainment for Around $400m," Music Business Worldwide, December 16, 2021, https://www.musicbusinessworldwide.com/warner-buys-300-entertainment-for-around-400m/.

[9] "Lyor Cohen Talks Migos Issues with 300 Ent, Kanye West + more!" Breakfast Club Power 105.1 FM, YouTube, August 1, 2018, https://www.youtube.com/watch?v=sitMVitcB8c.

[10] Nathan McCall, "My Rap Against Rap," Washington Post, November 13, 1993.

Acknowledgments

This book was five years in the making, and I am deeply grateful to all who supported its creation. My heartfelt thanks to editors and contributors Dana Sanchez and Ann Brown, whose insights and dedication were invaluable throughout this journey. I'm especially grateful to my patient and loving wife Anita, whose unwavering support made this work possible.

This book is dedicated to my children Elijah, Imani, and Niya. May the Science vs. Spook framework help you beyond political understanding and propel you faster and smarter toward your DREAMS, wherever they may lead you.

This book is also dedicated to the fallen soldiers who touched my life and inspired me: Martha Nelson, Lisa Johnson, Alfred Clark, Michael Brown (my childhood friend, not of Ferguson), Dr. Victor Kuo, Auntie Darlene, and Herman Muhammad.

I also wish to express my sincere appreciation to the Lineage-Based Reparations organizations such as American Descendants of Slavery (ADOS) and LEAP, scholars like Dr. William "Sandy" Darity Jr. and Kirsten Mullen, and activists and leaders such as Attorney Kamilah Moore, Yvette Carnell, Chris Lodgson, Chad from Politics in Black, Nyheim (Lord Abba), along with many others whose commitment continues to advance the cause of freedom, justice, equality, and political efficiency for Black Americans.

Your collective wisdom and commitment to truth have shaped not just this book, but my understanding of what's possible when we replace spook with science in our pursuit of freedom, justice, and equality.

Bibliography

Books and Major Publications

Abdul-Jabbar, Kareem. (2015). Prosperity gospel is war on the poor. *Time Magazine*.

Alexander, Carol. (2001). *Market models: A guide to financial data analysis*. John Wiley & Sons.

Anderson, Claud. (2001). *PowerNomics: The national plan to empower Black America*. PowerNomics Corporation of America.

Baradaran, Mehrsa. (2017). *The color of money: Black banks and the racial wealth gap*. Harvard University Press.

Barboza, Steven. (1993). *American jihad: Islam after Malcolm X*. Doubleday.

Berry, Mary Frances. (2005). *My face is Black is true: Callie House and the struggle for ex-slave reparations*. Knopf.

Blackstock, Nelson. (1988). *Cointelpro: The FBI's secret war on political freedom*. Pathfinder Press.

Coates, Ta-Nehisi. (2014). *Between the world and me*. Spiegel & Grau.

Covel, Michael. (2007). *The complete turtle trader: The legend, the lessons, the results*. Collins.

Cuba, Prince A. (2004). *Our Mecca is Harlem: Clarence 13X (Allah) and the Five Percent*. Self-published.

Darity, William A., Jr., & Mullen, A. Kirsten. (2020). *From here to equality: Reparations for Black Americans in the twenty-first century.* University of North Carolina Press.

DeGruy, Joy. (2017). *Post traumatic slave syndrome: America's legacy of enduring injury and healing* (Rev. ed.). Joy DeGruy Publications.

Evanzz, Karl. (1992). *The Judas factor: The plot to kill Malcolm X.* Thunder's Mouth Press.

Evanzz, Karl. (1999). *The messenger: The rise and fall of Elijah Muhammad.* Pantheon Books.

Faith, Curtis. (2007). *Way of the turtle: The secret methods that turned ordinary people into legendary traders.* McGraw-Hill.

Fishman, Ted C. (2006). *China, Inc.: How the rise of the next superpower challenges America and the world.* Scribner.

Garvey, Marcus. (2020). *Message to the people: The course of African philosophy.* Dover Publications.

Glaude, Eddie S., Jr. (2016). *Democracy in Black: How race still enslaves the American soul.* Crown.

Greene, Lucie. (2018). *Silicon states: The power and politics of big tech and what it means for our future.* Counterpoint.

Greider, William. (1989). *Secrets of the temple: How the Federal Reserve runs the country.* Simon & Schuster.

Jones, Ricky L. (2008). *What's wrong with Obamamania? Black America, black leadership, and the death of political imagination.* State University of New York Press.

Kelton, Stephanie. (2021). *The deficit myth: Modern monetary theory and the birth of the people's economy.* PublicAffairs.

Kiley, Dan. (1983). *The Peter Pan syndrome: Men who have never grown up.* Dodd Mead.

King, Martin Luther, Jr. (1967). *Where do we go from here: Chaos or community?* Harper & Row.

Krauthammer, Charles. (2013). *Things that matter: Three decades of passions, pastimes and politics.* Crown Forum.

Krauthammer, Charles. (2018). *The point of it all: A lifetime of great loves and endeavors.* Crown Forum.

Marrs, Jim. (2017). *The illuminati: The secret society that hijacked the world.* Visible Ink Press.

McWhorter, John. (2001). *Losing the race: Self-sabotage in Black America.* Harper Perennial.

Mearsheimer, John J., & Walt, Stephen M. (2008). *The Israel lobby and U.S. foreign policy.* Farrar, Straus and Giroux.

Muhammad, Elijah. (2006). *Message to the Blackman in America.* Secretarius MEMPS Publications.

Muhammad, Silis. (2023). *Silis Muhammad's United Nations interventions on behalf of Afrodescendants.* Self-published.

Obama, Barack. (2008). *Change we can believe in: Barack Obama's plan to renew America's promise.* Crown.

Obama, Barack. (2020). *A promised land.* Penguin Books.

Rasiel, Ethan M. (1999). *The McKinsey way.* McGraw-Hill.

Rasiel, Ethan, & Friga, Paul N. (2001). *The McKinsey mind: Understanding and implementing the problem-solving tools and management techniques of the world's top strategic consulting firm.* McGraw-Hill.

Reed, Adolph, Jr. (2001). *Posing as politics and other thoughts on the American scene.* The New Press.

Robinson, Randall. (2000). *The debt: What America owes to Blacks.* Dutton Adult.

Rothstein, Richard. (2017). *The color of law: A forgotten history of how our government segregated America*. Liveright.

Schwager, Jack D. (2012). *Market wizards: Interviews with top traders* (Updated ed.). Wiley.

Seykota, Ed. (2013). *Govopoly in the 39th day*. Trading Tribe.

Shabazz, Malik Zulu. (2020). *The book of Khallid: The untold story of Khallid Abdul Muhammad*. Self-published.

Spence, Lester. (2015). *Knocking the hustle: Against the neoliberal turn in Black politics*. Punctum Books.

Steele, Shelby. (1999). *A dream deferred: The second betrayal of Black freedom in America*. Harper Perennial.

Steele, Shelby. (2006). *White guilt: How Blacks and whites together destroyed the promise of the civil rights era*. HarperCollins.

Stern, Carl W., & Deimler, Michael S. (Eds.). (2012). *The Boston Consulting Group on strategy: Classic concepts and new perspectives* (2nd ed.). John Wiley & Sons.

Stout, Martha. (2005). *The sociopath next door*. Broadway Books.

Sullivan, William C. (1979). *The Bureau: My thirty years in Hoover's FBI*. W.W. Norton.

Truman, Edwin M. (2010). *Sovereign wealth funds: Threat or salvation?* Peterson Institute for International Economics.

Vogel, Ezra F. (2013). *Deng Xiaoping and the transformation of China*. Harvard University Press.

Wax, Amy L. (2009). *Race, wrongs, and remedies: Group justice in the 21st century*. Hoover Institution Press.

Weiner, Eric J. (2011). *The shadow market: How sovereign wealth funds secretly dominate the global economy*. OneWorld Publications.

Whipple, Chris. (2025). *Uncharted: How Trump beat Biden, Harris, and the odds in the wildest campaign in history*. Harper Influence.

Academic Articles and Reports

Abel, Martin, & Burger, Rulof. (2023). Unpacking name-based race discrimination. *IZA Discussion Paper No. 16254*. IZA Institute of Labor Economics. https://doi.org/10.2139/ssrn.4469326

Austin, Algernon. (2016). The color of entrepreneurship: Why the racial gap among firms costs the U.S. millions. *Center for Global Policy Solutions*.

Bostic, Raphael. (2022). The case for considering reparations. *Federal Reserve Bank of Atlanta Working Paper Series*.

Chen, Meng-Jinn, Miller, Brenda A., Grube, Joel W., & Waiters, Elizabeth D. (2006). Music, substance use, and aggression. *Journal of Studies on Alcohol, 67*(3), 373-381. https://doi.org/10.15288/jsa.2006.67.373

Chen, Tian. (2023). An analysis of Amazon's high turnover rate. *Proceedings of Business and Economic Studies, 6*(3), 31-38. https://doi.org/10.26689/pbes.v6i3.5096

Darity, William A., Jr. (2008). Forty acres and a mule in the 21st century. *Social Science Quarterly, 89*(3), 656-664.

Darity, William A., Jr. (2019). A direct approach to eliminating the racial wealth gap. *Federal Reserve Bank of Boston Conference on Race and Inequality*.

Darity, William A., Jr., Addo, Fenaba R., & Smith, Imari Z. (2021). A subaltern middle class: The case of the missing "Black bourgeoisie" in America. *Contemporary Economic Policy, 39*(3), 494-502. https://doi.org/10.1111/coep.12476

Darity, William A., Jr., Hamilton, Darrick, Paul, Mark, Aja, Alan, Price, Anne, Moore, Antonio, & Chiopris, Caterina. (2018). What we get wrong about closing the racial wealth gap. *Samuel DuBois Cook Center on Social Equity.*

Darity, William A., Jr., & Mullen, A. Kirsten. (2023). Calculating the reparations amount. *Journal of Economic Perspectives, 37*(3), 107-124. https://doi.org/10.1257/jep.37.3.107

Dietrich, Bryce J., & Hayes, Matthew. (2023). Symbols of the struggle: Descriptive representation and issue-based symbolism in US House speeches. *Journal of Politics, 85*(4).

Drumetz, Françoise, & Pfister, Christian. (2021). Modern monetary theory: A wrong compass for decision-making. *Intereconomics: Review of European Economic Policy, 56*(6), 355-361. https://doi.org/10.1007/s10272-021-1013-7

Emmons, William, & Ricketts, Lowell. (2017). The link between family structure and wealth is weaker than you might think. *Federal Reserve Bank of St. Louis.*

Fairlie, Robert W., & Robb, Alicia M. (2010). Disparities in capital access between minority and non-minority-owned businesses. *U.S. Department of Commerce, Minority Business Development Agency.*

Hamilton, Darrick. (2019). Neoliberalism and race. *Democracy Journal.*

Hamilton, Darrick, McMillan Cottom, Tressie, Darity, William A., Jr., Aja, Alan A., & Ash, Carolyn. (2015). Still we rise: The continuing case for America's historically Black colleges and universities. *The American Prospect, 25*(4), 54-60.

Hussain, Khuram. (2020). Dreaming differently about freedom: Malcolm X and Muhammad speaks. *Journal of African American Studies, 24,* 427-444.

Kobayashi, Shigeo, Baobo, Jia, & Sano, Junya. (1999). The 'Three Reforms' in China: Progress and outlook. *Sakura Institute of Research, Inc.*, No. 45.

Krupnikov, Yanna, & Piston, Spencer. (2016). The political consequences of Latino prejudice against Blacks. *Public Opinion Quarterly, 80*(2), 480-509. https://doi.org/10.1093/poq/nfw014

Lee, Harry F. (2019). Cannibalism in northern China between 1470 and 1911. *Regional Environmental Change, 19*(8), 2573-2581.

McManus, Michael. (2016). Minority business ownership: Data from the 2012 Survey of Business Owners. *U.S. Small Business Administration Office of Advocacy.*

Meschede, Tatjana, Taylor, Joanna, Mann, Alexis, & Shapiro, Thomas. (2017). Family achievements?: How a college degree accumulates wealth for whites and not for Blacks. *Federal Reserve Bank of St. Louis Review, 99*(1), 121-137. https://doi.org/10.20955/r.2017.121-37

Muñoz, Ana Patricia, Kim, Marlene, Chang, Mariko, Jackson, Regine O., Hamilton, Darrick, & Darity, William A., Jr. (2015). The color of wealth in Boston. *Federal Reserve Bank of Boston.*

Perry, Andre, & Stephens, Hannah, & Donoghoe, Manann. (2024). Black wealth is increasing, but so is the racial wealth gap. *Brookings Institution.*

Perry, Andre, Rothwell, Jonathan, & Harshbarger, David. (2018). The devaluation of assets in Black neighborhoods: The case of residential property. *Brookings Institution.*

Rashid, Hakim M., & Muhammad, Zakiyyah. (1992). The Sister Clara Muhammad Schools: Pioneers in the development of Islamic education in America. *The Journal of Negro Education, 61*(2), 178-185. https://doi.org/10.2307/2295418

Ray, Rashawn, & Galston, William A. (2020). Did the 1994 crime bill cause mass incarceration? *Brookings Institution.*

Sloan, Allan, & Podkul, Cezary. (2021). How the Federal Reserve is increasing wealth inequality. *ProPublica.*

Stewart, Delarious O., Maiden, James L., & Mizelle, Nathalie. (2020). Violent and angry in the age of hip hop: Exploring the relationship between the behavior and the music. *Journal of Liberal Arts and Humanities, 1*(8), 18-25.

Traub, Amy, Sullivan, Laura, Meschede, Tatjana, & Shapiro, Thomas. (2017). The asset value of whiteness: Understanding the racial wealth gap. *Demos and the Institute on Assets and Social Policy.*

Whatley, Warren C. (2018). The gun-slave hypothesis and the 18th century British slave trade. *Explorations in Economic History, 67*, 80-104. https://doi.org/10.1016/j.eeh.2018.01.002

Government and Organizational Reports

Alaska Permanent Fund Corporation. (2023). Annual report FY 2021: Distributions to Alaska residents. *Alaska Department of Revenue.*

Columbia School of Law. (2024). A survey of free AI tools: Chat GPT and Deep Seek. *Columbia Law Technology Review.*

Consumer Affairs Commission. (2024). Report on AI capability misrepresentation (2019-2021). *Consumer Protection Quarterly.*

Darity, William A., Jr. (2019). The case for reparations: Addressing the racial wealth gap. Testimony to the *House Judiciary Subcommittee on the Constitution, Civil Rights, and Civil Liberties.*

Federal Trade Commission. (2024). Report on digital marketing fraud: The $143 billion industry. *Federal Trade Commission.*

Goldman Sachs. (2023). Generative AI could raise global GDP by 7 percent. *Goldman Sachs Research.*

Harvard Business Review. (2024). Privacy in the age of AI: Subscription models for data protection. *Harvard Business Review.*

Henderson, Kaitlyn. (2022). The crisis of low wages in the US. *Oxfam America.*

Million Family March. (2000). Public policy issues, analyses, and programmatic plan of action, 2000-2008. Washington, D.C.

MIT Technology Review. (2024). Chrome extensions for AI: The Awesome Screenshot plugin. *MIT Technology Review.*

National Urban League. (2023). Annual report 2023. *National Urban League.*

The Moguldom Nation. (2025). Digital media company growth report. *The Moguldom Nation Annual Report.*

Urban Land Institute. (2025). Historical land valuation: Grove Hill plantation property assessment. *Urban Land Institute Economic Brief.*

World Justice Project. (2021). Rwanda ranked 42 out of 139 countries on rule of law. *World Justice Project Rule of Law Index.*

News and Media Articles

Adams, Lorraine. (1995, January 21). Farrakhan aide blasts U.S. probe of business. *Washington Post.*

Bala-Gbogobo, Elisha. (2012, December 20). Nigeria sovereign wealth fund to start investing in March. *Bloomberg.*

Barkan, Ady. (2019, February 12). What Ilhan Omar said about AIPAC was right. *The Nation.*

Bedekovics, Greta. (2024, April 29). How the racist history of the filibuster lives on today. *Center for American Progress.*

Bender, Bryan, & Meyer, Theodoric. (2020, November 23). The secretive consulting firm that's become Biden's cabinet in waiting. *Politico*.

Bertuca, Tony. (2021, January 11). Austin discloses financial ties to defense contractors. *Inside Defense*.

Birch, Kean. (2017, November 2). What exactly is neoliberalism? *The Conversation*.

Blankfort, Jeffrey. (2016, September 6). Congressional Black Caucus: Deep in the Israel lobby's pocket. *Black Agenda Report*.

Blest, Paul. (2020, April 2). Leaked Amazon memo details plan to smear fired warehouse organizer: 'He's not smart or articulate'. *VICE*.

Bloomberg News. (2022, July 20). China's $1.2 trillion wealth fund reorganizes key investment arm. *Bloomberg*.

Blow, Charles M. (2020, January 19). The agitated M.L.K. I came to love. *New York Times*.

Bohrer, Becky. (2023, October 5). Alaskans get a $1,312 oil dividend check this year. The political cost of the benefit is high. *Associated Press*.

Bolton, Alexander. (2019, June 26). Senate Democrats wish talk on reparations would go away. *The Hill*.

Bose, Nandita. (2024, August 2). Harris adds top Obama aides to her presidential campaign team. *Reuters*.

Brown, Ann. (2019, August 13). 10 things you need to know about the Nation of Islam's position on reparations. *The Moguldom Nation*.

Brown, Ann. (2019, November 12). What Hillary Clinton, Bernie Sanders and Barack Obama have said about reparations for slavery. *The Moguldom Nation*.

Brown, Ann. (2020, October 27). 5 things MSNBC brunch Democrats won't tell Black America about the 1994 Biden crime bill. *The Moguldom Nation.*

Brown, Ann. (2020, November 6). What is a bougie buffer? 3 things to know about the concept of the buffer class. *The Moguldom Nation.*

Brown, Ann. (2020, December 16). $10.6B+ was given to Black Lives Matter causes: Where did the money go? *The Moguldom Nation.*

Brown, Ann. (2021, April 9). BLM co-founder Patrisse Khan-Cullors buys million dollar home and the streets have questions. *The Moguldom Nation.*

Brown, Ann. (2021, May 28). BLM co-founder Patrisse Cullors suddenly resigns after defense of expanding real estate portfolio. *The Moguldom Nation.*

Brown, Ann. (2021, July 29). Remembering 'Reparations Ray': 5 things to know about reparations pioneer Raymond Jenkins. *The Moguldom Nation.*

Brown, Ann. (2021, August 6). Remembering when Caucasians united for reparations and emancipation supported Silis Muhammad at the U.N. *The Moguldom Nation.*

Brown, Ann. (2021, November 17). 7 things to know about how Wallace/Warith Dean Muhammad removed nation-building from NOI. *The Moguldom Nation.*

Brown, Ann. (2021, November 18). A warning to Black America about scammy 'artificial intelligence' hype: 5 things to know. *The Moguldom Nation.*

Brown, Ann. (2022, July 19). Remembering Dr. Robert Brock's fight for reparations in the '90s. *The Moguldom Nation.*

Brown, Ann. (2022, August 9). Remembering Callie House: 7 things to know about the organizing pioneer and reparations advocate. *The Moguldom Nation.*

Brown, Ann. (2022, October 18). Tavis Smiley: If Obama looked like Isaac Hayes or Rick Ross, he wouldn't have been president. *The Moguldom Nation.*

Brown, Ann. (2022, December 20). What did Father Allah (Clarence 13X) mean when he said he's "not pro-Black or anti-white." *Moguldom Nation.*

Brown, Ann. (2023, February 21). Why Kwame Ture hated political reactionaries and why Bill Clinton hated him. *Moguldom Nation.*

Brown, Ann. (2023, September 21). Karen Hunter vs Marc Morial: Interview ends abruptly after sharp questioning. *Moguldom.com.*

Brown, Ann. (2023, November 16). Fact check: The 'dollar only stays in Black community 6 hours' is urban myth. *Moguldom.*

Brown, Ann. (2023, December 27). Who will defend us? 3 Black American leaders and organizations who are financially compromised by Wells Fargo. *Moguldom.com.*

Campbell, Sean. (2022, April 4). Black Lives Matter secretly bought a $6 million house: Allies and critics alike have questioned where the organization's money has gone. *New York Magazine.*

Châtelot, Christophe. (2024, May 28). The dark side of Paul Kagame, the Rwandan autocrat who fascinates the West. *Le Monde.*

Coates, Ta-Nehisi. (1999, May 14). Schism nation: Black Muslims in D.C. are in the midst of a Holy War. *Washington City Paper.*

Coates, Ta-Nehisi. (2016, January 19). Why precisely is Bernie Sanders against reparations? *The Atlantic.*

Cooper, Ryan. (2017, January 7). The White House's dirty campaign against Keith Ellison. *The Week.*

Cousens, Maryann. (2024, December 11). 2024 post-election survey: Racial analysis of 2024 election results. *Navigator Research.*

Cunningham, Vinson. (2018, January 28). The politics of race and the photo that might have derailed Obama. *The New Yorker.*

Daniels, Eugene. (2021, March 2). Biden privately tells lawmakers not to expect much on reparations legislation. *Politico.*

Darcy, Oliver. (2021, July 21). Bezos donates $100 million each to CNN contributor Van Jones and chef José Andrés. *CNN Business.*

Darity, William A., Jr. (2016, December 22). How Barack Obama failed Black Americans. *The Atlantic.*

Doherty, Erin. (2024, October 8). Harris: "Not a thing" she'd have done differently than Biden. *Axios.*

Donovan, Lydialyle, Cucho, Lyka, & Gordon, Ariana. (2024, February). 40 acres and a lie. *Mother Jones.*

Emmons, Alex. (2019, March 30). In leaked recording, Cory Booker says he and AIPAC president "text message back and forth like teenagers." *The Intercept.*

Epstein, Reid J. (2024, November 8). Pelosi laments Biden's late exit and the lack of an 'open primary'. *New York Times.*

Farmer, Ashley D. (2019, June 24). The Black woman who launched the modern fight for reparations. *Washington Post.*

Fears, Darryl. (2008, May 9). Black community is increasingly protective of Obama. *The Washington Post.*

Felton, Emmanuel, Hatzipanagos, Rachel, & Wilson, Scott. (2023, June 29). An obstacle to Black reparations in California: Convincing Latinos and Asians. *Washington Post.*

Fields, Hannah. (2021, March 31). Lawmakers renew effort to study slavery reparation. *Capital News Service.*

Freeman, David. (2012, August 27). Are politicians psychopaths? *Huffington Post*.

Gaskins, Kayla. (2023, May 31). BLM finances under fire: Only 33% of donations given to charities as execs paid millions. *ABC 15 News*.

Gass, Nick. (2015, August 31). Obama: It hurts when people call me antisemitic. *Politico*.

Gaynor, Gerren Keith. (2020, April 1). Amazon worker on strike over COVID-19: 'Dildos are not essential items'. *The Grio*.

Gerstein, Josh. (2015, December 31). How Obama failed to shut Washington's revolving door. *Politico*.

Ghaffary, Shirin. (2022, June 7). Amazon fired Chris Smalls. Now the new union leader is one of its biggest problems. *Vox*.

Goldstein, Steve. (2024, October 4). The bond king, Jeffrey Gundlach, says the economy isn't working after seeing a Hamburger Helper ad. *MarketWatch*.

Goodman, J. David. (2019, July 14). When big tobacco invoked Eric Garner to fight a menthol cigarette ban. *The New York Times*.

Goudreau, Claire. (2024, November 20). The impact of inflation on the 2024 presidential election. *Johns Hopkins University Hub*.

Greenwald, Glenn. (2017, February 24). Key question about DNC race: Why did Obama White House recruit Perez to run against Ellison? *The Intercept*.

Greenburg, Zack O'Malley. (2013, April 19). Jay-Z sells Nets stake, earns Warren Buffett-like return. *Forbes*.

Grimaldi, James V., & Ballhaus, Rebecca. (2015, February 17). Foreign government gifts to Clinton Foundation on the rise. *Wall Street Journal*.

Harris, John F. (1998, March 25). Clinton says US wronged Africa. *Washington Post.*

Harrison, Isheka N. (2019, May 29). Alyssa Milano says she thought America had moved beyond race because Obama was elected. *Moguldom.*

Herndon, Astead W. (2020, July 13). George Soros's foundation pours $220 million into racial equality push. *New York Times.*

Herndon, Astead W., & Glueck, Katie. (2020, May 22). Biden apologizes for saying Black voters 'ain't Black' if they're considering Trump. *The New York Times.*

Holmes, Steven A. (1996, February 22). Farrakhan's angry world tour brings harsh criticism at home. *The New York Times.*

Hu, Rollin. (2016, January 28). Spence talks neoliberalism and Black politics. *The Johns Hopkins News-Letter.*

Huang, Jacky. (2023, March 30). Why Black founders continue to not be funded in Silicon Valley. *Harvard Technology Review.*

Huang, Zheping, & Lahiri, Tripti. (2017, September 21). China's path out of poverty can never be repeated at scale by a country again. *Quartz.*

Huszar, Andrew. (2013, November 20). Tim Geithner and the revolving door. *The New Yorker.*

Jackson, David, & Gaines, William. (1995, March 25). Farrakhan's murky finances. *Greensboro News & Record.*

Jan, Tracy, McGregor, Jena, & Hoyer, Meghan. (2021, August 23). Corporate America's $50 billion promise. *The Washington Post.*

Jaschik, Scott. (2007, January 31). The immigrant factor. *Inside Higher Ed.*

Jessop, Julian. (2020, August 6). Beware the siren call of modern monetary theory. *Institute of Economic Affairs*.

Jones, Joyce. (2011, August 11). Steve Harvey suggests that Smiley and West are 'Uncle Toms'. *BET*.

Jones, Joyce. (2011, July 25). Tavis Smiley calls attention to Obama's failings. *BET*.

Jones, Zoe Christen. (2020, October 16). Ice Cube defends advising Trump on plan for Black Americans. *CBS News*.

Kane, Alex. (2021, Fall). Ritchie Torres is the future of 'pro-Israel' politics. *Jewish Currents*.

Kantor, Jodi, & Weise, Karen. (2022, April 2). How two best friends beat Amazon: The company's crackdown on a worker protest in New York backfired and led to a historic labor victory. *The New York Times*.

Karni, Annie. (2025, March 14). Schumer, facing backlash for not forcing a shutdown, says he'll take 'the bullets'. *The New York Times*.

Kellman, Laurie. (2019, June 18). McConnell on reparations for slavery: Not a "good idea." *Associated Press*.

Kirsanow, Peter. (2024, February 13). Illegal immigration and Black voters. *National Review*.

Krauthammer, Charles. (1990, December 31). Essay: Reparations for Black Americans. *Time Magazine*.

Krauthammer, Charles. (2001, April 6). A grand compromise. *Washington Post*.

Krishna, Mrinalini. (2021, December 12). The Amazon effect on the U.S. economy. *Investopedia*.

Lacy, Akela. (2023, September 21). AIPAC targets Black Democrats — while the Congressional Black Caucus stays silent. *The Intercept*.

Lacy, Akela. (2024, July 31). AIPAC used distorted photo of Cori Bush in $7 million negative ad blitz. *The Intercept*.

Landers, Peter. (2021, August 22). Japan's love of debt offers a view of U.S. future. *Wall Street Journal*.

Lane, Charles. (2019, August 12). Would reparations for slavery be constitutional? *The Washington Post*.

LaVecchia, Olivia. (2017, February 7). How Amazon undermines jobs, wages, and working conditions. *Institute for Local Self-Reliance*.

Lau, Tim. (2021, April 26). The filibuster explained. *Brennan Center for Justice*.

Lee, M.J. (2012, January 9). Tavis Smiley booted from MLK event. *Politico*.

Longley, Robert. (2021, July 28). What is neoliberalism? Definition and examples. *Thought Co.*.

Los Angeles Times. (1995, October 19). Farrakhan sets Black vote goal of '3rd political power'. *Los Angeles Times*.

Lumpkin, Lauren, Kolodner, Meredith, & Anderson, Nick. (2021, April 18). Flagship universities say diversity is a priority. But Black enrollment in many states continues to lag. *Washington Post*.

MacDonald, Cheyenne. (2017, March 15). Silicon Valley is full of psychopathic CEOs who are 'charming and manipulative' but have no empathy, experts claim. *Daily Mail*.

Mandel, Bethany. (2018, April 2). The troubling connections between Scientology and the Nation of Islam. *National Review*.

Manzullo, Brian. (2016, May 4). Michael Moore calls Barack Obama drinking Flint water 'disappointing'. *Detroit Free Press*.

Markay, Lachlan. (2021, February 18). Juul spins vaping as 'criminal justice' issue for Black lawmakers. *Daily Beast.*

Martin, Jamarlin. (2018, October 8). Revisiting the $100M+ economic blueprint of Elijah Muhammad and Malcolm X. *Moguldom.com.*

Martin, Michel. (2010, March 11). Smiley: Black America deserves an agenda with the president. *NPR.*

Mascaro, Lisa, & Amiri, Farnoush. (2023, October 3). Speaker McCarthy ousted in historic House vote, as scramble begins for a Republican leader. *Associated Press.*

McCall, Nathan. (1993, November 13). My rap against rap. *Washington Post.*

McCabe, Bret. (2015, Winter). Lester Spence argues that African Americans have bought into the wrong politics. *Johns Hopkins Magazine Hub.*

McGreal, Chris. (2022, August 4). Pro-Israel groups denounced after pouring funds into primary race. *The Guardian.*

McWhorter, John. (2010, August 10). What hope? *The New Republic.*

Medina, Jennifer. (2020, July 3). Latinos back Black Lives Matter protests. They want change for themselves, too. *New York Times.*

Moore, Antonio. [@tonetalks]. (2020, August 5). August 5, 2020 [Tweet]. *X.*

Moorcraft, Bethan. (2024, September 26). Nancy Pelosi's husband sold Visa shares 2 months before a DOJ lawsuit — some say the trade shouldn't have been allowed. *Yahoo Finance.*

Mosley, Tonya. (2020, February 27). Tom Steyer thinks his progressive policies will win big in South Carolina. *Here & Now, WBUR.*

Mwanza, Kevin. (2019, July 19). 'Juul doesn't have African-Americans' best interests in mind': Backlash following $7.5M gift to medical school. *The Moguldom Nation*.

Mwanza, Kevin. (2021, April 29). 5 things to know about the African Akata slur against Black Americans. *Moguldom.com*.

Natarajan, Sridhar, & Martin, Eric. (2022, August 11). Biden ties to BlackRock deepen with latest Treasury hire. *Bloomberg*.

Newsweek. (2024, December 19). Democrats face 'gerontocracy' crisis amid ageing leadership. *Newsweek*.

Noel, Peter. (2000, September 5). The shame of Mosque No. 7. *Village Voice*.

Oder, Norman. (2012, April 26). Bloomberg promises 2,000 jobs at the Barclays center, sort of. *New York Magazine*.

O'Donnell, Tim. (2021, February 7). Just how much leverage does Joe Manchin actually have? *The Week*.

Owen, Laura Hazard. (2016, January 22). A Howard project is debunking myths about African-Americans and teaching students fact-checking. *Nieman Lab*.

Peoples, Steve. (2024, November 26). Harris' campaign leaders say there was a 'price to be paid' for shortened campaign against Trump. *Associated Press*.

Peralta, Eyder. (2013, May 19). Two excerpts you should read from Obama's Morehouse speech. *NPR*.

Picchi, Aimee. (2023, September 29). How much was Dianne Feinstein worth when she died? *CBS News*.

Pitcher, Jack. (2024, November 4). Why $11 trillion in assets isn't enough for BlackRock's Larry Fink. *Wall Street Journal*.

Prince, Kathryn J. (2020, July 11). Student leaders at historically Black US colleges join Israel advocacy effort. *The Times of Israel.*

Rabouin, Dion. (2021, June 29). America's first Black billionaire wants his reparations check, now. *Vice Media.*

Rahman, Khaleda. (2016, May 5). Beso for Bezos! Jill Biden plants a kiss on Amazon billionaire at the White House. *Daily Mail.*

Reed, Adolph, Jr. (2014, March). Nothing left: The long, slow surrender of American liberals. *Harper's Magazine.*

Reid, Sytonia. (2022). Revisiting C. Delores Tucker's war on rap: Too much smoke, not enough flowers. *Medium.*

Redden, Elizabeth. (2021, January 3). A fairy godmother for once-overlooked colleges. *Inside Higher Education.*

Rojas, Nikki. (2023, March 16). Are drill musicians chronicling violence or exploiting it? *Harvard Gazette.*

Rosen, Armin. (2019, March 6). How influential is AIPAC? Less than beer sellers, public accountants, and Toyota. *Tablet Magazine.*

Rosenberg, M.J. (2019, February 14). This is how AIPAC really works. *The Nation.*

Rogers, Zachary. (2023, July 6). Ice Cube warns rap record labels encourage criminal behavior and help fuel private prisons. *ABC 15 News.*

Roosevelt, Margot. (2022, August 22). In California's largest race bias cases, Latino workers are accused of abusing Black colleagues. *Los Angeles Times.*

Russ, Valerie. (2020, January 18). Forget the notion of MLK as "Dreamer," say activists. He was a radical, whose rhetoric is used. *Philadelphia Inquirer.*

Sanchez, Dana. (2019, June 10). Swamp thang: JUUL vaping firm hires Ben Jealous to lobby D.C. *The Moguldom Nation*.

Sanchez, Dana. (2020, June 9). When the money printers go crazy: Gold investors go on the attack as new modern monetary theory book is released. *The Moguldom Nation*.

Sanchez, Dana. (2021, August 2). The most influential trader in crypto, Sam Trabucco, works with FTX exchange: Some see manipulation. *The Moguldom Nation*.

Santa Clara University School of Business. (2023, May 8). What is corporate restructuring? *Santa Clara University*.

Schleifer, Theodore. (2019, February 22). Silicon Valley loves Cory Booker. That could be a problem for him. *Vox*.

Schlesinger, Jacob M. (2020, July 26). Reparations to Black Americans for slavery gain new attention. *The Wall Street Journal*.

Schrader, Adam. (2021, February 25). Obama calls for reparations for Black Americans because the 'wealth of this country was built on the backs of slaves'. *Daily Mail*.

Scott, Eugene. (2016, December 3). Haim Saban: Keith Ellison 'is clearly an antisemite and anti-Israel individual'. *CNN*.

Scott, Eugene. (2019, July 9). What Obama actually said in his rejection of reparations. *Washington Post*.

Seaton-Msemaji, Ken. (2021, October 28). Marketing menthol cigarettes to Black Americans is a racial injustice. It must end. *San Diego Union-Tribune*.

Shapiro, Bruce. (2016, April 11). Nothing about the 1994 crime bill was unintentional: In the '90s, Bill Clinton exploited fears about crime in the same way that Donald Trump uses immigration today. *The Nation*.

Silsby, Gilien. (2001, January 8). Law scholar links civil rights to cold war embarrassment. *USC News.*

Sippell, Margeaux. (2018, November 2). Friends of the Israel Defense Forces gala raises record $60 million for soldiers. *Variety.*

Sirota, David. (2015, May 26). Clinton Foundation donors got weapons deals from Hillary Clinton's State Department. *International Business Times.*

Sirota, David. (2016, April 5). Oil companies donated to Clinton Foundation while lobbying State Department. *International Business Times.*

Smiley, Tavis. (2017, January 10). My criticism of President Obama was always rooted in love. *Time.*

Smith, David. (2021, November 28). How Manchin and Sinema's status as Senate holdouts is proving lucrative. *The Guardian.*

Stassen, Murray. (2021, December 16). Warner buys 300 Entertainment for around $400m. *Music Business Worldwide.*

Steele, Shelby. (2009, August 1). From Emmitt Till to Skip Gates: Black victim, white oppressor. It's a narrative we know well. *Wall Street Journal.*

Stein, Jeff. (2016, August 25). 4 experts make the case that the Clinton Foundation's fundraising was troubling. *Vox.*

Stockman, Farah. (2019, November 8). 'We're self-interested': The growing identity debate in Black America. *The New York Times.*

Stringer, Sam. (2015, March 16). Minister Creflo Dollar asks for $60 million in donations for a new jet. *CNN.*

Taibbi, Matt. (2015, July 8). Eric Holder, Wall Street double agent, comes in from the cold. *Rolling Stone.*

Tankersley, Jim. (2021, December 19). The path ahead for Biden: Overcome Manchin's inflation fears. *The New York Times*.

Taylor, Keeanga, & Spence, Lester. (2016, January 13). Black people's state of the union missing from Obama's address. *The Real News Network*.

TeamEBONY. (2017, November 1). Steve Harvey's TV shows took a hit after that Trump meeting. *Ebony*.

Thompson, Derek. (2010, October 1). Google's CEO: 'The laws are written by lobbyists'. *The Atlantic*.

ToI Staff. (2023, July 27). Ex-Mossad chief: Netanyahu allies worse than KKK, overhaul is his 'master plan'. *The Times of Israel*.

Vaidhyanathan, Siva. (2017, January 15). Was Obama Silicon Valley's president? *The Guardian*.

Wagner, Daniel. (2014, July 18). Congressman defends payday lending industry. *The Center for Public Integrity*.

Wallace-Wells, Benjamin. (2022, January 31). The Marxist who antagonizes liberals and the left: The renowned Black scholar Adolph Reed opposes the politics of anti-racism, describing it as a cover for capitalism. *The New Yorker*.

Wallsten, Peter. (2010, March 17). Obama's new partner: Al Sharpton. *Wall Street Journal*.

Weisenthal, Joe. (2013, January 18). Newsweek likens Obama to Jesus—calls second term "the second coming." *Business Insider*.

Weissert, Will. (2024, October 14). Harris announces a new plan to empower Black men as she tries to energize them to vote for her. *Associated Press*.

Wessler, Seth Freed. (2012, January 18). The Israel lobby finds a new face: Black college students. *Color Lines*.

West, Cornel. (2017, December 17). Ta-Nehisi Coates is the neoliberal face of the Black freedom struggle. *The Guardian*.

Whipple, Chris. (2025, April 8). Uncharted: How Trump beat Biden, Harris, and the odds in the wildest campaign in history. *Harper Influence*.

Woodpop, Mikael. (2022, February 11). Jay-Z's Roc Nation remade the Super Bowl halftime show, but NFL's record on race casts long shadow. *Los Angeles Times*.

Zahn, Max. (2024, March 28). A timeline of cryptocurrency exchange FTX's historic collapse. *ABC News*.

Zeitlin, Matthew. (2020, July 18). Federal Reserve policy has failed Black Americans for decades. Now is the time to fix that. *Business Insider*.

Primary Sources, Speeches, and Interviews

Andreessen, Marc. (2008, March 3). An hour and a half with Barack Obama. PM Archive.

Bostic, Raphael. (2020, June 12). Institutionalized racism and economic potential [Speech]. Federal Reserve Bank of Atlanta.

Clement, Douglas. (2019, April 29). William "Sandy" Darity Jr. interview: "If you think something's the right thing to do, then you pursue it." Federal Reserve Bank of Minneapolis.

Darity, William A., Jr. (2018, February). Obama and the politics of reparations [Interview]. The Root.

Gates, Bill. (2023, March 21). The age of AI has begun. GatesNotes.

King, Martin Luther, Jr. (1967, April 4). Beyond Vietnam [Speech]. Riverside Church, New York.

Liu, Jennifer. (2023, October 3). JPMorgan CEO Jamie Dimon says AI could bring a 3½-day workweek. CNBC.

Malcolm X. (1964, April 3). The ballot or the bullet [Speech]. Cleveland, Ohio.

Malcolm X. (1963, January 23). Malcolm presents the Nation of Islam call for reparations. Michigan State University.

Muhammad, Elijah. (1962, March). Put the Muslim program before Congress. *Muhammad Speaks.*

Muhammad, Elijah. (2023, July 4). Who is God? *The Final Call.*

Muhammad, Khallid Abdul. (1992, May 19). Not even invited to the party [Speech]. Malcolm X Day Celebration.

Obama, Barack. (2008, January). NAACP questionnaire responses. NAACP.

Obama, Barack. (2013, May 19). Morehouse College commencement address. NPR.

Sanders, Bernie. (2016, January 17). Town hall meeting on racial justice [Speech]. Myrtle Beach, South Carolina.

Schmidt, Eric. (2024, December 15). Interview by George Stephanopoulos. This Week, ABC News.

Transcript of CNN Late Edition with Wolf Blitzer, Q&A with Barack Obama. (2008, July 27). CNN.

Ture, Kwame (Stokely Carmichael). (1968, April 15). Revolution is creating, not destroying [Speech]. Howard University.